# THE ARCHITECTURE OF WALES

## SERIES

**General Editor**

– Mary Wrenn
 *Former Director, RSAW*

**Series Editors**
– Bella Kerr
– David Thomas

**Advisory Panel**
– Irena Bauman, *Consultant, Bauman Lyons Architects;*
 *Director, MassBespoke*
– Richard Parnaby, *formerly Professor of Architecture, UWE Bristol*
 *and University of Wales Trinity Saint David*
– Alan Powers, *author and architectural historian*
– Ian Pritchard, *Secretary General, Architects Council of*
 *Europe (ACE)*
– Professor Damian Walford Davies, *Deputy Vice-Chancellor,*
 *Cardiff University*

Architecture.com/wales
**Published in cooperation with**
The Royal Society of Architects in Wales –
Cymdeithas Frenhinol Penseiri yng Nghymru

# Frank Lloyd Wright
## The Architecture of Defiance

Jonathan Adams

www.uwp.co.uk

British Library CIP Data

A catalogue record for this book is available from the British Library

ISBN        978-1-78683-913-8

eISBN       978-1-78683-914-5

**THE
ARCHITECTURE
OF WALES**
SERIES

To Hazel and to Harri and Lowri and their Mamgu and Tadcu

# Contents

# Taliesin

## Frank Lloyd Wright 1867–1959

A house on a hill, Spring Green, Wisconsin.
From an outcrop of rock, an outcry of water,
he would curb the stone, harness the light of the sun,
bridle the great horse of the river,
raise walls, wings, walkways, terraces, a tower,
slabbed stone horizons on the shining brow.

The mark was on him before birth,
that single drop of gold his mother brought
across the Atlantic in the hold of her heart
from the old home in Ceredigion,
for her imagined boy, her child,
man of her making who would shape a world.

Raised in the old language, the old stories,
he learned his lines from the growth-rings of trees,
wind over water, sandbars, river-currents,
rhythms of rock beneath the ground he stood on,
colours of the earth, his favourite red
the rusting zinc of old Welsh barns, of *twlc* and *beudy*.

*Taliesin*, house of light, of space and vista,
corners for contemplation, halls for fiesta.
He sang a new architecture
from the old, in perfect metre.

*Gillian Clarke*

*twlc* and *beudy*: pigsty and cow house

Reproduced courtesy of Gillian Clarke and
Carcanet Press Ltd.

# General Editor's Preface

Given the conventional image of Wales as a land of song and poetry, architecture and the visual arts can be easily overlooked, a neglected poor relation to the country's seductive musical and literary traditions. Relatively little has been published about the architectural heritage of our nation, despite the fact that buildings and places have been created in Wales that bear comparison with contemporaneous examples elsewhere, produced by architects engaged in the same wider cultural currents and discourse. There are many reasons for this: Wales has so often been judged as being too small, too homely, or simply not distinctive or fashionable enough to attract the sustained attention of architectural critics and historians. Add to this a lack of consistent patronage and a deeply ingrained Nonconformist tradition that discourages any form of showing off, and it is not surprising perhaps that we lack a more complete record of the architectural achievements of past generations.

Of course, the truth is that Wales has a rich built heritage, from the medieval to the modern. Its architectural character is very different from that of the other nations of the British Isles, and it is this very distinctiveness that deserves to be celebrated. In 2016 the Royal Society of Architects in Wales and the University of Wales Press launched a series of books exploring the architecture of Wales, seeking to add new chapters to the evolving story of the buildings, places and spaces of our 'damp, demanding and obsessively interesting country'.[1]

Now, in the third book in the series, we are delighted to extend the scope of the project beyond the geographical boundaries of Wales, by exploring the influence of Frank Lloyd Wright's Welsh roots and Unitarian upbringing on his creative achievements.

*Mary Wrenn*

[1]   Jan Morris, *Wales: Epic Views of a Small Country*.

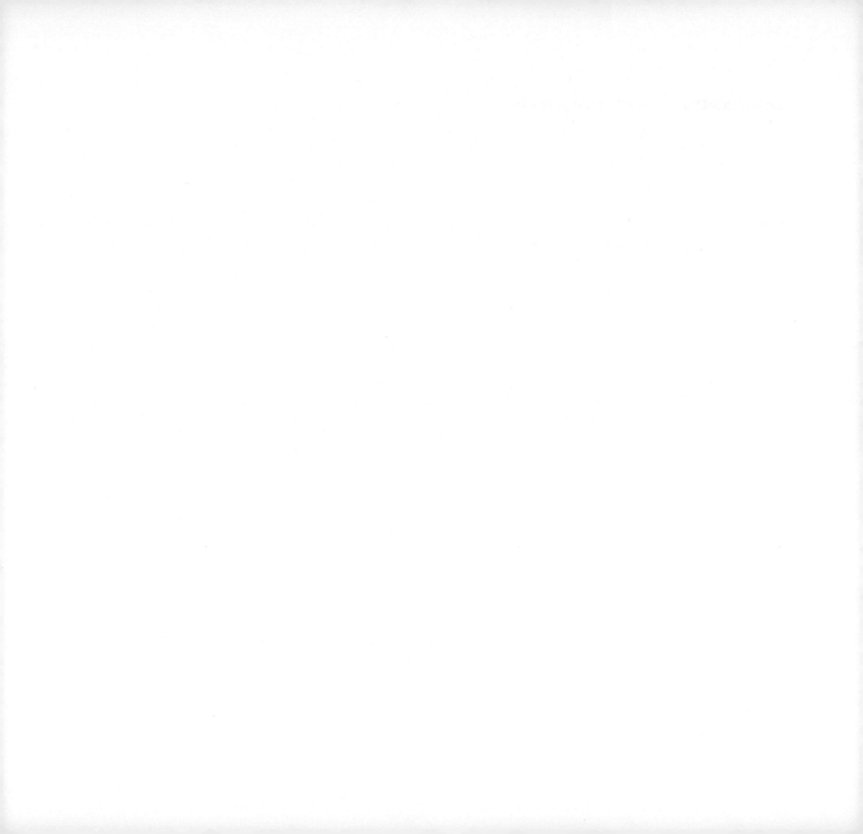

# List of Illustrations

# Family Tree

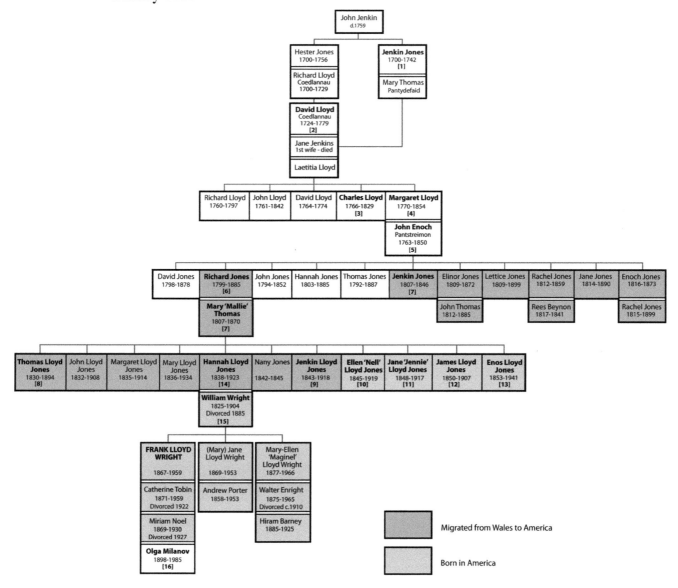

**John Jenkin** d.1759

**Hester Jones** 1700-1756

**Richard Lloyd** Coedlannau 1700-1729

**Jenkin Jones** 1700-1742 **[1]**

**Mary Thomas** Pantydefaid

**David Lloyd** Coedlannau 1724-1779 **[2]**

**Jane Jenkins** 1st wife - died

**Laetitia Lloyd**

**Richard Lloyd** 1760-1797

**John Lloyd** 1761-1842

**David Lloyd** 1764-1774

**Charles Lloyd** 1766-1829 **[3]**

**Margaret Lloyd** 1770-1854 **[4]**

**John Enoch** Pantstreimon 1763-1850 **[5]**

**David Jones** 1798-1878

**Richard Jones** 1799-1885 **[6]**

**John Jones** 1794-1852

**Hannah Jones** 1803-1885

**Thomas Jones** 1792-1887

**Jenkin Jones** 1807-1846 **[7]**

**Elinor Jones** 1809-1872

**Lettice Jones** 1809-1899

**Rachel Jones** 1812-1859

**Jane Jones** 1814-1890

**Enoch Jones** 1816-1873

**Mary 'Mallie' Thomas** 1807-1870 **[7]**

**John Thomas** 1812-1885

**Rees Beynon** 1817-1841

**Rachel Jones** 1815-1899

**Thomas Lloyd Jones** 1830-1894 **[8]**

**John Lloyd Jones** 1832-1908

**Margaret Lloyd Jones** 1835-1914

**Mary Lloyd Jones** 1836-1934

**Hannah Lloyd Jones** 1838-1923 **[14]**

**Nany Jones** 1842-1845

**Jenkin Lloyd Jones** 1843-1918 **[9]**

**Ellen 'Nell' Lloyd Jones** 1845-1919 **[10]**

**Jane 'Jennie' Lloyd Jones** 1848-1917 **[11]**

**James Lloyd Jones** 1850-1907 **[12]**

**Enos Lloyd Jones** 1853-1941 **[13]**

**William Wright** 1825-1904 Divorced 1885 **[15]**

**FRANK LLOYD WRIGHT** 1867-1959

**(Mary) Jane Lloyd Wright** 1869-1953

**Mary-Ellen 'Maginel' Lloyd Wright** 1877-1966

**Catherine Tobin** 1871-1959 Divorced 1922

**Andrew Porter** 1858-1953

**Walter Enright** 1875-1965 Divorced c.1910

**Miriam Noel** 1869-1930 Divorced 1927

**Hiram Barney** 1885-1925

**Olga Milanov** 1898-1985 **[16]**

Migrated from Wales to America

Born in America

## Significant Ancestors of Frank Lloyd Wright

[1] Rev. Jenkin Jones established the first Arminian (non-Trinitarian) Chapel in Wales at Llwynrhydowen in 1733.

[2] Rev. David Lloyd was the nephew of Rev. Jenkin Jones. His first wife was Rev. Jenkin Jones's daughter, Jane, his cousin. Jane died at a young age. His second wife, Laetitia, was also a Lloyd by birth. Rev. David Lloyd took over the leadership of Llwynrhydowen Chapel after the death of Rev. Jenkin Jones.

[3] Rev. Charles Lloyd led the Unitarian breakaway from the Arian tradition, establishing two new purely Unitarian chapels in 1802..

[4] Margaret Lloyd was a descendent of Cardiganshire nobility who married the farmer John Enoch of Pantstreimon. She took the name Margaret Jones after marriage.

[5] John Enoch, like his wife Margaret, was a dedicated Unitarian, and one of the founders of Pantydefaid Chapel.

[6] Richard Jones migrated to America with his family in 1844. He changed his surname to Lloyd Jones circa 1850.

[7] Jenkin Jones was Richard's closest brother. He migrated to America two years before Richard and his family joined him there.

[8] Mallie Thomas was born on the farm Pen-y-Wern, neighbouring Pantstreimon. She and Richard married in 1829, and lived at the farm 'Blaenralltddu' before they migrated to America.

[9] Thomas Lloyd Jones was the eldest of Richard and Mallie's children. He became responsible for the design and construction of the majority of the family's homes and farm buildings.

[10] Hannah Lloyd Jones was Frank Lloyd Wright's mother. She married in 1866, and from then on took the name Anna Lloyd Wright.

[11] Jenkin Lloyd Jones was the most famous of his siblings in his lifetime. He became the leader of the Western Unitarian Conference. Jenkin provided the opportunity for Frank Lloyd Wright to pursue his architectural career in Chicago.

[12] Ellen Lloyd Jones, with her sister Jane, established Hillside Home School in the Lloyd Jones Valley.

[13] James Lloyd Jones was Frank's favourite uncle. Frank lived on his farm through every summer from the age of 11 to 18.

[14] Jane Lloyd Jones established and led Hillside Home School, jointly with her sister Ellen. Ellen and Jane were among Frank Lloyd Wright's most important early clients.

[15] William Wright was Frank Lloyd Wright's father. He was born in Massachusetts, the son of a Baptist Minster.

[16] Olga (Olgivanna) Ivanovna Lazović was a native of Montenegro. She was estranged from her first husband, Vladimar Hinzenberg, when she first met Frank Lloyd Wright. They became a couple in 1924 and married in 1928, remaining together until Frank's death in 1959.

# Introduction

I had the good fortune, a few years ago, to be asked by BBC Wales to develop a television documentary looking at the life and work of Frank Lloyd Wright from the viewpoint of a Welsh architect.[1] In preparation I immersed myself in Wright's original autobiography, written in the late 1920s at what seemed the dead end of his career. Among the memories of his early life, it contains an account of his design of Unity Temple, in Oak Park, Chicago, a building regarded as revolutionary in its time, and a genuine precursor of modernism in architecture. Our first days' filming took us to south Ceredigion, to Llwynrhydowen, the mother-chapel of the Unitarians, Wright's ancestral homeland and Wright's people. As I took in the form and pattern of the Old Chapel, it became apparent to me, gradually, that the revolutionary Unity Temple of 1904 was its deliberate simulacrum.

Although no architect has been more written-about than Frank Lloyd Wright, this surprising fact appeared to have passed without mention. If something so significant could be missed, something that so clearly expressed Wright's identification with his Welsh roots, then surely, I suspected, there would be more to find. Indeed, there was.

Frank Lloyd Wright has every right to be considered the greatest architect of the modern age. The story of his life is no less astounding than his most remarkable architectural works. He enmeshed himself eagerly in myth and hearsay and revelled in the extravagance of his creative defiance. As a 'brand', as the projection of a cultivated persona, it has often been said that he was a signpost to the future, even that he invented the contemporary notion of the architect-as-artist. As an architect he was certainly ahead of his time. In fact he, more than anyone, calibrated the modern clock of architecture.

This book investigates two elusive aspects of his life. Firstly, the question asked at some stage by most Welsh people with an interest in architecture: just how Welsh was Frank Lloyd Wright? To what extent did he think of himself as one of us? The second theme concerns his behaviour, personal and creative: what exactly was it that he was trying to do, and why? Why was he so compelled, so determined to make himself exceptional? These are questions that can only be answered by looking far back through the generations that preceded Frank Lloyd Wright's time. They will be answered here.

I have divided the story into three sections. The first is set in eighteenth-century Cardiganshire, in the compass of Alltyrodyn, an estate of the ancient Lloyd dynasty. The second takes in the Atlantic Ocean, and a vast expanse of the western frontier of America, as it shifted through the course of the mid-nineteenth century. The third section begins with a young country boy stepping off a train into the cauldron of the world's fastest-growing city, a cauldron of inspiration …

Wright was first and foremost an American architect, so it is no surprise that all his serious biographers are American. All discuss his Welsh background, which they could hardly avoid as Wright often alluded to it, but none of them has recognised the significance of the connections between his Welsh roots, his religious beliefs and his childhood experience that reveal the clear map of his creative motivations.

According to the historian Robert M. Crunden, 'Wright's architectural theory verges on the incomprehensible unless it is understood in terms of the literary and religious ideas that dominated New England during the mid-nineteenth century.' Transcendentalism and Unitarianism were prominent among those concerns. In *Ministers of Reform*, Crunden's account of the Progressive Era in America, he also observes how essential it was to the achievements of great American figures like Frank Lloyd Wright, John Dewey and Jane Addams that they found themselves among the right people, in the ideal place and at a unique moment in the evolution of American society. Crunden makes the following point about Dewey, which could be applied in identical terms to Wright:

> Had he been born two decades earlier such a path would have been far harder to follow and the questions asked and the answers given would have been different. Had he been born two decades later, the pioneer work would have been done, perhaps along other lines, and a far different, less original career could have resulted. Both the people and the ideas were rooted in the place, problems and opportunities of their times.

It is true that Frank Lloyd Wright was fortunate to find himself in the right place at the right time, but he was just one young architect among many. It was by chance that he followed a path that led him into architecture. The work that survives from his early apprenticeship displays all the familiar, touching incompetence of an architectural novice. And yet, within a decade of taking his first awkward steps, he was briefly abreast of the foremost architectural innovators in the world – before leaving them in his slipstream. It was he who emerged to become the architect who 'probably deserves more credit, and more blame, for what modern America looks like than any other single figure in American history'.[2]

The aesthetic and design influences that Wright drew upon have always been a rich area for speculation. Despite his efforts to deny and to obfuscate them, some sources are clear to see, in particular the vernacular traditions of Asia and Meso-America. It is evident, also, that he applied methodical systems in his draughting that enabled him to develop architectural ideas efficiently in three dimensions. These aspects of his practice have been pored over meticulously by academics, and they help us to understand, to an extent, the sheer abundance and diversity of his work. But regardless of the depth of their scholarship, all have ultimately retreated from trying to account for his achievements. It seems enough to say that he was an unfathomable genius, that his ideas came, as if by magic, from thin air. Wright liked to encourage this view himself. When he was asked about the origins of his ideas, he used to say that he 'shook them out of his sleeve', like a stage conjuror.

Architecture involves teams of people, pulling and pushing over months and years towards their divergent goals under the gaze of an anxious client. It offers endless opportunity for inventive thinking and for ingenuity; it can be a wonderfully creative discipline, but it provides little space for the unprecedented flash of original insight that we associate with the individual genius. Nonetheless, Frank Lloyd Wright enjoyed leading people to infer the presence of genius in his work. Throughout his long career he strongly resisted the suggestion that his accomplishments owed anything to earthly influences. As much as he wanted his achievements to be recognised, he wanted them to be unaccountable. But they are not. Even Wright's extraordinary work can eventually be accounted for, provided we trace the many tangled branches of his story back to their roots. What we will find, then, is that everything that sets him apart has its origins in the radical religious and philosophical attitudes, and an appetite for hard work that were deliberately and methodically embedded into his personality during his childhood by his Welsh Unitarian family, by his mother, his many aunts and uncles, and through them, by his grandparents, Richard and Mallie Lloyd Jones. Without these influences he might still have become an architect, possibly a good architect, but he would not have become the greatest architect of modern times ∎

# Introduction
## *Notes*

1  'Frank Lloyd Wright: The Man who Built America', Wildflame Productions (Cardiff), 2018.

2  R. M. Crunden, *Ministers of Reform* (Champaign: University of Illinois Press, 1984), pp. 64, 133–62.

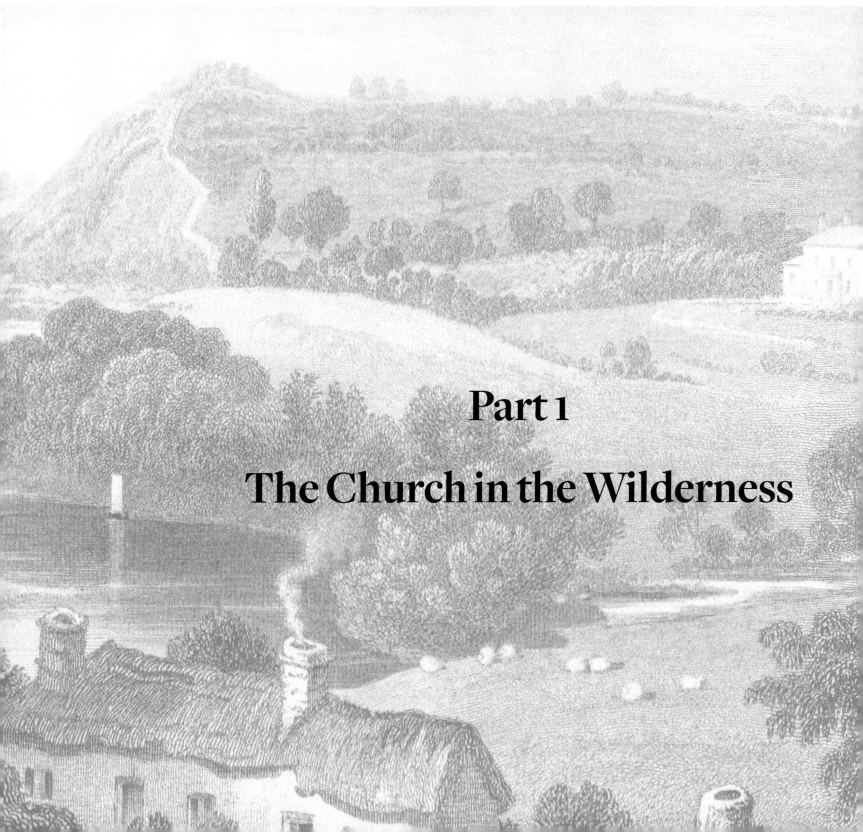

# Part 1

# The Church in the Wilderness

# 1

# A Rural Enlightenment

## Early October, 1926.
## Wildhurst, Lake Minnetonka, Minnesota

Frank Lloyd Wright was on the run from the law, pursued by state police, federal agents; by a posse of tabloid journalists and voracious lawyers, all energised by the calculated fury of his estranged wife. He had laid a false trail, heading way south to the desert of New Mexico and, as far as he knew, his tormentors had followed it.[1] The prospect that he looked out upon from his safe house was cool, watery, sparkling in early autumn sunlight; islets and jetties and the low,

wooded shoreline of the lake, far to the north-west of the Lloyd Jones Valley and Taliesin, the home that he had built there.[2] He was reminded of the view along the shore of Lake Mendota: the view from the backyard of his boyhood home, the first proper home that he could remember. He let his mind drift back, across the placid water. The muttering of his mother's hens, the fruit trees and the shuffling of the cow in the barn. Was it a happy time? Perhaps not entirely, but it was a time of revelation, and the memories were still vivid.

He supposed that it was as good a moment as any to start writing his autobiography. Despite everything: his flight, the reality that at any time he might lose everything, he felt warm contentment. In the next room the beautiful, young Olgivanna, his would-be wife and the unwitting cause of his legal predicament, was resting with her ten-year-old daughter Svetlana, and with their baby, Iovanna. The book was Olgivanna's idea, a good idea. He had nothing to draw with, and no projects to work on anyway. Maude, the stenographer, was sitting patiently at his side, waiting for him to start his dictation. He had been giving it some thought. He had a good story to tell, the right kind of story, and he was in the right mood to tell it.[3] Sunlight, sparkling water, willows turning gold, for the moment, peace. Time to begin: *'Back in Wales, in the Victorian Era, there lived a hatter.'*[4]

## 1840. South Cardiganshire, Wales (Fig. 1.1)

At every chapel meeting there was talk about liberty, the rights of man, a new and better society. It was getting harder for Richard Jones to be satisfied with the life that he was born into (Pl. 1).

Richard had five children and another due soon. He had to find some way to improve their lot while still keeping the farm going. With the help of his younger brother, Jenkin, he'd branched into hat-making at what had seemed the right time. It required no large investment, and only a little space.[5] They were beaver hats: easy to make. Tapering stove-pipes with a buckram shell and black silk covering. Just a few years before, it had only been the gentry, but now all the respectable women wanted to wear them. They had been

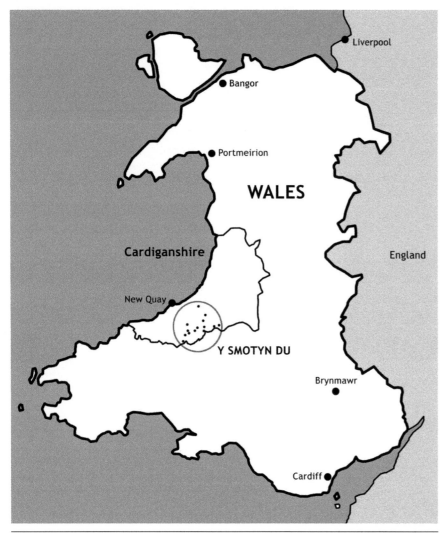

Fig. 1.1. A map of Wales. The locations identified are all significant to the story of Frank Lloyd Wright and his Welsh forebears. The circle encloses *Y Smotyn Du*, the 'Black Spot' of Unitarianism in south Cardiganshire (now Ceredigion).

Pl. 1. Richard Lloyd Jones. A portrait from the 1932 edition of Frank Lloyd Wright's *An Autobiography*.

busy at the fairs and had made a good profit, but that had quite suddenly changed. They found themselves competing with merchants who came to the fairs with hundreds of hats, thin, light and very cheap, hats made in factories, in England.[6] Richard's hats may have been heavier and stronger; he would even stand on top of them to prove their quality, but he couldn't compete on price.[7] He knew that his business, like those of the other small milliners of south Wales, was destined for the hat-box of history. But Richard was not downhearted. He believed that God was always present in the world around him and that He could always be trusted. God would provide, as long as Richard would follow his own instincts and remain true to his faith. This was a conviction that he shared with almost all of his neighbours. Like him, they were Unitarians, Rational Dissenters, followers of the enlightened philosophy of Joseph Priestley, Theophilus Lindsey and of Richard Price, the Welsh protagonist of the American Revolution.

In the rest of Britain Unitarianism was the faith of urban radicals, aligned with the struggle for universal suffrage and workers' rights. It was a fringe denomination, its chapels greatly outnumbered by those of the Methodists and Baptists. Richard's neighbourhood was quite different. Within barely twenty square miles, centred on the parishes of Llandysul and Llanwenog, there were a dozen flourishing Unitarian

chapels, a greater concentration than anywhere else in Britain (Fig. 1.2). The Methodists referred to it as *Y Smotyn Du*, the Black Spot, a disturbing example of what could go wrong if radicals and free thinkers could get a foothold in a community. Beyond their enclave they were regarded as heretics, 'people without hope'. They often felt embattled, even oppressed, but this only gave strength to their conviction that it was they, the Unitarians, who were in possession of the Truth, while the rest of society was stuck in the superstitious past, blindly following derelict religious and social conventions. Within their close-knit community they shared pride in their own resilience and a deep commitment to the importance of moral purity and liberal education.[8] The 'Black Spot' of south Cardiganshire was, 'an almost unique example of an enduring rural Enlightenment', a wonderfully fertile spiritual landscape. Richard's ancestors – Frank Lloyd Wright's ancestors – were responsible for planting its first seeds.[9]

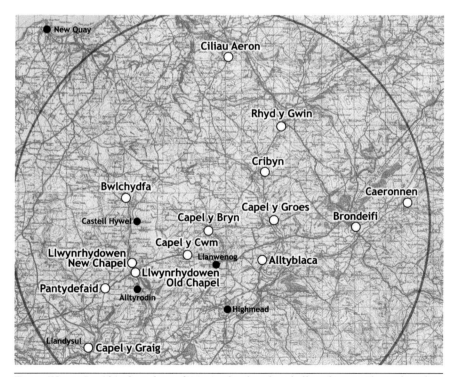

Fig. 1.2. *Y Smotyn Du* with its dense cluster of Unitarian chapels, each marked by a white spot. The circular outline is enlarged from the map of Wales (Figure 1.1). The other locations identified are significant in the history of the Lloyd Jones family.

## Mid-Eighteenth Century, South Cardiganshire, Wales

The name of Jenkin Jones recurs through the life story of Frank Lloyd Wright. The most famous of them was Jenkin Lloyd Jones, Frank's uncle, the leader of the Unitarian cause in the west of America in the latter decades of the nineteenth century, but the first Jenkin was a young idealist, the son of a blacksmith, born in 1700 and ordained as a minister in 1726, soon after his graduation from the Presbyterian Academy of Carmarthen.[10] In common with other Dissenting colleges, Carmarthen Academy encouraged its students to develop their independence of thought. It had an international perspective, with a keen focus on technological progress, particularly in the natural sciences. Thomas Perrot, the principal of the academy during Jenkin's time, encouraged his students to question conformist doctrine. This led some, Jenkin among them, to the ideas of the sixteenth-century theologian Arminius, a man who had outraged the established Church by arguing that there was nothing in the Bible that supported the doctrine of predestination. He believed that anyone could be 'saved'; it was up to each individual if they wanted to be saved or not. When Jenkin returned from college to his family home he did so as a confirmed Arminian, with an urgent compulsion to spread the good news.

The initial reaction was not encouraging. His Arminianism was dismissed as a 'faith for the young and roughians because it allowed everybody to go to heaven'.[11] He was able to preach on only a few occasions at Pantycreuddyn Independent, his home chapel, before the members banned him. He then began preaching outdoors, in the garden of his parents' home at Penybanc, just south of the manor house of Alltyrodyn[12] (Pl. 2 ). Once he could be heard, hostility softened. Jenkin was charismatic: word spread and people were drawn to his message. Although Jenkin's father was a blacksmith, he had married into modest wealth. In 1732, with support from his father and from Dafydd Thomas, an affluent neighbour, Jenkin built a new chapel a short distance to the north of Alltyrodyn.[13] That chapel was Llwynrhydowen, dedicated in

Pl. 2. Alltyrodyn House (centre) and its hinterland. The farm in the top right corner is Pantstreimon, the birthplace of Richard Lloyd Jones. The fields at the bottom right belong to Pen-y-Wern, the birthplace of Mallie Lloyd Jones. The village of Llwynrhydowen can be seen at the top left.
Photograph Toby Driver, © Crown copyright: RCAHMW.

Frank Lloyd Wright: The Architecture of Defiance

1733, the first Arminian chapel in Wales.[14] Over the course of the following decade the membership of Llwynrhydowen grew to over four hundred. A second chapel was built at Alltyblaca, a few miles to the east, and Arminian services were preached from at least three other shared Nonconformist pulpits in the neighbourhood. The cause was growing steadily when Jenkin succumbed to a common illness, and died. He was only forty-two years old.

As it had been ignited by his charisma, it might have been expected that the Arminian light would die with Jenkin, but ill fortune was turned unexpectedly to good. A succession had been planned a few years before. The lead ministry was to pass to Jenkin's young nephew, David Lloyd, the son of Jenkin's sister Hester. It had been assumed naturally that this would happen at some time in the future, after David's ordination, but at the time of Jenkin's death, the boy was less than two years into his seminary training. David's family knew that he was gifted, a brilliant scholar since his childhood, a born leader perhaps.[15] So it was that David Lloyd found himself propelled to the head of a thriving, radical religious community, aged just eighteen. He never did go back to college, but combined active ministry with his own scholarship from then through the rest of his life.[16] He became a remarkably learned man, fluent in Greek, Latin and Hebrew as well as English, Italian and French, and with many correspondents in European academic circles. He came to be thought of in his day as 'the greatest religious genius and the greatest influence in the cause of religious freedom in Cardiganshire, if not in the whole of Wales'.[17] He also began a significant tradition among the leaders of rational Dissent in the area by setting up his own school to provide an enlightened education to the children of his congregation. Crucially, David Lloyd was also Cardiganshire nobility, a descendent, on his father's side, of the Lloyds of Castell Hywel. The Lloyd name carried ancient prestige.[18] For the first rational Dissenters of Cardiganshire, David Lloyd's leadership lent a new authority to the Arminian cause.

The Arminian congregation continued to grow and, in 1754, Llwynrhydowen Chapel was rebuilt, much enlarged (Pl. 3). The network of chapels prepared to host his services also grew steadily, for the first time raising real alarm among the leaders of the established Church and of the Calvinist societies who had their own ambitions for Wales. In the late 1760s David Lloyd began to share ministerial duties with a capable assistant, the Rev. David Davis. Like Jenkin Jones, Davis was a graduate of Carmarthen Academy but, unlike Jenkin, he had come under the influence of an Arian tutor, a believer in the doctrine of Arius, an Egyptian priest of the third century AD. Although the roots of Arianism are far older than those of Arminianism, Arianism represents an even more radical set of beliefs, the most controversial of which is that the Holy Trinity does not exist, that there is only one God, and that the Father's deity could be shared with no other.[19] In the late eighteenth century in Britain, because of its association with anti-establishment politics, Arianism remained a dangerous persuasion. Despite this, as the two Davids spent more time together, it was the elder theologian who came to accept the younger minister's more progressive convictions.

David Davis was another brilliant and persuasive man: a great scholar, multi-lingual like his mentor and a gifted poet in modern and classical languages. It was David Davis who made a celebrated translation of Thomas Gray's 'Elegy in a Country Churchyard' into Welsh, considered by many to be an improvement on the original. The memory of this translated poem had a special significance for Frank Lloyd Wright's family which resonated into the twentieth century. In 1782 David Davis made a surprising move: he bought a farm around two miles north of Llwynrhydowen, which included the ruins of the ancient seat of the Lloyd family, Castell Hywel. He then converted most of the farmhouse into a preparatory school. Over the thirty years of its existence this 'Athens of Cardiganshire' built a high academic reputation, preparing pupils for Carmarthen Academy and for Oxford and Cambridge.[20] Through his educational mission, David Davis did more than any other Dissenting minister in Wales to forge the link between liberal religion and liberal education, to make spiritual Truth inseparable from innovation in science, politics and the humanities.

The Rev. David Lloyd died in 1779, at the age of fifty-five. David Davis assumed the leadership of the Arminian chapels and benevolently led his membership onto the more radical path of Arianism.[21]

While David Davis easily filled the gap left by David Lloyd at the head of the Dissenting community, the hole torn in the Lloyd family proved more difficult to repair. David Lloyd's widow Laetitia was left with six children to provide for, with a fraction of the means she had been used to. Their third son, Charles, was twelve years old when his father died. David Lloyd's brother John paid for young Charles to be taught at David Davis's Castell Hywel school, but when he matriculated his uncle's largesse ran out without warning, leaving Charles distraught and having to fund his own way through theological training at Carmarthen Academy. Charles had to manage the full four years with less than £20, the whole of his inheritance.[22] He graduated as a frustrated and conflicted young man, by turns terrified of his own vulnerability and driven to fury by the laziness and conservatism of the society in which he was expected to make a living.

Charles Lloyd took his first pastorate at a Presbyterian Chapel in Worcestershire, where he struggled to cope with the fact that his personal understanding of scripture was at odds with the traditional rituals of his role. He went along with it reluctantly at first, grateful for the salary. But his conscience eventually asserted itself when he refused to baptise a dying baby on the grounds that there was no such thing as 'original sin' and therefore the child did not need to be 'saved' from anything. He told the dismayed parents that it was a 'superstition which it is high time to explode'. He was dismissed from his post very soon after, but he reflected later that the 'event had a great influence on all my opinions and on my future destiny'.[23] He had determined that he should live the life of his true convictions while resenting, but accepting, that they could lead him onto a dangerous path.

For the next few years he abandoned his clerical vocation and turned to teaching, keeping his counsel as his private sentiments veered increasingly towards extreme radicalism. Around him, English society grew more brittle and reactionary, fearful that republican upheavals in France would spread across the Channel. Then, in 1791, Joseph Priestley, the prominent Dissenter and republican, was forced to flee from his Birmingham home as it was set ablaze by a royalist mob. A year later, their monarchy dispatched,

Pl. 3. *'Yr Hen Gapel'*, Llwynrhydowen. The 'Old Chapel'. The present building dates from 1834.

the leaders of the Republic of France made it known that they intended overthrowing the British monarchy too. There were many in the Dissenting community, including Joseph Priestley, who had openly supported the revolution in France. From 1793 any public statement of that kind would be regarded as an act of treason, punishable by death. Charles took the greatest care not to draw attention to himself.

Charles Lloyd had left Cardiganshire because there had been nothing for him there. He might never have returned, but for another untimely death. While he had inherited £20 from his father, his older brother, Richard, had inherited the large family farm, Coedlannau Fawr. The farm had provided a living to supplement Richard's work as junior minister at Llwynrhydowen, but then, aged just thirty-seven and still unmarried, Richard himself passed away. Charles found unexpectedly that Coedlannau Fawr now belonged to him. At this time Charles was settled in Exeter, married with two young children.

He knew nothing about farming, but he sensed that Coedlannau Fawr might provide an opportunity, for once, to make a reasonable living. He wondered, also, if he could take over the junior minister's position at Llwynrhydowen that his late brother had vacated. David Davis, his old schoolmaster, was still senior minister at the chapel. Richard died in 1797. Earlier that year, the French had actually attempted an invasion of Britain, a venture that ended shambolically where it began, at Fishguard on the Pembrokeshire coast, just south of Cardiganshire. For a while the region had crackled with aggressive royalism, but once the excitement had dissipated the far south-west of Wales settled back to being the 'obscure district' it had always been.[24] In 1799, with his wife and, now, three children, Charles Lloyd turned his back on urbane Exeter, and away, perhaps wisely, from the baleful scrutiny of the English establishment, feeling safe enough at last to take to the pulpit again. Wisely, because Charles had had plenty of time to think when he had been leading his quiet life on the south coast. He had been reading the works of the leading Unitarians. He had even corresponded with Priestley, and had become convinced by a proposition that would have outraged the vast majority of decent folk: that Jesus was not the Son of God at all, that he was a great teacher, a human being only, and furthermore that the Bible was not the word of God but the work of ordinary men, with all the flaws that that would entail. By the time he returned to his home country he had become fully Unitarian.

Charles Lloyd was Frank Lloyd Wright's great-granduncle. He was an awkward man, curmudgeonly at times, but strong on principle even when his own convictions made him nervous. When he wanted to write an autobiography, he was too wary to put his name to it, and published it anonymously. This makes it a strange book to read, as he omits any reference to names, places or information that might allow a reader to identify him. It ends with a memory of Cardiganshire, and a significant note of triumph: 'I thank God for having made use of me in a work which I consider most conducive to the information, to the moral worth and to the happiness of the country ... this was the most important era of my life. And here I close my narrative.'[25] The

events that he alludes to were not what he expected when he returned to Wales. First he had to deal with the failure of his farming experiment. He had read as much as he could in preparation, but found the reality a very different prospect. A first wet summer and poor harvest were followed by another. He found himself deep in debt and had to put the property up for rent. The chapel was his familiar ground and his real profession, but he ran into problems there too.

Although two years had passed since Richard's death, Charles had been relieved to find that his brother's post at Llwynrhydowen had not been permanently taken. Supply pastors were still being brought in to provide cover. But Charles was dismayed when it dawned on him that David Davis had not kept the post open for him, but had been keeping it free until Davis's own son Timothy was ready to graduate from Carmarthen Academy and fill the vacancy. David Davis knew that Charles Lloyd was highly regarded by his congregations because he was the son of the revered David Lloyd. Everyone assumed that Charles would be the obvious successor to his elder brother. Each of the ministers felt intimidated by the other. Davis compromised by asking Charles to deliver some services, provided he did so as another supply pastor. Charles claimed that he accepted this with good grace. He had to rein in his Unitarian views, but it did at least give him the opportunity to develop a relationship with the local community. He did this very effectively, to the extent that chapel members began to get impatient for Davis to promote Charles to the vacant pastorate. But then Charles heard a rumour that David Davis had told some influential members that Charles was secretly a Baptist, and could not be trusted with a permanent role at Llwynrhydowen. Charles was appalled: 'the falsity, the calumny and malignity displayed on that day changed every sentiment in my breast!'[26]

Charles refused to be defeated. He would not risk destroying the trust of the Llwynrhydowen membership by telling his tale of treachery, but he instead appealed discreetly to supporters among the congregations to whom he had confided some of his more extreme liberal views. One of his keener advocates was David Jenkin Rees, the owner of a prosperous farm in the Aeron valley, called 'Lloyd Jack', an hour's ride north of Llanwenog. Rees had attended David Davis's Arian services for years, but he had recently been excited by the more radical, truly Unitarian ideas that Charles had expressed. He had been trying gently to put forward the same ideas in many conversations with David Davis, and earlier with David Lloyd, Charles's father. They had been sympathetic but not to the point of further liberalising their Arian message. In Charles he saw real hope for change. Rees invited Charles to visit him at Lloyd Jack so that they could discuss the prospects for the Unitarian cause.[27]

It is most likely that it was at Lloyd Jack that David Jenkin Rees first introduced Charles to his influential friends Thomas Evans and Edward Williams, men who would be important allies in their cause. Charles knew that in some circles they were also notorious men who, unless he was careful, could get him into trouble. Both were better known by other names. Evans was Tomos Glyn Cothi, also known as 'Priestley Bach' (little Priestley). In 1796, with financial support from the eminent Theophilus Lindsey, Tomos Glyn Cothi had established the first pure Unitarian chapel in Wales at Brechfa, across the county border in Carmarthenshire. His good friend Edward Williams was better known as Iolo Morganwg, Wales's greatest antiquarian, and most dangerous seditionary: the Bard of Liberty himself[28] (Pl. 4).

## 20 October 1926. Wildhurst, Lake Minnetonka, Minnesota

Frank Lloyd Wright had just dictated the closing paragraphs of Book 1 of his autobiography, the story of his childhood. His mind was still full of memories of the Lloyd Joneses, of The Valley, and of Madison and Chicago in the early days. Dusk had fallen across the lake, another peaceful night lay ahead. Then, a loud crack on the door, shouts from outside. He hadn't expected that at all. The local sheriff pushed past Maude as she opened the door, followed by more state police and men in suits, led by his estranged wife's lawyer, and journalists, some with cameras. He kept his composure, as he always did, as he was goaded by the posse, and even when he was handcuffed and pushed into a police car. Barely an hour later he was marched along a steel gallery, led by

Etched by Robert Cruikshank. _ from a memoriter drawing by E.W.

Edward Williams.
Bardd Braint a Defod.

Pl. 4. Edward Williams, better known as Iolo Morganwg.
Frontispiece to Elijah Waring's *Recollections and Anecdotes of Edward Williams, The Bard of Glamorgan or Iolo Morganwg* (1850).

torchlight in the darkness of Hennepin County Jailhouse in the centre of Minneapolis. As the warden locked him into his cell, Frank asked for a message to be sent back to the house on the lake, to tell Olgivanna that she shouldn't worry, that he was going to be fine. 'No need', the warden replied, 'they are all here.' Frank was outraged: not just Olgivanna and the baby, but little Svetlana too. They had all been brought in another car and locked in cells as disgusting as his[29] (Pl. 5).

Svetlana was the focus of the first hearing in the County Court the next morning. The young girl's father was Vlad Hinzenberg, Olgivanna's ex-husband. He had been convinced by the lawyer acting for Frank's estranged wife that Frank was planning to take Svetlana out of the country, maybe never to return. Hinzenberg was aghast. He offered a reward of $500 for the capture of his daughter's abductors. It worked: the reward had led directly to their arrest. But even before the arraignment had taken place Hinzenberg had realised that there had been no abduction planned at all. Frank and Olgivanna had no intention of leaving America; they had been hiding in Minnesota for weeks. Those charges at least could be dismissed, but they weren't free yet. In

Pl. 5.  The arrest of Frank Lloyd Wright, Lake Minnetonka, 20 October 1926.
Courtesy of Hennepin County Library.

the afternoon they appeared in the neighbouring Federal Courthouse to answer more charges brought against them under the Mann Act, a law intended originally to prevent the trafficking of women for prostitution. A worthy legal instrument, but in the view of many too often abused to persecute innocent unmarried couples who made the mistake of travelling across state lines. They were reassured by their lawyer. He told them that Olgivanna was only required to give a full account of her movements with Frank to convince the judge that it was entirely consensual. Frank went into the hearing feeling relaxed. He took the stand first. To Olgivanna's acute discomfort, when asked to give his name and standing he said, 'I am Frank Lloyd Wright, the world's greatest architect.'

The Federal Court hearing was not as straightforward as their lawyer had led them to expect. In her candour, Olgivanna mentioned that she and Frank had spent a short while in Puerto Rico, to escape the Wisconsin winter, two months after their baby had been born. American citizens could travel to Puerto Rico without a passport, but it wasn't actually American territory. The young federal prosecutor was elated: that would mean she had violated her status as an 'alien resident'. More charges were suddenly thrown at them. They were trapped: there would have to be another Federal Court hearing, and another night in the hideous County Jail. Back in court the following day, the judge recorded the new charges. They would take weeks to prepare, so he agreed to release them on deposit of a substantial bond. Frank couldn't pay it. Not for the first time, devoted friends and family came to his rescue. Despite the cloud still over them, the couple, their lawyers and their generous supporters adjourned to a nearby hotel to celebrate their freedom. Olgivanna had been badly affected by the experience. She felt ashamed and severely frightened, while Frank was his usual good-humoured self. She rankled at his nonchalance. 'Why did you have to say that about being the world's greatest architect? You should have shown more modesty!' Frank consoled her: 'But Olgivanna, what else could I tell them? I was under oath!'[30]

# First Years of the Nineteenth Century. South Cardiganshire, Wales

TRUTH. The word meant more to Iolo Morganwg than any other in the English language. Truth that could be held up against tyranny, against prejudice and against the suffocating self-interest of the establishment. Truth to confront superstition and ignorance. The truth of pure holiness in the beauty and harmony of nature: the truth of one God, the Unitarian TRUTH. To any intelligent person, he believed, these truths should be obvious. But throughout his lifetime he pursued another more elusive truth with relentless determination: the truth of the primacy of the Welsh nation in the Isles of Britain, and of the pre-eminence of her language and poetry. Frank Lloyd Wright has roots that go back to the ancient Lloyds of Castell Hywel, but for reasons that will become clear, the story of the making of Wright, of his character and his creative brilliance seems really to begin with the meeting of Charles Lloyd and Iolo Morganwg at Lloyd Jack, at the dawn of the nineteenth century. Frank and Iolo are not just strongly connected in history; they are exceptionally similar people. Each was a lifelong advocate and follower of Truth, and each understood Truth to be a statement of defiance. Each was also clear, in his own mind, that Truth was a powerful creative and spiritual force, and that it should never be confused with mere fact.

In 1801, with the encouragement of Iolo Morganwg, Charles Lloyd made the most courageous move of his life. He began to deliver Unitarian services on his own, away from the protection of Llwynrhydowen and its sister chapels. David Jenkin Rees and other sympathisers licensed their farm buildings so that Charles could preach from them. Against a backdrop of aggressive loyalist persecution in the world outside, Charles Lloyd's congregations grew steadily, and as they grew, those of the Arian chapels began to shrink. 'Our success was rapid and considerable. The whole country was roused to inquiry; and curiosity, or a better principle, brought people to our assemblies from a distance of many miles.'[31] As the mood of south Cardiganshire became more radical, so the pressure from Anglicans, Methodists, magistrates and loyalist militias increased. Charles Lloyd had hoped that Cardiganshire would provide relief from royalist persecution. For a short while it had, but by 1801 reactionary sentiment eventually reached Carmarthen Academy itself: the governors announced that they would no longer take students from non-trinitarian families. Then, in a move that sent a tremor through the Unitarian community, the authorities in Carmarthen arrested Tomos Glyn Cothi on a charge of sedition.

The Unitarians knew that the charges were spurious. In the course of a rowdy drinking party, it was alleged, Glyn Cothi had entertained the crowd by singing *The Carmagnole*, a Jacobin anthem extolling the destruction of the monarchy. He was supposed to have sung an English translation, making George III the intended target – an unlikely scenario at a very Welsh gathering.[32] The judge was a well-known scourge of Dissenters, especially Unitarians whom he believed to be supporters of the French Revolution: he was determined to eradicate them from society. Despite the efforts of Iolo Morganwg to defend him, Tomos Glyn Cothi was sentenced to two years in Carmarthen jail and two sessions in a public pillory, leaving his young family to depend on the charity of the Unitarian community. The disturbing affair had another momentous consequence: with the hope of greater strength in union, Iolo Morganwg and a group of Unitarian allies, including Charles Lloyd and David Rees of Lloyd Jack, met to establish the first Welsh Unitarian Society[33] (Pl. 6).

David Davis's continued resistance to the blossoming Unitarian cause led, eventually, to outright secession. Under the dark cloud of the Glyn Cothi trial, work began on the construction of two new pure Unitarian chapels on sites that were carefully chosen for proximity to Jenkin Jones's pioneer chapels. The first, Capel y Groes, was just a mile and a half from Alltyblaca, and the second, Pantydefaid, was even closer to Llwynrhydowen. Iolo Morganwg, who for many by that time was a popular hero, was present in 1802 at the opening of both, and for each he carved a handsome dedication stone (Pl. 7).

At Pantydefaid, Iolo Morganwg was introduced, by the Rev. Charles Lloyd, to the most committed of his congregation, the generous donors and founders. One of the seven founders of Pantydefaid was Charles Lloyd's

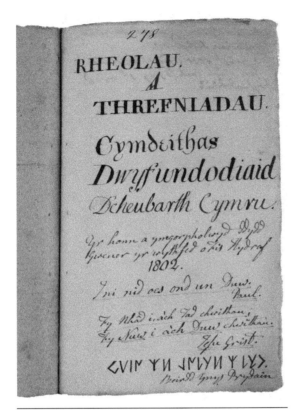

It was his triumph in leading the successful Unitarian breakaway from Llwynrhydowen that Charles Lloyd remembered with such satisfaction ten years later, when he came to write the final words of his autobiography. By then he had the added satisfaction of knowing that, one by one, the other Arian chapels in south Cardiganshire had all become Unitarian, but he was far away at the time. After leading his two breakaway chapels for just one year, he gave them up and returned to the south of England. His reasons for leaving are not recorded, but the curious approach that he took to writing his memoir suggests that he left because he could not live with the fear that he might end up, like Tomos Glyn Cothi, in the pillory outside Carmarthen jail.

In the course of his many tramping visits to Cardiganshire, long after Charles Lloyd's premature departure, Iolo Morganwg would make a point of visiting Pantydefaid. It is possible that he became further acquainted with Charles Lloyd's sister Margaret, and with her husband, John Enoch. Even if they did not know Iolo well personally, their close relative Charles Lloyd certainly had done. Their

brother-in-law, a farmer named John Enoch, the husband of Charles's sister Margaret. They were tenants of an old farm called Pantstreimon, just to the east of Alltyrodyn Manor. The small group also included their immediate neighbours, the brothers David and Thomas James of Pen-y-Wern. A few years later Thomas James would find himself the father of a baby daughter, Mary, known as Mallie. John Enoch and Margaret may even have had with them their three-year-old son, Richard, who, in the fullness of time, would become Mallie's husband. Later still Richard and Mallie would become the grandparents of the 'world's greatest architect'.[34]

proximity to Iolo Morganwg was deeply important to them. Before Iolo had given it an ancient cultural context and romanticised it, in the circumscribed existence of the small farmer the landscape of Wales meant little more than something that had to be struggled with. Richard and Mallie Jones, Frank Lloyd Wright's grandparents, were among the earliest generations to inhabit fully the Wales that Iolo had revealed. This meant that when they left for America they took with them a very particular sense of their own nationhood. It was a vision of Wales that was deeply interwoven with their language, their Unitarian faith, their landscape, a community and a unique way of life, an enlightenment persisting in the shadows of English dominion. Although it was rooted in the ancient past, Iolo's was a progressive vision that demanded action to resist discrimination, oppression and anglicisation. To the Unitarian community of south Cardiganshire it was a vision that sustained a beacon of hope, an inner strength that would only grow in the face of adversity, a drive towards liberty that could propel a family half way around the world.

In his autobiography Frank Lloyd Wright recalled that his grandfather had a 'family crest, the old Druid symbol: /|\ "TRUTH AGAINST THE WORLD"'. Frank understood the deep meaning in these words, the meaning that Iolo Morganwg invested them with. It was a Truth that would inevitably bring the believer into direct conflict with the accepted norms of wider society, that had the power to burn through the shallow pretensions and oppressions of the establishment. It was this expression of Truth that Iolo had kindled and then carried aloft as a torch, and it was the same Truth that lit the way for Frank through his extraordinary life and career. Although the idea of 'Truth Against the World' had been passed on to Frank through two generations, and of course to many other Welsh people since 1792 when they had first appeared in print, no one else among Frank's family, and few others anywhere, perhaps since Iolo himself, so deeply and completely inhabited the meaning of 'Truth Against the World' as did Frank Lloyd Wright.[35]

The words were invoked by Iolo Morganwg, as was the three-line symbol. Perhaps they were indeed from the rubric of ancient Druids: if they were, the evidence is absent. It is certainly evident that the words expressed Iolo's defiant personality, his willingness to stand up to authority and his contempt for convention. In these respects Frank's personality and attitudes seem identical to Iolo Morganwg's. It should come as no surprise, then, that the revolutionary vigour and spiritual clarity of 'Truth Against the World' appealed so powerfully to Frank Lloyd Wright.

Both Frank and Iolo presented themselves as autodidacts, developers of their own distinctive brilliance, whereas, in fact, each was largely home-schooled by an intelligent, articulate and dominant mother. They both thrived under intense maternal attention and, as a consequence, came to regard formal education as empty and unnourishing.[36] Each thought of his father as being relatively marginal to his upbringing, although in both cases their fathers taught them skills that they prized. Frank's father taught him about music; Iolo's father taught him how to work stone. From their similar backgrounds each evolved an extravagant, solipsistic personality. Each was often excessively passionate and provocative, but at the same time desperate to be appreciated. Both cultivated a flamboyant persona, a public image that, as they became better known, made them vulnerable to caricature. Each was in no doubt that the world owed them a living.

Iolo and Frank both identified themselves and energised themselves creatively by taking a strong contrapuntal position. In Iolo's case the opposition was England: its monarchy, its class system and its established religion. For Frank, in his early career at least, the opposition was the establishment of New England: its decadent Europhilia, its dreary Puritan conventions and its superior attitude as expressed so deplorably in its enthusiasm for Beaux-Arts, neo-classical architecture. Later in his life Frank directed his righteous anger at more substantial political and social targets, flirting occasionally with disaster. Although each of them was at times obsessed with nation building, in Iolo's case the nation of Wales and in Frank's, America, their own brand of patriotism led both to be investigated for treasonous activity: Iolo by the Privy Council in 1794,[37] and

Frank by the FBI in 1941, for his anti-war statements and again in 1955 for his pro-Russian stance.[38] Each of them was a vigorous public advocate of pacifism at inconvenient times. Although Frank narrowly avoided prosecution during World War II, five of his loyal students did serve prison sentences. For both Iolo and Frank, hostility to England added piquancy to their rebellious instincts. Over years of suffering abuse and discrimination in stoneyards and taverns in the south of England, Iolo developed a 'moral hatred of the Saxons', to which he gave vigorous expression in many poems and songs.[39] During the Second World War Frank's FBI investigators were at first baffled by his attitude, but eventually concluded that he was not un-American at all, just 'violently anti-English'.[40]

Iolo Morganwg was born in 1747, in the Vale of Glamorgan. He spoke English as a child but learned Welsh as a youth from unusual teachers. His godfather, Edward Williams of Middle Hill, Llancarfan, was a poet and scholar of Welsh literature. He became a literary mentor, leading Iolo into a small scholarly community with a shared interest in ancient Welsh verse. By the time he was ready to head to England to make a living from stonemasonry, he was not just a fluent Welsh-speaker but an expert in historic Welsh literature.[41] His first sojourn in England led him, as it leads so many with artistic talent and ambition, to London. Masonry skills were in high demand. His work provided him with a steady living, which bought him time to spend in the library of the British Museum, where he indulged his delight in ancient British writing. His social life revolved around chapel and the Gwyneddigion, one of the city's 'London Welsh' societies. It was based at a tavern in Walbrook, next to the magnificent Mansion House. He was something of a misfit among the wealthy membership, but he soon endeared himself by entertaining his compatriots with crude drinking songs of his own composition.

The president of the Gwyneddigion was a wealthy fur trader named Owen Jones, known better by his bardic name, Owain Myfyr. He was intrigued to discover that the rowdy stonemason they knew as plain Ned Williams claimed to be an expert on the historic literature of Wales.

Myfyr had established the society to be more than a drinking club: his ambition was to use it to promote Wales and Welsh causes in London. Nothing excited him more than the possibility of discovering literary artefacts, ancient manuscripts that the society could publish to demonstrate the cultural precedence of his own nation and its people over the Anglo-Saxons. Owain Myfyr believed that he had discovered a scholar who could help him, and he was prepared to fund the young stonemason to achieve his goal. It was from this point that Ned Williams stonemason, began his transformation into Iolo Morganwg poet, scholar, myth maker and revolutionary.

There is little to suggest that Iolo had developed a political consciousness before he first left his homeland for England. When he returned seven years later, he did so as a fully formed Jacobin, a republican activist and a devout Unitarian. Like Frank Lloyd Wright a century later, his innate character was receptive to anti-authoritarian sentiments, but something in Iolo's experience of England sparked that potential into explosive expression. To Iolo, the whole of England was synonymous with Anglicanism, monarchy and the confident presumption of superiority. It was a confidence that he both envied and despised. He felt an outsider even in his own country, and doubly so as a Welshman on English soil. Like Frank Lloyd Wright, he gravitated to other outsiders. In 1774 he found himself among a host of the spiritually marginalised when he attended a chapel in Essex Street, off the Strand, in central London. This was the new Unitarian Chapel led by Theophilus Lindsey, the first to be registered in the British Isles. Essex Street Chapel attracted an early congregation of some two hundred people, many drawn by the, 'combined attractions of heresy and novelty',[42] but there were others with serious principles and missions to perform, including Joseph Priestley, Richard Price and Benjamin Franklin, who just two years later was on the small committee that drafted the American Declaration of Independence.[43]

Franklin's presence at Essex Street was no coincidence. Even as Unitarianism emerged defiantly into the open in Britain it was already associated with rebellious intentions. For many among the early Essex Street congregations, Iolo Morganwg included, the political implications of Unitarianism were as invigorating as the transgressive theology itself. It was around this time, as the possibility of American independence began to crystallise, that the *idea* of America acquired a heady significance among those who were liberally inclined. The incipient nation was a social and cultural *tabula rasa*, with the potential to become the ideal free society: a land of unmapped vastness and immeasurable wealth. The members of the Gwyneddigion had their own claim on the American future. As educated Welsh patriots they were aware that America had been discovered first by Prince Madog ab Owain Gwynedd in the twelfth century, and that his mariners had established a colony with local natives which continued to flourish somewhere deep in the American wilderness.[44] Later, in the 1790s, they funded an extraordinary expedition to find the 'Welsh Indians', but in the meantime, as revolutionary spirit came to the boil in America, the broad church of British Dissenters, republicans and Jacobin sympathisers invested heavily in their hopes and dreams of a utopian American future.

Iolo Morganwg lived to an old age and never lost his fascination with the possibilities that America could offer. As he rhapsodised on the themes of American liberty his excitement passed as a contagion into the minds of his admirers among Welsh Unitarians to such an extent that some congregations were decimated by emigration. Those migrants all shared the thrill of the possibility of freedom, and a deep belief that they could each play a part in the creation of the new nation.[45]

Frank Lloyd Wright's grandparents went to America with expectations that pushed well beyond the liberal intentions of the Declaration of Independence. To them, slavery was an abomination, notwithstanding the ambivalence of the Founding Fathers. To them, also, the native American was their equal to be honoured and respected as any other neighbour, whether or not they were descended from the household of Prince Madoc. They believed in equality of opportunity for women and men alike and, without reservation, in universal suffrage. In America they believed that they could build a society that would prosper according to these principles. Their hopes and expectations were shared throughout the Dissenting congregations of Britain, but where they gained traction among the Unitarian communities of south-west Wales, it was due largely to the efforts of early visionaries like Charles Lloyd, Tomos Glyn Cothi and, because he was such an effective conduit of heterodox ideas from London and Glamorgan, Iolo Morganwg.[46]

When Richard and Mallie Jones took their children to America, they went with the intention of shaping the land specifically to Iolo's vision of an ideal, free Wales. When their children grew up their minds were ruled by the same ambitions. Many of their grandchildren, none more so than Hannah's son Frank, would be preoccupied with the making of the ideal America throughout their own lives. Frank's architecture was 'an Architecture upon which true American society will eventually be based if we survive at all'.[47] This was not an obsession that gripped Frank as a young American; it was there in the minds of his ancestors, in Cardiganshire, generations before he was born ∎

# 01  A Rural Enlightenment
## *Notes*

1   Robert C. Twombley, *Frank Lloyd Wright: An Interpretive Biography* (New York: Harper Colophon, 1974), p. 151.

2   Historic weather data from Minnesota Department of Natural Resources, *https://www.dnr.state.mn.us/climate/twin_cities/listings.html* (April 2021).

3   Roger Friedland and Harold Zellman, *The Fellowship: The Untold Story of Frank Lloyd Wright and the Taliesin Fellowship* (New York: HarperCollins, 2006), p. 116.

4   The first words of F. L. Wright, *Family*, Book One of *An Autobiography (Edition 1)* (New York: Longman, Green & Co., 1932), p. 3.

5   UK Census 1841. Both Richard and Jenkin Jones are listed as hat-makers.

6   From the mid-nineteenth century onwards the great majority of hats sold in south Wales were mass produced by either Christy of London or Carvers of Bristol. M. Freeman, *Welsh Hats* (Ceredigion Museum, 2008).

7   Chester Lloyd Jones, *Youngest Son* (Madison WI: self-published, 1938), p. 12.

8   D. Elwyn Davies, *They Thought for Themselves: A Brief Look at the History of Unitarianism in Wales and the Tradition of Liberal Religion* (Llandysul: Gomer Press, 1982), p. 28.

9   M. Fitzpatrick, 'Enlightenment', in I. McCalman (ed.), *The Oxford Companion to the Romantic Age: British Culture 1776–1832* (Oxford: Oxford University Press, 1999), p. 303.

10  The Academy was one of those established after the restoration of the monarchy had led to the 'Great Ejection' of 1662, in which thousands of Nonconformist ministers were expelled from the established Church.

11  Davies, *They Thought for Themselves*, p. 34.

12     Penybanc was attached to an area of marshy fields known as Wernhir.

13     Rev. Aubrey J. Martin, *Hanes Llwynrhydowen* (Llandysul: Gwasg Gomer, 1977), pp. 22–3.

14     The site of Llwynrhydowen Chapel is now within the settlement of Rhydowen. However, when the chapel was first built it occupied a corner on a crossroads opposite the Alltyrodyn Arms. The small village of Llwynrhydowen was a short distance to its south, and the settlement of Rhydowen was a short distance to the east. During the nineteenth century the name of Rhydowen was transferred from the settlement to which it was originally applied to the group of buildings that accumulated around the Alltyrodyn Arms and Llwynrhydowen Chapel.

15     David Barnes, *Llwynrhydowen and its Radical Tradition* (Welsh Religious Buildings Trust/Royal Commission on the Ancient and Historical Monuments of Wales, 2005).

16     Rev. Thomas O. Williams, 'Lloyd, David (1724–1779), Arian Minister', in *Dictionary of Welsh Biography*, https://biography.wales/article/s-LLOY-DAV-1724 (April 2021).

17     B. Clarence (Lord Aberdare), writing in the Unitarian newspaper *Yr Ymofynydd* in 1946.

18     The Lloyd family's reputation was established in the twelfth century when Lord Rhys ap Gruffydd played a crucial role in the Welsh uprising that had recaptured Cardiganshire and then won liberty for the nation, for a while, from Henry II of England. Lord Rhys claimed Castell Hywel for his family. His descendants took the name Llwyd (Grey) in the fourteenth century. In the sixteenth century there was a branching of the family as all four sons of Llewellyn Llwyd established their own estates. One of the sons, Gwion, founded the Llanfechan estate from which David Lloyd claimed descent. Another son, Rhys, founded the Alltyrodyn estate which was so significant to the background of both of Frank Lloyd Wright's maternal grandparents. Lucy Theakston and John Davies (eds), *Some Family Records & Pedigrees of the Lloyds of Allt yr Odyn, Castell Hywel, Ffos y Bleiddiaid, Gilfach Wen, Llan Llyr and Waun* (London: Fox, Jones & Co., 1913).

19     Author's correspondence with D. Densil Morgan, Emeritus Professor in Theology, University of Wales Trinity St David. Prof Morgan provides this further elucidation: 'Arianism, in the context of patristic (especially fourth century) theology was a belief in a radical duality between God and creation. Christ, though pre-existent as the divine logos, did not share full deity with the Father but was the means through which God had created the world. Born of the Virgin, sinless and resurrected from the dead, his sacrificial death was redemptive. Consequently, although the greatest of God's creatures, the medium of all other created things and the means of human salvation, Christ was not fully divine.'

20     Davies, *They Thought for Themselves*, p. 35.

21     C. Lloyd, 'David Davis (Obituary)', *The Monthly Repository and Review of Theology and General Literature* (New Series 1, 1827), 693.

22     Charles Lloyd, *Particulars of the Life of a Dissenting Minister* (London: self-published, 1813), p. 6.

23     Lloyd, *Particulars of the Life of a Dissenting Minister*, p. 100.

24     C. Lloyd, 'David Jenkin Rees (Obituary)', *The Monthly Repository and Review of Theology and General Literature*, 12 (1817), 743.

25     Lloyd, *Particulars of the Life of a Dissenting Minister*, p. 166.

26     Lloyd, *Particulars of the Life of a Dissenting Minister*, p. 154.

27     Lloyd, 'David Jenkin Rees (Obituary)', *The Monthly Repository*.

28     Geraint H. Jenkins, *Bard of Liberty: The Political Radicalism of Iolo Morganwg* (Cardiff: University of Wales Press, 2012), pp. 223–4; Davies, *They Thought for Themselves*, p. 177; G. H. Jenkins, 'The Unitarian Firebrand, the Cambrian Society and the Eisteddfod', in G. H. Jenkins (ed.), *A Rattleskull Genius: The Many Faces of Iolo Morganwg* (Cardiff: University of Wales Press, 2005), p. 278.

29     Frank Lloyd Wright, *An Autobiography (Edition 1)* New York: Longman, Green & Co., 1932).

30     Each of the serious biographies of Frank Lloyd Wright gives a different account of the court hearings, but none of them makes entire sense and none is entirely consistent with Wright's own in *An Autobiography*. The account given here is an attempted reconciliation only. The quotation, 'I was under oath', and the story around it come from an interview with Wright published in *Look Magazine* (17 September 1957), and written by John Peter.

31     Lloyd, *Particulars of the Life of a Dissenting Minister*, p. 165.

32     Jenkins, *Bard of Liberty*, p. 157.

33    National Library of Wales, Iolo Morganwg Papers, MS 13145A,
      Rule book of the South Wales Unitarian Society.

34    Jix Lloyd Jones, *The Welsh Backgrounds*, from *www.UnityChapel.org*
      (April 2021). The statement that David James was a founder of
      Pantydefaid originates in a memoir written by Jane Lloyd Jones,
      Frank Lloyd Wright's aunt. It has been corroborated, during the
      writing of this book, by Rev. Cen Llwyd, who was able to find a list
      of the first Trustees of Pantydefaid in *Yr Ymofynydd* (April 1902),
      77–8. John Enoch, Thomas James and David James are all on
      that list.

35    The first appearance of the phrase 'Truth Against the World' in
      print is most likely in William O. Pughe, *The Heroic Elegies and
      Other Pieces of Llywarç Hen* (London: 1792), a book based on
      material provided to the author by Iolo Morganwg.

36    Jenkins, *Bard of Liberty*, pp. 3, 12.

37    Jenkins, *Bard of Liberty*, p. 111.

38    Meryl Secrest, *Frank Lloyd Wright: A Biography* (Chicago:
      University of Chicago Press, 1998), pp. 490, 543.

39    National Library of Wales, Iolo Morganwg Papers, quoted in
      Jenkins, *Bard of Liberty*, p. 168.

40    Secrest, *Frank Lloyd Wright: A Biography*, pp. 490, 264.

41    Jenkins, *Bard of Liberty*, pp. 20–1.

42    Alexander Gordon, *Addresses Biographical and Historical*
      (London: Lindsey Press, 1922), p. 285.

43    Davies, *They Thought for Themselves*, p. 21.

44    The evidence to support this story is scant and ambiguous, but
      'absence of evidence is not evidence of absence'.

45    Kathryn J. Cooper, *Exodus from Cardiganshire: Rural–Urban Migration
      in Victorian Britain* (Cardiff: University of Wales Press, 2011),
      pp. 191–9.

46    Jenkins, *Bard of Liberty*, pp. 79–86.

47    Frank Lloyd Wright, *The Natural House* (New York: Horizon
      Press, 1954).

# 2

# Bards of Liberty

## 27 April 1957.
## University of California,
## Berkeley, San Francisco

Frank Lloyd Wright always enjoyed speaking to students. Their uncritical enthusiasm was life-affirming, and it gave him a good reason to reflect on what was truly important to him in his work. In 1957, a few weeks before his ninetieth birthday, he was at the University of California in Berkeley. He spoke for a while about the responsibilities of the architect and the idea of organic design, and then he moved on to the subject of his childhood, his memories of his Welsh ancestors and the wisdom that he believed had been passed down through them to him:

*I want to give you something now that will be worth the evening if I don't succeed in saying anything else ... the definition of a genius for you all. A genius is a man who has an eye to see nature. A genius is a man with a heart to feel nature. And a genius is a man with a boldness to follow nature. There is the wisdom that's come down and never have I heard a more appropriate definition of what constitutes human genius.*

This is not a mere aphorism, it is a 'triad', an ancient form of three-line verse that formed a vital part of druidic training. It is presumed that the triads were part of an oral tradition, devised to be learned by listening and repetition, not to be written down. The oldest surviving collection of triads in text form dates from the thirteenth century, but it is likely that some at least were composed in the Iron Age, and that they were passed on for centuries by word of mouth alone.[1] The words of this 'Genius Triad' were impressed upon Frank Lloyd Wright in his youth, and they enfolded a guiding principle for him still as a ninety-year-old. The triad appears again in his last written work, *A Testament*, published in 1957.

The Genius Triad first appeared in print in 1794, in Iolo Morganwg's literary debut, *Poems, Lyric and Pastoral*. Its two volumes contain ninety-five poems, the fruits of many years of poetic endeavour, notes on druidic tradition and his own translations of one hundred druidic triads. Many of the poems address radical themes. Thomas Paine himself, the author of *The Rights of Man*, was among its subscribers along with a host of other notable revolutionary figures. In the Preface Iolo justified the provocative nature of his poetry:

*I have always, with an Ancient Briton's warm pride preserved the freedom of my thoughts and the independence of my mind: these shall not be subjected to anything but my own conscience ... I doubt not that numberless errors of judgement may be found in some things that I have written. Other things may be deemed* imprudent: *but* prudence *and* conscience *never walk hand in hand.*

Apart from the self-deprecation, the sentiments could have come from the pen of Frank Lloyd Wright. In an explanatory note following the poem *The Happy Farmer*, Iolo explained that his approach to creativity was to seek the absolute and pure essence of the natural world and to present it free of 'artistic' elaboration:

> *A Poet in the character of a shepherd, an occupation the most proper of all others to represent primeval simplicity and virtue, describes objects as they naturally present themselves to the senses, and affect the mind; or utters sentiments that spring from the simple notions and inborn feelings of those that are unacquainted with the abstractions of philosophy and the complex ideas derived from art ... It would perhaps not be amiss if our modern critics and poets would take into consideration the following maxim of the Welsh Bards, from their poetic triads ...*

> *The three primary and indispensable requisites of poetic genius are,*

> *An eye that can see nature*
> *A heart that can feel nature*
> *And a resolution that dares follow nature.*

> *This, I will venture to say, is the best, the most just and philosophical definition of Genius that was ever given by any writer in any language.*[2]

Both Iolo himself and Frank Lloyd Wright could be embodied in the figure of the shepherd, with a perception of nature uncontaminated by bourgeois pretensions, with creativity expressed in the truest, most simple and most personal terms: *organically*, as Frank would have it.

Several decades after the publication of *Poems, Lyric and Pastoral*, it was established by diligent scholars that many of the triads that Iolo had translated, including the Genius Triad, were not ancient at all, but composed by Iolo himself. In fact, almost everything that Iolo had purportedly discovered from ancient sources concerning the rites and customs of the ancient Druids was also created by Iolo. This in no way diminishes the significance of the influence of his words on the attitudes and the sense of nationhood of generations of Welsh partisans. For Frank Lloyd Wright and his Welsh family, the historical accuracy of Iolo's vision could never be proved, any more than anyone else's legend, but that didn't diminish its essential Truth. Neither does it devalue Iolo's literary achievement. *Poems, Lyric and Pastoral* was admired by other radical literary figures of his time, including the leaders of the emerging Romantic movement. Its influence seeps into Wordsworth's contributions to *Lyrical Ballads*,[3] and the Genius Triad in particular was deeply admired by Samuel Taylor Coleridge.[4]

In the course of his emotionally charged Preface to *Poems, Lyrical and Pastoral*, Iolo Morganwg discussed his intention to go to America to find Prince Madoc's descendants, and he also referred, in passing, to the fact that as a young man his 'studies were during this time chiefly *Architecture* and the *other sciences* that my trade required'. Almost as a rejoinder, Frank Lloyd Wright said: 'Every great architect is necessarily a great poet. He must be a great original interpreter of his time ... True architecture ... is poetry. A good building is the greatest of poems when it is organic architecture.'[5] It would be easy to become convinced that Frank Lloyd Wright had his own copy of *Poems, Lyric and Pastoral*. Although he left no mention of it, or indeed of Iolo Morganwg at all, at least not by name, there is abundant evidence to show that his mother and her brothers and sisters were aware of Iolo's legacy, and because of that it is reasonable to presume that his name was also known to Frank.

*Poems, Lyric and Pastoral* reaches its climax with an 'Ode on the Mythology of the Ancient British Bards', a long poem that Iolo recited aloud at the first modern *Gorsedd Beirdd Ynys Prydain*, the Meeting of British Bards, which he convened on Primrose Hill in London on the summer solstice of 1792. This was the original enactment of the ritual which, years later, became the theatrical centrepiece of the National Eisteddfod, the annual celebration of Welsh arts that is today among the largest cultural festivals in Europe. The opening line of the ceremony, which precedes the Ode, is *Y Gwir yn Erbyn y Byd*,[6] translated by Iolo as 'Truth Against all the World', the motto adopted by the Lloyd Jones family in America. The closing line of the Ode, and of the ceremony, is *Yn enw Duw a phob daioni*, translated as 'In the name of God and all that is good'. This is a much less familiar phrase than 'Truth Against the World', even though it has identical provenance. If the Lloyd Joneses knew where 'Truth against the World' had originally come from, then they might also be expected to be familiar with *Yn enw Duw a phob daioni*. And indeed, when Frank Lloyd Wright's aunts Nell and Jennie established their progressive Hillside Home School, the school that Frank designed for them, it was this exact phrase that they used as their school motto[7] (Pl. 8).

Poems, Lyric and Pastoral is also an early printed source of the name 'Taliesin': not the first, as Taliesin was among the greatest of the ancient Welsh Bards, a sixth-century poet in the court of King Urien of Rheged, but Iolo's efforts greatly broadened awareness of Taliesin in Wales and beyond.[8] In 1911 Frank Lloyd Wright gave the name Taliesin to the beautiful new home that he built on his ancestors' land in Wisconsin. In *An Autobiography* (1932) he explained:

> *Taliesin was the name of a Welsh poet. A druid-bard or singer of songs who sang to Wales the glories of Fine Art. Literally the Welsh word means 'shining brow'. Many legends cling to the name in Wales. And Richard Hovey's charming masque 'Taliesin' had made me acquainted with his image of the historic bard. Since all my relatives had Welsh names for their places, why not for mine?[9]*

Even the most perceptive and knowledgeable of Wright's American scholars have found this subject slippery. Antony Alofsin, for example, suspects that it is indeed Richard Hovey's *Taliesin: A Masque* that may be the most relevant source.[10] Hovey was an Illinois-born poet of the late nineteenth century.

Pl. 8. Hillside Home School Yearbook, 1913–14 with the school's bardic motto prominently displayed.
Courtesy of Douglas M. Steiner, Edmonds, WA, USA.

His long poem *Taliesin* is presented as an Arthurian drama, a setting that the author uses to impart a 'highly charged meditation on the nature of poetry'.[11] Alofsin's position is reasonable, given the comment in Frank's autobiography, but there is nothing in Hovey's *Taliesin* that refers to Wales.[12] The nation of Frank's forebears is entirely absent. There is no doubt, as Frank clearly implies in the quotation from his autobiography, that he knew that Taliesin was Welsh, and that he knew about Taliesin before he encountered Hovey's work. This exemplifies a consistent and understandable tendency of Frank Lloyd Wright: his instinct to prioritise a proximate American source or reference rather than admit there were more important sources of inspiration that came to him from beyond America's shores. The magical story of Taliesin and Ceridwen would certainly have been familiar to Frank's aunts and uncles, as it would be to most with a Welsh childhood at that time.

In this story Ceridwen, a sorceress, brews a potion that will confer the gift of poetic genius upon her son, Morfran, who had the misfortune to be born hideously ugly. His mother, Ceridwen, hopes that the poetic gift will compensate for his physical shortcomings. The potion has to be stirred over a flame for a year and a day. Ceridwen employs a boy, Gwion Bach, to stir it. The vessel is *Awen*, the 'cauldron of inspiration'. Just as the preparation comes to its climax three boiling drips splash onto Gwion's thumb. Without thinking he puts his thumb in his mouth, and is instantly infused with poetic genius. He flees from Ceridwen's fury, turning into a hare, then a fish, then a bird and eventually into a grain of wheat. Ceridwen, transformed into a hen, swallows Gwion. But the seed inside her then transforms into a baby. When the child is born she puts him in a bag and tosses him into a river. The child is rescued by Elffin, son of King Gwyddno. He names the foundling Taliesin. The boy grows into a prodigiously gifted poet with magical powers of versification.

The most potent elements of the story are that Taliesin is a creative genius, and that he has inherited the gift of shape-shifting. It is his ability to transform himself, apparently to disappear and then re-emerge many years, even centuries, later through Welsh history that captivates.

As the Lloyd Jones family identified so deeply with *Y Gwir yn Erbyn y Byd* and with the cultural and historical background of the proclamation, there can be no doubt that they were also familiar with both the real and the mythical Taliesins.[13] It is a story that left a lasting impression on Frank Lloyd Wright, and in time came to influence the formation of his personal identity. This vital part of Frank's story will be revisited further on.

Frank's younger sister Maginel recalled that among the mistletoe and holly that were carved into the stone fireplaces in the homes of her Welsh aunts and uncles she also saw the /|\ symbol. Possibly under the influence of Frank's autobiography, she took this specifically to mean 'Truth Against the World'.[14] The words and the symbol are tightly interconnected within the rituals of the Gorsedd of Bards created by Iolo Morganwg, but they have distinct meanings. Iolo referred to the /|\ symbol as *Y Nod Cyfrin*, which he translated as the 'Mystic Mark'. It was important to Iolo Morganwg that the Gorsedd was a hermetic community with an esoteric system of governance. Beginning with the meeting at Primrose Hill on midsummer's day in 1792, he set out to revive the Gorsedd, convening it at each solstice, summer and winter, and conducting events in precise accordance with the ancient ritual that he had conjured. He explained to those who were drawn to his gatherings that the Gorsedd had never actually died out: that in fact it had endured in secret for centuries, and that he, Iolo Morganwg, was bearer of the honorific *Bardd wrth fraint a Defod Beirdd ynys Prydain*, in English 'Bard according to the Rites and Institutes of the Bards of the Island of Britain': 'I have been trained in a cultural institution that can be traced back to primitive times, in a bardic school, and I am the last of the bardic teachers.'[15] It was vital to Iolo that the ancient heritage he claimed to embody would be shielded from the habitual cultural appropriation of the English. Like many of his educated compatriots he was needled by the manner in which English academics and authorities routinely conflated the words 'Britain' and 'England' to suit the Unionist agenda, regardless of the indisputably Welsh origin of the word 'Britain'; not to mention the slipshod assimilation of Arthurian legend, and even druidic lore into England's invented past.[16] He hoped that symbols such as /|\ would be more resistant to misappropriation, provided its mystery could be maintained. He used it in his Gorsedd regalia and occasionally in correspondence with Welsh colleagues, but it would not be seen in a publication until 1812, nearly twenty years after *Poems, Lyric and Pastoral*. Its appearance then had particular significance to Frank Lloyd

Wright's grandparents, because it was at the head of the title page of *Salmau yr Eglwys yn yr Anialwch*, a collection of 204 Unitarian hymns in the Welsh language, all written by Iolo. In English the title reads *Hymns for the Church in the Wilderness*. Migrants were obliged by simple practicality to travel with few possessions. Aside from their bible, Iolo's *Salmau* is one of the few books that would almost certainly have travelled with them to America.[17] A typical Victorian hymnal, it fits easily into a small pocket. Its title evokes the poignant image of the migrant family, exhausted, depleted in number, making slow progress across unmapped frontier territories in search of a place to settle, finding comfort in Iolo's image of the welcoming prayer house that was waiting for them somewhere in the empty vastness (Pl. 9).

It may seem inconsistent that this symbol, which belonged to druidic doctrine, was used to introduce a Unitarian hymn book. This shows that the two nature-religions, in Iolo's mind, had at some stage merged into one. The Unitarian scholar D. Elwyn Davies explained that Iolo 'knew that according to the classical writers, the religion of the Druids was monotheistic and concluded that the bards, after the coming of Christianity, became Unitarian in theology'. Furthermore, the recondite aspects of Iolo's Druidism, the privileged knowledge and resilience, clearly echoed the cloaked existence of the Unitarians, at least until 1813 when the legal ban on their faith was eventually repealed.

Iolo may have used /|\ originally as a 'mason's mark'. Although it was a custom of medieval masons, every stone carver of more modern times would be familiar with these secret signatures, and it would have appealed to Iolo to devise one of his own. The three simple downward cuts are similar to many other recorded medieval marks. Iolo's accounts of the druidic meaning were more elaborate: as the tangible universe shimmered into existence, God's 'shout of joy' was manifested both as 'the most exquisite melody that could possibly exist' and as three rays of light which beamed from the origin of His emergence.[18] Most significantly, the invocation of this first inscribed mark led directly, in this mythology, to the development of the first written

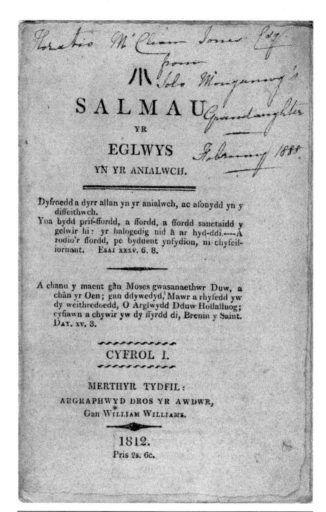

Pl. 9. The title page of Iolo Morganwg's '*Salmau yr Eglwys yn yr Anialwch*'. This is the earliest known appearance of *Y Nod Cyfrin*, the 'Mystic Mark', above the title at the top of page. The Jones family would almost certainly have taken at least one copy of this hymnal with them when they emigrated. NLW.

alphabet, known as *Coelbren y Beirdd*, the Bards' Alphabet, which in turn gave definition to the original language of the 'Cimmeri' tribe, the first people of the Isles of Britain: the Welsh. *Coelbren y Beirdd* had another practical application. It could be used as a cypher if it became necessary to protect communications. In 1802, when Iolo Morganwg, Charles Lloyd and their colleagues met to agree the rules of the Unitarian Society of Wales, Iolo put a bold heading above his record of the meeting in his notebook, and at the foot of the page, equally bold, *Gwir yn Erbyn a Byd*, 'Truth Against the World', written in the strange, stick-like characters of *Coelbren y Beirdd*.

There are few remnants of the original Lloyd Jones farmhouses in their home valley now, and there is no evidence to be seen of the engraving of /l\ on foundations and hearths that the family memoirs recall. It can, however, be seen prominently on the gatepost of the family church, Unity Chapel, which was dedicated in 1886, the year after Frank's grandfather, Richard Lloyd Jones, died. In 1900, Frank Lloyd Wright was commissioned by his Aunts Jennie and Ellen to design a new building to replace their original Hillside Home School in the Lloyd Jones Valley. They had built the first school on the site of Richard and Mallie's old farmhouse, a building that the two aunts had inherited. The building and the educational institution were both far in advance of their time, while also being rooted deeply in the noble past of primitive Wales. There is more to be said in due course about this extraordinary school. In her own memoir Aunt Jennie recalled that they asked Frank to give the central Assembly Hall

*a Welsh feel ... which the material, oak druid and stone, would make possible. Over the stone fireplace a tablet was inserted, inscribed with an appropriate stanza of Gray's Elegy, for the mother's sake. The fire fender was formed of the conventionalized Welsh hat. Over the base of the ... balcony was carved a selected verse from the 40th chapter of Isaiah, a favourite chapter of our father.*[19]

This, within the Lloyd Jones family, was a residual memory of the celebrated 1789 Welsh translation of Gray's 'Elegy' made by the Rev. David Davis, minister of Llwynrhydowen and passive adversary of their real ancestor, Charles Lloyd.

According to Jennie's memory the translation was the work of Mallie's own grandfather: David Davis was not Mallie's grandfather. The verse above the fireplace is, anyway, in Gray's original English, the better to be understood by the pupils. The 'conventionalized Welsh hat' that Aunt Jennie refers to is another innocent but strange subversion of the original story of Richard the hatter. The steel 'hats' that support the fireplace are tall pointed cones, not the subtly tapering cylinder of a real Welsh beaver hat (Pl. 10). Was this a misunderstanding that began with Frank? Or with his two aunts? In his autobiography Frank describes the hats that his grandfather made as being, 'high pointed cones. The witches wore them when riding on their broom-sticks', an image which is bafflingly at odds with the anecdote, repeated by Frank, that his grandfather would demonstrate their quality by standing on their crowns. The one feature of their Welsh legacy that is clearly and accurately represented is /l\, the mystic mark. It is carved into the face of the timber balcony in several places, so that it can be seen all around the Assembly Hall (Pl. 11).

Writing in the 1950s about his memory of building the second Hillside Home School, Frank recalled:

*One of the best foundations I know of, suitable to many places ... was devised by the old Welsh stone-mason. Instead of digging down ... four feet below the frost line as was the standard practice in Wisconsin ... he dug shallow trenches about sixteen inches deep and slightly pitched them into a drain. These trenches he filled with broken stone about the size of your fist. Broken stone does not clog up, and provides drainage beneath the wall that saves it from being lifted by frost ... I have called it the 'dry wall footing', because if the wall stayed dry the frost could not affect it ... if there is no water there to freeze, the foundation cannot be lifted. Ever since I discovered the 'dry wall footing' I have been building houses that way.*[20]

The old Welsh stonemason was David Timothy. Frank's sister Maginel remembered Timothy as being *really like an Uncle too ... he was the stone builder for all of the clan. He made the walls and the foundations of their houses, their fireplaces and chimneys. He carved their mantels with ... the family emblem: the old druid symbol /|\ which means 'Truth Against the World'.*

She also recalled that 'he was a loyal advocate for my brother. If there was ever a controversy concerning Frank's building, later on when he was becoming an architect, Timothy would nod his old head gently and say "Trust the boy, he knows".'[21] David Timothy was born in 1840, the illegitimate son of Hannah Timothy, whose grave can be found at Pantydefaid Chapel. He had worshipped at the chapel himself, and through contacts there had arranged to join the Joneses in America around 1880. David Timothy's own grave is to be found among those of the Lloyd Jones family at Unity Chapel, a short distance from the grave of Frank Lloyd Wright.[22]

The assumption of Iolo's /|\ symbol, and of his words 'Truth Against the World', by Frank Lloyd Wright's Welsh family has, until now, generally been dismissed as a presumptuous affectation. The American author Brendan Gill accuses the Joneses of 'not noticing its intrinsic fatuity', and furthermore, 'for a family to see itself as the embodiment of some grandly undefined truth that pits itself against the entire world implies arrogance on a colossal scale'.[23] More recently another American academic, Donald Leslie Johnson, wrote that /|\ was 'printed on British prisoner's uniforms in the eighteenth and nineteenth centuries', and that it was 'not old or valid', all of which is incorrect and misses the point that it was only its validity to the Jones family that is relevant to the story of Frank Lloyd Wright, and to the Joneses it was indeed deeply meaningful.[24] The mark and the motto were not intended to be significant to those outside the circles for which they were created, so it was only to be expected that, within the larger narrative of Frank Lloyd Wright's life, the story of the mark and motto has been a convenient anecdote to marginalise. In doing so, a vital part of the

Pl. 10. The fire-place and fender in the Assembly Hall at Hillside Home School. The cones are supposed to represent Welsh hats. *Y Nod Cyfrin* is formed in the steel projections at the base. A verse from Gray's 'Elegy' is inscribed, in English, above the fire-place.
Photograph Melinda Larson.

story has been missed. Not only do they shed light on the spirit of Rational Dissent that suffused his extraordinary ancestors; they also signify a compelling source of Frank's own spiritual and creative philosophy and, ultimately, the most useful insight into his 'genius'.

The direct influence of Rational Dissent can be seen as two beams of light that divide, initially in Britain in the late eighteenth century, and which then reconverge upon Frank Lloyd Wright in his childhood several decades later. The family's roots in Unitarian Cardiganshire, the Lloyd lineage and

Pl. 11. *Y Nod Cyfrin* engraved into the oak front of the parapet that crowns the Hillside Home School assembly hall.

Pl. 12. Ralph Waldo Emerson's visiting card, *circa* 1873.
National Portrait Gallery.

their interaction with Iolo Morganwg are the first source of enlightenment. This was the inherited history that cemented the identity of the Lloyd Jones family and which brought Frank to the revelation that he found among them in the summers of his childhood, in the rural idyll of south Wisconsin.

In the early 1850s, as they acclimatised themselves to America and to the English language, and before they became the *Lloyd* Joneses, the family had been enthralled to find that America had its own spiritual philosophers who spoke to them in warmly familiar terms. The most compelling of those voices came from the Bostonian Ralph Waldo Emerson. To the younger children of Richard and Mallie Jones, this second source of enlightenment provided a vital modern and accessible endorsement of their deeper inherited spirituality (Pl. 12).

It is evident from Frank's later writing that he, like his mother, his aunts and his uncles, was aware that their American enlightenment and the light that came with their family from Wales were kindled from the same original Romantic flame. Iolo Morganwg's revelation of the primitive nature religion of Bardism harmonised sweetly with the emerging poetic vision of the Romantic poets, Coleridge and Wordsworth. The English poets admired Iolo's efforts to reveal, by a simplification of language, the sanctity of nature and of God's presence within it, and in their collaboration, *Lyrical Ballads* of 1798, they embraced Iolo's themes and his simple sincerity. Just as Iolo had endeavoured to do, Wordsworth expressed himself 'in unparalleled nature poetry, declaring the life of mountains and rivers, rocks and stone and trees ... recording the spiritual history of the race ... binding the present and the past in natural piety'.[25] In 1818, during a lecture entitled *Shakespeare, a Poet Generally*, Coleridge remarked:

> *the form is mechanic when on any given material we impress a predetermined form, not necessarily arising out of the properties of the material; – as when to a mass of wet clay we give whatever shape we wish it to retain when hardened. The* organic *form, on the other hand, is innate; it shapes, as it develops, itself from within, and the fulness of its development is one and the same with the perfection of its outward form. Such as the life is, such is the form.*[26]

It was within this milieu, around the dawn of the nineteenth century, that the fundamental precepts of modernism began to coalesce. From the veneration of Truth in nature came the notion of authenticity of expression, that things should appear as they really are, in organic continuity within and without. From the belief that past human societies lived lives of spiritual purity in truthful harmony with nature emerged the ideas of the wise, noble and self-reliant primitive, a man identified so closely with his environment that he would shape it naturally, organically to his needs. It followed that the decline of Western civilisation could only be arrested if creative people, the shapers of society, could achieve access to the perspicacity of their unspoilt, primitive souls.[27]

The network of Unitarians, republicans and Romantic poets was a tight one. Connections were direct;

mutual influence was powerful. Ideas gained momentum as they crossed the Atlantic. In the 1780s the elder William Hazlitt, a Unitarian Minister, had spent three years in Boston. While there, he had supported John Freeman in establishing America's first Unitarian church. Joseph Priestley established his own Unitarian church in America in 1794, after migrating from England to escape the imminent threat to his life. By that time, little more than a decade after Hazlitt and Freeman had established the first cause, Unitarianism had spread across New England. At the beginning of the nineteenth century, with only one exception, every church in the city of Boston hosted a Unitarian congregation. William Emerson was minister of the First Church in Boston, the most venerable of the American Unitarian churches; Ralph Waldo Emerson was his son. Both William Hazlitt the elder and his son were active participants in the 'Priestley Circle'. The elder Hazlitt corresponded with Priestley, Richard Price and even Benjamin Franklin. The Hazlitts were also friends of Coleridge, and Coleridge was, of course, a friend of Iolo Morganwg. To Coleridge, Joseph Priestley was a hero.[28] Coleridge himself was no less a hero to Ralph Waldo Emerson. The American academic Samantha C. Harvey has observed that Emerson's

> *intellectual engagement with Coleridge was so intense and encompassing that it almost amounted to a kind of collaboration ... Emerson turned to Coleridge for a fundamental armature of Romantic ideas and an intellectual and literary method that informed his entire oeuvre.*[29]

Emerson's most influential text, one of his earliest, is *Self Reliance*. It was first published in 1841 in a collection called *Essays: First Series*. Even today it is a quite breathtaking exhortation. It appeals powerfully to an instinct that each of us must occasionally acknowledge, that we are too content to live our lives according to rules imposed upon us by others. But it goes further: Emerson's proposal is that the future of America, the destiny of the new nation, actually depends on the rare individuals who would be bold enough to reject every convention that society seeks to impose upon them, and instead grasp the earth in their own hands and mould it organically into a truthful expression of American spirituality:

> *Whoso would be a man must be a non-conformist ... Nothing is at last sacred but the integrity of our own mind ... No law can be sacred to me but that of my nature ... A man is to carry himself in the presence of all opposition as if everything were titular and ephemeral but he ... I ought to go upright and vital and speak the rude truth in all ways ... Your goodness must have some edge to it – else it is none.*

Emerson's essay is relentless:

> *The other terror that scares us from self-trust is our consistency; a reverence for our past act or word ... Suppose you contradict yourself; what then? ... Trust your emotion ... A foolish consistency is the hobgoblin of little minds ... if you would be a man, speak what you think today in words as hard as cannon-balls, and tomorrow speak what tomorrow thinks in hard words again, though it contradicts everything that you said today ... To be great is to be misunderstood.*

He demanded new leaders, new creative heroes to proclaim themselves, men who could summon forth a truly American civilisation from the vastness of unspoilt nature that only America possessed:

> *a true man belongs to no other time or place, but is the centre of things. Where he is, there is nature ... Every true man is a cause, a country and an age; requires infinite spaces and numbers and time fully to accomplish his thought; – and posterity seems to follow his steps like a procession ... He cannot be happy and strong until he too lives with nature in the present, above time.*[30]

It will certainly have occurred to Richard and Mallie Jones that they had known of people, back in Wales, who might fulfil Emerson's ideal, and in the case of Iolo Morganwg, a maverick spirit who truly personified it. Speaking the 'rude truth', Iolo often took aim at English society:

> *[It] has hardly anything in view but the improvement of fortune, the sordid acquisition of wealth, not the attainment of virtue and pure morality. Its objects are those of avarice, ambition, power; the means not of instructing those who are destitute of knowledge, but of trampling upon them and more effectually holding them in that state of degradation, slavery and blindness that best suits its own superciliousness, arrogance and self-conceit.*[31]

Emerson was equally contemptuous:

> *the [English] system is an invasion of the sentiment of justice and the native rights of men, which, however decorated, must lessen the value of English citizenship. It is for Englishmen to consider, not for us; we only say, let us live in America.*[32]

When they emigrated, Richard and Mallie Jones did so with the explicit intention of establishing a new Wales free from the oppressive influence of the English establishment, a new Wales in which they and their children could live and grow unconstrained, to realise their absolute creative and spiritual potential. It was a time and place in which countervailing ideas were easily excluded, in which every clan could live by its own beliefs, and they believed unreservedly in the promise of their American Wales. But they still depended deeply on their spiritual philosophies, on Unitarianism and Transcendentalism for moral reassurance and to bolster their physical and emotional resilience. From the moment of his birth, Frank's mother immersed him in Welsh Bardic Unitarianism and Emersonian Transcendentalism, the two enlightenments that shared the same origin, and he was transfigured in the gleam of their confluence.

In Frank's autobiography, he summoned up a memory from the first year of his architectural career, when he was a lowly tracer at the Chicago office of the architect Joseph Silsbee. Speaking with Cecil Corwin, his colleague and closest friend, Frank questioned Silsbee's commitment to his art in terms that invoked the radical faith of his forebears and the self-reliance of Emerson:

> But he's not doing the right thing if he is not doing as well as he knows how to do ... Because if there is GOD he can be trusted to use the best he has made ... HE can be trusted to make the modifications ... not Silsbee. This GOD of our Grandfathers – the first thing he would put upon every member of creation ... would be ... to do the best he knew how to do. Not as he was told to do it, but as he saw it for himself ...

> Cecil laughed 'That mother of yours is going to have occasion to weep for you Frank.'

> 'Maybe Cecil, but not on that account, **not if she is Grandfather's daughter. And she is.**'[33] ∎

## 02 Bards of Liberty
### *Notes*

1    National Library of Wales, Peniarth Manuscripts Collection.

2    Edward Willams (Iolo Morganwg), *Poems, Lyric and Pastoral*, two vols (London: 1794), vol. 1, pp. 173–6; vol. 2, p. 218.

3    Richard Gravil, *Wordsworth's Bardic Vocation* (London: Palgrave Macmillan, 2003), p. 81. See also D. W. Davies, 'At Defiance: Iolo, Godwin, Coleridge, Wordsworth', in G. H. Jenkins (ed.), *A Rattleskull Genius: The Many Faces of Iolo Morganwg* (Cardiff: University of Wales Press, 2005), pp. 147–72.

4    Author's interview with Dr Mary-Ann Constantine, University of Wales Centre for Advanced Welsh & Celtic Studies, 2018.

5    Frank Lloyd Wright, from a lecture delivered at the RIBA, London in 1939, published as *An Organic Architecture: The Architecture of Democracy* (London: Lund Humphries and Co., 1939), p. 14.

6    It is important to think of this as a line of poetry with its own alliteration and assonance. It should be pronounced something like 'uh-gweer-unn-airbin-uh-beed'.

7    The motto can be seen on the covers of every annual prospectus issued by Hillside Home School.

8    *The Myvyrian Archaiology of Wales,* jointly authored by Edward Williams (Iolo Morganwg), Owen Jones and William Owen Pughe, was, 'the major published source of Taliesin material for a good deal of the 19th century'. See Gwyneth Lewis and Rowan Williams, *The Book of Taliesin: Poems of Warfare and Praise in an Enchanted Britain* (London: Penguin Classics, 2019), 'Introduction', p. xxxvi.

9    'Shining Brow' was an established translation of the name 'Taliesin'. See, for example, the popular poem written in celebration of the 1858 Llangollen National Eisteddfod by James Kenwood (Elfynydd), printed in several anthologies, c.1860. Scott Gartner's essay, 'The Shining Brow: Frank Lloyd Wright and the Welsh Bardic Tradition', in N. Menocal (ed.), *Wright Studies*, vol. 1: *Taliesin 1911–1914* (Carbondale: Southern Illinois University Press,

1992), pp. 28–43, points out that the name Taliesin is translated as 'Radiant Brow' in Lady Guest's first translation of the *The Mabinogion*. He further suggests that Frank Lloyd Wright obtained the translation 'Shining Brow' from a book called *The Boys' Mabinogion* (New York: Charles Scribner's & Sons, 1881), which also contains Iolo's 'Genius Triad', just as Lady Guest's original *Mabinogion* collection had done. 'Shining Brow', was, however, a popularly accepted translation of 'Taliesin' long before the publication of *The Boys' Mabinogion*.

10    Richard Hovey, *Taliesin: A Masque* (Boston: Small Maynard and Co., 1900).

11    Lewis and Williams, *The Book of Taliesin*, p. xxxvii.

12    A. Alofsin, 'Taliesin: To Fashion Worlds in Little', in N. Menocal (ed.), *Wright Studies*, vol. 1, pp. 44–65.

13    In the summer of 1926 Frank's friend and patron Darwin Martin sent him a 'handbook about Wales'. Frank wrote back to him: 'I am glad to have it from your hand and only now learn just what the word Taliesin means. It is worth knowing.' He may have intended his remark to flatter Darwin Martin. Another possibility is that the 'handbook to Wales' provided information about Taliesin that Frank was genuinely unaware of, even sixteen years after giving the name to his house (Secrest, *Frank Lloyd Wright: A Biography*, p. 327). There is only one 'handbook' that it could have been. This was *Muirhead's Wales*, published in 1922 and reprinted in 1926, one of the highly popular Blue Guides. It offers the following: 'Taliesin is popularly regarded as the greatest of all Welsh bards (6th cent.), but is more probably a mythical character, or at most, like Homer, a composite personification' (p. 139). It is now understood that the poems attributed to Taliesin are not the work of a single author, but this may have been the first time that Frank became aware of the idea. This seems the most probable explanation of his remark to Darwin Martin.

14    Maginel Wright Barney, *The Valley of the God Almighty Joneses* (New York: Appleton Century, 1965), p. 85.

15    D. E. Davies, 'Iolo Morganwg (1747-1826): Bardism and Unitarianism', *Journal of Welsh Religious History*, 6 (1998), 4.

16    Cathryn Charnell-White, *Bardic Circles: National, Regional and Personal Identity in the Bardic Vision of Iolo Morganwg* (Cardiff: University of Wales Press, 2007), p. 3.

17    In her memoir *The Valley of the God Almighty Joneses*, Frank's sister Maginel Wright Barney recalled the Lloyd Jones family singing hymns together in the open air: 'I remember the Welsh hymn *Hyfrydik Y Delyn Aus*' (*sic*). This appears to be the names of two very popular hymn tunes joined together, 'Hyfrydol' (composed by Roland Prichard in 1844) and 'Y Delyn Aur' ('The Golden Harp'), a very old tune with an unknown composer (Barney, *The Valley of the God Almighty Joneses*, p. 103).

18    Charnell-White, *Bardic Circles*, p. 67. Prof D. Densil Morgan points out that 'for classic Unitarianism God, as uncreated Being, is and always has been eternal'. Iolo's imagining of God's own inception was presumably a personal vision.

19    Thomas Graham (ed.), *Trilogy: Through Their Eyes* (Spring Green, WI: Unity Chapel Publications, 1986), p. 39.

20    Bruce Brooks Pfeiffer (ed.), *Frank Lloyd Wright Collected Writings*, vol 5: *1949-1959* (New York: Random House, 1995), p. 114.

21    Barney, *The Valley of the God Almighty Joneses*, p. 85.

22    Ceredigion Archive/UK Census.

23    Brendan Gill, *Many Masks: A Life of Frank Lloyd Wright* (London: Heinemann, 1988), p. 34.

24    Donald Leslie Johnson, *Frank Lloyd Wright: Early Years: Progressivism: Aesthetics: Cities* (Abingdon: Routledge, 2017), pp. 28, 7. In that it comprises three converging lines, *Y Nod Cyfrin* is similar to the 'King's Broad Arrow', but in detail and in provenance it is distinctly different. The King's Broad Arrow was used to mark British state property of all kinds. Its three straight lines typically meet in a point.

25    Gravil, *Wordsworth's Bardic Vocation*, p. 90.

26    Samuel Taylor Coleridge, *Coleridge's Essays and Lectures on Shakespeare and Some Other Old Poets and Dramatists* (London: J. M. Dent, 1907), p. 46.

27    R. P. Adams, 'Architecture and the Romantic Tradition: Coleridge to Wright', *The American Quarterly*, 9/1 (Spring 1957), 46–62. The Swiss philosopher Jean-Jacques Rousseau (1712-78) first proposed the 'noble savage' as the embodiment of incorrupt human nature. The idea became of central significance in Romantic thought.

28       Samuel Taylor Coleridge, *To Priestley*, a sonnet (1794).

29       Samantha C. Harvey, *Transatlantic Transcendentalism: Coleridge, Emerson and Nature* (Edinburgh: Edinburgh University Press, 2013), pp. 1–6.

30       Ralph Waldo Emerson, 'Self Reliance', in *Essays: First Series* (New York: Houghton Mifflin & Co., 1899), pp. 41–76.

31       National Library of Wales, Iolo Morganwg Papers, MS 13121B, 'On the Welsh Literature', p. 473, undated. Quoted in Charnell-White, *Bardic Circles*, p. 273.

32       Ralph Waldo Emerson, 'The Young American', *The Dial*, 4 (April 1844), 507.

33       Frank Lloyd Wright, *An Autobiography (Edition 2)* (New York: Duell, Sloan & Pearce, 1943), p. 83. The emphasis on the last two sentences is mine.

# 3

# Remittance

Llanwenog Church is perched on a steep east-facing slope. Rimmed with ancient hedges, low hills ripple away to a green horizon. Grass grows thick between tightly grouped headstones. Mowing must be a challenge. It is an Anglican church, the cynosure of its parish for at least seven centuries, and quite possibly for twice as long. For centuries, also, it has been associated with the Llanfechan branch of the Lloyd family whose estates skirt the village and dominate the south of the parish. To the north lie Brynllefrith and Coedlannau and to the south the sprawling estate of Highmead, also known as Dolebach. The Llanfechan lineage is well represented in the graveyard at Llanwenog, and the splendid condition of the church reflects their generous patronage. In 1779, despite his prominence as an Arminian Dissenter, the great David Lloyd was buried among his ancestors in this densely Anglican ground. This is not as surprising as it first seems. It was only after the passing of the Doctrine of the Trinity Act in 1813 that Unitarian worship became legal, allowing the Unitarian chapels to have burial grounds of their own, and even then it was not until 1834 that the first burial took place at Llwynrhydowen. In the intervening years, at a local level, discreetly, the Anglican gentry was tolerant of the Old Dissenters, acknowledging their shared anxiety that the 'dark cloud' of Methodist fanaticism, the New Dissent, might smother them both (Fig. 3.1).

David Lloyd's presence in the precinct of Llanwenog seems to have opened the way for others of his persuasion. Among many Unitarians, Mallie Thomas's grandfather, James Griffiths, was buried there in 1800, despite having lived his life from birth in the neighbouring parish of Llandysul. David Lloyd's protégé, the Rev. David Davis, was buried there in 1827. Even the expatriate Charles Lloyd is there, beneath a characteristically reticent inscription, having had the good sense to expire while on a visit to his Welsh family in 1829. Another headstone is squeezed in, between David Davis's expansive memorial and the edge of the footpath that loops the church, as if it occupies a space that was not intended to be used. It is the grave of John Enoch, husband to Margaret Lloyd and father of Richard Jones, once hat-maker of the parish (Pl. 13).

John Enoch died in 1850, six years after Richard and Mallie had emigrated and long after Unitarianism had been legalised. The logical resting place for him would have been in the spacious grounds of Pantydefaid Chapel's Unitarian cemetery, but instead he was interred at Llanwenog, on Anglican territory, because it mattered more to him and to his family that he should take a place as close as possible to the two great pioneers of Rational Dissent, one of whom, David Lloyd, had been his wife's father. It was common in the nineteenth century for headstones to be inscribed with verse, most often from the Bible, less so from contemporary poets, and on those occasions when an earthly source was set in stone, the name of the poet is, by convention, omitted, superfluous. David Davis's stone follows this rule. It has a lengthy verse from the prize-winning poet Daniel Ddu.[1] Despite this, the author's name does not appear. John Enoch's headstone, fittingly, breaks with this convention. It is inscribed

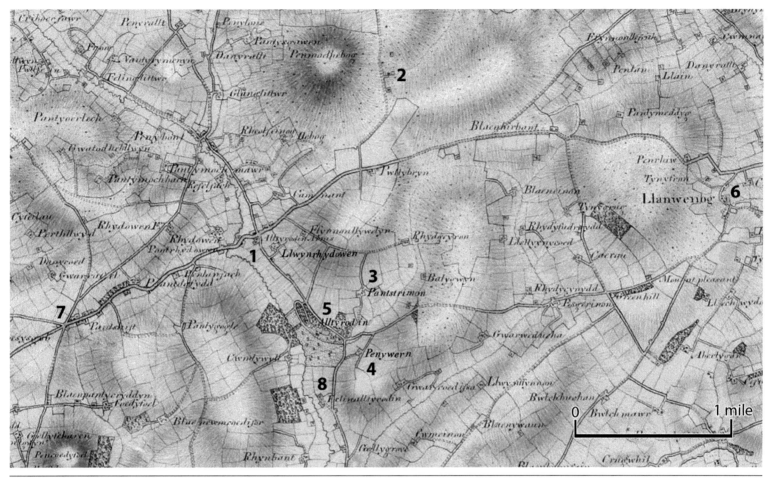

Fig. 3.1. A detail from Thomas Budgen's map of Cardiganshire, 1811.
   (1) Llwynrhydowen Old Chapel (Yr Hen Gapel).
   (2) Blaenrallthddu home of Richard and Mallie Jones.
   (3) Pantstreimon home of John Enoch and Margaret Jones (*née* Lloyd), birthplace of Richard Jones.
   (4) Pen-y-wern, birthplace of Mary Jones (*née* Thomas).
   (5) Alltyrodyn Manor House.
   (6) Llanwenog Church (Anglican), family church of the Lloyds of Llanfechan.
   (7) Pantydefaid Chapel, established by Charles Lloyd in 1802.
   (8) Felinguron, the last home of John Enoch, and the likely home of Richard Jones before his marriage to Mary Thomas (not labelled on map).
   British Library Board / Open Government License.

with lines from a funeral hymn, Psalm 91 from the 1827 edition of *Salmau yr Eglwys yn yr Anialwch*, the 'Hymns for the Church in the Wilderness', and the author's name is inscribed boldly at the base: 'IOLO'. This is another striking testament to his family's preoccupation with the life and the philosophy of the 'Bard of Liberty', the devotion that was passed on to Richard Jones, that fortified him and his family for their tumultuous journey. It sustained them throughout the long years before their settlement in south Wisconsin, was passed on as a mixture of ardent faith and family honour to their children and their grandchildren, and then unexpectedly emerged in dazzling physical expression from the extraordinary mind of Frank Lloyd Wright.

Frank Lloyd Wright died in 1959, aged ninety-two. A few years later, thousands of miles away in London, England, a letter was found inside a wooden box, in the attic of a house. The letter had been sent in 1852 by Margaret Lloyd, Richard Lloyd Jones's mother, to her third son, John, who had been living in London for many years by that time. The letter revealed that, of Margaret Lloyd and John Enoch's eleven children, no fewer than five had left Wales to settle in America during Margaret's lifetime.

*25th July 1852*

*My dear Son,*

*To my great surprise I received a letter from you, not believing that you were on the land of the living. You blame me for not writing and I can blame you for your neglect. You knew where we were. I did not know in the world where you were so let us renew our correspondence from henceforth. I am very happy to hear that you and your children are doing so well at present and I will give you an account of your relations. In the first place we have lost your dear father. He has been dead these two years and is buried at Llanwenog on the 12th day of May 1850 being ninety years of age ... There has not been a moment hardly past that he is not uppermost in my thoughts. Your brother David is married these twenty years and lives in the same place near Aberaeron ... He gets his livelihood tolerably well by his trade as a blacksmith. Richard and his wife and six children went to America seven years ago next autumn.[2] Jenkin and Rachel went four years before them and bought 80 acres of land and built a handsome house on it. Soon after the house was finished my poor dear Jenkin died and was buried on his own land.[3] He made a will and left all his property to Richard. So Richard and his family live now in the house that dear Jenkin built in Wisconsin ... Nell and her husband, she was married to the son of Oernant,[4] and ten children*

*went to America. They are settled within a quarter of a mile of Rachel and are doing exceedingly well so that I have 30 to 40 between children and grandchildren in America living all in the same neighbourhood and close to Watertown in Wisconsin.[5] There is a house of worship built close to Jenkin's grave where I hope they all flock on Sundays ... Hannah as you know is married to the son of Dolebach three miles nearer than Llansawel [6] (Pl. 14). A brother of her husband died last winter and left them a very good tenement of land so that Hannah and her husband have from 60 to 70 pounds a year of landed property. Now there is none but Enoch who lives with his mother single.[7] We have left Felinguron.[8] We live now in a house called Blaencwmarch opposite Pantydefaid Chapel [9] ... The paper is too small for me to write any more. Write very soon. Why can't you come to see us. Try to get yourself a suit of clothes and come. How glad we would be to see you. We have plenty of provisions.*

*Margaret Jones.*

Pl. 14. Highmead Mansion, known locally as Dolebach. According to the 'Margaret Letter' Richard Lloyd Jones's sister Hannah was married to John Evans, one of the heirs of this estate.
NLW.

The contents of the 'Margaret Letter' came as a surprise to the American descendants of Richard and Mallie Lloyd Jones.[10] Until then they had understood their family history to have been more straightforward, along the lines of the family memoir, *Youngest Son*, which had been assembled from the sermons of his uncle Jenkin Lloyd Jones, and from other collected memories and anecdotes, by Chester Lloyd Jones, the eldest son of Frank Lloyd Wright's uncle Enos, and published privately in 1938. In Chester's version of the story it was only Jenkin who had preceded Richard and Mallie to America, acting as their pathfinder, and there was no mention of any that followed them. This led naturally to the formation of an image of Richard and Mallie as courageous pioneers who had found themselves isolated in the remote west, and who, despite their lonely predicament, had managed to prevail and eventually to take control of the wilderness, and to flourish. From today's vantage point, the fact that Richard and Mallie and their seven children were only small figures

in a vast migratory enterprise, a rush that swept up many of their brothers and sisters along with thousands of other Welsh families, and millions more from across Europe, still does not diminish their astonishing bravery and resilience. It is a story that had a formative influence on the young Frank Lloyd Wright, one that frequently led him to find within himself an equivalent spirit of fortitude, a spirit that he knew he could call upon, because it was his inheritance.

Chester Lloyd Jones's book *Youngest Son* contains a collection of extraordinary photographs, which set the scene beautifully for the story of Richard and Mallie's journey and the events that led up to it. They are interesting not only for their own sake but also because most of them have been misinterpreted and wrongly labelled by the author. They serve as an illustrative microcosm of the way in which the migration story as a whole has evolved in the telling, in some cases far away from what must have been the reality. It is likely that the photographs were taken in the summer of 1882 when Frank's uncle Jenkin Lloyd Jones, the famous Unitarian Minister, made a celebrated visit to Wales from Chicago.[11]

The first photograph shows a building identified as the 'Llwynrhydowen Church' (Pl. 15). It is an unusual chapel because it is built in the form of a house.[12] It is larger than a typical farmhouse, perhaps a doctor's house or that of a modest landowner. The plan is in the shape of a 'T': a short gabled frontage projects from the lateral façade of the rectangular main body of the building. There is an attractive fanlight above the front door. Without the prominent burial ground in front, there would be nothing to identify it as a place of worship. But, if we look very closely, there is the suggestion of a panel set into the wall above the front door, between the top of the fanlight and the sill of the window above. The building is actually Pantydefaid Chapel, the second building on the site, completed in 1836, and the panel in the wall may be the inscribed block that Iolo Morganwg set into the wall above the door of the first chapel in 1802.[13] This was how Pantydefaid Chapel appeared in 1844, when Richard and Mallie Lloyd Jones last saw it, and how it appeared in 1882 when Jenkin Lloyd Jones preached there, in the course of his visit. None of the other Unitarian chapels in the region looked like this: only Pantydefaid was built deliberately to resemble a house, with the purpose of emphasising the forthright domesticity of the Unitarian faith.

Pantydefaid Chapel made a deep impression on Jenkin Lloyd Jones. Two years after his visit he delivered a sermon on *The New Problems in Church Architecture* in which he set out his vision for his new All Souls Church, to be built in the Oakland district of Chicago: 'The modern church, built after the conventional cathedral type, is an obvious anachronism.' The traditional form of church provided, 'no place to listen, to work or to think. It kindled a mystic imagination but strangled the judgment.' Jenkin asked for a new type of church that could accommodate 'the finer ideal of many smaller homes, where those of like mind and taste band themselves together with home-like ties', in which the church community would be 'the larger family, and its building must be made the larger home.' As he concluded his sermon, Jenkin made a plea directly to those that he felt should respond:

> *Would you build us a house of worship? O architect, build it low with humility, and make it warm with human tenderness ... Build us, O architect, a building whose very walls will be instinct with human fellowship and human needs. Flood it with sunlight and fill it with pure air.*

Just like Pantydefaid Chapel, it would not recognisably be a church, but it would still be beautiful: 'the line of beauty ever tends to be the line of truth. The rational faith will only demand that the architect recognize the broad distinction between the conventional and the genuine in art.'[14]

In this sermon, preached by his Uncle Jenkin shortly before Frank Lloyd Wright first took up his architectural apprenticeship, it is apparent that Uncle Jenkin was more than just a spiritual mentor. He was also the inspiration for Frank's way of thinking about architecture, a supremely articulate and persuasive advocate for innovation and for progressive transformation who, through decades of preaching in churches across America, had arrived at a deep understanding of the power of architecture to influence human behaviour and to be a vehicle for social change. The sermon also reveals a note of respect for, and focus upon, the architectural profession

THE LLWYNRHYDOWEN CHURCH FOUNDED BY REVEREND JENKIN JONES (D 1742) His Nephew Reverend David Lloyd (1724-1779) was the Second Minister. Reverend David Lloyd was the Grandfather of Richard Lloyd Jones.

Pl. 15.   The first photograph in Chester Lloyd Jones's book *Youngest Son* shows the second Pantydefaid Chapel, not Llwynrhydowen Church. This is the only known photograph of the building, a chapel that resembles a house more than a place of worship.

that leads one to presume that Jenkin may well have been instrumental in guiding his young nephew towards it. All Souls Church was opened in 1886, the same year that Frank Lloyd Wright moved to Chicago to begin his apprenticeship. Later, in his autobiography, Frank recalled that his Uncle Jenkin had got the building that he had envisaged. It looked 'in no way like a church, more like a 'Queen Anne' dwelling'.[15]

The second photograph in *Youngest Son* is of a large, two-storey farmhouse, again a little more grand than would be typical for Cardiganshire in the nineteenth century (Pl. 16). It is identified as 'Blaen-yr-alt-ad, the birthplace of Richard Lloyd Jones'. 'Blaen-yr-alt-ad' is meaningless, so we have to presume that it is a distortion of 'Blaenralltddu', the farm that was the home of Richard and Mallie in the decade before their emigration. Richard was not born at Blaenralltddu, however. He was born in December 1799 at the farm called Pantstreimon, situated just a few hundred metres to the east of Alltyrodyn Manor. The Alltyrodyn

BLAEN-YR-ALT-AD
Birthplace of Richard Lloyd Jones.

Pl. 16. The second photograph actually shows Pantstreimon, not 'Blaen-yr-alt-ad'. Pantstreimon was indeed the birthplace of Richard Lloyd Jones.

Alltyrodyn were their landlords. The house in this photograph is of a much more familiar form, single-storey, heavy set with blunt features, a typical Cardiganshire tenant farm with a pond in the foreground, overhung by large trees. The house was demolished a few years after the photograph was taken; it can be identified on the 1886 Ordnance Survey map, but in the 1904 map there is a new house in its place, the more decorous late Victorian villa that stands there today.

Throughout the period of the growth of the Unitarian 'black spot', the Lloyds of Alltyrodyn held firmly to the conservative Anglican principles that validated their life of privilege, and by the standards of the time and place, they were very rich indeed. For centuries the tenants on the Alltyrodyn estate would have fulfilled their subservient role without question, but as Rational Dissent began to flower on their very doorstep the nature of the relationship changed. Increasingly their tenants began to view them with resentment, as the embodiment of a corrupt system that belonged to the past. The same tensions were manifest between landlords and tenants across Cardiganshire, made worse by increasing demands for tithes and tolls, a rapidly growing rural population, and, as a consequence, widespread hardship.

For a few years in the early 1840s, under the tacit leadership of a Unitarian minister, the friction ignited the

estate spread over miles and encompassed dozens of farms, but Pantstreimon was not one of them. It had been a stately home itself in the pre-Tudor era and had managed somehow to avoid being absorbed by its dominant neighbour. By the time John Enoch's family took over the tenancy it was owned by yet another branch of the Lloyd family, the Price-Lloyds of Glansevin, Carmarthenshire. Richard's father, John Enoch, had himself been born at Pantstreimon in the early 1760s. Pantstreimon is the house in the photograph. The farmhouse is still there. It has been robustly remodelled but it can easily be recognised by its outline and its setting above the high retaining wall and the steeply sloping track (Pl. 17).

A few pages on we come to the third photograph, showing 'Pen-y-Wern, the birthplace of Mary Thomas James, wife of Richard Lloyd Jones' (Pl. 18). Pen-y-Wern and Pantstreimon were neighbouring farms, separated by a stream, Afon Geyron. Pen-y-Wern was also directly adjacent to Alltyrodyn Manor, embedded in the estate. The Lloyds of

Pl. 17. Pantstreimon as it appears today. It has been altered, but it is unmistakeably the same house that appears in the photograph in *Youngest Son*.

Rebecca Riots, a flurry of destruction that specifically targeted the property of rich landowners and English corporations. Uncomfortable as it must have been, the security and the status of local gentry, like the Lloyds of Alltyrodyn, were always assured by the might of the state. Troops sent from England snuffed out the Rebecca Riots, an echo of the state suppression that had stifled republican sentiment in the area fifty years earlier. Mallie's and Richard's families were both poised, physically and emotionally, on the threshold between political revolt and the establishment, as embodied in Alltyrodyn. When Mallie's father died, he left the tenancy of Pen-y-Wern to his wife, and as Mallie's six brothers and sisters grew up and moved away, most of them went to other farms on the Alltyrodyn estate. Richard's mother, Margaret, a Lloyd herself, was related, albeit distantly, to the Lloyds of Alltyrodyn. Despite their religious and political differences there are indications that it was a relationship that Richard's parents valued. They left their tenancy at Pantstreimon in 1814 to move to a farm on the Alltyrodyn estate called Rhydyceir, so that the Lloyds of Alltyrodyn became their landlords too, and some time before 1826 they moved again to the mill house on the Afon Geyron, almost as if they wanted to be as close as possible, again, to Alltyrodyn Manor.

The last of the architectural photographs in *Youngest Son* is the most mysterious (Pl. 19). It shows a house shrouded in ivy from the ground up almost to the ridge of its roof, standing in an overgrown meadow. It seems unlikely at first that anyone could be living in it, but it has an intact, glazed front door, and a small window just to its side. The title identifies it as 'Blaen Strimon, the home of Richard Lloyd Jones in Wales'. The 'Strimon' in the supposed name must come from Pantstreimon, but there was no house called 'Blaen Strimon'. Looking through the ivy we can discern the outline of a cottage with a low, single-storey front wall supporting an unusually high-pitched roof, as if the back part of the cottage contains two storeys. These features make it possible to identify the house as 'Blaenralltddu', Richard and Mallie's married home, the home they left to travel to America[16] (Pl. 20). Below this photograph, on the same page, there is a picture from a postcard, a photograph of

PEN Y WERN
The Birthplace of Mary Thomas James, Wife of Richard Lloyd Jones.

Pl. 18. This photograph, from *Youngest Son*, is correctly identified as Mallie's birthplace. The pond still exists but the house has been replaced..

BLAEN STRIMON
The Home of Richard Lloyd Jones in Wales.

Pl. 19. The farmhouse, Blaenralltddu, overgrown by foliage, as pictured in *Youngest Son*.

Pl. 20. Blaenralltddu today.
Photograph David Thomas.

the coastal town of New Quay, taken from the air. A small black 'X' has been drawn on the line of New Quay's historic harbour wall. The title on the photograph explains: 'New Quay Cardiganshire. Richard Lloyd Jones set sail at X.' The picture was taken in 1923 by Airco Aerials Ltd, the year in which Frank Lloyd Wright's mother Anna (Hannah) died, and nearly forty years after the death of her father, Richard Lloyd Jones.[17] This late addition serves to show that, despite the many faded and misremembered details of their shared history, communication between the Welsh and American branches of the family continued well into the twentieth century.

At the time that the aerial photograph was taken, almost the whole of Frank Lloyd Wright's surviving family, on both sides of the Atlantic, had come to think of him as a embarrassment to their name. The scandal-hungry press of Chicago and Wisconsin had revelled in the eccentricity of his private life. It was easy for them to present him as a scoundrel, a libertine and a womaniser, whereas in truth he was none of

these things. If anything, he was painfully keen to stand up to his responsibilities and to answer publicly for his private actions. Although he was adept at misplacing financial liabilities, he never dodged an emotional debt. Throughout his long life he always kept the company of strong women. He was only truly himself with the women that were closest to him. But he had high expectations of them. The devoted support of a woman meant little to him unless he believed that that woman could be his equal intellectually, creatively and even physically. The only woman whom he walked away from, much as it genuinely hurt him to do so, was his first wife, Kitty, and he left her for no better reason than that she had seemed to settle into a life of comfortable domesticity, caring for their five children, rather than prioritising her role as his spiritual muse and creative champion. Frank's mother, Anna Lloyd Jones, provided the template for this vital feminine role. As we will see, it was she, more than anyone else, that provided the foundation for her son's achievement, and throughout his life he sought out other women who could liberate his creativity as fully as his mother had done.

There is a suggestion of reciprocal narcissism in Frank's relationship with his mother, and it would be easy to see Frank's attitude to women as being an expression of insecurity, consistent with a narcissistic nature. But there is more to it than this. Among their cherished family anecdotes there is the story of an ordinary man who, in defiance of social conventions, wins the heart of a young lady of the gentry and marries her. Male descendants appreciated the message in the parable: a Lloyd Jones man was blessed with charisma that could open doors to a privileged life, and the right marriage would enable him to realise his full potential. Because of his mother's influence upon him, Frank seems to have been more receptive to the messages in his family history than his many cousins, and his attitude to the women in his life does seem to have been directed in part by a feeling that he should be elevated by marriage, as his celebrated ancestors had been. There was the Rev. Jenkin Jones's father, the blacksmith who married the daughter of a rich landowner. Then Jenkin Jones himself had married Mary, daughter of another landlord, Dafydd Thomas of

Pantydefaid; and then, of course, there was the marriage of Frank's great-grandparents, John Enoch, the farmer, and Margaret Lloyd, daughter of the Rev. David Lloyd of Brynllefrith: their families really did inhabit opposite slopes of a class and linguistic valley.

Margaret Lloyd had grown up at Brynllefrith, still a prestigious address at that time. She was a Llanfechan Lloyd, a fluent English-speaker. John Enoch was the son of a tenant farmer and monoglot Welsh. Both had grown up as members of the Llwynrhydowen Chapel when it was led by the Rev. David Davis and by Margaret's eldest brother, the Rev. Richard Lloyd. Margaret was the youngest of David Lloyd's children. She had been only nine years old when her father had died. Her mother, Laetitia, had also been the youngest of a large family. To her great discomfort, Laetitia had found herself without a single surviving brother or sister to help support her and her children after her husband's death. It was for this reason that her late husband's brother, John Lloyd, found himself compelled to step forward and become the children's guardian.[18] This was the same Uncle John who cut off support to his nephew Charles Lloyd just as he began his ministerial training. It is easy to imagine that John Lloyd, frustrated at his burden, would have been receptive to the idea of Margaret 'marrying down', if it would free him from his duty to his late brother. Even in these awkward circumstances, in any other part of Wales the marriage of Margaret Lloyd and John Enoch would have been quite unlikely, but in their corner of south Cardiganshire, liberal religion and radical politics bridged the class divide. Margaret was twenty-seven and John was ten years older when they married, both surprisingly old. The marriage must have come as a relief to all of those close to them. While Margaret had privileged roots, John Enoch was certainly the wealthier. Pantstreimon was a prosperous farm. Margaret moved there to live with her new husband, and her mother, the *grande dame* Laetitia Lloyd of Llanfechan, moved in with her. So it was that Richard Lloyd Jones was raised from birth by two generations of Welsh gentry.

The tracing of Welsh family trees can be a challenging process. In English convention it is a matter simply of following the surname through generations, but most Welsh surnames were patronymic. The surname for each generation was taken from the father's forename. Hence John Enoch's father had been Enoch Jacob, and in December 1799, when Richard was born, he took his first name from his late uncle, the Rev. Richard Lloyd, and, as was usual when the father's name was John, he was given the surname Jones. It was only the gentry that followed English convention in passing on their surname: this is why the Lloyds appear to have proliferated. They kept their name while those of the families all around them constantly changed, flickering through familiar biblical appellations to the point where a name on its own did little to identify a person, and it was essential to append it, informally, with the name of their farm or their trade. The eleven children of John Enoch and Margaret Lloyd all took the name Jones, and although she was ineluctably a Lloyd down to the roots of her being, Margaret gave up her illustrious surname and also became a Jones.[19] It is a quirk of history that, at just this stage, as a result partly of patronymic confusion but also as a consequence of the spread of the English language, Welsh habits began to change. After the first generation of Joneses were born to John Enoch, Jonés was retained as the family name. It was decades later, in America, that Margaret's maiden name was retrieved from history by Richard, her son. There was a day, around 1850, when he opened the family's bible and carefully amended his name and those of each member of his family, adding the prestigious 'Lloyd' to their quotidian 'Jones', the married name that had been good enough for his mother.

Pantstreimon was a farm of 234 acres, one of the larger tenancies in the parish of Llandysul. Rhydyceir was two miles south, down the vale of the Afon Clettwr, and half the size of Pantstreimon. In 1814, when John Enoch and Margaret Jones moved to Rhydyceir, they went with their nine children, all under the age of sixteen. It was at Rhydyceir that young Richard Jones learned the skills of the land that served him so well on the American frontier. The move to Felin Guron in the mid-1820s was the last that John Enoch was to make: he lived there at the mill house until his death in 1850. There is no record of Richard's whereabouts after his parents moved from Rhydyceir, but it is likely that he moved to the mill house with them. This brought him back very close again to Pen-y-Wern, the home of Thomas James and of his daughter, Mallie, the family who had been their neighbours when they had lived at Pantstreimon.

In the years between, Richard and Mallie had both grown up as members of Pantydefaid Chapel, but with their new proximity they began to enjoy a much closer familiarity. Richard and Mallie's marriage is recorded in the Llandysul parish register on 14 July 1829 (Pl. 21). Richard was twenty-nine years old and Mallie had recently turned twenty-two. It would not have seemed poignant at all to Mallie or to her husband, as it does in our times, to recognise that she was illiterate. This was something that she had in common with the great majority of rural women. Her name is recorded on the ledger as a clumsy 'X'. According to family memoirs Mallie never did learn to read or write, and she remained a monoglot Welsh-speaker for the whole of her life.

Richard and Mallie's first child, Thomas, was born a year after the wedding. By that time they were resident at

Pl. 21. The registration of the marriage of Richard Jones and Mary Thomas, on 14 July 1829. Mallie has signed her name as 'X', showing that she was illiterate at that time. The witnesses are Richard's brother David, who was a blacksmith at Llyfanog, near Llanarth, and Mallie's brother James, a farmer at Pen-y-Wern, Mallie's family home.
Ceredigion Archive.

Blaenralltddu, on the boundary of the parishes of Llandysul and Llanwenog.[20] Blaenralltddu was on the southern edge of the Coedlannau estate, the large property that had belonged to the Rev. Charles Lloyd. After his death in May 1829, Coedlannau had been inherited by Charles Lloyd's eldest son, also named Charles. Hence, Richard's landlord was also a first cousin. Blaenralltddu was an unusually small tenancy, only twenty-three acres in its entirety.[21] In Cardiganshire at that time it was generally reckoned that a farmer required at least thirty-five acres of productive land to support himself and his wife - unless he had a supplementary income.[22] There is a possibility that they rented fields on neighbouring farms to increase their grazing and, despite the hastening of land enclosure, there were still areas of upland commons in the south of the county that could be grazed in the summer. Without access to these extra land resources there is only the unlikely conclusion that, for several years at least, it was Richard's millinery that enabled them to make ends meet.[23]

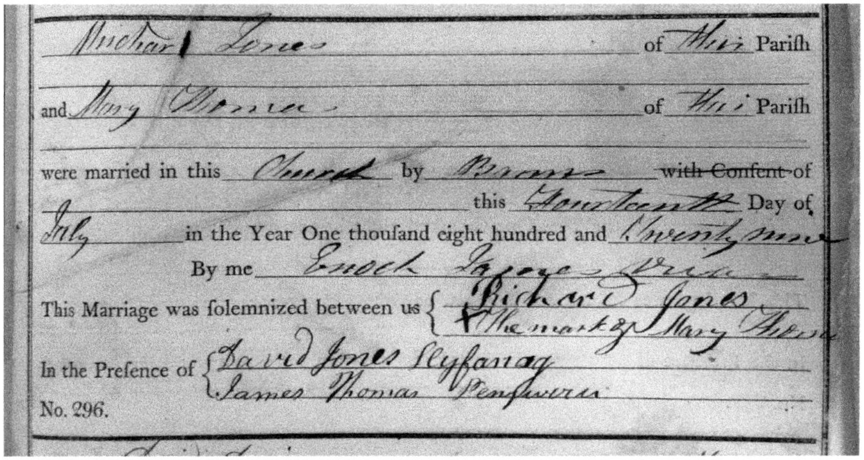

The first chapter of Chester Lloyd Jones's book *Youngest Son* is titled 'Wales'. It is drenched in a foggy drizzle of ennui. Richard is pictured making his way on foot, soaking wet and weary, back to Blaenralltddu after an unsuccessful day at a local fair, presumably with a quantity of unsold hats. His pace quickens when he hears Mallie's voice, from inside the farmhouse, singing 'Men of Harlech'. Maginel's later book borrowed substantially from *Youngest Son*, but she shows the scene from Mallie's viewpoint, the dutiful wife waiting patiently for her husband's return. She has food to prepare, and by 1843 she has six children to attend to. She has better things to do than singing songs that would not be written until twenty years later, and in a language that she didn't understand. But in Maginel's version, too, their decision to emigrate is presented as a reluctant inevitability, the only way out of a deepening economic predicament. Farming livelihoods in Cardiganshire were always under pressure, always a balancing act. The harvests of 1837 and 1838 had both been reduced by bad weather, forcing farmers like Richard Jones to buy overpriced imported corn to feed their livestock and their families. At the same time, though, prices for the sheep and butter they produced were unusually high, and remained so into the early 1840s. Then, in 1842 Robert Peel's new Tory government relaxed tariffs on imported livestock and meat. The price of livestock that had sustained farmers in Cardiganshire since the late 1830s immediately slumped. That same summer of 1842 delivered the best harvest for years, leading to a sudden fall in corn prices. The double price fall had a severe impact on farming income, and for a short while many came close to disaster. But despite this period of hardship, and even the sporadic destruction of tollbooths that it inspired, the population of the county continued to grow, and people generally managed.[24] It is recorded that the quality of healthcare and housing was improving, and, with the expansion of the metal mining industry in the north of the county, a new and prosperous market began to emerge for the farmers in the south. By 1844 the worst of the crisis in Cardiganshire had passed.

The American view of European immigration is coloured by the legacy of the rural Irish who fled in their hundreds of thousands to America in the late 1840s. For those Irish migrants the choice was stark: they had either to leave for America, with almost nothing to sustain them, or remain in Ireland and starve to death. It is little wonder that such an extreme experience has come to characterise a phenomenon that, in the years before the Irish famine, was driven by more affirmative motivations. Richard and Mallie were faced with a situation in which they felt something needed to change. Their farm was not big enough to sustain them, and Richard's hat-making enterprise was heading for failure, unable to compete with English mass production. Over generations before, however, their families and their neighbours had sustained livelihoods despite bad harvests and price falls by changing properties, learning new trades and, in time, benefiting from inheritances. America was by no means the only way out for them, nor was it for the great majority of Cardiganshire migrants at that time. Nevertheless, during the 1840s, they were leaving in large numbers. The total population of the county averaged around 67,000 during the 1840s, and during the same decade nearly three thousand left for America. The 1840s accounted for almost half of all emigration from Cardiganshire between 1795 and 1860.[25]

In her 1852 letter, Richard's mother Margaret remarked that her daughter Rachel had emigrated in 1840 with her husband Rees Beynon and their two children, and that Jenkin Jones, Richard's younger brother, had gone with them. However, census records show that Jenkin was still resident with Richard and Mallie at Blaenralltddu in the summer of 1841, so Margaret's recollection is imprecise. It made most sense to emigrate in the spring or early summer, in order to reach America well before winter. If this logic is followed it would suggest that this first group of Jones migrants probably departed in 1842, just before the damaging agricultural price falls. Rachel and Rees Beynon stayed in the Welsh settlements of Oneida County in northern New York State for long enough to have two more children, but Jenkin went on.[26] He found his way a few hundred miles west into Pennsylvania, passing through slate- and coal-mining areas, where Welshmen with the right skills were in demand, but they were not the skills of a Cardiganshire farmer. He moved on almost a thousand miles further westwards, perhaps via the 'little Cardiganshire' settlements in the Jackson and Gallia Counties of Ohio, to Galena and Mineral Point, lead-mining towns near the Mississippi River. All the Welsh settlements that he visited were welcoming, but few were prosperous. He had looked out over endless flat prairie in the south of Wisconsin to a remote and bare horizon, concluding that it could never sustain a crop if it couldn't grow a tree, and so he turned his back on what would become the richest farmland in the state. The last leg of his journey took him a hundred miles back eastwards, where he settled among a sparse Welsh community in the marshy forested territory of the Rock River valley, forty miles inland from the western shore of Lake Michigan. In the few, infrequent letters that Jenkin sent back to Richard, he was honest about the hardships, but more often enthusiastic about the opportunities, the sense of being part of a great enterprise, the opening up of new territories and the building of a new republic.[27]

Jenkin's enthusiasm gave credence to the reports they had both read before Jenkin had emigrated. There was a pamphlet called *Y Teithiwr Americanaidd* ('The American

Traveller') by 'Edward Jones o Cincinatti', which had been published in Aberystwyth in 1837. It gave solid, practical advice about the routes to follow, living conditions in the various Welsh colonies and the prospects for work. It was followed, in 1840, by the Rev. Benjamin Chidlaw's popular pamphlet *Yr American*, which made the case for emigration much more persuasively:

> Parents who are bringing up families and have some property, but are almost unable to pay their way in spite of every effort, should go to America where they would doubtless, ere long, see a great change for the better in their circumstances ... Many difficulties overtake strangers in a distant land ... sometimes sickness and disappointment, but for all this, having endured and striven untiringly, there will be for the family a better recompense and in a year's time they may rejoice that God's smile is upon them.

It could almost have been aimed directly at Richard and Mallie. Chidlaw's fervour was leavened by cautionary observations, in particular the tendency of Welsh migrants to choose mediocre land on which to settle, simply because it reminded them of Wales. Although he was from Ohio, where the Welsh had been settled for decades, Chidlaw observed: 'Far away in the West ... in the new states of Iowa and Wisconsin is found the best land for the least money.'[28] Both pamphlets were read, shared and discussed throughout Cardiganshire. When Jenkin and Rachel left for America they had followed precisely the route that Chidlaw recommended. For Richard and Mallie it was becoming increasingly real, the idea of America that had, since the days of Iolo Morganwg, become a byword for liberty and tolerance within the Unitarian community, the promise of religious and political freedom that would never be attainable in Wales under English control. Mallie became pregnant for the seventh time early in 1843. The baby, inevitably named Jenkin, was born in mid-November. From then on, inexorably, they put their plans in place to leave.

## Summer 1844. 'Blaenralltddu', Llanwenog, Cardiganshire

They had no property to sell, just their livestock, crops, some farm equipment and chattels. To raise as much as possible from the sale they had to leave after their final harvest. They would join Jenkin in Wisconsin before winter set in, so that they could clear their ground of stones and trees, ready to sow as soon as the snow melted in the following spring. They packed three wooden cases with clothes, boots, pots and pans and cutlery, all the things which they knew would be expensive to buy in America. Mallie tucked in a collection of seeds from the flowers in their garden, and then they had to choose the books. *Y Bibl* was part of the family and had to go with them regardless of its bulk. There was almost certainly a copy of Iolo's *Salmau yr Eglwys yn yr Anialwch*; it took up very little space, and probably also *Rheolau a Threfniadau Cymdeithas Dwyfundodiaid yn Nheubarth Cymru*, Iolo's Unitarian Rule Book.[29] Richard also found space for his most reliable hand tools, including a precious smooth-edged sickle that had, most likely, been made for him by his older brother David, the blacksmith.[30] In late August 1844, Richard and Mallie and their seven children left Blaenralltddu in two wagons to make the fifteen-mile journey to the harbour at New Quay. Their daughter Hannah had just had her sixth birthday. With her were her two older brothers, Thomas who was thirteen and John who was nearly twelve, and her older sisters Margaret and Mary, nine and eight years old respectively. Nany, her younger sister was only three and happily oblivious of what was happening, and there was Jenkin, just a babe in arms. Everything they took with them was packed into the three wooden chests except for their bedding, which was wrapped in a sheet, and a large copper dough trough that served as a cot for Jenkin.[31] At New Quay they boarded a coastal paddle-steamer, one of the many small passenger boats that worked the Welsh ports between Bristol and Liverpool. At Liverpool they would find a ship to take them to America. The journey to Liverpool would have taken two days. It was the beginning of a turbulent autumn season.

*Remittance* was a Baltimore clipper, built for the Atlantic packet service, sailing under the captaincy of J. R. Silsby. According to the advertisement in the *Liverpool Mercury*, she was 'still quite new' and 'remarkably fast'.[32] Although steamships had proved themselves on the ocean, the larger vessels were still few in number and not yet entirely trusted on the open sea. Passengers were more confident with wind and sail. *Remittance* had docked at Liverpool on 19 August.[33] She waited until the last week of September before she was sufficiently laden to sail west again. The voyage to America from Britain, against the prevailing winds, typically took twice as long as the journey in the other direction. Richard, Mallie and their children were among around a hundred other migrants lodged below deck in steerage. Around a week out from Liverpool, hundreds of miles into the ocean, *Remittance* was attempting to run before a violent storm.

It seems impossible to find any account of the experience of steerage passengers on an Atlantic crossing that is anything less than hellish. The steerage compartment was below the ship's deck and above the hold. The only daylight and fresh air came through hatches that opened onto the deck above. Toilets were up at deck level. In *Yr American* Benjamin Chidlaw advised that, 'the Welsh should prepare bread, oatmeal, butter, cheese and meat before leaving ... tea, coffee, sugar, treacle, salt etc. may be had at Liverpool.' Food preparation was communal, carried out in the centre of the steerage deck. Passengers had to be strict with their allowances. As Chidlaw again advised, it was better to arrive in New York with a surplus than to run out at sea. Fresh water was tightly limited and replenished by rain. Although saltwater was in generous supply, bathing was impractical and privacy impossible. According to Chidlaw, 'low spiritedness, lethargy and indolence cause half of the sea-sickness, and the best doctor for preventing it is to go on deck, walk about and converse cheerfully with one another.'[34] In calm weather this was manageable, but for much of the journey, particularly approaching winter, the opportunities for a pleasant walk were few.

The passengers lived for most of the time in their berths, open bunks on three levels arranged along each side of the ship. At the best of times it was crowded, badly ventilated, malodorous and heaving constantly in all directions. Sea-sickness was, of course, endemic. During storms the deck hatches would be firmly secured. No cooking or boiling of water was allowed and lamps were strictly controlled to avoid fires. The passengers would be in near-darkness. Some, like Richard and Mallie, were fortunate enough to know the scripture that they relied upon by heart. There was no access to the toilets up on deck: buckets had to be used instead and made to last usually for two to three days until the sea had settled. In churning seas the buckets often spilled, and with that came cholera, typhoid and dysentery. Every migrant knew that of all the dangers and discomforts they had to endure, it was disease that would be most likely to bring their journey to an end before landfall. Death by shipwreck was a lesser risk, but as *Remittance* grappled with the high wind and waves it became an alarmingly real prospect. At the peak of the storm the main mast collapsed.

We might consider, at this moment, the previous life experience of six-year-old Hannah Jones. It was a life of some hardship, but also of limited horizons, reliable routines and home comforts, very little that might lead her to question the reassuring message of her family's faith. How must she have felt to be huddled in the darkness as the sea crashed and the world rolled around her, holding on to her parents' words of comfort, then to be terrified by the explosion of noise, and the inevitable panic of all the adults whom she trusted to protect her, as the toppling mast struck the deck above her head? With a jury rig it took *Remittance* another two weeks to stumble back to Liverpool. To take rooms in the town while the ship was repaired was out of the question. Every penny had to be kept for America, so Richard, Mallie and the children lodged in the steerage deck, in port for another week with the rest of the passengers, replenished their food supply and prepared their souls to begin the voyage once more. *Remittance* left Liverpool for the second time near to the end of October on a route that was once again marbled with cyclones ∎

# 03  Remittance
## *Notes*

1    '*Awdl ar Sefydliad Coleg Dewi Sant*', by Daniel Ddu o Geredigion (Daniel Evans), from the collection *Gwinllan y Beirdd* (1823).

2    They took seven children with them.

3    The small Welsh graveyard still exists, in Ixonia, Wisconsin.

4    A farm on the Ceredigion coast roughly half way between New Quay and Aberaeron.

5    The township of Ixonia.

6    'Dolebach' is the estate of Highmead Manor, a little more than three miles from Llansawel. John Evans, Hannah's husband, was a grandson of Herbert Evans, a Conservative Anglican High Sheriff of Cardiganshire and collector of taxes for the county.

7    In 1855 Enoch Jones also left Wales to join his brother and sisters in Ixonia. It may have been at the same time that his mother, Margaret, moved from Blaencwmarch to live with her daughter Hannah and her husband, John Evans (n. 6, above), at Dolecanol, neighbouring Dolebach.

8    Felinguron was an old mill house on the Alltyrodyn Estate, half a mile to the south of Pantstreimon, John Enoch's birthplace.

9    The house, now known as 'Cwm March' still exists. It is located around 100 m due south of Pantydefaid Chapel.

10   This transcript of 'The Margaret Letter' appears in *A Lloyd Jones Retrospective* (Spring Green, WI: Unity Chapel Inc, 1986), pp. 43-6.

11   Chester Lloyd Jones, *Youngest Son* (Madison, WI: self-published, 1938). The photographs appear on pp. 16-19.

12   Quaker societies gather at meeting houses rather than places of worship. The Pantydefaid Unitarian Chapel of 1836 does bear some resemblance to a Quaker meeting house.

13   I am indebted to the Rev. Cen Llwyd for his help in identifying this building by means of the headstones in the chapel yard.

14    Jenkin Lloyd Jones, 'The New Problems in Church Architecture', *Unity*, XV (June 1885), 202-5. Also quoted in J. Siry, 'Frank Lloyd Wright's Unity Temple and Architecture for Liberal Religion in Chicago 1885-1909', *The Arts Bulletin*, 73/2 (June 1991), 257-82.

15    Frank Lloyd Wright, *An Autobiography (Edition 2)* (London: Faber and Faber, 1945), p. 65.

16    The Rev. Jenkin Lloyd Jones was accompanied by his friend the Rev. F. L. Hosmer of Cleveland, Ohio, for his July 1882 visit to Wales. In the Unitarian journal *Unity*, 9/12 (16 August 1882), Hosmer recalled climbing 'over the green hills to the ivy-clad cottage where the boy [Jenkin Lloyd Jones] was born'. Their visit to Wales was funded by the Western Unitarian Conference, and the two travellers sent regular reports back to their colleagues, some of which were printed in *Unity*.

17    I am indebted to the photographer Gary Roberts for his help in identifying this image.

18    Charles Lloyd, *Particulars of the Life of a Dissenting Minister* (London: self-published, 1813), p. 6.

19    In the 1841 Census her name is listed as Margaret Enoch. In the 1851 Census it is listed as Margaret Jones. She also signed the 'Margaret Letter' as Margaret Jones.

20    Unpublished research of Evan James.

21    Llanwenog Tithe Apportionment, 1840 (National Library of Wales).

22    David R. Jenkins, *The Agricultural Community in South-West Wales at the Turn of the Twentieth Century* (Cardiff: University of Wales Press, 1971), p. 43.

23    Evan James recorded that there were references in the Unitarian journal *Yr Ymofynydd* to some of Richard and Mallie's children being born at Blaencathal. This is a larger farm immediately to the south of Blaenralltddu. Blaencathal was also regularly identified on maps. Hence the journal was most likely referring to it as the name of a place, rather than a specific house. In other words Blaenralltddu was seen as being located in Blaencathal.

24    D. Howell, 'The Rebecca Riots', in T. Herbert and G. E. Jones (eds), *People and Protest: Wales 1815-1880* (Cardiff: University of Wales Press, 1988), pp. 113-38.

25    William. J. Lewis, *An Illustrated History of Cardiganshire* (Aberystwyth: Cymdeithas Lyfrau Ceredigion, 1970), pp.73-9

26    Richard Lloyd Jones et al., *A Lloyd Jones Retrospective (Second Edition)* (Spring Green, WI: Unity Chapel Inc.,1986), pp. 47-51.

27    Jones, *Youngest Son*, pp. 14-19.

28    Benjamin W. Chidlaw, *Yr American*, English translation (Llanrwst: John Jones, 1840).

29    Emyr Humphreys, 'Taliesin and Frank Lloyd Wright', *Welsh Books and Writers* (October 1980), 3-4.

30    Jones, *Youngest Son*, p. 25.

31    Thomas Graham (ed.), *Trilogy: Through Their Eyes* (Spring Green WI: Unity Chapel Publications, 1986), p. 19.

32    *Liverpool Mercury*, advertisement (27 September 1844), 4.

33    *New York Herald* (3 September 1844), 3.

34    Jones, *Youngest Son*, pp. 19-20.

Part 2

Lloyd Jones

# 4

# Lessons in the Land of the Free

## December 1844.
## Port of New York, America

*Remittance* docked at New York on 7 December, after six weeks of almost relentless winter storms, its sails in shreds and its hull leaking badly. It was little Nany's fourth birthday.[1] Before they could set foot on land, they were led through a registration process, where the name, age and occupation of each new arrival was carefully recorded. Richard gave his occupation as 'labourer' (Pl. 22). No longer a hatter, no longer even a farmer. After almost three months of unimaginable torment, all nine of the Jones family, eight of them on unsteady legs and one in a dough trough, found themselves at last on the filthy pinewood apron of the Port of New York, their plans for the onward journey as ravaged as the ship that had brought them there.[2] As they waited for their cases to be pulled out of the hold a crowd of young men, held back by a rope, yelled across to the disoriented passengers, pressing their services as 'runners' or street porters. Richard's attention was caught by one of them because he had shouted to them in Welsh. They had barely been there an hour before Richard was blindsided by the runner, acting in cahoots with a money-changer. They fleeced him of three silver dollars, enough to feed the family for a month, and then left him lost for a few hours alone within the dark grid of south Manhattan. Back at their dour immigrant boarding house, Mallie and the children were in despair at the looming prospect that he would never return, but he somehow found his way back. The sight of such a cheerless, insanitary tenement could rarely have been more gratefully welcomed. As Richard's grandson Chester put it many years later, 'First lesson in the land of the free.'[3]

Steamboats ran daily, in large numbers up the Hudson River from New York to Albany, the state capital 150 miles to the north. The glide of the ornate paddle-steamer through rich farming country allowed them a glimpse for the first time of what it might really feel like to be free, unconfined.[4] The torment of the ocean crossing and the menace of New York soon fell behind, to be revisited only as chastening memories. The river boat was wonderfully fast, at times reaching twenty miles per hour. It took them only ten hours to reach Albany. Perhaps they began to hope that, if they could keep up that pace, they might get to Wisconsin before the waterways turned to ice. But as the winter swept down from the north they were headed straight into it.

At Albany they had planned to take the Erie Canal westwards, 350 miles to Buffalo and the Great Lakes, but there had to be another change of plan. The Albany end of the canal was closed for engineering works, so for the first sixteen miles they were diverted onto a railway. Another new experience: a short-lived but breathtaking burst of controlled noise and speed that left them wishing they could have stayed on the whole way to Wisconsin. As it was, they had to unload again, close to the town of Schenectady, and find a berth on a narrow boat which, they hoped, would take them the rest of the way along the canal. The channels being too small and shallow for steam, the canal boats were horse-drawn and progress was unavoidably slow, so slow in fact that it was common for passengers to stroll alongside their boats when they felt the need to stretch their legs. After three days on the canal they had made it as far as Utica. They were two weeks into December when news reached them that the canal was frozen ahead. They weren't going to make it. They would have to stop and begin the journey again when the ice thawed which, if they were lucky, could be towards the end of April the following year.

If they had to stop, Utica was as good a way-station as any. Since the early nineteenth century, Oneida County had been home to thousands of Welsh migrants, many of whom held important civic roles.[5] Among them, somewhere, was Richard's sister Rachel with her young family. It is possible that Richard knew where to find her, but there is no account of their meeting at the time. Richard and Mallie and their children were used to cold and snowy winters, having lived through several, but they had seen nothing like a winter in the north of New York State. For every inch of Cardiganshire snow a foot would fall on Utica.[6] Richard was a big man, six foot two inches, and powerfully built. He quickly found work as a labourer, shovelling snow, holding the winter at bay. It paid for their lodgings, and the children attended school, but they could never really be themselves. Their compatriots in Utica were largely Calvinistic Methodists, deluded, oppressed by their own conservatism.

It was still bitterly cold in April 1845, but the ice was loosening its grip on the canal. As it often did, the thaw exposed damage. The canal was soon closed again for repairs to the north of the town. Richard wouldn't wait. He hired horses and a wagon large enough to take the family and their belongings around the blockage to meet the canal again near to the old military settlement of Rome. It was a journey that should not have taken longer than a day, but

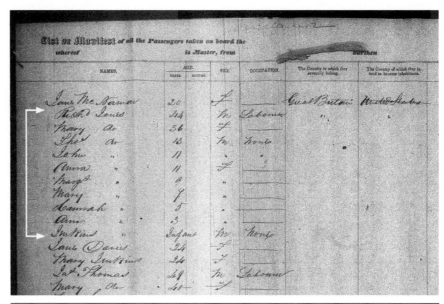

**Pl. 22.** The Jones family recorded on the Passenger List of the *Remittance*. The name of the ship is written faintly in pencil at the head of the page. An eighth child has mistakenly been added to the family, an eleven year old named Anna. (Hannah was six years old, but listed here as five. She would change her own name to Anna later in her life.)
US National Archive.

as the ice thawed the roads were at their worst, treacherous with thick mud. It was dirty, freezing cold, and their progress was painfully slow. The wagon offered minimal shelter. Towards the end of the first day it was clear that Nany was struggling. She had developed a bad cold, and overnight it became worse. Over the course of the second miserable day she declined into a high fever. They were a long way from shelter or help. Little Nany died early the following day. Her loss was a crushing blow. How quickly she had gone, along with the innocent hope that God would see them all safely to their journey's end. We can only guess at the impact Nany's death may have had on her nearest sister, Hannah, only six years old herself and just beginning to understand the world around her. Nany was buried in the earth bank alongside the trail, her grave lined with strands of the last summer's grass. Her brother Jenkin recalled, when he was seventy-one years old, that the memories *touched me with peculiar tenderness, and suggest the unwritten and too often cruelly-neglected pathos in the life of the immigrant pioneer, much of which I have seen, part of which I have been. A little sister, two years my senior,[7] a fair blossom, wilted on the journey and the little body was left in a roadside grave in Utica, New York. I was too young to remember her, but through all the succeeding years that unmarked and unvisited grave has left a hallowed touch of tenderness in the home.[8]*

Within a few hours of leaving Nany's grave, they were at the canal side in Rome, among the first of the west-bound migrants that season. From Rome westwards the canal skirted the south of Lake Oneida and then followed the Seneca River valley, a sinuous course that added days to the journey time, days in which to reflect on their sacrifice and to find some consolation in their faith. Richard was a wholehearted optimist, with little time for introspection, but the loss of his daughter was the worst experience of his life. They drifted through a landscape that was well cultivated, thoroughly settled, punctuated by thriving towns. He set his mind on practicalities, sought advice from the boatmen about the way ahead and kept his sights on the western horizon. The wilderness was getting closer.

They reached the port at Buffalo, at the eastern end of Lake Erie, five days after leaving Rome. It was the last dropping-off point for the passage of west-bound migrants. From Buffalo onwards the migratory routes fanned out into the new territories from the various Great Lakes ports. The dock at Buffalo was crowded with steamships. They found one that was set to depart imminently. After only a few hours in Buffalo they were on the water again, with a welcome surge of speed into the vast inland sea of Lake Erie. The shores were too distant to see except when they docked to take on more wood fuel, and on those occasions, as they approached land they had a brief foretaste of an increasingly wild and foreign interior, the unsettled territory that they were searching for, exhilarating, daunting. At the western end of Lake Erie they turned north up the St Clair River, past

the burgeoning sprawl of Detroit into the shallow wetland of the upper river and Lake St Clair, teeming with water birds, a profusion of life, an abundance of nature beyond their imagining. They were now heading due north, deeper into the cold, the shore of Lake Huron just occasionally visible, a faint line to the west. At almost 600 miles into the voyage they reached Mackinaw at the narrow coupling of Lake Huron and Lake Michigan. It was the northernmost point of their migration; they would never go so far north again (Fig. 4.1).

Eight days after leaving Buffalo their ship chugged slowly through the breakwaters into the harbour channel of Milwaukee. Dense morning fog lifted to reveal the town, divided by its river into 'two sides of almost equal unattractiveness'.[9] Their arrival, a week into the month of May, coincided with the outbreak of a violent squabble between the two larger wards of the town, inflamed by an abundance of firearms and the ambition of competing colony leaders, each hoping to obstruct the other's harbour business by building low bridges over the river.[10] A timely memorandum for the arriving migrants: it was up to them and people like them to bring civility to their new world. Jenkin had been at the harbour for days, waiting for them to arrive. There was huge relief and joy when they found each other at last, and then deep sadness as it dawned on Jenkin that they had arrived without little Nany, his dear niece, whose birth had been one of his last happy memories of Wales. Jenkin had brought a wagon and a team of oxen with him. Mallie, the children and their battered cases were hoisted up into the open carriage and the men walked alongside as they turned their backs on lowly Milwaukee and struck out, due west into the open country.

Anyone who visits America for the first time from Wales will find themselves jolted by the need to adjust to an entirely different order of spatial scale. As their wagon struggled along the narrow westward trail from Milwaukee the Jones children could look up to catch sight of a narrow strip of sky high above them, the line of the trail lit by the gap that it cut through the solid mass of towering trees. To each side of them the dense gloom of endless forest; forest

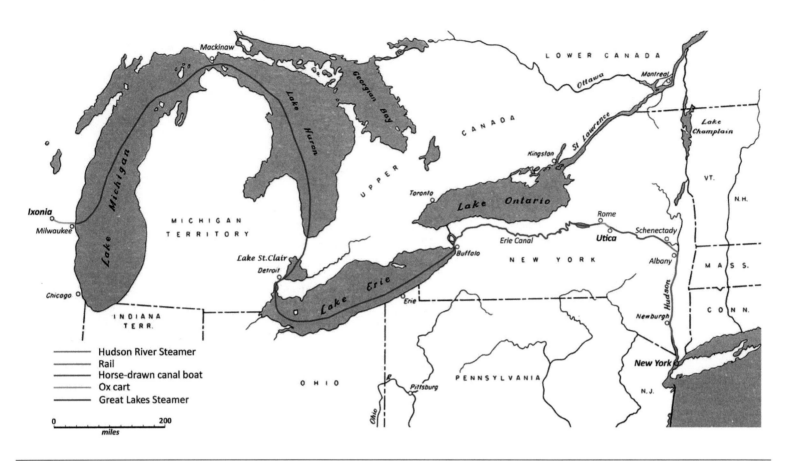

Fig. 4.1. Inland Migration journey of the Jones family. The overall distance travelled from New York to Ixonia was circa 1,550 miles.

behind them, and forest as far as they could see ahead. Then after hours of darkness the trees would suddenly give way to open meadow, carpeted with brilliant flowers, but what appeared to be meadow was just the margin between forest and swamp. Where it crossed marshland the trail beneath the wheels was reinforced with the closely packed trunks of willow saplings. Without the bone-jarring 'corduroy roads' it would have been impassable.[11] This was the character of the wilderness that enveloped their first home in the new world: mile after mile of alternating forest and swamp, punctuated by the deeply worn paths of the native

Americans, still present in large numbers, cutting across the trail from north to south.[12]

As Margaret Jones explained in her letter of 1852, Jenkin was already living in the settlement, called Union at that time, and had built a log house for himself there. It had been his task to go ahead of the rest of the Blaenralltddu household, to secure a plot of land in one of the new states where, as Benjamin Chidlaw had said, they could purchase the best land for the least money. He had to establish himself, find work, build a home and only then would it be safe for Richard and Mallie and all of the children to follow him. They arrived there, eventually, on 12 May 1845. Jenkin's house was on a small plot at the north-west edge of the settlement, deliberately alongside unclaimed land. He had to hope that no one else would try to buy near to him before Richard could join him. As soon as he could after arriving, Richard went to Watertown to hand over the bulk of his capital to a government official to secure the 120 acres of forest and swamp that would become his home and farm for the next decade. It cost him $150, more than thirty pounds sterling. He then went with Jenkin to buy a yoke of oxen, two cows and the best tools that he could afford to improve his land, saving his last gold sovereign against the unforeseen.

Union was actually two scant townships that had merged in 1841. Less than a decade before their arrival there had been not a single European settler anywhere in the 4,000 square miles of the Rock River basin. The settlements of Watertown and Oconomowoc, each of them originally developed around a single pioneer cottage, were the first to coalesce. The settlement of Union lay between Watertown and Oconomowoc, but it lacked a centre of its own. The two original communities had continued along culturally divergent paths, one of them increasingly Welsh and the other predominantly German. Within a few months of Richard and Mallie's arrival, the residents agreed to split Union into two separate townships again. In January 1846, following weeks of good-natured disagreement between the residents, a new name, Ixonia, was decided by asking a child to pick individual letters randomly from a hat. Population records of this time are as insubstantial as the settlements themselves, but it is safe to assume from census data that Ixonia's populace in 1846 was well below one hundred. The Joneses' farm was on the fringe of the town, which was itself no more than a scatter of homesteads among forest, and they involved themselves tentatively in the life of the community, wary of advertising their Unitarian beliefs.[13]

Each Sunday they attended a Welsh service at the German Baptist chapel, the only church in the town. If called upon, they would help their neighbours, and they received the support of their neighbours in return. They were preoccupied throughout the summer of 1845 with the immense physical task of felling and processing the dozens

of soaring oak, elm and basswood (lime) trees that grew on their acreage. Most of the work was done by Richard and his older boys. The fields and hedgerows, stone walls and streams of Cardiganshire had served little to prepare them for their new life of trees and timber. Trees frustrated them, but also sheltered and sustained them in almost every aspect of their lives. Respect for the trees became embedded there, among the Jones family, in the thick of the Rock River forest. It was passed down to the generations that followed (Fig. 4.2).

## The 'Machine Age'. Midwest of America

Among the lyrical and reflective passages of Frank Lloyd Wright's autobiography, the fictions and the flights of fancy, there are a few potent aesthetic propositions. The briefest of them has the heading 'A CULTURAL IDEAL'. It reads as follows:

> I now propose that ideal for the architecture of the machine age, for the ideal 'American' building. Grow up in that image. The TREE. But here is pure appeal to the imagination for I do not mean to suggest the imitation of the tree.[14]

Tree, leaf and flower forms in two and three dimensions proliferate through Wright's early work as abstract motifs in glass, in stone, timber and concrete. They are the most recognisable and most popular features of his work, transposed onto hundreds of marketable products, earning funds that support the preservation of his buildings. It was the natural structural integrity of trees, their perfect and sacred physicality that, through his whole creative life, seemed to provide him with the ideal model for a true, organic architecture: 'The structure will now put forth its forms as the tree puts forth its branches and foliage – if we do not stultify it, do not betray it in some way.'[15]

Frank Lloyd Wright was captivated by the formal and the natural splendour of trees. As he grew older, and the architectural world around him changed, they became central to his notion of 'organic architecture', perhaps because trees showed that structural purity could give rise to complex and poetic expression, and not just to mute geometry. From early in his career he was reluctant to move trees to make way for his buildings, despite the fact that the buildings themselves were made substantially or entirely of timber. Most of those earliest cottages and summer houses are long gone and, in the few old photographs that survive, it is often difficult to discern useful detail because the buildings are hidden by dense foliage. When he first built a house of his own he chose a plot of land in Oak Park, a prosperous new suburb of Chicago that cherished the trees from which it took its name: 'a certain profusion of foliage characterized the village. I remember that I came to Oak Park to live for no other reason than that.'[16] The first house that he built as an independent architect was the Winslow House in River Forest, a wealthy and beautifully wooded precinct of the city. His drawings of the house show it against a rich backdrop of tall trees.

In designing the stable block at the rear, he took care to preserve the trees that were so important to the overall composition (Pl. 23). To make his intention clear, the overhanging roof of the stables was designed around one of the larger trees, as if the tree had grown up through it. That was in 1894. Four years later he moved his practice from the centre of Chicago to his home in Oak Park, and extended his house to create the workspace that he needed for his growing team. Before its enlargement he had located the north elevation of his house as close as possible to a handsome multi-stemmed willow tree. The passageway connecting home and studio went directly through the willow tree, but the tree was allowed to remain and the passage was built around it (Pl. 24). Both the roof and the tree were, obviously, compromised by this and it was not an easy thing to construct, but it conveyed perfectly the lightness of heart and the spirituality in the integration of nature and building that Frank always sought to express and it was there, at the physical axis of his work life and his home life where it would remind him, and everyone that lived and worked with him, of what he was trying to achieve.

In 1908 he designed a house for Isabel Roberts and her mother. Isabel was part of his architectural team, and it is very likely in the circumstances that she worked with him on the design. The entrance had an extended open porch,

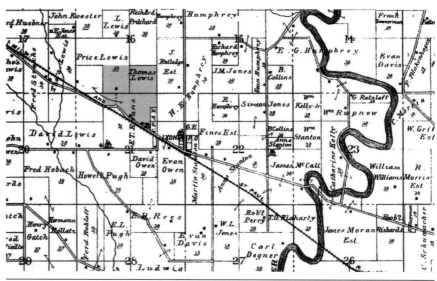

Fig. 4.2. Plat map of Ixonia Township, 1887. This is over thirty years after the Joneses moved from Ixonia. The town is still small. The small black dots are the buildings. The shaded area is the approximate location of the Jones farm. The Welsh cemetery is at the bottom right corner of the farm. The railroad came in the early 1860s and ran along its south boundary, only yards from the Jones farmhouse. LOC.

Pl. 23. Winslow House Stables 1894. The edge of the roof is built around a tree trunk. Courtesy of Rayerson and Burnham Archives, Arts Institute of Chicago.

built around a large elm tree (Pl. 25). Nearly fifty years later, after several families had lived in it and moved on, he was commissioned to restore and extend the house. The base of the elm tree, by then almost a metre in diameter, found itself fully inside the house where it has remained ever since. The crown of the tree was only removed in 2015, after it had been dying for several years. The desiccated trunk is now part of the woodwork of the house.

> The tree lives and fulfills its destiny, its 'design' inevitably. The life principle of the tree seems fixed and simple. Ours is really as simple though perhaps more flowing, and it is a song in our hearts, the Symphony of Nature.[17]

## Late Summer 1846. Rock River Basin, South-east Wisconsin

Jenkin worked at the Rockwell sawmill in Oconomowoc from Monday to Friday and boarded in Oconomowoc during the week. He walked the six miles through thick forest back to Ixonia each Saturday evening bringing news of the outside world and the wages without which the family might have starved. Even though it was already too late to hope for a useful harvest, the older sisters helped with tilling and sowing between the tree stumps, while Mallie, who by midsummer was visibly pregnant again, saw to it that all of them were fed, clothed and prepared each morning to begin work.[18] In that first year their only valuable crop was the timber. The owner of the general store in Oconomowoc was also the owner of the sawmill, Jenkin's employer. Knowing Jenkin to be trustworthy, he agreed to supply Richard with the flour and salt that he needed through to the following spring in exchange for Richard's promise to float all of his logs down to his sawmill when the next winter's ice was gone.[19] The logs were hauled to the river bank, ready to go. They must have used some of the timber to enlarge the house, and after storing all that they needed from the cut branches for fuel they burned the remainder and sold the ashes to a travelling trader for a cent a bushel, to be sold on, back in the east, as potash.

Their daughter Ellen was born in December. By the following summer they were beginning to see the rewards for their exertions of the year before. They concentrated their efforts on a first few acres, which yielded an encouraging crop. It seemed, towards the end of the summer of 1846 as if they had got through the hardest part, but on the last Saturday in August Jenkin didn't come home from the sawmill.

It is revealing of the vulnerability that the family must have felt in their isolated home, that Richard didn't leave the house immediately to look for Jenkin. They received a message on the Monday that Jenkin was still at the sawmill, and that he was ill. By the time Richard found him there, Jenkin was dreadfully anaemic and barely conscious. Richard stayed with him, helpless. Two days later Jenkin was gone, killed by malaria. Autumn was malaria season. By that time it was inevitable that the whole family had been exposed to the parasite, but Jenkin was the only one to become seriously ill and to die. It was only Jenkin who worked every day alongside the sluggish waters of a dammed stream, the water that powered the sawmill. He would have been infected many times over.

South-east Wisconsin, where they had settled, was peppered with small lakes and swamps. It had the highest incidence of malaria across the entirety of the northern states. In *Yr American* Benjamin Chidlaw, from Ohio, did mention that 'ague' was the most common disease, but he dealt with it lightly, reassuring Welsh migrants that they would be well cared for when ill. There was no reason to think that it would be any more of a threat in America than it was in Wales, where only a dozen or so would die from malaria each year in the entire country. But south-east Wisconsin was very much worse, so bad in fact that in 1844 a Norwegian counterpart of Chidlaw wrote urgently to his own countrymen telling them to go anywhere else but there. The Norwegian writer knew personally of sixty-eight fellow colonists who had been killed by the parasite.[20] The Welsh migrants knew nothing of this until they arrived, and from then on it became such a routine aspect of their American lives that it was taken entirely for granted. Each autumn there would be chills and fever. 'India Cologogue', 'Wahoo Bitters', possibly wet sheets or one of many other spurious therapies were tried and, once they could afford it, quinine, the only medicine that actually helped.[21]

Jenkin was buried in a plot marked out by Richard at the south-east corner of the farm, just behind their house. His headstone was inscribed '*Pe lladdai efe fi eto mi a obeithiaf ynddo ef.*'[22] Jenkin's loss was catastrophic. He had been their bridgehead to America, and their vanguard on American soil. They were on their own now. 'Yea though he slay me yet will I trust in Him', said the inscription. They are really Richard's words, not Jenkin's: although You slew my brother and my daughter, I *still* trust You. Weather has erased the inscription but it is believed that Jenkin's headstone still stands in the little Welsh cemetery, in Ixonia (Pl. 26).

The first profound shift towards a Welsh-American culture had begun in the winter of 1845 as the children acclimatised to their new school. Nothing they could be taught was considered as important as the English language, the language of America. Their mother Margaret had raised

Pl. 26.  The Welsh Cemetery, Ixonia. Jenkin Jones is buried here. The area beyond the cemetery was the Jones farm between 1845 and 1856.
© Google 2020 / Google Earth.

Richard and Jenkin in Welsh and English, but their English had become weaker during the years at Blaenralltddu, away from Margaret's influence. Jenkin had been two years ahead of Richard in adapting to America, relearning his second language and picking up Yankee idioms. When Jenkin died Richard had also lost his interpreter. Fortunately English came quite easily to the younger children, and they had a good teacher – according to the younger Jenkin, 'a bi-linguist [who could] dispel the forlorn feeling which her English inspired by some soothing sentences in [their] mother tongue'.[23]

Young Jenkin was bitterly frustrated that he had to miss weeks to work on the farm at the beginning and end of the school year while his sisters were allowed to attend, but the blow was softened by the fact that the teacher would board at their house. It was the norm on the frontier that the teachers, always young women, would live in the houses of their pupils' parents, staying one week for each child, each year.[24] There were usually four Jones children at the school, sometimes more, so she was with them for weeks at a time. She didn't mind that the children kept her working during meals, around the fire, before bed. Hannah was entranced by her: a woman of intellect, self-reliance and charm, completely different from the careworn women of the village. Hannah was quick to learn to read and write in both languages. She was bright, strongly motivated, at times impatient to better herself, to rationalise her way out of her recent, traumatic past. The teacher provided her for the first time with the model of a life that would be fulfilling to lead. The whole family admired the teacher, Jenkin adored her, but her influence on Hannah seems to have been profound.

In the early years the small, scattered and culturally disparate community of Ixonia was content to use the German Baptist church in turns, and among the Welsh settlers no one was much bothered by the mix of denominations, they were all just glad to be together as Welsh Christians. Richard was candid with the minister about their faith, and they were welcomed regardless. Richard is sometimes referred to in the family memoirs as a minister himself. He wasn't trained, certainly not ordained, but this memory suggests that at times, in Ixonia, he may have been invited to address the congregation. He would have had the presence and the scriptural knowledge to have made a strong impression, but his message must have been uncomfortable for some. However it came about, inexorably as the congregation grew, whispers began to spread and fingers to be pointed at the Joneses.

Sometime around 1850 a group of Methodist ministers arrived at the door of the Joneses' house. There was no central authority behind their visit. They came from other settlements in the area, and they had convened themselves in response to complaints that had reached them from concerned members of the Ixonia community. Richard and Mallie welcomed them into their home, gave them space to sleep and fed them three times a day. In return the posse of Methodists interrogated Richard vigorously about his heretical beliefs. Between bouts of argument they retreated to the chapel to rehearse their next attack. Richard almost relished the confrontation. From his infancy he had been immersed in religious argument; his dialectical skills were advanced compared to those of his interrogators. Young Jenkin recalled that all the children and their mother listened intently as the debate rolled on day after day, quietly elated that their father seemed always able to get the upper hand. When they realised that their arguments were exhausted, the inquisitors changed tack. Instead of persecuting the Joneses they arraigned the Welsh minister of the chapel himself, on the grounds that he should not have allowed the Unitarians to join the congregation in the first place. Richard couldn't stand to see this happen to the gentle parson who had welcomed the family into his fold, despite their religious differences. He abandoned the argument and accepted the banishment imposed on them by the visitors that they had fed and housed for the week before. The Methodist ministers went away, satisfied with the outcome. The Joneses did not attend chapel in Ixonia again. They were their own congregation from then on, and their place of worship was their own home.[25] This extraordinary episode was referred to by the Jones family for many years after as

'Black Week'. It had been a humiliation, a social martyrdom, but also a transformative experience, one from which they were to grow stronger.

## Late December 1911.
## Taliesin, The Valley,
## Wisconsin

Frank Lloyd Wright and his partner Mamah Borthwick were settled in for their first winter at Taliesin, the exquisite house that he had built for them overlooking the Lloyd Jones Valley. They were far away from Chicago, safe from the scandal that had hurt so many two years previously, when their romance first became public. The architect had a few important commissions to think about, but made time also to involve himself in Mamah's work. She had become captivated by the writings of the Swedish feminist philosopher Ellen Key and, with Key's assent, had taken it upon herself to translate them into English for publication in America. Frank and Mamah immersed themselves in the task, extracting the social and political manifesto from Key's sometimes obscure and romantic texts. They explored these intellectual and emotional realms together as equals, as they had dreamed of doing, and as neither had felt able to in the marriages they had abandoned.[26] It would be Christmas in a few days: they had everything to look forward to. The headline in the *Chicago Tribune* came as a jolt: 'Architect Wright in New Romance with "Mrs. Cheney".'

The *Tribune* of 1911 was a 'yellow paper', revelling in scandal and quite prepared, where no real story existed, to invent one. The newspaper reported that the architect and his mistress had been in hiding for months in a remote part of Wisconsin. It was claimed that a journalist had observed him there wading through an icy stream, carrying a lady in his arms and, in doing so, revealing 'a good deal of lingerie of a quality not often seen on display in that part of Wisconsin'. It was the sort of fictitious detail that its readers relished. Although the basics of the story were true it was of no great interest without the lascivious extras.[27] Acting on a tip, the *Tribune* had sent a telegram to Frank, catching him unawares, inviting

him to deny that he had, 'deserted his wife and (was) living in Spring Green with the divorced wife of E. H. Cheney'. Mamah and her husband had indeed divorced, without rancour, in August of that year. If they had kept their counsel and waited for Christmas to go by, the 'story' would surely have gone no further. But that was not Frank's way. He replied: 'Let there be no misunderstanding, a Mrs. E. H. Cheney never existed for me and now is no more in fact. But Mamah Borthwick is here and I intend to take care of her.'[28] Christmas had come early for the *Chicago Tribune*. Frank had written their headline for them; within hours reporters were dispatched to Spring Green to whip up a story to go with it. They tried, at first, to provoke some outrage from local residents. Mamah had taken time to get to know their neighbours; she was well liked. They would say nothing bad about her, so the journalists turned their attention to Taliesin. There were more teasing phone calls and surprise visits, all rebuffed by the household. The pressure was deeply uncomfortable and the patience of their neighbours was becoming strained. Frank and Mamah decided to face down their tormentors. They called a press conference at Taliesin, insisting that journalists should attend on Christmas morning.

The most damaging accusation against Frank was that he had no care for his wife and children. He explained that they had married too young, that it was a mistake from the start. He would always support them financially, regardless, and he had done the best for them all by leaving when he did. If he had stayed with Catherine, he explained, he would have been living a lie, and in doing so he would have set a poor example to his children. It was in their interests that he should act with integrity, even if that meant leaving the family for the love of another woman. He went on to explain that his relationship with his children was quite different from his wife's, that he felt a greater emotional bond to his work:

*In a way my buildings are my children ... If I could have put aside my desire to live my life as I build my buildings – from within outward – I might have been able to stay ... [but] I would be honestly myself first – and take care of everything else afterwards.*

Naturally, though, his thoughts turned to the impact of the publicity on his work:

> It will be a waste of something socially precious if this thing robs me of my work. I have struggled to express something real in American architecture. I have something to give. It will be a misfortune if the world decides not to receive what I have to give.

He concluded his prepared statement with a vigorous Emersonian clout:

> Laws and rules are made for the average. The ordinary man cannot live without rules to guide his conduct. It is infinitely more difficult to live without rules, but that is what the really honest, sincere, thinking man is compelled to do. And I think when a man has displayed some of his ability to see and feel the higher and better things of life, we ought to go slow in deciding he has acted badly.[29]

It is hard to believe that Frank Lloyd Wright really intended, by making this statement, to bring an end to his persecution. There may have been some part of him, and perhaps of Mamah too, that saw it as a chance to promote their new sexual philosophy, the opportunity for an earnest public debate. Either way, they were to be disappointed. The Christmas Day statement only made things worse. Over the next few days the story was taken up by coarse journals and newspapers from Alaska to New York, each cheerfully adding its own embellishments to provide delightful fireside entertainment to millions of Americans between Christmas and New Year. On 30 December, in an attempt to bring the commotion to a close, Frank called another press conference. Calling the reporters 'mutts' and 'boobs', he was no longer under the illusion that the lowbrow press would host a serious debate on his and Mamah's behalf. His second statement, he said, would be his 'last word' on the matter:

> Here we are, four people – a wife and a man and a husband and a woman, who each assumed earlier in life the responsibility of marriage and children. Then the thing happened that has happened since time began ... as soon as the situation developed its inevitable character, a frank avowal to those whose lives were to be affected by a readjustment was made. Time was asked and the man and the woman agreed to make it plain that their love was love ... The man knew that only with the woman could he carry out life's purpose. A place was found for the woman. It is this place [Taliesin]. There are no family obligations, no family deserted, no duties undone. But the hue and cry of the yellow press was raised, the man and the woman defamed.[30]

The story of Frank and Mamah's 'love bungalow' faded from the pages as the newspapers celebrated the first day of 1913. It had run its course.[31] The great Wright scholar Anthony Alofsin has observed that through the course of this encounter with his accusers Frank 'had begun to see himself as a member of the Nonconformist American tradition who would pay the price for speaking against the status quo'.[32] It was actually the Nonconformist Welsh tradition that he was drawing from, the tradition of the Unitarian Joneses. Frank talked of it later as his own 'Black Week', but very much darker days were soon to come ∎

# 04

## Lessons in the Land of the Free
### *Notes*

1    In the Preface to the published version of *An Artilleryman's Diary*, Jenkin Lloyd Jones mentions that the ship docked at Castle Garden. This could not have been the case since Castle Garden, America's first immigration centre, did not open until 1855.

2    C. W. Garrison, 'Waterfront Construction in New York Harbor' (unpublished M.Eng. thesis, Newark College of Engineering, New Jersey Institute of Technology, 1949), 52-7.

3    Chester Lloyd Jones, *Youngest Son* (Madison, WI: self-published, 1938), p. 26.

4    The *New York Tribune* (10 December 1844), 2, reported that the *Remittance* was badly damaged by fire in the Port of New York, the day after her arrival from Liverpool. Richard and Mallie Jones were apparently unaware of this as they travelled upriver to Albany.

5    David M. Ellis, 'The Assimilation of the Welsh in Central New York', *New York History*, 53/3 (July 1972), 299-333.

6    The north of New York State has the heaviest average annual snowfall of anywhere in America. Utica receives an average of 2.4 metres of snow every winter.

7    Nany was more than three years older than Jenkin.

8    Jenkin Lloyd Jones, *An Artilleryman's Diary* (Madison: The Wisconsin History Commission, 1914), pp. 4-8.

9    Jones, *Youngest Son*, pp. 29-30.

10    The 'Milwaukee Bridge War' broke out on 5 May 1845 and lasted into June. A good account can be found at *https://shepherdexpress.com/arts-and-entertainment/ae-feature/bridge-wars/* (April 2021).

11    Jones, *Youngest Son*, p. 35.

12    'Early History of Oconomowoc', *Daily Freeman* (Waukesha, WI, 10 October 1935).

13     John H. Ott, *Jefferson County, Wisconsin and its People: A Record of Settlement, Organization, Progress and Achievement*, vol. 1 (Chicago: S. J. Clarke Co., 1917), p. 45.

14     Frank Lloyd Wright, *An Autobiography (Edition 1)* (New York: Longman, Green & Co., 1932), p. 146.

15     Olgivanna Lloyd Wright, *Frank Lloyd Wright: His Life, his Work, his Words* (New York: Horizon, 1966), p. 47. This is a long overdue correction of a line from p. 159 of Frank Lloyd Wright's 1932 autobiography. The original sentence had the word 'not' instead of 'now', making an accidental double negative. (It is omitted from the 1946 edition *of An Autobiography*.)

16     F. L. Wright, 'Concerning Landscape Architecture' (lecture to Oak Park Fellowship Club, 1900), in B. B. Pfeiffer (ed.), *Frank Lloyd Wright: Collected Writings*, vol. 1 (New York: Rizzoli, 1992), p. 56.

17     F. L. Wright, 'To my European Co-Workers', *Wendingen* (Santpoort, Netherlands: C. A. Mees, 1925); also in Pfeiffer (ed.), *Frank Lloyd Wright: Collected Writings*, vol. 1, p. 207.

18     Meryl Secrest,: *Frank Lloyd Wright: A Biography* (Chicago: University of Chicago Press, 1998), p. 36.

19     Thomas E. Graham (ed.), *Trilogy: Through Their Eyes* (Spring Green, WI: Unity Chapel Publications, 1986), p. 3.

20     P. T. Harstadt, 'Sickness and Disease on the Wisconsin Frontier: Malaria 1820-1850', *The Wisconsin Magazine of History*, 43/2 (Winter 1959-60), 83-96.

21     Graham, *Trilogy: Through Their Eyes*, p. 8.

22     Graham, *Trilogy: Through Their Eyes*, p. 6.

23     Graham, *Trilogy: Through Their Eyes*, p. 16.

24     M. Day, 'Boarding Round' from the website of the Country School Association of America, *https://www.countryschoolassociation.org/* (April 2021).

25     Graham, *Trilogy: Through Their Eyes*, pp. 12-13.

26     Ron McCrea, *Building Taliesin: Frank Lloyd Wright's Home of Love and Loss* (Madison: Wisconsin Historical Society Press, 2012), pp. 147-62.

27     Secrest, *Frank Lloyd Wright: A Biography*, p. 212.

28     McCrea, *Building Taliesin*, p. 123.

29     McCrea, *Building Taliesin*, p. 125. Frank was arguing here that he, and people like him, should be allowed to live without the shackles of convention. Many other artists of the era expressed similar views. It is unfortunate that, some decades later, his position was misconstrued as a claim to superiority over the 'average man'. The Russian-American author Ayn Rand chose to understand him this way. The central character of her fantastical 1943 novel 'The Fountainhead' was modelled on her misreading of Frank Lloyd Wright's beliefs and intentions. Frank was, at first, flattered when Rand told him that her hero had been based on him, but when he read the novel, he insisted that he should be dissociated from it.

30     Brendan Gill, *Many Masks: A Life of Frank Lloyd Wright* (London: Heinemann, 1988), pp. 222-3.

31     McCrea, *Building Taliesin*, pp. 123-9.

32     Anthony Alofsin, *Frank Lloyd Wright: The Lost Years, 1910-1922: A Study of Influence* (Chicago: University of Chicago Press, 1993), p. 95.

# 5

# The Valley

While their isolation from chapel life prevented the Joneses from sharing their Unitarianism with their neighbours, it also enabled them to exclude contrary influences from their own lives. They would still welcome travellers to lodge with them, piecing together, from the stories that they were told, a picture of the accelerating migrant tide and the transformation of the state beyond their forested horizons, but their most valued source of information came in the post. Every Saturday one of the younger children would make the two-mile trek to the grocer's store at the opposite end of Ixonia to collect the mail as soon as it had been dropped. It would sometimes include letters or packages from Wales, but the bulk of it was newspapers. There was a farming journal, a magazine for the children called *The Youth's Companion* and *Y Drych*, the Welsh newspaper published in Utica. There was also *Yr Ymofynydd*, the monthly journal of the South Wales Unitarian Society, published in Cardiganshire and posted to them from the mother country. But of all of the regular papers it was the *New York Tribune* that was most anticipated. It was their main source of news and opinion, one of the most respected newspapers in the country and, most significantly, with its Unitarian editor and his staff of Unitarian and Transcendentalist columnists, it allowed the Lloyd Joneses for the first time to feel part of the vibrant, progressive Unitarian community of America. It is also significant that the *Tribune* was written in English.

Within the American Lloyd Jones household, reading aloud and listening became a cardinal preoccupation, never just a passive attendance but a penetrating, immersive engagement with the written and spoken word. Evening recreation for the brothers and sisters was to take turns reading aloud around the kitchen table, picking from books or newspaper articles that interested them. Richard and Mallie would retreat into their own room, where Richard read to Mallie from *Y Bibl*, leaving the children to their autodidactic entertainment.[1] It was these kitchen-table lessons in philosophy and literature, dealing often with challenging progressive ideas from the pages of the *New York Tribune*, that seem to have given Hannah a first real focus for her intellect and definition to her forceful instincts.

The American Census of 1850 provides a snapshot of the family's progress over the five years from their arrival in Ixonia. There were two more children, named Jane (Jennie) and James. They had more cows, more oxen, a small flock of sheep and a team of pigs. They had successfully grown oats, wheat, corn and potatoes in large quantities, along with 24 tons of hay. They had produced 24 pounds of wool and 300 pounds of butter. The land that Richard and Jenkin purchased for $150 was worth ten times as much, according to the enumerator, despite the fact that only 30 of their 120 acres had actually been improved. The remainder was still either forest or swamp. The Census also records that five of the children attended school in that year: Thomas, John, Margaret, Mary and Hannah. Thomas and John were nineteen and seventeen years old respectively. Although Thomas finished his schooling during that year, he and John still evidently continued their education long after boys, or young men, would usually have left it behind. Hannah was eleven years old, and it is here, in the 1850 Census, that the initial 'L.' for Lloyd first appears in the middle of Richard's name.

Sometime before 1850 Richard's sister Rachel and her family had followed Richard from Utica to Jefferson County, Wisconsin. They had settled in urban Watertown, only a few miles away from Ixonia but a very different place. Perhaps the attractions of rural life had faded during their time in the cosmopolitan east.[2] In 1851 Richard's sister Eleanor, or Nell, also arrived bringing her husband and seven children with her and, as their mother, Margaret, mentioned in her letter of 1852, they found a home, initially, within a quarter of mile of Rachel and her family in Watertown. Both of Richard's sisters gravitated towards their brother, bringing children and husbands with them. Just as Richard and Mallie had been, the Jones sisters were carried along in a gathering torrent of migrants, from overseas and from the eastern states, to fill the West in an unprecedented period of growth. Between 1840 and 1850 the population of Wisconsin increased from 31,000 to 305,000. Nevertheless it was still sparsely peopled. While it was eight times the size of Wales, in 1850 Wales had four times the population of Wisconsin. In the next decade the population of Wisconsin more than doubled again as the migrant tide moved further west, an irresistible pull that eventually uprooted the Lloyd Joneses from Ixonia and carried them closer to the valley of their dreams.

The catalyst for their next move west was the arrival of the railroad in 1855. It seemed almost unbelievable that the remote colony of ten years before was now just a stop on the line between Milwaukee and Watertown, a line that was to be laid all the way to the Mississippi River. Richard's sister Nell and her husband John G. Thomas, were alert to the opportunity that the railroad would provide. Even as the track was being laid, they moved from their home in Watertown a hundred miles along the line of the future railroad to an incipient village where a train stop was to be established. It was in the township of Spring Green, Sauk County. They bought a tract of unimproved, high-quality land that straddled the track, as close as they could get to the future train stop, and set up there to wait for prosperity to bloom around them. Back in Ixonia, the Lloyd Joneses also found themselves with the railroad as a neighbour. The track was laid along the southern boundary of their farm, within a few yards of their house.[3] Jenkin recalled a neighbourhood in which villagers could once rarely be seen through the trees, their presence only inferred from the knocking of axes or the soft clunk of cow bells. The Milwaukee and Watertown railroad was opened in 1886, and from then on the ground beneath their feet would shake with the raucous passage of enormous steam trains twice a day heading west, and twice heading back. The railroad boosted the value of the Lloyd Joneses' deficient, swampy land, but each train passing was a reminder to them that better land might be found further west, if they could summon up the will to go on again and find it. Richard was fifty-six years old but he was still unsettled by the thought that, if they stayed where they were in Ixonia, they might miss a greater opportunity. It was a troubling dilemma, and it had been made more complicated, in the summer of 1855, by the arrival of Enoch, Richard's youngest brother.

Enoch had married, probably in late 1852. Back in Cardiganshire their mother, Margaret, in her mid-eighties, moved from Blaencwmarch, the house opposite Pantydefaid Chapel, to spend the rest of her days with her eldest daughter, Hannah, at prosperous Dolecanol on the Highmead estate.[4] Enoch had migrated with Rachel, his wife, and their baby daughter Margaret. He had declared himself a shoemaker as he disembarked in New York, but once on American soil he too would become a farmer.[5] There was no cheap land in Ixonia or anywhere in the area in 1855, so it is likely that Enoch and his family made a house of their own on Richard and Mallie's property, and that Enoch lent his efforts to improving the farm.[6] Just a year later, as soon as the trains started running Thomas and John, the two oldest

Lloyd Jones boys, took a ride west to visit Aunt Nell and see for themselves the quality of the land that could be found in her neighbourhood. They came back with disconcerting news: the prospects were excellent; decent farmland could still be acquired there quite cheaply, but they had to move quickly because the village was growing apace.

It must still have been difficult to leave behind the unpromising land that they had worked so hard to improve, and to leave Uncle Jenkin, the sole occupant of the family graveyard. They had far more belongings to take with them on this occasion, but they were all loaded on the train with five adult children to help. Enoch would not go with them. He had been living in his own house for just a year, and was evidently reluctant to uproot himself again so soon. Richard sold the majority of his farm and his livestock for the impressive sum of $3,500, leaving Enoch with a small acreage to live on.[7] It seems that the terms of this separation became awkward for both brothers: Richard and Mallie's last-born child had been christened Enoch. He had been born four years before they left Ixonia, but such was the bad feeling between Richard and his brother that the youngster's name was changed from Enoch to Enos, and Enos he remained. Sadly, Enoch's trajectory after 1857 was downward. He was over forty years old with just one child, an infant daughter. It was too much for one man to manage. Census records show that his farm fell steadily in value over the course of the next sixteen years, until he died in 1873, aged fifty seven. He is buried in the Welsh cemetery in Ixonia, near to his brother Jenkin.[8]

The Lloyd Joneses left Ixonia as the snow began to melt in March 1857. Their first migration had taken eight months; the move from Ixonia to Spring Green took them well under eight hours. Spring Green had been established in 1850 by the initiative of a speculator named William Barnard. His purchase was on the northern bank of the Wisconsin River, arranged along its meanders, and surrounded by a landscape of gently rolling hills. Everyone who passed through the area agreed that it was a perfectly beautiful place, wooded rather than forested, and blessedly free of malarial swamp. It was also 'driftless'. Most of Wisconsin bore colossal scars of glaciation, as if a titanic rake had been scraped diagonally across it. The linear dips and bumps around Ixonia were typical: marshy and forested respectively and, for good measure, retreating ice had left the earth thickly studded with broken rocks, known as glacial drift, all of which had to be pulled out before it could be cultivated. By an accident of nature, Spring Green and its stretch of the Wisconsin River valley had escaped glaciation. It was this that accounted for the familiar softness of the contours and the gratifying smoothness of the soil.[9] It seemed the embodiment of a European settler's dreams. Within a few years of its establishment, the township had been subdivided, part sold on and part retained through stages, until it had begun to take on the characteristic checkerboard pattern of a frontier settlement. Funds raised through land sales by some of the early owners were invested in the construction of public buildings, and by 1855 a village began to appear near to the centre of the township. A unique account of the early days of Spring Green can be found in a 1918 compendium of the history of Sauk County compiled by Harry Elsworth Cole.[10] It quotes from a lecture delivered to the 'Old Settlers Association' in 1907 by their official historian, Miss Maud Lloyd Jones. This was Frank Lloyd Wright's cousin Maud, the daughter of his favourite uncle James. It would be nice to think that Frank was present at the event, but it's unlikely. He was living in Chicago and working on Unity Temple, at that time the most important project of his life.

In her lecture Maud explained that it was when the railroad company came to survey the township that interest in Spring Green intensified; more settlers arrived and land values began to rise. Her great-aunt Nell had been among the first of the incomers. In the early 1850s, before the railroad came, the village was a few small structures clustered around a post office built by a Welshman, Thomas Jones, on one of the government-reserved sections and known as 'Jonesville'. Once the railroad arrived, the centre of the village moved a mile north towards the track. Jonesville got left behind, eventually to be worn away by the river. With the only railroad station in Sauk County, an area larger than

Cardiganshire, Spring Green became a focal point of trade for Sauk and for large parts of the neighbouring counties. By the time the Lloyd Joneses arrived, it was home to around two hundred settlers, including a variety of professionals, manufacturers and tradesmen, most of whom had come in the previous two years to live in the growing village near to the railroad.[11] Jonesville did leave one notable legacy: it drew many other Welsh families to the settlement.

There were numerous Cardiganshire farms of 100 to 200 acres. Some, like Coedlannau Fawr, were over 300, but not many. At Spring Green the Lloyd Joneses were able to acquire 415 acres. By then most of the township had been settled, so their land was not the best that Spring Green could provide. Their new home was a mile and a half south of the village, close to the remnants of Jonesville.[12] The property spread across a peninsula, bounded on three sides by a loop of the Wisconsin River. As the land was now divided between the parents and their older sons, it was referred to as the River Farms. Roughly half of the acreage was level, clear of obstructions, sandy but reasonably fertile, at least initially. The land to the south, nearer to the river banks, was lightly wooded with an alluvial dampness that might be drainable, not the sucking, peaty mire of Ixonia. It was less useful for growing, but suitable for their buildings.

The arrival at the River Farms was also the start of the dispersal of the family. Shortly before they left Ixonia, Margaret, the eldest daughter, married a Welshman, Thomas Evans. Instead of moving to Spring Green, she had gone farther west with him to settle in Minnesota. In 1861 Thomas, the eldest son, married Esther Evans, who had come from Wales to Spring Green via the Welsh colony in Pennsylvania. Thomas soon built them a house of their own a short distance along the river bank, beginning a tradition that would be followed by each successive son, and by which the family eventually grew to become a village.

All women of rural Nonconformist families would learn from childhood the essential skills that enabled them to transform raw wool into textile and from textile into garments, cloth and bedding. These domestic artists were capable at times of producing work of exquisite abstract design and superb craftsmanship. The men of the family were expected to practise their own craft skills, to make wooden utensils, furniture, leatherware and light metalwork. Richard had, of course, been a hat-maker. His elder brother David was a blacksmith, and Enoch had made shoes, so there appears to have been a proclivity of sorts among the Lloyd Joneses for creativity, for making. During his teenage years in Ixonia, as his family improved and expanded their homestead, Thomas became absorbed by the processes of design and construction. He provides the first tangible expression of Lloyd Jones creativity following their emigration. According to his son Edward, when Thomas left school he was apprenticed to a carpenter and 'by intense application obtained a sufficient insight in geometry and advanced mathematics which, when applied to his architectural work, placed him much in advance of the usual country carpenter'.[13]

As the oldest son, Thomas naturally took the lead on the construction of the new buildings for the River Farms and once they were settled he began to offer his design and building services to their neighbours. Edward recalled that his father's diaries 'indicate that he was in demand, and was kept busy in the construction of homes and buildings throughout the countryside where he lived'.[14]

With horizontally lapped timber sidings, a roof of timber shakes and often also a shady veranda, these were houses of a type quite unknown in Wales, but becoming ubiquitous across the American West. Builders' guide books had become increasingly popular since the 1830s, offering house patterns, stylistic advice and technical instruction, all in accordance with the aims of raising aesthetic standards and developing the architectural consistency that was understood to be essential to the civic life of the proliferating townships and villages. Some of the most influential of these practical guides were underpinned by a naturalistic philosophy that would have resonated in the mind of the bookish, romantic and deeply religious Thomas Lloyd Jones. Andrew Jackson Downing was the most respected of the design guide authors. In the Preface to his *Cottage Residences* of 1842, he explained that his intention was to help his readers to build houses that would 'harmonise with our lovely rural landscapes', and embody a, 'pure moral tendency ... a domestic feeling that purifies the heart', and he went on to discuss in detail the principles to be applied in the 'ordering of rooms' within the floor plan to enable the harmonious interaction of the family. In *The Architecture of Country Houses* (1850) he invited his readers, the majority of whom were, like Thomas, budding carpenter-architects, to consider two types of beauty: firstly the 'relative beauty' that, 'expresses moral, social or intellectual ideas', and secondly the 'absolute beauty' of the abstract ideas of 'Proportion, Symmetry, Variety, Harmony and Unity'. The ideal picturesque house would express the balance of absolute and relative beauty, and the natural means of achieving that balance, the 'American Style', was to design and construct according to the true nature of the most abundant material:

> *If we call this style American, it is only because we foresee that our climate and the cheapness of wood as a building material, in most parts of the country, will, for a long time yet, lead us to adopt this as the most pleasing manner of building rural edifices of an economical character.*[15]

It is easy to imagine Thomas, with his intense religious convictions, drawing up his house designs while contemplating the proper ordering of rooms to encourage family interaction and the notions of the truthful expression of materials, of proportion, of harmony and, most important of all, of organic Unity and its implicit connection to his faith.[16] It is easy to imagine, also, that at some point in later years he might have shared these concepts with his young nephew Frank, for whom in due course they would become a driving obsession.

The stories of their time at the River Farms add up to a picture of the Lloyd Jones family at ease with itself. Most of their children were grown up and able to take on the greater part of the agricultural labour and domestic duties, allowing some relief at last to their parents, while the younger children, even little Enos, were all at school. Notwithstanding the occasional accident, they were healthy, well fed and free, on their own territory, to practise their faith

without having to endure the spite of neighbours. For the first time, also, they were in a position to hire labour. They really had no choice: the farm was too big and too productive for even a large family to manage, but their workers found themselves drawn into the family, eating with them, praying and singing with them, joining them for regular walks and picnics. They worked together as family, colleagues and friends, a community bonded by trust, equality and loyalty to Richard, the household's head – in fact, a proper *teulu*, a peculiarly Welsh form of fellowship.[17] In years to come it would take the boy Frank Lloyd Wright into its prodigious embrace, and embed in his mind for ever the spirit of motivation and collective joy that came from being part of it.

## 8 May 1930.
## Princeton University,
## New Jersey

Frank Lloyd Wright was facing scrutiny of a new kind. He was addressing the scholarly community of the Department of Art and Archaeology at one of America's oldest and most prestigious educational institutions. He had given countless public talks over the course of a career that had begun in the early 1890s, but this audience was likely to be more discerning and more critical than most that he had previously addressed. The lecture that day was the second in a series of six that he had agreed to present over the course of a fortnight, to be followed by a new exhibition of drawings of his most important projects.

The lecture series took place in the aftermath of the Wall Street Crash. Work of every kind, and building work in particular, had ground to a halt. There were two projects that had once had huge promise for him. They were very different, but with similar names. One was a complex of tall buildings in New York, St Mark's in the Bowery, and the other a palatial resort in the wilds of Arizona, San Marcos in the Desert. Both were cancelled within weeks of the crash. If either had been built it would have established him firmly as the leading architect in America. He would have to wait for several more years before that would eventually happen. Undaunted by his prison experience, he had finished his autobiography, but it had not yet been published. He was so deeply in debt that he had agreed to sell himself to a group of investors, all good friends and supporters of his work, in return for their commitment to ensure that he could continue to live and work at Taliesin, and that his many creditors would be kept from his door. He was no longer Frank Lloyd Wright: he was Frank Lloyd Wright Incorporated. Princeton offered him a fee of $125 per lecture, a figure that he considered 'less than merely nominal'. He desperately needed every dollar that would come his way, but the time and the expense involved in preparing, travelling and delivering the lectures at Princeton possibly outweighed the humble stipend. Like all professional architects, he knew the value of 'casting bread on the water'. Princeton was a prestigious platform: there was a chance that his presence there, if he acquitted himself well, would lead him to other opportunities. The second lecture was titled 'Style in Industry'. In the concluding section of the talk he introduced a notion that had been taking form in his mind for several years before:

*The Machine as it exists in every important trade, should without delay be put, by way of capable Artist interpreters, into student hands ... to put the Machine, as the modern tool of a great civilization, to any extent into the hands of a body of young students, means some kind of school ... Sensitive, unspoiled students ... should be put in touch with commercial industry in what we might call Industrial 'STYLE' Centers ...*

*Such a school should be in the country, on sufficient land so that three hours a day of physical work on the soil would ensure the living of the students ... There would remain, say, seven hours of each day ... in which to unite in production ... Architecture, without hesitation, or equivocation, should be the broad, essential background of the whole endeavour.*[18]

The site of the experimental school that he described was unmistakably that of his home, Taliesin. In May 1917 he had been in Japan negotiating the early design stages of the Tokyo Imperial Hotel. While he was away, his beloved Aunt Jennie had died. The wonderful Hillside Home School, designed by Wright just after the turn of the century was, by then, derelict.[19] The Imperial Hotel project dominated his life and work for the next five years. While he was back in America, briefly, late in 1919, his Aunt Nell, who had shared the running of the school with Aunt Jennie, had also died at Taliesin, and so was cut the last significant tie with the pioneering school that had for three decades been the heartbeat of the Jones Valley.[20] Frank began to think about the school while he was in Japan: was there a way for him to revive it? The English designer and architect Charles Robert Ashbee had become one of his closest confidants during his early career. There was much that they admired in each other. Frank was impressed by Ashbee's talent and by his creative philosophy, which was broadly aligned with the English Arts and Crafts manifesto. He was impressed by Ashbee's charisma and his sartorial style but, more than anything, he was impressed by Ashbee's 'Guild of Handicrafts', the way that he had drawn a community of craftsmen and apprentices into an orbit around his personal radiance. As he thought about the future of the Hillside buildings, he came to see himself in a similar role, attracting young disciples, becoming the centre of their lives. He envisaged students working closely with him, working for him, and perhaps paying him for the privilege.[21]

By 1928 he was married to Olgivanna, his third wife, and settled again at Taliesin, but searching for work, weighed down by his debts and striving to free himself from his 'Incorporation'. Olgivanna had her own intense experience of communal education at Georges Gurdjieff's 'Institute for the Harmonious Development of Man' on the outskirts of Paris. She had become very close to her 'Master', rising through the ranks to become his lead dancer, and she had been in the vanguard of Gurdjieff's efforts to establish a commune in America. She met Frank in strange circumstances, which will be revisited later in this story. At their first encounter she could discern will-power and self-possession that far surpassed her own, that could even be the equal of her Master's. But while Gurdjieff had made a career out of it, the architect had used his powers to create marvels. Olgivanna did, however, remain a committed believer in Gurdjieff's methods of human improvement and longed for the opportunity to pass on what she had learned to a suitably selected group of young Americans.[22]

Just days before his Princeton lecture Frank had visited the Roycrofters Community in Aurora, New York, the mission of Edwin Hubbard who, decades before, in his previous life as a senior executive of the Larkin soap corporation, had been instrumental in commissioning Frank to design his first great commercial building, the Larkin Administration Headquarters. In its heyday, Roycrofters was a thriving handicraft community modelled on William Morris's Art Workers' Guild. When Frank spoke about a school, he found himself thinking about a working commune, like Roycrofters, like Ashbee's Guild; and a little like Gurdjieff's institute. But what kind of school requires three hours each day of farm work in the core of its curriculum? When he looked out over the landscape of the Jones Valley he could picture the harrowed earth, the green haze of emerging spring wheat, the cattle on the slopes, the school filled with vigorous youngsters. He could revive The Valley to its best, as it had been in the farm years of his grandfather, and as it had been when the Hillside Home School was in its prime. Whereas it had been a side-project in the years before the Crash, it was now his driving preoccupation, his only business plan.

Frank wrote a prospectus in collaboration with one of his most committed European advocates, the Dutch architect Hendrik Wijdeveld. Wijdeveld was also a writer and editor of the journal *Wendingen*. In 1925 he devoted seven consecutive editions entirely to Frank's work. For a while, Frank had it in mind to ask Wijdeveld to move to America to become Dean of the school. It was only when the Dutchman eventually seemed set to make the move that Frank began to have second thoughts. Perhaps it was Olgivanna's influence: she wanted to work with the young people herself, and with her husband in charge, her opportunities would be far less constrained. Frank came to accept that he should lead the school himself, despite his concern that it would take time away from his own work. Frank and Olgivanna rewrote the prospectus. The revised manifesto of the 'Taliesin Fellowship' was infused with Gurdjieffian terminology from its beginning: 'The

Fellowship aims first of all to develop a well-correlated human individual. It is this correlation between the hand and the mind's eye that is lacking in the modern human being.' One of Wijdeveld's contributions had been retained: the young recruits were to be *apprentices* to the fellowship, not students. The apprenticeship had no timescale, there were no lessons and no degrees would be awarded. 'Apprenticeship will be the condition and should be the attitude of mind of all the Fellowship workers.' The three hours of labour that the apprentices would provide each day, either on the farm or on the renovation of the buildings, would entitle them to 'the privilege of participation in the experimental work in the studios and [work]shops'. Each apprentice would have his or her own room; meals would be taken communally. There would be regular talks from eminent visitors, music and film shows. Most importantly, the 'inspirational fellowship of the genuinely creative artist' would be enriched by 'constant contact with the nature of the ground'. The fee for the first year was $675. It was more expensive than Harvard.[23]

Young, talented students, many of European and Japanese origin, wrote frequently to Taliesin, appealing for a chance to work with Frank Lloyd Wright. There was never a lack of enthusiastic potential recruits, just a lack of work and of funds from which to pay them. The Fellowship achieved the trick of making the funds flow *into* Taliesin while still providing a workforce, albeit one with very little architectural experience, and recruited largely from prosperous East Coast families. The prospectus generated interest, but it was the eventual publication in 1932 of Frank's autobiography that really captured the necessary attention. Within weeks of its first adulatory reviews, eager young Americans began to arrive at Taliesin, happy to part with their parents' money for the promise of a life-changing adventure. Most of them got what they were seeking, although for many it did not, and was never really expected to, lead to an architectural career.[24]

Why would an architect feel such a strong urge to establish a school of his own? Although his mother and his aunts had been ardent educationalists, he didn't seem to be motivated to follow their example. It was never really an academic institution that Frank had it in mind to create. He certainly had a powerful social and philosophical message to convey to the world, but in this he was not unique among architects at that time. Most were satisfied to use their buildings as the medium for those messages, and Frank did that more effectively than any other. The most meaningful purpose of the Taliesin Fellowship was that it brought Frank back to the feeling of communal solidarity that he had sought to rediscover since his childhood in The Valley – the poetry of Nature, the fields being cultivated, the buildings rising again, the collective life of the youth and their elders, working together, eating together and growing spiritually together. It was Frank's own *teulu*, that distinctly Welsh form of fellowship drawn together by the captivating brilliance of an autocratic, inspirational patriarch, and it was the bedrock of the astonishing architectural achievements that were to follow (Pl. 27).

Pl. 27. Frank, in hat and striped blazer, at the centre of a picnic with apprentices of the Taliesin Fellowship, 1940. Photograph Pedro Guerrero courtesy of Dixie Guerrero.

# 1860. River Farms, Spring Green, Sauk County, Wisconsin.

The Decennial Census showed Richard Lloyd Jones to be one of the leading farmers in Spring Green. The size of his farm, the value of his livestock and equipment and his productivity were all well above the average in the township. The mixed agriculture that was the convention in Cardiganshire was seen, in modern America, as the prudent application of diversification. It was the only way that the Lloyd Joneses knew. In 1860 the River Farms produced thousands of bushels of cereals, almost half a ton of butter and cheese and hundreds of pounds of potatoes, pork, mutton and beef. An impressive yield, despite the fact that the soil at the River Farms was bulked with sand.[25] This must have been new to the Lloyd Joneses; they may not have realised how difficult it would be to keep loose, sandy soil moist through a hot summer, or how quickly its fertility would dwindle. In that third year of growing it is possible that crop yields were already in decline. It is significant also that this was the output of less than half of their land. The Census records that 255 acres were still unimproved. The problem areas were those closest to the river to the south. Even today, it is dotted with ponds, incised by narrow sloughs and thickly overgrown. Richard was in his sixties and his older sons, Thomas and John, had gradually taken over leadership of the farm work. They must have walked the paths through the riverside brush each day and wondered when it could be improved; how they could spare the time and, perhaps increasingly, could they justify the effort when a more practical option appeared close to hand?

The first development in the area had been in Wyoming Township, directly across the waters of the Wisconsin from the River Farms. The heart of Wyoming was the village of Helena, so close that from their bedrooms the Lloyd Joneses could hear the sounds of late night carousing drifting across from the ferrymen's saloons.[26] In the 1830s a shot tower had been built there to take advantage of nearby lead mining and of the river that led to the markets in the east. Many years later Tower Hill, the site of the shot factory, became the summer home of the Rev. Jenkin Lloyd Jones and the base for an extraordinary series of religious convocations, but in 1857, when the Lloyd Joneses arrived at Spring Green, the factory was at the peak of production, its workers unaware that it was rapidly approaching its twilight. Late in 1857 a financial panic began to sweep through the urban centres of the northern states prompting a recession that lasted for three years and decimated the market for lead shot. To consolidate the crisis, the new railroad through Spring Green had taken a large share of the river trade. As the industry disappeared the residents of Helena began just as quickly to drift away. In 1861, the shot tower closed, the saloons fell silent and the village dwindled into ruin, leaving Wyoming township almost deserted.[27] The Lloyd Joneses were aware that there were still hundreds of acres of government land waiting to be settled immediately to the west of the fading Helena village. Their attention became drawn to the convergence of three small valleys, just a mile south of the river. Part of the land was heavily wooded with ancient oaks, but it was a sumptuous territory of rich, loamy soil and clean, beautiful streams. Three prominent hills rose up around a hundred metres on the eastern side, and more hills rolled close by, to the west. There was a palpable sense of enclosure and a natural definition to the valley basin, space to expand but with tight, reassuring horizons all around. More than anywhere else they had seen, it reminded them of Wales. It seemed to offer all that they wanted, but it was still a difficult decision to make, one that led to a short and bitter squabble between the two elder brothers and their father, who at first couldn't face the prospect of another move. Then there was another argument about the fair value of their respective shares, as it had a bearing on the division of the land across the river. Lloyd Jones life was as variable, and at times as turbulent, as that of any large family. They kept careful account of debts and favours owed[28] (Fig. 5.1).

The hills on the east side of The Valley would become known, within a few years, as Bryn Canol, Bryn Mawr and Bryn Bach.[29] In due course The Valley itself would be labelled on maps as 'Jones Valley', but before they could move across the river, they had to take time to clear the best of the land and to build the new houses (Fig. 5.2).

They had learned from Ixonia that it was a miserable task to farm among tree stumps, to sow and to saw at the same time. They settled their arguments and sold the River Farms in 1862 to buy 425 acres in The Valley, which they would divide into three separate farms, one each for Thomas and John and one for the rest of the family. Over the course of the next two years they rented land almost ten miles west of the the River Farms across the border into Richland County, in a township called Buena Vista.[30] The nearest village was Lone Rock, just a mile away to their south. At another time and in other circumstances the family might have pressed on collectively, as they had always done, until the trees in The Valley were processed and the stumps blasted from the ground, but the early 1860s were years of upheaval for all Americans.

The Civil War has been characterised in many ways. It was seen by the great majority of recent European settlers in the Midwest as an existential struggle between those like them, who had come to America with high ideals, to build a republic of freedom and equality, a more civilised world than the one that they had left behind; and those in the South, the old colonial America that had become dependent on its slave economy, trapped in a culture of pre-modern barbarism. The Unitarian Lloyd Joneses had been active abolitionists for generations. Like the millions of Europeans who had emigrated since the 1830s, they had come to America knowing that slavery still existed on the southern fringe of the republic but expecting it soon to wither away, as it had from the rest of the civilised world. They could not have imagined that they might have to sacrifice their lives to make it happen.

The Lloyd Joneses found themselves tied in ethical knots. They were as deeply opposed to slavery as anybody, but they were just as steadfast in their opposition to war. Their participation in the conflict reflects this ambivalence. Both Thomas and John, the two elder brothers, considered volunteering and were turned down, or perhaps thought better of it. Thomas had been weakened by a childhood illness and had never regained full strength. A work accident had left John with a stiffened index finger that would struggle to pull a trigger. They could probably have gone if they had really wanted to. Medical checks were so cursory that hundreds of women were able to enlist in disguise. For Jenkin it was

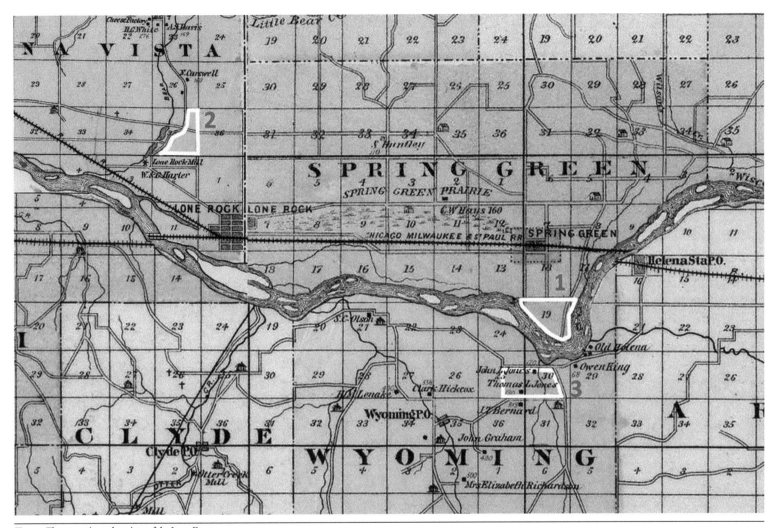

Fig. 5.1. The approximate locations of the Jones Farms.

    (1) The River Farms 1857–63.

    (2) The rented farm on Little Bear Creek, north of Lone Rock, Richland County 1863–65.

    (3) The first Lloyd Jones property in The Valley.

    The houses of John and Thomas Lloyd Jones are identified in The Valley. Each of the numbered squares is one square mile.

    Composite from 1878 Snyder, Van Vechten & Co. *Atlas of Wisconsin*.

    LOC.

different. He was sixteen, vigorous and a zealous abolitionist. Like most of the older boys of the village he had been roused to the cause by their schoolteacher. Whereas Thomas and John were essential to the farm, more so than ever as they planned their move across the river, Jenkin was not yet so critical to the enterprise that he could not be spared for the duration of what everyone hoped would be a short conflict. Jenkin was too young to enlist in the first year of the war, but went at the end of the following summer, 1862, to join old schoolfriends on the battlefront.[31] Jenkin said his farewells as his family was in the process of packing up to leave the River Farms for the tenancy in Lone Rock, and he stayed with the 6th Battery of the Wisconsin Artillery for three grim years, until the rebels surrendered.[32] The family gathered to welcome him to their new Valley home in August 1865 when he at last made it back to Wisconsin:

> *three years had brought a change here as well as upon me. The locks of my aged father were considerably whiter than when I left. Mother I was rejoiced to find looking so well. Thomas, John, Margaret, Mary, Hannah and Ellen were the same in appearance as when I left, but Jane had grown from a school girl to the full proportions of a woman, and I scarcely could recognize her. The little boys [James and Enos] are grown and much changed, but yet the same.*
>
> *And this is not all the change. I left them without a place to call home, but found them situated in a lovely location, a pleasant house and expanding fields, for which I felt very thankful.*[33]

John Lloyd Jones was married before the end of 1865. Mary would later marry an Aberdonian, James Phillip, and move to her own home in The Valley, but at that time she was still with Richard and Mallie, helping her mother to run the house and to raise the two young boys, Enos and James, who both still had a few years of schooling ahead. Ellen and Jane, very much a pair, were in their late teens and both deeply absorbed in teaching. They were also exposed to its hazards: while she was a young assistant in Lone Rock, Ellen was caught by an outbreak of smallpox that left her with a badly scarred face and hair that had turned pure white.[34] With characteristic compassion, Jenkin chose not to mention this in his diary

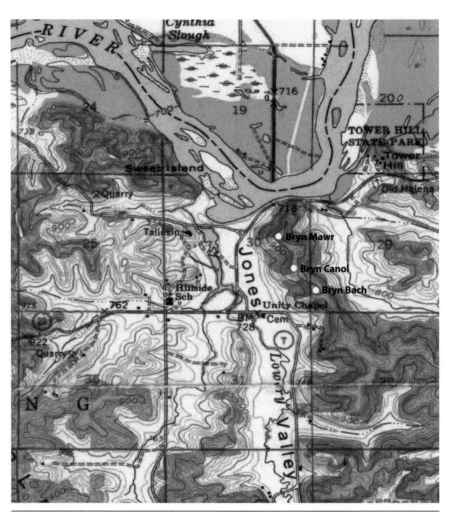

Fig. 5.2. Topography of 'Jones Valley', from the US Geological survey map 1960, with labels added for the hills Bryn Mawr, Bryn Canol and Bryn Bach. The quarry in the top left quarter of Section 36 is the most likely source of the stone used in buildings in The Valley.
LOC.

account of his return home; as far as he was concerned, she hadn't changed at all. There were many dividends from the end of the war. Strengthened government authority gave real impetus, for the first time, to federal disease control, and the days of smallpox were numbered. It also gave momentum to a nationwide mission to improve teaching standards through a system of public teacher-training colleges, known as State

Normal Schools. The funds for these institutions came from the government's sales of largely useless swampland to eager settlers – a tacit admission to a degree of guilt on the government's part for the struggles endured by so many families who had, like the Lloyd Joneses, innocently paid for unimprovable land.[35] In October 1866 Ellen and Jane were delighted to embark on three years of rigorous training from which each would gain a professional teaching qualification. They were among the first intake at the Wisconsin State Normal School at Platteville, a prosperous zinc-mining town forty-five miles south-west of The Valley.

As soon as he had reacclimatised to normal life, Jenkin also plunged into teaching, but before long he too felt the urge to move into higher education. The journey ahead of him was that of the first Jenkin Jones, his destination the pulpit rather than the classroom. In 1866 he enrolled at the prestigious Unitarian Seminary at Meadville, hundreds of miles to the east, in Pennsylvania (Pl. 28).

With the war behind them and the promise of a prosperous future ahead, Richard and Mallie approached their old age with the satisfaction of knowing that their long journey from Cardiganshire, to Ixonia and from there to Spring Green and eventually to The Valley had delivered to them and their children everything that they had hoped for: freedom, independence and unlimited opportunity. The children all seemed settled on their respective ambitions, and blessed with the robust physicality, intelligence and confidence they needed to achieve their goals.

But what of Hannah? Somehow the story of the middle sister became lost among those of the adventurous younger siblings and the land-taming older brothers. Hannah was twenty-five years old when the Lloyd Joneses moved to The Valley. Where had she been in the years before? In her definitive biography of Frank Lloyd Wright, Meryl Secrest echoes her predecessors in saying, 'nothing is known of her life as a young woman.'[36] This is enormously frustrating, because the woman that Hannah had become would give birth to her son Frank only two years after the end of the Civil War. If we know so little about her life in the years before, we can really only guess how her experience contributed to the moulding of Frank. It seems that the safest guess in the circumstances, for all of Frank Lloyd Wright's biographers, is that Hannah was little more than a bystander while those around her led their extraordinary lives, despite the fact that her own son's life was the most extraordinary of all. There is an obvious inconsistency in this version of the story that his many biographers have been reluctant to acknowledge. As Frank was the most remarkable scion of the Lloyd Joneses, how could it be that Hannah was the least of them? Until now there has been no plausible answer to this question, but it now appears that Hannah was just as motivated and as capable as any of her sisters and brothers. Given the exceptional hardships of her childhood it is reasonable to suggest that Hannah was, in some ways, the most impressive of them all and that she can be revealed now as a woman whose ambitions, discipline and poignant compromises ideally disposed her to become mother of a modern genius ∎

**Pl. 28.** Meadville Unitarian Seminary, Pennsylvania *circa* 1863. Jenkin Lloyd Jones studied here after his return from the Civil War. He probably became acquainted with some of the gentlemen in this photograph. Courtesy of Meadville Lombard Theological School.

# 05

## The Valley
### *Notes*

1      Thomas E. Graham (ed.), *Trilogy: Through Their Eyes* (Spring Green, WI: Unity Chapel Publications, 1986), p. 33.

2      Richard Lloyd Jones et al., *A Lloyd Jones Retrospective (Second Edition)* (Spring Green, WI: Unity Chapel Inc., 1986), p. 48.

3      US Census and Wisconsin State Census data.

4      Margaret Jones née Lloyd died 3 June 1858. I am indebted to the historian David Barnes who shared a note that he had made from the diary of the Rev. John Thomas, minister of Pantydefaid Chapel in the late 1850s:

        *4 June 1858: Margaret died at daughter Hannah's home at Dolau Canol, Rhydcymerau.*
        *7 June 1858: Have heard that Mrs Jones, Dr Lloyd's aunt is to be buried at Llanwenog today.*
        Her grave is not marked.

5      US Immigration Record 1855. Enoch and his family came from Liverpool on a sailing ship, *The Southampton*. It was around twice the size and of better quality than *Remittance*.

6      This is supported by the 1850 and 1860 US Census records: the Evans family, recorded in 1850 as being neighbours to Richard and Mallie, are also recorded as being neighbours to Enoch in 1860, implying that Enoch was living on property previously owned by Richard.

7      Meryl Secrest, *Frank Lloyd Wright: A Biography* (Chicago: University of Chicago Press, 1998), p. 36.

8      Enoch's first daughter Margaret died in 1858, aged three according to her grave marker. However her immigration record lists her as being two years old in 1855. A second daughter, Sarah was born in 1857, shortly after Richard and Mallie left Ixonia (US Census 1870 and *A Lloyd Jones Retrospective*).

9      Ron McCrea, *Building Taliesin: Frank Lloyd Wright's Home of Love and Loss* (Madison: Wisconsin Historical Society Press, 2012), p. 32.

10    Harry E. Cole, *A Standard History of Sauk County Wisconsin* (Chicago: Lewis Publishing Co., 1918), pp. 495–505.

11    Wisconsin State Census 1855.

12    Chester Lloyd Jones, *Youngest Son* (Madison, WI: self-published, 1938), pp. 51–4.

13    Thomas Edward Jones (1867–1939). It may be significant that the Welsh word for carpenter is *saer,* and the word for architect is *pensaer,* literally 'head carpenter'. As 'head carpenter' in a Welsh-speaking community, Uncle Thomas had the status of an architect.

14    Graham, *Trilogy: Through Their Eyes,* p. 46.

15    Andrew J. Dowling, *Architecture of Country Houses* (New York: D. Appleton, 1851), pp. 10, 163. Also quoted in Vincent Scully, *The Shingle Style and the Stick Style (Revised Edition)* (New Haven: Yale University Press, 1971), pp. xxvi–xlvii.

16    Graham, *Trilogy: Through Their Eyes,* p. 45.

17    Jane Aaron, 'Welsh Keywords: Teulu', *Planet: The Welsh Internationalist,* 232 (Winter 2018), 45–52.

18    Frank Lloyd Wright, *Modern Architecture: Being the Kahn Lectures for 1930* (Princeton: Princeton University Press, 1931; repr 2008), p. 41.

19    Secrest, *Frank Lloyd Wright: A Biography,* p. 253.

20    K. Smith, 'Frank Lloyd Wright and the Imperial Hotel: A Postscript', *The Art Bulletin,* 67/2 (June 1985), 296–310.

21    Roger Friedland and Harold Zellman, *The Fellowship: The Untold Story of Frank Lloyd Wright and the Taliesin Fellowship* (New York: HarperCollins, 2006), pp. 25–7. The most complete account of the Taliesin Fellowship is to be found in this important book.

22    Friedland and Zellman, *The Fellowship,* pp. 49–71, 103.

23    Friedland and Zellman, *The Fellowship,* pp. 159–71.

24    The Fellowship continued up to Frank's death twenty-seven years later, and beyond under the control of Olgivanna until her death in 1985. It evolved over the decades to become the School of Architecture at Taliesin, before its eventual closure in June 2020, following a failure to agree terms with the Frank Lloyd Wright Foundation for the school's continued use of the two houses.

25    US Department of Agriculture Soil Survey Map of Sauk County, 1925.

26    Graham, *Trilogy: Through Their Eyes,* p. 54.

27    B. Folkedahl, 'Forgotten Villages: Helena', *Wisconsin Magazine of History,* 42/4 (Summer 1959), 288–92.

28    Thomas E. Graham, *Unity Chapel Sermons 1984–2000* (Winnipeg: New Colgrove Press, 2002), p. 32.

29    Maginel Wright Barney, *The Valley of the God Almighty Joneses* (New York: Appleton Century, 1965), p. 49.

30    Jones, *Youngest Son,* p. 63.

31    Jenkin Lloyd Jones, *An Artilleryman's Diary* (Madison: The Wisconsin History Commission, 1914), p. xiv.

32    There are differing accounts of the date of the Lloyd Joneses' move from the River Farms to Lone Rock. In his contemporaneous diary account Jenkin says that he left Spring Green with the militia in July 1862 and that the Lloyd Joneses were 'without a place to call home' when he left. Other sources say that they moved from Spring Green in 1863, e.g. *A Lloyd Jones Retrospective,* p. 51. I have worked from the date implied in Jenkin's account.

33    Jones, *Artilleryman's Diary,* p. 364.

34    Barney, *The Valley of the God Almighty Joneses,* p. 118.

35    *Alumni Today* (University of Wisconsin-Platteville, 2015), pp. 11–15.

36    Secrest, *Frank Lloyd Wright: A Biography,* p. 48.

# 6

# Anna Had Chosen
# an Englishman

Frank Lloyd Wright's autobiography first appeared in print in 1932. It was greeted with unexpectedly positive reviews. The first printing, a conservative 500 copies, quickly sold out. A second edition of 2,000 appeared a year later and many reprints followed. The popularity of Frank's version of his past prompted further memoirs from members of his family, each of which was complementary to a degree, while offering in some aspects a contradictory perspective. The first was Chester Lloyd Jones's *Youngest Son*, privately published in 1938. For reasons that, at the time, would still have been raw, it contains no mention of his cousin Frank.

Frank's second son, John, wrote his own story, *My Father who is on Earth*, published in 1946.[1] It depicts his father as an emotionally sequestered *Übermensch*. It is also lovingly and woundingly candid. In the early 1960s, shortly after his death, Frank's sister Maginel wrote *The Valley of the God Almighty Joneses*.[2] Maginel had made a successful career of her own as an illustrator, specialising in children's books. Her story of her childhood, and of her brother's youth is written for young readers. Despite its soft-focus glow and relaxed attitude to facts, it is delightful and uplifting; and it reveals her brother to be a singular boy cast cleanly in the mould of his remarkable forebears.

All of these versions of the family story drew from Jenkin Lloyd Jones's sermons and correspondence, spoken recollections of the generation before and the few, short written accounts that the other children of Richard and Mallie Lloyd Jones left behind. Jenkin often talked about the family's journey from Wales to America in his sermons. He also gave a short, vivid account of it in the Introduction to *An Artilleryman's Diary*, published in 1914. The body of this book is a direct transcript of the journal that Jenkin kept through the Civil War. Although it is the Introduction that is most informative for anyone interested in Frank Lloyd Wright's family background, the diary itself provides a few comments, almost in passing which, in the process of the writing of this book, have turned out to be revelatory, and which overturn much that has been assumed and written over the past several decades about the personality and significance of Frank Lloyd Wright's mother, Anna Lloyd Wright.

While Frank himself is sometimes a dominant presence in the Lloyd Jones family histories, at other times he is utterly absent. She, on the other hand, is always there, as Hannah, the young girl and older sister, or as Anna, the mother and grandmother. While she is always present, she is rarely in the foreground. She has proved to be a difficult woman to understand, but all too easy, for some of Wright's male biographers at least, to caricature in demeaning terms and even to traduce. To Brendan Gill, author of the Wright biography *Many Masks*, Anna was, 'ambitious, half-mad, sexually cold and drearily self-righteous'. Her husband,

William Carey Wright, 'made but one single irremediable error in his long lifetime', which was 'consenting to marry her'. Furthermore, in Gill's judgement, 'no matter how vehemently she pressed her claim to total possession of Frank, genetically he was a Wright and not a Lloyd Jones.'[3] Donald Johnson, author of many Wright books and essays, believes that 'the genetic and practical source of Frank's artistic genius and intellectual fervour was his father. The drive for fame ... was obtained from his mother ... a result of [her] overweening ambition.'[4] Paul Hendrickson, a recent biographer, is just as bluntly tendentious: 'the vote here will always be cast for William and against the cruel Anna', a woman who 'with her awful and inborn ... temper, with her terrifying will, suffered a prolonged siege of mental illness', which of course, if it were true, would mean that we should not take her seriously.[5]

The circumstances of Anna's marriage to William Wright have been the subject of speculation since the publication of their son Frank's autobiography. They aren't obviously compatible, so what brought them together? Although there is no evidence to support it, the unanimous presumption, until now, has been that Anna, at that time in her late twenties, pursued William and sought him for her husband; and the basis of this is that William was formally educated, accomplished and charismatic, whereas Anna, for all her native acumen, was of plain stock, untutored and lacking social graces.

As Frank's mother, Anna was in fact, and not surprisingly, the single most important influence on the making of the 'architectural genius' that her son became. To his credit, Frank said as much himself in his autobiography. Perhaps his devotion to his mother has goaded those biographers who argue that her influence was negative. They are compelled to dispute Frank's account of his mother for two reasons. Firstly, because they find it hard to accept that a woman - an assertive, Welsh woman - could be more important in his creative achievements than his father would have been. Secondly, because they know that Wright's own account of his childhood is full of deliberate fictions. In fact, much of the scholarship on Wright is engaged with the discovery of the real stories that underlie the long-standing myths.

Anna and William contributed equally to the genes of their son. Genetic inheritance also influences the nurturing behaviour of parents, traits they inherit from their own parents.[6] It was Anna who dominated Frank's nurturing. She was the one most responsible for moulding him into what he became, a task that she stuck to all her life. More so than his father, she was the making of him, but not in the way that he would later have his readers believe. To get closer to Anna's true story we must review its beginning, back in Ceredigion where she was born in July 1838.

By the time of Hannah's (Anna's) birth, Unitarianism had come through the precarious period of its legal repression, and was flowering openly and abundantly in south Cardiganshire. Although it was still regarded by other denominations as an extreme form of Dissent, within their neighbourhood it was the comfortable norm. Hannah's infancy was suffused with radicalism, although she, of course, would not have known it. Religion would have been the foundation of her schooling, but not in the conventional form of catechistic rote. She would have learned to read in Welsh first, but it is likely she also learned basic English, and she would have been taught maths and encouraged to learn from nature. Like everyone else growing up in the Unitarian faith, she would have been encouraged from her earliest years to think for herself. Blaenralltddu, a compact, three-room cottage was home to her parents, to her brothers and sisters and to her Uncle Jenkin. Jenkin had shared responsibility for bringing up the children, becoming a third parent to them, in his heart and in theirs. The first upheaval in Hannah's young life came in the summer of 1842 when Uncle Jenkin left the household, and didn't come back. A typical child will begin to develop her emotional and intellectual independence at around six years of age. Familiarity of surroundings and relationships becomes increasingly important as her engagement with her surroundings extends beyond immediate familial warmth to the challenges and uncertainties of real life in the wider world. But for Hannah, this was when everything changed. In the late summer of 1844 her parents loaded the wagons with their seven children and their few belongings and set off towards New Quay, the first steps of their agonising migration journey.

It was not until around April of the following year, eight months after they left their home in Wales, that they were reunited with Uncle Jenkin and the travelling stopped at Ixonia, the scant township of forest and malarial swamp. The first six years of Hannah's life had been a time of comfort and security. The following years were a struggle with an extreme environment, agricultural toil, poverty and the coldness of neighbours that came to a head during their 'Black Week'. Social and physical isolation were relieved by occasional correspondence with family in Wales, and by the weekly and monthly journals. Without her appreciating it, the words she read in both languages came almost exclusively from the radical, progressive viewpoint. There was simply no other source of ideas accessible to her, and she, perhaps more than her brothers and sisters at that time, was particularly receptive to them.

Hannah was nineteen years old and deeply radicalised, spiritually and politically, by the time the family arrived in Spring Green. Her childhood was behind her, punctuated by intense struggle and trauma. She had taken her share of daunting domestic duties since her infancy and had by that time, according to Maginel, 'assisted the midwife in half a dozen family births'.[7] With young mouths to feed, Hannah had to take a larger share of the workload. She shared the responsibility for raising the youngsters, teaching them to read and write. Enos, in particular, recalled how difficult he found it to learn anything at Spring Green's 'pioneer school', and how Hannah led him gently towards literacy at home: 'He long remembered gratefully the sister's patience which at last raised him from his low orthographic state.'[8]

She tended the livestock on foot and on horseback, fed them, milked them. She sowed and weeded, hoed and harvested and made every type of food with the produce. A share of the clothes-making and blanket-making fell to her, as it had done to generations of women before. She provided first aid for the frequent injuries, and when infections took hold she knew the natural remedies. Even for a woman of her time, a pioneer, she was tremendously self-reliant. She had a sharp intellect, a deep mistrust of social conventions and pretences, and a profound spirituality that, at times,

tormented her. She also felt a powerful drive to improve herself, to map out her individual destiny and to follow it to its truest fulfilment. To her lasting frustration, she couldn't help but expect the same of others. There is a memorable passage in Maginel's book that describes Hannah in her in early womanhood (Pl. 29). She was:

> *tall and lovely looking. She had a wide brow, great brown eyes and strong, wilful curly hair ... she could ride like a man and would ride anywhere in any weather to pursue her passion, which was teaching. Education obsessed her, and she would teach anyone who had even the vaguest desire to learn ... Nature and knowledge: those were her early and abiding passions ... She was emancipated before the emancipated woman became the vogue: perhaps she was a little formidable, though, in her adherence to principle.*[9]

There are many accounts of Hannah's story that accompany her to this point, and then lose track of her. The presumption has always been that she took on irregular teaching work, as a classroom assistant or as an occasional home governess. The next point of general agreement is that she married William Carey Wright in 1866, after the death of his first wife, and that the marriage probably took place at Lone Rock, the small township a few miles to the west of Spring Green, where he was practising as a lawyer, and where, between 1863 and 1865, the Lloyd Joneses were living on their rented farm.

None of the published accounts of her life before marriage are correct. In Maud Lloyd Jones's 1907 presentation to the Spring Green Old Settlers Association, there is a tantalising reference to the earliest teachers at Spring Green School: 'the first school building was erected in 1857. Miss Franklin of Wyoming was the first teacher; Miss Hubbard the next; then Aunt Anna Wright.'[10] No date is given for the period in which Anna led the school, but it was probably at the end of the 1850s. This record indicates that Anna was in charge of the school, not just an assistant, certainly not an itinerant governess. Where did she go

Pl. 29. Hannah Lloyd Jones, a young woman *circa* 1865.
From *An Autobiography* (1932).

1864 he eventually heard from her. She was 'off to Albion again'. Significant entries are recorded in 1865:

*14 May 1865: Wrote home and to sister Hannah. I am troubled much in regard to her, have not received any letter from her for over two weeks and I fear she is sick again. Her ambition is too much for a frail nature.*

From this it is clear that Hannah was not at the family home at that time, and that whatever she was engaged in was providing her with a challenge that even she was struggling to overcome.

*21 May 1865: Wrote two long letters, one to brother John, my ever faithful weekly correspondent, the other to Sister Hannah at Albion. Have not received a word from her this month. I fear she has overtaxed herself again by arduous study.*

Finally, on 20 June, he received a reply from Hannah,

*jubilant at the immediate prospect of the relief from her confinement.*

It is possibly this last reference to Hannah that has led some biographers to infer that she was receiving some kind of medical care shortly before her marriage. Albion is a small town seventy miles to the east of Spring Green. In the mid-nineteenth century there was only one institution of note in Albion. Not a psychiatric hospital, but a prestigious teaching college, Albion Academy (Pl. 30).

The village of Albion was established by Seventh Day Baptists in 1840. These particular settlers had moved west from the civilised eastern states, looking for new opportunities, in most ways no different from the foreign migrants that so greatly outnumbered them. They did bring a different attitude, though: many had already benefited from a good American education, and were ambitious to fulfil themselves in leadership roles within their new pioneer communities. It is a consistent pattern across the Midwest frontier in this period that the majority

when she moved on from Spring Green School? Her actual whereabouts between 1861 and 1865, are hinted at in the *Artilleryman's Diary* of Jenkin Lloyd Jones, in which he kept a record of his sporadic correspondence with his brothers and sisters. He wrote to Hannah more often than she wrote to him, causing him to worry for her wellbeing. On 28 August of civic leaders of all types are from the eastern American states, the descendants of earlier immigrant generations. Once the founders of Albion felt sufficiently established, they set their minds to founding an educational institution that was:

*more than just the reading, writing and arithmetic that the one-room school house offered. Education to them meant the best that had been thought and said in the world, and they were determined that their children should be so educated.*[11]

The residents shared the job of constructing the Academy, felling the trees, cutting the stone and making bricks from local river clay. Set within a twelve-acre campus, its two buildings dominated the township. It was opened to its first students in the autumn of 1854.

*Albion Academy was the first educational institution in Wisconsin to give equal standing and equal treatment to female and male students. Its founders had the then revolutionary idea that women should be educated in the same manner and in the same subjects as men.*[12]

In the first two decades of its existence it was recognised in Wisconsin that the qualities of teaching and of the graduates of Albion Academy were at least equal to the standards achieved at the State University in Madison, and the university would not accept female students until the late 1860s.

It is likely that Hannah would have shared a dormitory with one or two other women. Tuition cost $6 per term and she would have paid $1.50 per week for her accommodation, a significant financial commitment at that time. The core curriculum was directed towards the achievement of the four-year Academic Qualification, a degree that was intended to be the springboard to a high-level professional teaching career. For women this was known as the Laureate of Philosophy degree. To fulfil the degree requirements, the students had to complete studies in English, Mathematics, Natural Sciences, History and Metaphysics, along with three

Pl. 30. Albion Academy circa 1850.
Courtesy Nancy Durgin, Albion Academy Historical Society.

years in Latin, although as an alternative to Latin, female students were allowed to take either German or French.[13] It is difficult to discern which of the two Hannah might have chosen, for she loved French and German literature equally.

Jenkin's wartime diary, in a few short sentences, gives a clear picture of his concern that his elder sister had taken on more than she could handle at Albion Academy. The reference that he made to Hannah's 'frail nature' is most likely to allude to a recurring health problem: Hannah probably suffered from epilepsy. More evidence for this is discussed further on. Regardless of her health, Albion Academy was an extremely challenging environment for a woman who had grown up in such unsettled circumstances, and whose education, until her entry to the Academy, had been acquired as much in the fields and at the fireside as it was from the little school in Ixonia. As the third teacher to lead Spring Green School, she could not have enrolled at the Academy any earlier than autumn of 1860. She was only two months short of her twenty-seventh birthday when she graduated. From a student body of over 250 she was one of only seven students who achieved graduation in the Class of 1865.[14]

The Seventh Day Baptists had their own national journal, *The Sabbath Recorder*. Each summer it reported on the 'Anniversary Exercises' of Albion Academy. These ceremonies took place over the course of three days, culminating in a 'closing exercise' which, in 1865, took place on the last Wednesday in June, in the village church, as heavy summer rain fell outside. The seven students of the graduating class all read essays specially prepared for the event. The last to read was 'Miss H. L. Jones of Wyoming Valley' on the subject 'On the Heights', a presentation that was 'well prepared and admirably read with self possession and refined modesty'.[15] Hannah appears to have been highly thought of by her tutors. She had also been asked to present an essay at the Exercises of 1864, a year before her graduation, on the theme 'The Holy Prisoners'. At that time she was Miss H. L. Jones of Lone Rock.[16]

The record of Hannah's graduation from Albion Academy identifies her as 'Hannah L. Jones (Wright) of Wyoming Valley'. It was amended to provide her married name. Her wedding took place, according to most sources, in August 1866, a year after her graduation.[17] With this evidence of Hannah's formal education the long-accepted notion that she was a poorly educated farm girl who 'had grown tired of the drudgery of teaching' and who had a 'dread of failing to find a husband' is revealed as fallacy.[18] It becomes much harder to believe that it was Hannah who pursued William Wright as a husband than it is to believe that it was William who pursued Hannah for his second wife. So why has such a significant part of her story apparently been overlooked until now? The only plausible answer is that it was Hannah herself who chose to erase it from her history, and that it was her marriage to William Wright that caused her to do so.

The settlement of Lone Rock, Wisconsin, is seven miles west of Spring Green. Both towns were founded in the mid-1850s and both were, and remain, small communities. In 1880, when it first appeared in the US decennial census, the population of Lone Rock was recorded as 380. It is reasonable to assume that in 1860, when William Wright and his family arrived at Lone Rock, they would have found themselves among fewer than 200 fellow citizens, the great majority of whom were new settlers from Scandinavia and Germany who spoke little or no English.[19] An American from Connecticut, his arrival would have made a significant impression, and evidence suggests that this was his intention. There were some, like the first teachers at Albion Academy, who had been specifically called to the West by new settlers to contribute to the civilising of the wilderness. In *Many Masks*, Brendan Gill's popular biography of Frank Lloyd Wright, William Wright is portrayed as a saintly example of that

> *small group who accepted the opportunity to pioneer not as a means of growing rich but as a means of serving his fellow men in occupations – teaching and preaching – that would almost certainly guarantee him a lifetime of genteel poverty.*[20]

Again, the facts suggest the opposite. When William Wright arrived at Lone Rock, at the age of thirty-four with his wife and two sons, he set himself up as a lawyer. He had been admitted to the Bar in 1857, only two years before his move west.[21] Successive biographers have cited this as a marker of Wright's education, but this too is erroneous. Bar admission did not then require any legal qualifications, and he had none. The convention in the West of America was that anyone entitled to vote was entitled to practise law.[22] In the words of Robert Twombley:

> *His choice of residence was an apt one, because the residents of Lone Rock immediately recognised him as a potential leader ... He was ambitious, aggressive, made friends easily and elicited confidence and respect. Within a year he was appointed Commissioner of the Richland County Circuit Court.*[23]

This was a role without a fixed term that William could fulfil alongside his own legal practice. It provided an additional income and it gave him a wide range of public legal powers, second only to those of the Circuit Judge. In 1862 and 1863 he also served as a deputy US revenue collector, in both Richland and Sauk Counties. In 1861 he had put himself forward for another civic role, that of Richland County Superintendent of Schools. His first bid for this post was unsuccessful, but in 1863 he was given his turn. Before taking on his new role, he stepped down from his tax-collecting duties and, somewhat incongruously, also took his ordination to become a Baptist minister, evidently planning for a change in career. At that time the prospects for William Wright and his family must have seemed encouraging, but soon after they were to go sadly awry.

William had married Permelia Holcombe in 1851 in Utica, New York, where he had gone to teach music (Pl. 31). Permelia's family lived in Utica, the town with a prevalence of Welsh settlers.[24] After the marriage they moved back to Hartford, Connecticut, William's hometown, where they resided for the next five years. During that time Permelia had two children: the first died at birth, the second was their son Charles, born in 1856. All the biographers of Frank Lloyd Wright who have discussed his father's influence upon him have been perplexed by his behaviour from 1856 onwards, because over the course of his life he moved his family and latterly himself to dozens of different houses in towns spread across the Midwest and the eastern states, never settling at any for more than a few years. Even in that era of ambition and resettlement, it seems he was propelled by an eccentric impulse. The first of the moves was from Hartford to Providence, Rhode Island, where their son George was born in 1858. The following year they made their 1,200-mile move west to Lone Rock, Wisconsin, where, in July 1860, their daughter Elizabeth was born. In April 1864, while William was serving as Superintendent of Schools, Permelia had a fifth baby. Like her first birth, it was difficult, the baby was stillborn. On this occasion, within two weeks, Permelia herself died from the complications, aged thirty-eight. William couldn't manage his family alone, so Permelia's mother made the long journey west from Utica to 'keep house' for him, which she did for the next two years.

Death in childbirth was not uncommon at that time on the frontier, but given William's prominence in the county, news of his family's misfortune would have

Pl. 31. William Wright and his first wife Permelia *née* Holcomb
Courtesy Iowa Historical Society.

spread quickly through Lone Rock and its neighbouring settlements. It would certainly have reached the Lloyd Joneses. Between 1863 and 1865 they were in the near vicinity on their rented farm. It has been presumed until now that Hannah became acquainted with William Wright while working in a classroom somewhere in the south of Richland County, and that this probably happened in 1863 when the Lloyd Joneses made their temporary move to Lone Rock. Hannah's sisters, Ellen and Jane must have known William, because they were both granted Richland County teaching certificates in 1864, following a process that required them to be interviewed by William in his capacity as Superintendent of Schools.

There is no evidence, though, to show how Hannah divided her time between Albion Academy, Spring Green and Lone Rock in the years between 1860 and 1865, except that she would be with her family at Christmas and for eight weeks each summer. Although the circumstances of their meeting are not known, and may never be, there are at least the facts that in 1865 William was the Superintendent of Schools and Hannah had just graduated from the most respected teacher-training academy in the state; that she was surely hoping to progress her teaching career at the level that her qualification merited, and that they were neighbours in a small, rural community. Whatever the circumstances of their meeting, it is easy to imagine that each would have made a strong impression on the other.

Since the death of his first wife William had been looking for a second wife to care for his three children, to look after his home and, most important of all, to care for him. His outlook was formed by a conservative Baptist upbringing. His expectations of family and social hierarchy were deeply traditional, and very different from Hannah's. She had committed the major part of her young life to achieving a higher educational qualification that would equip her for a professional career. William's time at Baptist College in Hamilton, New York, had yielded a liberal arts degree, with a heavy emphasis on classics and with modest vocational value, but he did appear to have the beginnings of a promising career in public life.[25] He was forty-one, fourteen years older than Anna. He was light-boned, slight, around five feet five inches tall. She was three inches taller, strong and physically confident. The transactional nature of their marriage is unavoidable. From William's viewpoint the marriage would have been beneficial in every way. For Hannah it was a Faustian pact. The 'marriage bar' was a strict expectation among the professional class, which William aspired to represent. She knew that once she married, she would have to give up her teaching ambitions, the very ambitions that had carried her through years of rigorous college education. What she would gain in compensation was the promise of security, even prosperity. Most compellingly, it would also allow her to have children of her own, who would share the benefits of a stable and comfortable upbringing.

Hannah was deeply religious, her Unitarian faith was the axis of her identity, and her spiritual integrity was her anchor. The direction that her life was now about to take diverged sharply from the course that she had previously followed with such determination. Hannah was surely deeply affected by the adjustment she had to make. She made no reference thereafter to her time at Albion Academy; that part of her life all but disappeared from her history. She also changed her name from Hannah Jones to Anna Wright. As Maginel later put it, 'Anna had chosen an Englishman ... about that union there were some misgivings.'[26]

*W. C. Wright came to Richland County as a lawyer and settled at Lone Rock ... He was a hard worker and a good speaker, when he had time to prepare himself. He had a fair practice and was very successful at the bar. After practicing law for several years he gave it up and began preaching for the Baptist Church. For a number of years he was located at Richland Center (from the* History of Crawford and Richland Counties, 1884*).*[27]

William wouldn't return to his legal practice until many years later, after he and Anna had gone their separate ways. Once his time as Superintendent of Schools had come to an end he followed his father into the Baptist ministry. Despite his ordination three years before, it still seems an unexpected career change. His academic history shows little inclination towards a religious life. His one abiding passion was for music, so it seems plausible that his move to the ministry was made, in part at least, to allow him more time to work on his music and a regular audience to listen to it. The Wrights moved to Richland Center, the County Town with a population of almost a thousand, in May 1867. He had begun to preach there during his time as Superintendent of Schools, making the thirty-two-mile round trip on as many weekends as he could manage. Richland Center had no Baptist church at the time, but William was confident in his ability to build a congregation within the predominantly German community. We can only guess at the circumstances in which William's future prospects were discussed between the recently married couple. A minister's career was certainly held in high regard by Anna's family; her most illustrious ancestors had all followed that path. It seems reasonable to assume that she would have supported the venture. At the same time, his abandonment of his legal career must have seemed precipitate.

Anna's first child, their son Frank, was born at Richland Center in their small two-roomed bungalow a month after their arrival (Pl. 32). 'Lincoln' was the middle name he was given at birth. William delivered his ministry at Richland Center's Courthouse. His principal task should have been 'church planting', that is, raising funds for the new building, but this proved impossible for him. He struggled to find the support he needed from his small congregation merely to provide for himself and his family, and in March 1869, less than two years after his arrival, he relinquished his ministry and moved from the town, leaving behind him a set of half-built foundations.[28]

They travelled sixty miles west to settle at McGregor, Iowa, on the western bank of the Mississippi (Pl. 33). With a resident population of over two thousand, and thousands more passing through, it was large by frontier standards, with a thriving local economy based on its river port. It already had a Baptist church, where William was taken on as a temporary pastor. In late July 1870 the family was called back to The Valley for a short while. Anna's mother, Mallie, was gravely ill. There is a story that, in her last hours, she asked William to sing a hymn to her, a touching gesture on Mallie's part, as until her death she would only speak Welsh, and William could only speak English. Mallie died on 3 August 1870, and was laid to rest in the pine grove in the base of The Valley. There were two words only engraved on her headstone: *Ein Mam*, 'Our Mother'.[29] William led the music at her funeral. He was a seasoned musical performer, a fine singer and pianist. In his effort to establish himself in McGregor he delivered regular public lectures and gave music lessons. He even bought a share in a local music shop. But despite the initial promise, his temporary pastorate did not develop into a permanent appointment. Before two years had elapsed the Wright family was once more making plans to move.

By this time Frank was three years old and Anna had a second child, her first daughter, Mary-Jane (known as Jane), born in April 1869. She was also caring for her three stepchildren, Lizzie, George and Charles, then aged between ten and fifteen. In the late summer of 1871, William made the long trek alone, back to the richer and far more

Pl. 32.  The house in which Frank Lloyd Wright was born, the Wertz House, shown here *circa* 1930, after it had been removed from its original site and rebuilt in a new location several blocks to the south, on South Park Street, Richland Center. The house no longer exists.
Courtesy Richland County History Room.

Pl. 33.  The High Street of McGregor, Iowa, 1870. The Wrights resided here at this time.
McGregor Historical Museum/WC.

populous territory of New England, where he hoped to find a Baptist ministry that would for once provide him with a viable living.[30] Anna and the children moved temporarily to stay with the Lloyd Joneses in The Valley.[31] After making the necessary connections, William was taken on as Minister at the High Street Church of Pawtucket, Rhode Island. The accommodation that he found was far from ideal. It was so cramped that, in December 1871, when Anna and the children moved to join him there, they had to leave George with Anna's family in The Valley.

Pawtucket was a major town with an industrial economy. Anna was a very long way from everything that was familiar to her. Twelve difficult months later, Charlie was sixteen. Frank and Jane were infants, but Elizabeth was approaching her twelfth birthday and could no longer be treated as a child. She needed a room of her own, but they had none to give her. His late wife's sister had space in her house in New York. William arranged for Lizzie to move there. Her departure meant George could rejoin them from Wisconsin. Eight years were to go by before Elizabeth saw her family again.[32] As must be explored in due course, her subsequent reconstruction of the events of her childhood has cast a disquieting shadow over her stepmother's reputation.[33]

William engaged his new congregation with his characteristic initial vigour, sermonising and teaching, delivering lectures on moral and historical subjects, performing his music and even publishing a song. As always he needed to raise funds to support himself, and to commit to the rebuilding of a church. Anna hosted donation parties, but they tended to yield vegetable pies rather than dollars. Occasionally they even struggled for food. Inevitably, as it seemed, within two years of arriving William capitulated again.[34] In December 1873, they gave up Pawtucket and sought refuge with William's father in Connecticut. Frank was six years old; his grandfather's house was his sixth home.

The following September they were on the move again. Probably through his father's connections, William had been given the chance to preach a trial sermon at the First Baptist Church of Weymouth, Massachusetts, and had given his usual consummate performance. Weymouth was prosperous, and rich in history and culture. William's new pastorate began in November 1874. He had never had a better opportunity to make a success of his clerical career. He started well, cultivating the support of the local press and joining influential societies. He leavened his pulpit duties with secular activities, lectures and, inevitably, musical performances. In a 'Semi-Centennial' booklet published by the church in 1904, there is a note that it was 'during Mr. Wright's stay in Weymouth that the church put in the valuable pipe organ'. Until his time in Weymouth, the two territories of his public life had flowed together naturally. No one had thought the combination troubling. Weymouth was different, more conservative. Proprieties had to be respected. 'He had some wonderfully interesting musical Sundays at his Church, [although] they were not entirely to the satisfaction of his congregation. [He would] seat himself at the piano and, throwing his head back with its snow-white hair, sing and play to us some song of his choosing.'[35]

He lost the confidence of his congregation and was relieved of his pastorate in November 1877, three years after its promising start. Departing from their previous behaviour, the Wright family did not leave Weymouth immediately. Anna's stepchildren were gone, George to Law School and Charles to be an apprentice engineer in Pawtucket. Then, in April 1877, Anna gave birth to another daughter, Margaret Ellen (later to become known as Maginel).[36] Anna was thirty-nine years old. The baby had been born prematurely and struggled with poor health throughout her early years. William continued to give music lessons and occasional lectures. More significantly he began to attend the local Unitarian church, and even spoke from its pulpit. For a traditional eastern Baptist this was a dramatic change in spiritual outlook. In some accounts of William's journeys there is a suggestion that his conversion to 'liberalism' was a genuine spiritual awakening, and that it could account for his disappointment with the Baptist ministry, but this conjecture is based on comments that William made many years later. There is no doubt that it was convenient to him at the time as it meant that, when everything else had failed, he could turn to the Lloyd Joneses to give him a lifeline.

In April 1878 they were back in Wisconsin, at the farm in The Valley. Anna, once a proud and emancipated woman, was now attended frequently by humiliation.

*As for the times when they would have to pack up and leave, swallow their pride and beg their relatives for a roof over their heads, these were the unkindest of all. When Frank was snubbed by a relative and complained about it to his mother, Anna replied that it was nothing new. [She] did not reproach her relatives who, she implied, were justified. The person who had let them down was Frank's father.[37]*

Regardless of any misgivings they must have felt about William, the Joneses did their best to put Anna's family back on their feet. They were fed and housed at The Valley until the late summer. Anna's brother Jenkin had risen rapidly to become the Missionary Secretary of the Western Unitarian Conference, the leading promoter of Unitarianism across half of the country. He used his influence to help William secure part-time pastorates in two rural churches in the south of the state, a commitment that would require him to make a seventy-mile round trip every Sunday. William was also convinced that, if he could find a suitable place in a large town, he could supplement his income by teaching music. With the modest but secure salary his preaching would bring, and the comfort of knowing that the resources of the Lloyd Joneses were close at hand, they moved from The Valley in the late summer of 1878 to Madison, state capital of Wisconsin, a short train ride to the east.

The city of Madison aspired to be a cosmopolitan resort. It was run by 'codfish aristocrats', wealthy migrants from New England, the kind of people that William could identify with. He was good at making connections, so he had high hopes for his music teaching, and even that he could secure the leadership of the city's Unitarian Church. In the first year, they had two addresses in rented homes, and then eventually in October 1879 they bought a house with a long back garden that sloped down to the edge of Lake Mendota. It was a beautiful spot, and it was the last time that they would move as a family. They paid $2,000 for the property; the money was probably provided by Anna's brothers[38] (Pl. 34).

The geography of William and Anna's marriage can be followed in some detail through the local newspapers and church yearbooks of the towns they moved through. This aspect of their lives together has been well mapped. Much less is known about their married relationship and how it changed, but what little we do know suggests that the family environment in which Frank grew up was frequently turbulent and often quite wretched. William Wright was blessed with an easy charm, erudition and self-confidence, but ultimately he emerges as a man tormented by his own weakness, dissociated from his responsibilities and easily distracted into escapism through his music. He moved to the West, knowing that opportunities there, for someone of his background, were plentiful and that scrutiny would be superficial. He was quick to impress and to make new friends wherever he went, but he was incapable of persevering with his commitments to the point where the faith that others invested in him would be vindicated.

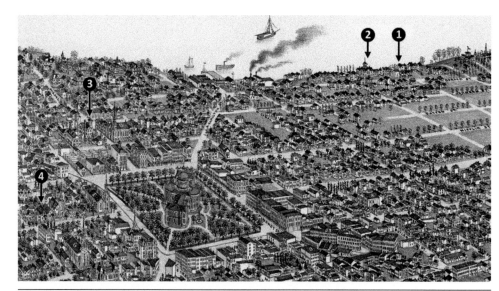

Pl. 34. A detail from an 1885 topographic map of Madison, Wisconsin. The large, domed building at bottom left is the State Capitol.
(1) The Wright residence from 1879 onwards, backing onto the shore of Lake Mendota.
(2) Second Ward School, attended by Frank between ages 11 and 13.
(3) Madison High School, attended intermittently by Frank to age 18
(4) Gates of Heaven Synagogue, used by the city's Unitarians until 1885.
LOC.

He was a beguiler. Apparently with the best intentions he beguiled the burghers of each new town to which he moved, and then he let them down. Just as he repeatedly beguiled civic leaders and congregations, he had of course beguiled Anna. With her, as with everyone else, the spell did not last. But by the time she saw through it, it was too late. In the 1932 edition of his autobiography, Frank recalls his adolescence in two voices: memories of his time with the Lloyd Joneses at The Valley are plentiful, vivid and lyrical, whereas his recollection of home life is terse, allusive and often awkward. While his father entertained his ambivalent Weymouth congregation with a programme of organ music, Frank explains that it was he, just seven years old at the time, who was forced into a dark cupboard behind the pipes to ply the pump handle, and that his father went on oblivious until his son collapsed in exhaustion and the recital came to a premature end.

> When they got home his mother, seeing the state the boy was in, looked reproachfully at the father. It was always so. The differences between husband and wife all seemed to arise over that boy. Mother on the defensive, father taking the offensive. And the boy grew afraid of his father.

His awareness of a division prevails throughout his childhood and adolescence. Reflecting on events that took place in their home in Madison when he was sixteen:

> Things were, by now, not so well at the small town house by the blue lake. There was no longer agreement between father and mother. Mother for some years had been ailing. Poverty pinched ... the father's earnings were small and shrinking. Music wasn't much of a livelihood in Madison, irregular preaching less so. And he grew irascible over cross-currents of family feeling. The Joneses didn't much care for Anna's privations. And he, being a proud man, resented their provisions.

William was a talented musician. He composed his own music and even built instruments. It appears that his ideal was to make a living from musical composition, by the publication of sheet music. It was a dream that he was unable to fulfil, and in the meantime he found that he had to compete with at least eighteen other music teachers in Madison, and the hoped-for city pastorate remained beyond his reach. The Joneses were so concerned about the welfare of Anna and her children that Frank's Uncle James presented them with a cow, to provide them with fresh milk. He brought it all the way from The Valley to their house in Madison. There is a later incident in which William attempted to 'thrash' his son as punishment for 'some disobedience'. But Frank was no longer prepared to be disciplined. He pinned his father to the ground, humiliated him.

> The youth hardly had known himself as his father's son. All had gone well enough on the surface that was now broken ... Something – you see – had never been established that was needed to make them father and son. Perhaps the father never loved the son at any time. Memories would haunt the youth as they haunt the man.

The inevitable happened:

> One day when difficulties between father and mother had grown unbearable the mother, having borne all that she could – probably the father had borne all that he could bear too – said quietly 'Well Mr. Wright' – always she spoke of him and to him so – 'leave us. I will manage with the children. Go your way ... we will never ask you for help.' The father was to disappear and never be seen again by his wife or his children.

He then reflects:

> Perhaps it was that their life together had worn its soul away in the strife of failure after failure added to failure. And an inveterate withdrawal on his part into the intellectual life of his studies, his books and his music, where he was oblivious to all else.[39]

Anna was deeply bitter about the situation she had endured. As her family had moved from one failed ministry to another, thousands of miles across America, rootless and impoverished, they had needed to maintain a picture of composure and respectability for every congregation they had served. Maintaining this façade would certainly have distressed Anna. She who believed more than anything in Truth was forced, by her marriage, to live a lie.

In 1967 the historian Thomas Hines uncovered the records of the divorce hearing, brought by William C. Wright against Anna Wright in the Dane County Court in April 1885. In his testimony William complained that their marriage had been 'unhappy from the start ... after suffering violence, indignity and abuse for years ... I could endure it no longer.' Anna had 'withheld [her] wifely duties'. She refused to cook for him or to mend his clothes: 'when I requested her to do anything it was often neglected ... or when it was done often thrown in my face or on the floor.' She had moved out of their bedroom two years before and 'protested against and refused me intercourse as between husband and wife'. Poverty was the main cause of the marriage breakdown. William claimed that Anna, 'wanted more money than I could furnish', and that any discussion of her spending would enrage her to violent anger: 'She told me "I hate the very ground that you walk on".' For her part, Anna willingly admitted, 'that she had no love for her husband'. It was a straightforward hearing; after eighteen years of marriage each was at last free of the other.[40] William was sixty years old, Anna forty-six.

Some of Frank's biographers have taken a degree of relish in the divorce record, because they see it as a truthful counter-narrative to his autobiographical version, in which Anna is depicted as an abandoned wife. Neither Frank's account nor the divorce record provides the complete picture. Anna and William both wanted to separate, but there were no legal grounds for divorce in Wisconsin at that time that would allow a mutually agreed separation. Furthermore, the grounds on which a wife could obtain a divorce from her husband were narrow. Proof of severe physical violence was required.[41] The divorce could only be obtained with William as plaintiff. This is not to say that his complaints were significantly exaggerated, but both parties wanted the separation. Anna and William Wright's divorce was as transactional as their marriage. At least with the divorce Anna obtained what she had been given to expect. The timing of the separation is intriguing too. Frank was in his final year at school, and during 1885 it had become

sadly clear to Anna and her brothers and sisters that their father was dying. In Maginel's memoir there is a melancholic account of Richard Lloyd Jones's decline, how he became increasingly oblivious of the world around him.[42] With the imminent passing of the elder generation, it seems plausible that Anna felt there was no reason to maintain any pretence about the state of her marriage. The terms of the separation were negotiated with William by Anna's brothers. William would be free to walk away from any future responsibility for Anna and their children, provided he allowed Anna to take full ownership of the house in Madison – the house that Anna's brothers had, most likely, paid for. It was an arrangement that suited them both.

The last word on the marriage of William and Anna Wright has been deemed by some to be the memoir of Elizabeth Wright Heller, the youngest of Anna's stepchildren. Some of Wright's biographers have seized upon Lizzie's story as if it is the one true testament, when in reality it is the most tendentious of all. It will be recalled that Lizzie was sent to live with her late mother's sister when she reached puberty. Everything that she claims to remember about her life in the household took place between the ages of six, when Anna and William married, and twelve, when she was moved away, and her unpublished memoir, *The Story of My Life*, was written when Lizzie was in her early seventies.

Lizzie had grown up with her mother until she was nearly four years old, and then for the next two years, following her mother's death, with Grandma Holcomb, her mother's mother. She felt herself to be her father's favourite. While her two older brothers seemed to adapt to the change, for Lizzie the sudden arrival of Anna, a stranger, an intruder, was deeply unsettling. Anna died in 1923, years before Frank's autobiography was written. Her version of the events of that time will never be heard. Lizzie has no doubt where the blame lay: 'I am sure that I would have loved her if she had been kind to me or at all affectionate; for I was hungry for love, but as she failed me, I lavished more and more on father.' Lizzie took advantage of what she saw as her father's split loyalty: 'She had a terrible temper and seemed to make no effort to control it. She vented it upon me mostly because she was jealous of Father's affection for me, and the boys could keep out of her sight, but she wouldn't allow me to.' She also claimed to recall that her stepmother often 'beat her black and blue' while they were living in the house at McGregor, and that she 'threatened me with some terrible things, and especially if I should tell my father about her treatment'. She was around nine years old at that time. According to Lizzie, things got worse during their time at Pawtucket. Their first home there, the one that was too small for all the children, was split between the lower-ground and first floors of an apartment house. Someone else occupied the more salubrious upper-ground floor in between, 'surely one of the most unpleasant living arrangements that can be imagined', as Meryl Secrest has observed.[43] Lizzie recalls two incidents in particular. Once, in an outburst of rage, Anna threw a bowl of water over her. Hearing the commotion from his study two floors above, her father came down to defuse the situation. On the second occasion Lizzie claims that Anna threatened to 'put her eyes out' with a cooking fork. 'I believe she would have done so if she had dared to, she seemed so full of venom and hate. I screamed "Papa!" with all my might and he came running down and stopped her.' She then adds: 'I think those were the only two times when Father was home.'[44]

This last sentence holds an intriguing implication. It suggests that these two anecdotes may have been related to Lizzie by her father some years after the alleged events, and that they were not her own first-hand recollections. It also allows the reader to infer that there may have been other unrecalled events that took place in her father's absence. In his divorce testimony William drew attention to Anna's emotional instability. At times, he claimed, she would have spells of 'hysterics' after which she would retreat to her bed for a day or two to recover. Likewise Lizzie, '[did] not know whether her [stepmother's] mind was just right or not'. These remarks appear to allude again to Anna's struggle with epilepsy.

There is no reason to doubt Lizzie's feelings, or her testimony about a dysfunctional relationship with her stepmother. No reason to doubt, either, that corporal punishment was inflicted upon her, as was common at the time. Parts of her memoir do make for very uncomfortable reading, but for each allegation of Anna's cruelty there is an anecdote that shows her in a different light. During their journey to Pawtucket, when Anna was on her own with the children, Lizzie developed rheumatic fever, a fiercely painful immune disorder. Anna patiently nursed her through it over the course of several days until she recovered. Of all of the harrowing experiences that Lizzie recounts, it is her memory of this illness that seems the most convincing. It is also Anna who takes control of her education: 'Father was very busy and seldom had time to teach me, and she didn't like to have him teach me either.' There are suggestions in her story that Anna developed Lizzie's political and social attitudes through her education along the same progressive, emancipated lines as her own. When Lizzie was around sixteen and living with her Aunt Nellie and Uncle Albert, her uncle took exception to her independent attitude: 'in [Uncle Albert's] day girls were not supposed to make their own living, but that was just what I had always wanted to do.' When Lizzie made her views known, Uncle Albert 'whipped me with a buggy whip … If he had just talked to me a little I would have apologised readily, but that was not his way and he felt that he was right.' Lizzie managed to be quite sanguine about the assault: 'it just showed his peculiar ways.' Her stepmother was not forgiven so easily.[45]

Most of Lizzie's memoir concerns her adulthood and her life in farming. But the manuscript is bracketed at start and finish by repeated damaging accusations against her stepmother. The first page of the retyped manuscript has the subheading 'Begun Portland Oregon April 8th 1929'. But this seems likely to be untrue. She tells her story without further reference to this date, or to its significance. It is actually the sixty-fifth anniversary of her mother's death. If she really had begun to write her memoir on such a significant date, she would surely have mentioned her reason for doing so. There are other clues in the text that suggest that parts of it, at least, date from after 1933, and that these parts include the allegations against her stepmother. After several decades, it was during 1933 that she was reunited with her half-sister Jane and her half-brother Frank. Jane had been close to Lizzie during their childhoods. She had managed to track Lizzie down and had invited her to visit The Valley, where she and Frank were both back in residence, she in the little square house Tan-y-Deri on the hill near to the Romeo and Juliet Windmill, and Frank at his incomparable Taliesin.

If she had not known of it before, this was when Lizzie would have become aware of Frank's autobiography. When she read it Lizzie would, without question, have been appalled. Her father, a good, kind man, was not only dismissed as a fool and a failure, but accused of abandoning his family. Lizzie's memoir is an impassioned rebuttal of Frank's version of events. She could not deny the facts of William's unfulfilled ambitions, or their dysfunctional family life, but she could at least excuse her father of the blame. If she had to traduce her stepmother's reputation in order to restore her father's, as far as Lizzie was concerned that would only be fair:

> Being a stepmother is not an easy job by any means, and there was no money in it as there had been in school teaching, but she must have known that before she undertook it ... It was a different life from what she was used to, being much more work about it, and I fancy she did not like that very much, but she should have known there would be, and my father could not afford to keep help all the time.[46]

In her adulthood perhaps it really did seem to Lizzie that it was her stepmother who had been jealous of the attention that her father gave to her. The evidence tells a different story. The first decade of the marriage was a time of relentless hardship and humiliation for Anna. Life was little improved when they eventually settled in Madison. Lizzie had left the household by then. For his part, in his testimony to the divorce hearing, William Wright admitted that the marriage had been 'unhappy from the start'. The emotional vectors are not difficult to discern. Lizzie's sadness began, of course, with the death of her mother, and deepened with the awareness that her father could not replace her mother's love. When Anna was presented to her as a new mother, it only sharpened her sense of rejection. It would have seemed obvious to young Lizzie that it was her stepmother who stood between her and the love of her father. She may never have understood that her father expected to maintain an emotional distance from his children, that this was the norm for families of respectable English descent.

Lizzie was deeply hurt. It would be natural for her to hold her stepmother responsible and to fight against her, and it appears that she did. Elizabeth Wright Heller's *The Story of My Life* undoubtedly holds a grain of truth about Frank Lloyd Wright's childhood environment, but no more than Frank Lloyd Wright's own account does. We should read them together and accept that the truth is somewhere in between.

It is not an uncommon circumstance today, or at any time in the past, for a child to be raised entirely by his or her mother. Some, but not so many, children are brought up entirely by their fathers, and of course there is every gradation between. Frank Lloyd Wright's recent biographers have, for the most part, concluded that Frank's achievements must have been built on foundations laid by his father. They have inferred that his father had the dominant role in his upbringing simply because they were able to find out so little about his mother, and because what they believed they had learned about her cast her in an unflattering light. There is now compelling evidence that the conclusions drawn by those biographers were incorrect, and that Frank Lloyd Wright's own account of a childhood, in which his mother was the dominant influence and the greater intellectual presence in their household, was much closer to the truth.

There is a telling passage in the statement that Frank made to the rapacious journalists assembled for his Christmas morning press conference at Taliesin in 1911. He was trying to explain how he had felt that his own life had become detached from the lives of his wife and his children: 'Mrs. Wright wanted children, loved children and understood children. She had her life in them. She played with children and enjoyed them. But I found my life in my work.'[47] In these words, perhaps deliberately, Frank raised the echo of his own upbringing: a mother utterly absorbed and delighted by the wonders of childhood. A father whose instinct was to be remote from his children, who often took trouble to avoid them, and who found his greatest fulfilment in his music ∎

# 06 Anna Had Chosen an Englishman
## *Notes*

1    John Lloyd Wright, *My Father Who Is On Earth* (New York: Putnam, 1946).

2    Maginel Wright Barney, *The Valley of the God Almighty Joneses* (New York: Appleton Century, 1965).

3    Brendan Gill, *Many Masks: A Life of Frank Lloyd Wright* (London: Heinemann, 1988), p. 35.

4    Donald Leslie Johnson, *Frank Lloyd Wright: Early Years: Progressivism: Aesthetics: Cities* (Abingdon: Routledge, 2017), p. 81.

5    Paul Hendrickson, *Plagued by Fire: The Dreams and Furies of Frank Lloyd Wright* (London: Bodley Head, 2019), p. 456.

6    Robert Plomin, *Blueprint: How DNA Makes Us Who We Are* (London: Allen Lane, 2018).

7    Barney, *The Valley of the God Almighty Joneses*, p. 61.

8    Chester Lloyd Jones, *Youngest Son* (Madison WI: self-published, 1938), p. 61.

9    Barney, *The Valley of the God Almighty Joneses*, p. 61.

10   Harry E. Cole, *A Standard History of Sauk County Wisconsin* (Chicago: Lewis Publishing Co., 1918), p. 497.

11   Svea Adolphson, *A History of Albion Academy* (Beloit, WI: Rock County Rehabilitation Services Inc., 1976), pp. 6–8; speech delivered by Dr Jerome Head at the Albion Academy Historical Museum, 22 June 1969.

12   Adolphson, *A History of Albion Academy*, p. 13.

13   Adolphson, *A History of Albion Academy*, p. 23.

14   Adolphson, *A History of Albion Academy*, pp. 13–14, 37–44. Hannah's graduation class, p. 44.

15   *The Sabbath Recorder*, 21/9 (20 July 1865), 114.

16    *The Sabbath Recorder*, 20/8 (14 July 1864), 110.

17    Meryl Secrest, *Frank Lloyd Wright: A Biography* (Chicago: University of Chicago Press, 1998), p. 48.

18    Gill, *Many Masks*, pp. 40–1.

19    C. W. Butterfield, *History of Crawford and Richland Counties, Wisconsin* (Springfield IL: Union Publishing Company, 1884), p. 860.

20    Gill, *Many Masks*, p. 36.

21    Robert C. Twombley, *Frank Lloyd Wright: An Interpretive Biography* (New York: Harper Colophon, 1974), p. 4.

22    C.M. Langford, 'Barbarians at the Bar – Regulation of the Legal Profession through the Admission Process', *Hofstra Law Review*, 36 (2008), 1193–1224.

23    Twombley, *Frank Lloyd Wright: An Interpretive Biography*, p. 4.

24    Gill, *Many Masks*, p. 30.

25    Madison University, a Baptist College in Hamilton, New York, was renamed Colgate University in 1890. William Wright graduated in 1849. His biographical data can be seen in *Colgate University: A General Catalogue, 1819-1919*, series 19/4 (Hamilton, NY: Colgate University Press, 1919.), p. 58. The prospectus for the BA course can be seen in the *Madison University Catalogue 1848–49*, p. 20 (reference A1327, Special Collections and University Archives, Colgate University Libraries).

26    Barney, *The Valley of the God Almighty Joneses*, p. 57.

27    Butterfield, *History of Crawford and Richland Counties*, p. 860.

28    Butterfield, *History of Crawford and Richland Counties*, pp. 1171–2.

29    Thomas Graham (ed.), *Trilogy: Through Their Eyes* (Spring Green, WI: Unity Chapel Publications, 1986), p. 38.

30    Elizabeth Wright Heller, *The Story of My Life* (unpublished, typed manuscript, *c.*1933).

31    Anna's stepdaughter Elizabeth did not go to The Valley with the rest of the family. 'Grandmother Holcombe', Permelia's mother, had remained at Lone Rock, after she had moved there to keep house for her bereaved son-in-law, and Elizabeth was sent to stay with her until William was ready for his family to join him in Rhode Island

32    Elizabeth moved to Madison, aged nineteen, to live with her own family for around six months during 1879, so that she could take music lessons from her father. This was the last time that she lived with them.

33    Heller, *The Story of My Life*.

34    Twombley, *Frank Lloyd Wright: An Interpretive Biography*, p. 9.

35    '100th Anniversary – First Baptist Church of Weymouth' (1954), quoted in Twombley, *Frank Lloyd Wright: An Interpretive Biography*, p. 9.

36    Many sources cite Maginel's birth year as 1881. Maginel did use this date herself. However, the correct year of her birth is 1877

37    Secrest, *Frank Lloyd Wright: A Biography*, p. 57. Reference to a letter from Anna to Frank sent in 1887, FLW Foundation Index no. W02501000.

38    Mary J. Hamilton and David V. Mollenhoff, *Frank Lloyd Wright's Monona Terrace: The Enduring Power of a Civic Vision* (Madison: University of Wisconsin Press, 1999), p. 46.

39    Frank Lloyd Wright, *An Autobiography (Edition 1)* (New York: Longman, Green & Co., 1932), pp. 47–50.

40    T. S. Hines, 'The Madison Years: Records versus Recollections', *Journal of the Society of Architectural Historians*, 26/4 (December 1967).

41    H.A. Hartog, 'Marital Exits and Marital Expectations in Nineteenth Century America', *Georgetown Law Journal*, 80/95 (1991-2), 95–129.

42    Barney, *The Valley of the God Almighty Joneses*, p. 94–5.

43    Secrest, *Frank Lloyd Wright: A Biography*, p. 55.

44    Heller, *The Story of My Life*.

45    Heller, *The Story of My Life*.

46    Heller, *The Story of My Life*.

47    Ron McCrea, *Building Taliesin: Frank Lloyd Wright's Home of Love and Loss* (Madison: Wisconsin Historical Society Press, 2012), pp. 124–5.

# 7

# A Child's Garden

Frank Lloyd Wright had a problem when he sat down to dictate his autobiography. He needed it to be compelling: the inexorable rise of a natural-born genius, always being true to himself, brushing adversities and opponents aside to achieve spiritual and creative transcendence. The story had to begin from suitably propitious foundations that set the right mystical tone. But who really remembers much about their early infancy? Frank didn't. His story of his early childhood is vivid and inspirational. It has become as much a part of his identity as his architecture, but it is clear now that significant parts of it are fictional. His mother, he says, was determined that her son would be a great architect before he was born. She both wanted this and somehow sensed that it was predestined. 'The boy, she said, was to build

beautiful buildings. Faith in prenatal influences was strong in this prospective mother.' In anticipation of his birth, he says, his mother 'took ten full-page wood-engravings of the old English cathedrals from "Old England", a pictorial periodical ... had them framed simply in flat oak and hung upon the walls of the room that was to be her son's'.

Maginel also remembered her mother reading to her from *Old England*, a heavy, two-volume history book famous for its early coloured illustrations, published in London, in 1845, and probably acquired by her father.[1] Anna enjoyed the first part, which described Britain in the time of the Druids. Among the later pages there are indeed many images of cathedrals, but none is larger than a postcard and to have cut any out would have been deplorable.[2] Anna was a very committed Unitarian. Why would she hang pictures of Anglican cathedrals around her son's room? She didn't, and furthermore, when he was born, Frank became the sixth member of his family, all of whom were sharing a very small, single-storey house in Richland Center. It is not possible that he had a room of his own. Intriguingly, early in the 1980s a collection of pictures was found in the Taliesin archives, images of English cathedrals that had been cut from the pages of *Harper's Weekly*. They had been published between 1877 and 1881, when Frank was in junior high school.[3] Why the pages were cut out and kept isn't known, but it seems possible, at least, that these images were the basis of Frank's mythical anecdote. Unitarianism also has strong views on the idea of predestination. Like the Holy Trinity, it is regarded as a corrupt fallacy. Anna did not believe that Frank was predestined to be an architect. Once he moved away from home, Anna wrote frequently to him. Many of the letters survive, and none of them mentions that she planned or hoped that he would become an architect. One letter in particular, written on the morning of Frank's twentieth birthday, stands out:

*I got up early today as I did twenty years ago. You came to me about 8 o'clock. My beautiful baby, I used to call you. You have one year more to become a man and you can do it too. I hope you are settled ere this. Don't neglect to write to me for we are all very anxious about you ... Don't get discouraged. Things will turn around for you when you take things right.*[4]

Frank had been working as an apprentice architect in Chicago for around six months when his mother wrote this to him. If she was ever to mention architectural predestination, she would surely have done so in this letter, but in all of her letters to her son, Anna's overwhelming concern is that Frank is living a decent, moral life within his means. She shows little interest in how he is earning a living at all, only that he is conducting himself decently and mixing with the right kind of people, ideally the community around her brother Jenkin's church.

Frank's early childhood, according to his autobiography, was filled with his father's music.

*Father sometimes played on the piano far into the night and much of Beethoven and Bach the boy learned by heart as he lay listening. Living seemed a kind of 'listening' to him – then. Sometimes it was as though a door would open, and he could get the beautiful meaning quite clear. Then it would close and the meaning would be dim or far away. But always there was some meaning. And it was the boy's father who taught him to see a symphony as an edifice – of sound!*

This particular passage from *An Autobiography* has often excited Wright scholars into wishful sophistry. Robert Twombley says that Frank's father 'taught him the structural similarities between music and buildings'.[5] Donald L. Johnson speculates that it was through his father's music that Frank 'may have appreciated the inherent structure of art'.[6] According to Brendan Gill, 'William Wright may have been paraphrasing for his son's benefit Browning's then newly written poem 'Rabbi Ben Ezra' in which the relationship between music and architecture is explored.' An evocative picture indeed: not only is William able to use his music to teach his son about architecture, he does it through the medium of a mystical poem! This is another instance of

Gill being both overspeculative and bizarrely inaccurate. Browning's poem doesn't mention music or architecture at all.[7]

As a work of creative retrospection, the autobiography freed Frank to transpose any idea that may have occurred to him or come to his attention at any time in his life onto his account of his childhood experience. He had, for example, been a keen reader of Goethe since his late teens. It was Goethe who famously said, 'I call architecture frozen music.'[8] Frank often expatiated on Goethe's metaphor to support his belief that the eye could 'appreciate the expression of *harmonies in form, line and colour*'. In one of his earliest recorded talks, delivered at the Arts Institute of Chicago in 1900, he bemoaned the fact that architecture had no rules of harmony or construction equivalent to the 'harmony in tones' and the rhythms of music.[9] In his childhood, he would say, he had come to recognise Beethoven and Bach as the two great 'masters'. When he sat down to play his own piano, it was Bach or Beethoven that he turned to. His early devotion to them is partly explained by the fact that his repertoire was limited. His father was unable to teach him to read music – he played by ear only.

When he had young children of his own Frank's prized possession was a player-piano, a technological marvel of its time. Although it would soon be superseded by the phonograph, at the time it was the only apparatus that would produce convincing music without a player. Frank loved to keep it playing for hours while he worked at his drawing board. Much later in his career, the apprentices of the Taliesin Fellowship would carry out their daily labours in the fields around The Valley to the accompaniment of music played through a system of outdoor loudspeakers. In the evenings they would scrub the soil from under their fingernails, change into ballgowns and dinner jackets, and convene at the main house for dinner and musical entertainment.

In his thoughtful thesis on Frank Lloyd Wright, Norris K. Smith draws attention to the obvious limitations of the music and architecture metaphors:

*Architecture is the most essential of the arts. It is associated with the basic needs of human survival and its serves as the*

*primary symbol of those institutions by whose agency we are able to participate with one another as members of society. Music, on the other hand, is furthest removed from the word and the idea ... it makes no reference to anything that exists for us 'objectively' in our world. It provides those occasions when we are most wholly absorbed in the 'experience of experiencing'.* [10]

Smith is persuasive, but he misses something that Wright seems instinctively to have grasped in his approach to spatial arrangement. This is the fact that music and architecture both work with anticipation and realisation. You only need to hear a few beats in a bar to begin to anticipate how a rhythm will play out. Likewise the first experience of a building – usually the appearance of the exterior – will initiate expectations of the experience that will follow. The joy of music and of architecture comes from the unexpected, the degree to which the successive experiences diverge from, or conform to, instinctive expectations. Few experiences are as pleasurable as that of being drawn through tantalising thresholds into a succession of carefully composed, expressive spaces, whether they are the metaphorical spaces of music or the real spaces of architecture.

Music was indeed important to Frank Lloyd Wright, but it didn't make him an architect or meaningfully shape the architect that he became. Music was by far the most popular art form of the western frontier. It was shared by everyone in its many sacred and secular forms. When Frank spoke about music he used it as a gentle means of introducing his audience to his thoughts about architectural design, thoughts he knew were challenging. In his home life and in his working life he valued music for its socialising 'soft power', the way that it brought the people around him together in a shared pleasure. Unusually, his tastes became less conservative as he got older, reflecting the influence of the youngsters who surrounded him. In a 1932 article that was supposed to be about his favourite books, he said: 'the greatest literature, after all, is not words but notes. Bach, Handel, and Beethoven, Stravinsky, Scriabin, Debussy, and

sometimes the Negro spirituals and jazz. Music gives me more now.'[11] Wherever he lived, even in his New York hotel during the building of the Guggenheim Museum, he would ensure that a piano was near to hand. Music became part of his persona, and he knew how to use it to his advantage.

After his parents' divorce Frank's musical father left their Madison home with his mahogany secretary desk, his violins and very little else.[12] The rest of the furniture he left behind, including the piano and his woodworking bench. If Frank's autobiography is to be believed, there might also have been an unusual table somewhere among the furnishings, a small, low table marked on top with a grid of one-inch squares. This table was one of the essential components of the Kindergarten teaching method invented in the 1840s by the German educationalist and philosopher Friedrich Fröbel. The surface was used for setting out the Fröbel 'gifts': patterns of coloured paper, wooden blocks and sticks, all in accord with carefully planned developmental steps.

When Fröbel first formalised his ideas about the education of young children he must have foreseen its revolutionary implications. He had been taught by another radical pedagogue, Johan Pestalozzi, and Pestalozzi had taken his inspiration directly from Jean-Jacques Rousseau, the author of *Social Contract* and the unwitting philosophical catalyst of the French Revolution.[13] Rousseau believed that young children should be given the freedom to learn at their own pace and in the way that most suited their instincts: 'Love childhood, indulge its sports, its pleasures, its delightful instincts.'[14] Most significantly, Rousseau believed that young children could learn everything that they needed to know from the natural world that surrounded them. This idea was a practical expression of Rousseau's broader preoccupation with the state of modern man, how depleted modern lives had become compared with those of man's ancient ancestors. His evocation of the nobility and freedom of the lives of primitive peoples became one of the dominant themes of the Romantic movement in the arts, a fundamental influence, as we have already seen, on Iolo Morganwg, and on Coleridge and Wordsworth, Thomas Carlyle and the Priestley circle, and an irritant to the

European political establishment. Naturally, it also appealed hugely to Unitarian thinkers like those in Cardiganshire, and provided the impetus for their own heterodox approach to childhood education.

When they first read about it, the Fröbel Kindergarten method seemed very familiar to Anna Wright and to her sisters Jane and Ellen Lloyd Jones. As Jane recalled, 'When I took up the study of early child development as voiced by Fröbel, I was astonished to find how very familiar the philosophy seemed. It was so nearly what I was brought up on.'[15]

According to his autobiography the Fröbel 'gifts' stimulated the first awakening of young Frank's architectural impulse: 'The smooth shapely maple blocks with which to build, the sense of which never afterwards leaves the fingers: so *form* became *feeling* ... What shapes they made naturally if only you would let them!'[16] In this short passage of his autobiography Frank set in motion an entire side-industry of academic study and merchandising, enthralled by the idea that a simple set of educational toys had the power to unlock creative genius. This is all the more remarkable in the present day, given that it is now becoming increasingly clear that Frank's story about his Kindergarten training is another of his fictions.

It should really have been obvious from the outset that something about Frank's story was incongruous. He recalls that his mother first became aware of the Kindergarten method on a visit to the International Centennial Exhibition at Philadelphia in 1876. The Philadelphia Exhibition was a typically vast undertaking, presenting many thousands of American and international exhibitors. Among them were at least six different Kindergarten exhibits, two of which had their own small buildings providing demonstration classes.[17] If it was really the case that Anna 'discovered' Fröbel in the summer of 1876, and then introduced it to her son, Frank would have been nine years old when he first picked up a maple block. The Kindergarten method was geared to the development of children aged from four to six. Frank would have been long past the stage at which the 'gifts' would have had a learning impact sufficient to provide the creative epiphany he claimed to recall. Frank added another layer of

confusion to the story by claiming that he had been born in 1869. This would have made him only seven in 1876, a little more plausible perhaps, but still really too old for Kindergarten. He was fully aware of this himself. In his 1957 retrospective, *A Testament*, he further embellished the myth, claiming that he started Kindergarten at the age of three when his family was living in Weymouth.[18] They had moved there in 1874 when he was seven years old (Pl. 35).

Notwithstanding the foregoing, beginning in 1958 with the first published biographical study, Grant Manson's *Frank Lloyd Wright to 1910: The First Golden Age*, the Kindergarten story has been put forward as the most convincing stimulus of his genius. Manson observed,

> There was little direct imitation of nature; natural objects were translated into the crispness of geometry. At the same time the child was encouraged to see that geometric forms underlie all natural manifestations ... Letting his mind run free in the pleasantly ordered world of the abstract, Fröbel's child could produce unlimited designs that were independent of 'nature' in the banal Victorian sense. It was an enormous advantage.[19]

As evidence, Manson provided some illustrations of wooden blocks arranged to resemble the basic forms of some of Wright's early buildings. Many other scholars have devoted significant thinking time to the same misconception.[20]

Before rejecting the story completely, it would be reasonable to ask whether Anna might have adopted the Fröbel method *before* 1876, in which case Frank might be recalling an experience from earlier in his childhood. In the years before her marriage, Anna devoted herself to progressive education and to liberal religion. Fröbel had the same preoccupations. Anna was an intensive reader of journals and books, and a diligent follower of domestic and world events. The Unitarian newspaper *The Christian Examiner* first carried an account of Fröbel's Kindergarten theory in 1859, when Anna was a twenty-one-year-old teacher living at the River Farms in Spring Green with her parents. She was deeply absorbed in Transcendentalist ideas, so there

can be little doubt that Anna would also have been familiar with the work of Elizabeth Palmer Peabody. Peabody was a Unitarian and a Transcendentalist, and she had been taught by Emerson himself. In 1860 she established America's first English-language Kindergarten in a prosperous Boston suburb.[21] She was a highly effective proponent of the Kindergarten mission, through demonstrations, lectures and several influential books.[22]

The established approach to infant education in America at the time was predicated on the Calvinist baseline: man was born in sin, and therefore depravity was innate in young children. An eternity of damnation awaited any child whose will could not be broken.'Here begin; here interpose your parental authority: accustom him to be denied, and to take it patiently; habituate him to submit his will to yours, and to take pleasure in gratifying you as well as himself.'[23] The young Anna would have found much that was loathsome in this approach, and much to be welcomed in Peabody's account of the Fröbel method. She was not only already inclined to teach in a similar, natural way, but had been raised that way herself. Fröbel's Kindergarten method effectively codified the informal Unitarian approach. If the circumstances had been different, the Fröbel method could have provided a good teaching vehicle for Anna, but she had already committed herself to the progressive pedagogy of Albion Academy – and then she consented to marry William Wright, and cut herself off from her teaching career.

The 'gifts' were perhaps a distraction from the more significant agenda of Fröbel's Kindergarten, the philosophy that must have appealed to Anna, which was that young children should be allowed to learn at their own pace and in their own way, with the teacher as their friend, not their governor. As Elizabeth Peabody put it,

*Any child can learn anything if time and opportunity is given to go step by step ... Every degree of knowledge must be practically used as soon as attained. It then becomes a power; makes the child a power in Nature and prepares him, when his spirit shall come into union with the God of Nature.*[24]

The model Kindergarten comprised two rooms and a garden. Whenever the weather allowed, activities would take place outdoors in the garden. Provided it was moderated and secure, Nature was the ideal classroom. Nature with a capital 'N', just as Iolo Morganwg had expressed it, and just as Frank would choose to express it, in the fullness of time.

Despite her success at generating interest, Elizabeth Peabody's own Boston Kindergarten couldn't consistently attract the number of children that it needed. The problem was her inability to convince enough well-to-do parents to take the risk of exposing their young children to an experimental process. After seven indifferent years she packed the 'gifts' away for the last time.[25] It was not until the early 1870s that momentum gathered behind the Kindergarten movement, and the transformation began in St Louis, Missouri, far away from the privileged suburbs of Peabody's Boston. Susan Blow's Kindergarten was different from Peabody's in two significant ways: firstly, it was public, requiring no fees and actively recruiting children from working-class families; secondly it was sceptical of Peabody's romantic idealism and her Transcendentalist fixation with spiritual individualism. Susan Blow and her patron, William Torrey Harris, had come to the Kindergarten via the secular Idealism of Georg Hegel, and they defined their approach as 'symbolic education'.[26] Notwithstanding their philosophical differences, it was the open public access to Susan Blow's St Louis system that brought about the rapid growth Peabody had failed to achieve. Blow's success led to a schism. This was why there were two separate Kindergarten buildings at the Philadelphia Centennial Exhibition: one was organised by Peabody and the other by Susan Blow, at which Blow herself presented demonstration classes (Pl. 36).

Family memoirs confirm Frank's story that his mother visited the Philadelphia Centennial Exhibition in 1876. She went there with her sisters Jane and Ellen, both by then experienced senior teachers. In the same archive that held the fading magazine prints of English cathedrals, there is a small box that contains a specimen of one of the coloured paper 'gifts' and a catalogue of *Kindergarten*

Pl. 36. A demonstration Kindergarten class with visitors watching at the rear. The exhibit was organised by Elizabeth Palmer Peabody.
From *Frank Leslie's Illustrated Historical Register of the Centennial Exposition 1876*, p. 118.

*Gifts and Occupational Material* that was published by E. Steiger and Co. of New York in May 1876.[27] The publisher had a stand in the main exhibition building.[28] Whatever they may have known about the Kindergarten method before, the products and the demonstrations they saw there evidently made a strong impression. After the exhibition, Frank recalled: 'Mother would go to Boston, take lessons of a teacher of the Fröbel method and come home to teach the children.' That teacher was Matilda Kreige, a German migrant who had been trained by Fröbel's widow, and who had been attracted to Boston by Peabody's initiatives.[29] Most of her students were mothers who wanted to teach their own children at home, avoiding the risk of handing them over to others. For their convenience Kreige condensed the basic two-year training into a seven-month crash course.[30] While Anna was attending Kreige's classes in Boston, her sister Jane (Jennie) moved

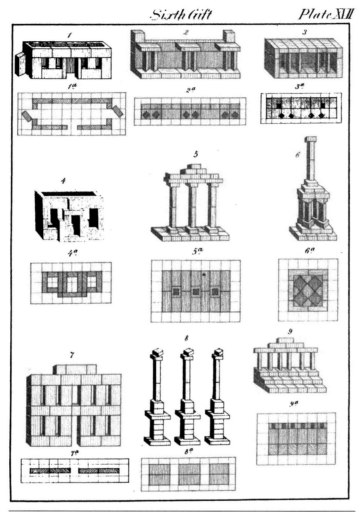

Pl. 37. 'Gift Six' from *Paradise of Childhood*, Milton Bradley, 1869. This illustration shows that architectural imagination was specifically encouraged in the Kindergarten curriculum.

whereas the limited training that Anna received was in the spiritually orientated, more authentic Fröbel method, as advocated by Elizabeth Peabody. By accident or by design this seems to reflect a recognisable difference in the outlook of the two sisters that was evident in other aspects of their lives.

To whatever extent the Kindergarten method made an impression on the young Frank, however, it was second-hand. Anna was interested in the method for its own sake, to satisfy her own intense curiosity and because it chimed so harmoniously with her Unitarian faith. She could have used it at home with Maginel, who would have been ready to start Kindergarten in 1880 when she was three years old. Frank was at junior high school level by then. Frank would also have been aware of his Aunt Jane's expertise: she and her sister Ellen both adored him. Frank's detailed, poetic description of the Fröbel 'gifts' in his autobiography could reflect a childhood memory. They may have been there in the background of his home life in Weymouth and in Madison, but they didn't play a part in his own education. As Edgar Kaufmann Jr correctly observed, 'One needs to forget Wright's family heritage, especially the strong Unitarian doctrine, if Fröbel is to be the one responsible for rousing the nine year-old boy's "powers of reason" and "sense of the harmony and order of God".[31] Frank didn't mention Kindergarten or write about it at all until 1901, by which time he was well established as a Chicago architect with a house full of his own children – a house from which his wife Kitty ran her own Kindergarten, under Anna's guidance. Through his mother and his aunts he would have known from his childhood years about Fröbel and about the kinship of Unitarian practice and Kindergarten philosophy, but it was almost certainly in Kitty's Kindergarten that Frank really became absorbed in the abstract, suggestive properties of the Fröbel 'gifts'[32] (Pl. 37).

The first formal education that Frank really could remember was at the private school run by a Miss Williams, in Weymouth, Massachusetts. The family had moved there a few months after his seventh birthday, so he was ready to start as a first-grade 'Abecedarian' as soon as

to St Louis, Missouri, to study the alternative Hegelian Kindergarten method with Susan Blow herself, a course that she completed in 1878. As it transpired then, the professional training that Frank's Aunt Jane received was in the refined psychological approach of Susan Blow, they had settled. His account of the school is dismissive. He shared his classroom with, 'the usual Snobbyists and Goodyites' and 'what he was taught in school made not the slightest impression that can be remembered as of any consequence.'[33] Apart from disagreeable classmates, there were other reasons why school might make a limited impression. The normal school year lasted only 132 days, and in most schools the 'day' was only five hours, from nine o'clock until two.[34] This left plenty of time for his mother's schooling, an education that was solely for him, and so much more enveloping. It allowed time, also, for his father's music lessons and for lessons in painting, provided by Miss Landers, a friend of his mother's. There is no mention before this, in his autobiography, of Frank having any graphic talent, and he was later disparaging of Miss Landers's approach: it was 'buckeye' painting, sentimental, kitsch. This type of painting was popular, however, and it had the potential to yield a reasonable living. It is, perhaps, the first indication that Anna may have suspected that visual art could provide her son with future opportunities.

When they moved into the house on the Madison lakeshore Frank enrolled in the seventh grade at the Second Ward School, just a few doors along the road, where his Aunt Jane had been appointed Principal. Jane's new post at the school and the Wright family's move to their new house are obviously connected. It seems likely that Aunt Jane lived with the Wrights while she was teaching so nearby. This was soon after she had completed her Kindergarten training in St Louis. It suggests that Jane was expecting to pursue her professional career in Madison for some time. It would have suited Frank, who of course benefited from the favour of his Aunt. But it was not to be: within two years she had progressed to a more auspicious role, as Head of Kindergarten Training in the city of St Paul, Minnesota, passing on to new teachers what she had only recently been taught by Susan Blow.

The Unitarian congregation in Madison met on Sundays at the city synagogue, near the domed Capitol building, a mile from the Wrights' home (Pl. 34).

Frank attended Sunday School there, following a curriculum that had been created by his Uncle Jenkin, which introduced the children to all of the world's major faiths, including Islam, Hinduism and Buddhism.[35] Frank moved up to Madison High School in 1882, when he was fifteen. The only records of his time there relate to the months from October 1884 to March 1885, his final year. They show that he achieved both 'good' and 'poor' marks in physics and poor to average marks in algebra, which resulted in his being 'put back'. In botany and rhetoric he managed an average score again. His parents' divorce was concluded during the Easter recess. There is no evidence that he went back to school for the final semester or that he graduated. One of the few vivid memories of his time at High School was traumatic. Just after lunch on 8 November 1883 the school shook to a thunderous crash. Frank joined the crowd that ran to the source of the noise. A new wing of the State Capitol building had been nearing completion, but columns in the centre had collapsed into the basement, bringing the building down. He watched for hours as the dead and injured construction workers were pulled from the wreckage. Frank reflected on the disaster for his autobiography decades later, 'The horror of the scene has never entirely left his consciousness and remains to prompt him to this day.'

Frank hoped that readers of his memoir would picture him as a sensitive and solitary young idealist, inclined to creative reverie, unconcerned with the mundanities of formal education and uninterested in making friends with other boys. In truth he really did have little in common with his classmates. His upbringing certainly differentiated him – the books he read, the way that he dressed, even the way that he wore his hair in long curls, an affectation that earned him the nickname 'Shaggy': all encouraged by his mother, all intended to set him apart. More significantly his mother had raised him to think differently, to question all that he was told and to avoid following the crowd, because the crowd was generally wrong. But he was certainly not a 'loner'; in fact, quite the opposite. Throughout his life he couldn't bear to be alone. His home life was energetic and boisterous, often fraught but also sometimes joyous. He liked nothing more than conviviality, provided he was its focus. He was not a loner, but he was an outsider, an instinctive nonconformist whose disengagement and distrust of authority are clearly evident in his lack of educational attainment.

As an outsider he was drawn to other outsiders. His one great boyhood friend had been disabled by poliomyelitis and was bullied by other boys at the school. Frank was inevitably drawn to him. He first befriended Robie Lamp when they were aged fourteen, when Frank intervened to rescue Robie from his tormentors.[36] He picked Robie up, consoled him and retrieved his crutches. Soon after, Maginel recalled, Robie was in their house almost as much as he was in his own. Frank recalls that 'both boys had a passion for invention'. Frank's father had an instrument workshop in the basement of the house, but Frank and Robie spent more time there than William did, building cross-bows, kites and sledges. As they grew older their attention shifted to a printing press. They used it to print visiting cards for friends, taking great pleasure in the technicalities of designing, composing and setting the type. In her memoir Maginel recalled 'trespassing' into her brother's room while he was away at The Valley:

> There was an odour of printer's ink, oil paints, shellac and turpentine ... a printing press and piles of visiting cards. Stock cards with sprays of flowers, some already printed with the names of girl friends ... there were blocks of paper, coloured inks and pencils.

Also, prominently hung were the 'buckeye' paintings that Frank had made with Miss Landers in Weymouth, the paintings that he dismissed as 'indubitably crime'.[37]

It wasn't until 1967 that the Wright scholar Thomas Hines tracked down Frank's dismal record at Madison High School. The grades are at least consistent with Frank's retrospective account:

> But of the schooling itself? Nothing he can remember! Except colorful experiences that had nothing academic

about them ... What became of it? What did it contribute to this consciousness-of-existence that is the boy? ... It may not have been positively harmful. It is difficult for one to say.[38]

It is clear that, even in his high school years, it was still Anna who guided his learning. Among the books that he recalls reading with her are Hans Brinker, a popular story about ice skating, works of Jules Verne and, most significantly, The Arabian Nights.[39] When his mother wasn't looking, he also revelled in the wild-west stories of the 'Nickel Library', books of only thirty-two pages that sold for five cents a copy.[40] The list of adventurous fictional entertainments accentuates the incongruity of the two other books that he claims to have read at the same time: Wilhelm Meister's Apprenticeship, Goethe's second novel, and Seven Lamps of Architecture, Ruskin's polemical and densely aphoristic study of gothic archetypes. Wilhelm Meister's Apprenticeship is, at least, a work of fiction. It concerns the escape of the central character from the threat of an empty bourgeois existence into a life of bohemian artistic expression and spiritual self-realisation. It is a complex book in which narrative and philosophical threads wander loosely, many remaining untied at the conclusion, and it was a favourite of the Transcendentalists, who found Goethe's preoccupations so similar to their own. According to Emerson, 'no book of [the nineteenth] century can compare with Wilhelm Meister in its delicious sweetness.' It is likely that Anna would have had a copy of Wilhelm Meister, either in German or in Carlyle's translation, but it is quite a different prospect from The Terror of Dead Man's Gulch. One might also ask why the Arabian Nights, rather than James Fenimore Cooper, Poe or Mark Twain? Again, there is a connection with Anna's preoccupations with the primitivism of Rousseau, with the 'all souls' liberalism of the Unitarians, as reflected by Uncle Jenkin's Sunday School curriculum, and with the Transcendentalists of Boston. Emerson's essays and poems in particular are peppered with references to Middle Eastern philosophy and literature. Wordsworth was another great advocate of the *Arabian Nights*.[41] Anna read it with all of her children: *The Arabian Nights* was also a favourite of her stepdaughter Lizzie.[42] The adventures of Aladdin would prove to be a surprisingly persistent influence on Frank's architectural career in a way that perhaps only childhood inspiration can be. As regards Ruskin and Goethe, it is much more likely that Frank came to them later in his life, but they serve, at this early stage in his autobiography, as symbols of his own devotion to Unitarian and Transcendentalist doctrine, of his admiration for his mother and, not least, of his intellectual pretensions.

Surprisingly, he makes no mention of reading Emerson during his adolescence, in essay or verse, which he surely did, or of reading the other leading Transcendentalist poets, Longfellow, Lowell, Whitman or Thoreau. Frank recalled that the Joneses were 'uncomfortable' with Thoreau, because he, 'seemed too smart'.[43] Thoreau's reputation was established by his long essay *Walden*. This is the account of a two-year experiment in which the author attempted to live on his own in the wilderness, in a shack that he built himself, and eating only the food that he could grow or catch. Thoreau's intention was to develop the sense of connection to nature and the self-reliance that the Transcendentalists eulogised. It is beautifully written, elegiac and richly visual. It is easy to understand why Frank would have been captivated, and how he might have imagined a similar adventure of his own. But Thoreau built his retreat in woodland at the edge of Walden Pond, just two miles from the centre of the academic enclave of Concord, Massachusetts, hometown of Ralph Waldo Emerson. He wasn't in the wilderness at all, and was never in any danger. It is not difficult to imagine how *Walden* might have come across to readers like Anna, her brothers and sisters, people who had truly lived the experience of self-reliant toil and, in the early years, the constant fear of starvation. Perhaps Thoreau was another enthusiasm that Frank kept to himself.

There is another striking passage in *Walden* that is echoed in Frank Lloyd Wright's autobiography. Thoreau describes a path that he made through deep snow from his hut to the highway, 'about a half mile long [which] might have been represented by a meandering dotted

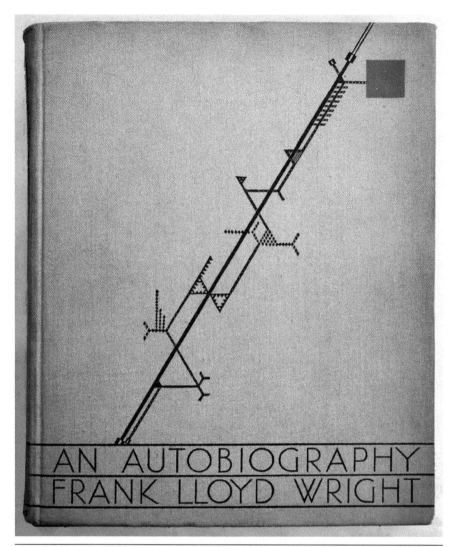

Pl. 38. 'The zig-zag line of a hundred tacks.' The cover that Frank designed for his 1932 autobiography represents his erratic path in the snow superimposed on the broad straight path of his Uncle John.

line, with wide intervals between the dots'. He also, 'frequently tramped … through the deepest snow to keep an appointment with a beech tree or a yellow birch or an old acquaintance among the pines'.[44] There is also a memorable line in Emerson's essay *Self Reliance*: 'The voyage of the best ship is a zig-zag line of a hundred tacks.' The front cover of the 1932 edition of Frank's autobiography bears a striking abstract graphic (Pl. 38).

A bold, straight diagonal runs from bottom left to top right and, overlying it, an arrangement of dotted lines that zig-zag across the bold straight line with occasional pauses and diversions. At the top right the dotted line leads to a red square, Frank Lloyd Wright's insignia, alongside, but separated from the bold diagonal. The significance of the image becomes apparent in the 'Prelude', an episode that precedes the body of the autobiography. Frank, as a nine-year-old, walks hand in hand with his Uncle John up a snowy hillside in The Valley. Freeing himself from his uncle's hold, he picks his way back and forth across the hillside, stopping intermittently to pull dried stems of weeds from the snow. When they reach the top they both look down at the tracks they have made. Uncle John's are straight, direct. Frank's are, 'wavering, searching ... embroidering the straight one like some free, engaging vine'. Wordlessly, with, 'gentle reproof', Uncle John looks down at Frank's erratic trail, and at the bunch of dry weeds in his hand. Frank feels ashamed: 'Uncle John's meaning was plain - NEITHER TO THE RIGHT NOR TO THE LEFT - BUT STRAIGHT IS THE WAY ... the boy was troubled. Something was left out.'[45]

The 'Prelude' sets the tone for *An Autobiography*, and establishes the character that Frank aspires to inhabit: that of a boy who, from his early childhood, is deeply sensitive to nature and at the same time a helpless transgressor within a family of radical Dissenters. Even if a nine-year-old had been alive to the symbolism of the moment, it seems unlikely that it would have struck so hard as to resonate within him half a century later. In the winter of 1876, his ninth year, he was living in Massachusetts, over a thousand miles from The Valley. Did it really happen? It is not important that it did, or did not.

The prologue to Maginel's memoir, *The Valley of the God Almighty Joneses*, recounts a visit that she made to see her brother at his hotel in New York, while the Guggenheim Museum was under construction. Frank was around ninety years old. While reminiscing, Frank exclaims:

> *'Uncle James! Now there was a man! ... You were only a baby – you don't remember the day Uncle James came to Madison in the wagon to get me. A summer's work on the farm! If I'd known what was in store for me I'd have lashed myself to the bannisters!'*

> *'But you loved it, Frank',*

Maginel reminds him.

> *'After a while I did, I suppose; not at first. After a while The Valley taught me everything. And Uncle James was responsible.'*

> *'Mother too'.*

Maginel reminds him again.

> *'Yes. sometimes I hated her for it, that first summer. I didn't know when I was lucky.'*[46] ∎

# 07

## A Child's Garden
### *Notes*

1    Maginel Wright Barney, *The Valley of the God Almighty Joneses* (New York: Appleton Century, 1965), p. 63.

2    Charles Knight, *Old England, A Pictorial Museum of Regal, Ecclesiastical, Baronial, Municipal and Popular Antiquities* (London: Charles Knight & Co., 1845).

3    E. Kaufmann Jr, 'Frank Lloyd Wright's Mementos of Childhood', *Journal of the Society of Architectural Historians*, 41/3 (October 1982), 232–7.

4    Letter from Anna Lloyd Wright to Frank Lloyd Wright, 8 June 1887. Frank Lloyd Wright Foundation Ref. W025A010000.

5    Robert C. Twombley, *Frank Lloyd Wright: An Interpretive Biography* (New York: Harper Colophon, 1974), p. 5.

6    Donald Leslie Johnson, *Frank Lloyd Wright: Early Years: Progressivism: Aesthetics: Cities* (Abingdon: Routledge, 2017), p. 44.

7    Brendan Gill, *Many Masks: A Life of Frank Lloyd Wright* (London: Heinemann, 1988), p. 35. 'Rabbi Ben Ezra' was first published in 1864 in Robert Browning's collection *Dramatis Personae* (London: Chapman and Hall), p. 87. Gill may have been thinking of 'Abt Vogler', a different poem from the same Browning collection. The poem, about the composer Vogler, does make metaphorical use of a few architectural terms, but to suggest that it played any part in William Wright's tutelage of his son is fantasy.

8    John Oxenford (translator), *Conversations of Goethe with Eckermann and Soret* (London: Smith, Elder and Co., 1850), p. 146. The original source of the statement that 'architecture is frozen music' continues to be debated. Some credit the contemporary German philosopher Friedrich von Schelling.

9    F. L. Wright, 'A Philosophy of Fine Art' (1900), in B. B. Pfeiffer (ed.), *Frank Lloyd Wright Collected Writings*, vol. 1: *1894–1930* (New York: Random House, 1992), p. 41.

10      Norris K. Smith, *Frank Lloyd Wright: A Study in Architectural Content* (Englewood Cliffs, NJ: Prentice Hall Inc., 1966), pp. 50-2.

11      F. L. Wright, 'Books That Have Meant the Most to Me', *Scholastic Magazine* (September 1932), in B. B. Pfeiffer (ed.), *Frank Lloyd Wright Collected Writings*, vol. 3: *1931-1939* -(New York: Random House, 1992).

12      Elizabeth Wright Heller, *The Story of My Life* (unpublished, typed manuscript, c.1933).

13      Pestalozzi was not a man to observe from the margins. He publicly argued on Rousseau's behalf when the Swiss establishment wanted him imprisoned, and sacrificed his legal career as a consequence.

14      M. Silber, 'From Seed to Mighty Tree: Susan Blow and the development of the American Kindergarten movement' (unpublished BA Honours thesis, Washington University in St Louis, 2012), 12.

15      Thomas E. Graham (ed.), *Trilogy: Through Their Eyes* (Spring Green WI: Unity Chapel Publications, 1986), p. 34.

16      F. L. Wright, *An Autobiography (Edition 1)* (New York: Longman, Green & Co., 1932), p. 11.

17      *Official Catalogue of the U.S. International Exhibition 1876* (Philadelphia: Centennial Catalogue Co., 1876).

18      Frank Lloyd Wright, *A Testament* (New York: Horizon Press, 1957), p. 19.

19      Grant Carpenter Manson, *Frank Lloyd Wright to 1910: The First Golden Age* (New York: Van Nostrand Reinhold Co.,1958), pp. 5-10.

20      E. Kaufmann Jr, 'Form Became Feeling: A New View of Fröbel and Wright', *Journal of the Society of Architectural Historians*, 40/2 (May 1981), 130-7.

21      The first American Kindergarten was a German-language school opened in 1856. By extraordinary coincidence it was located in Watertown, Wisconsin, just a few miles from the Jones family farm in Ixonia. Despite their close proximity, it seems unlikely that Anna would have been aware of it. At this early stage, the life of each immigrant group was conducted largely in isolation from others.

22      *Moral Culture of Infancy and Kindergarten Guide* (1864), *Kindergarten Culture* (1870), *The Kindergarten in Italy* (1872). Founder and editor of the journal *Kindergarten Messenger* (1873-5).

23      Michael S. Shapiro, *Child's Garden: The Kindergarten Movement from Fröbel to Dewey* (University Park: Penn State University Press,1983), p. 3.

24      Elizabeth Palmer Peabody and M. T. Peabody-Mann, *Moral Culture of Infancy and Kindergarten Guide* (Boston: T. O. H. P. Burnham, 1864), p. 104.

25      Silber, 'From Seed to Mighty Tree', p. 31.

26      Shapiro, *Child's Garden*, p. 3.

27      Kaufmann, 'Frank Lloyd Wright's Mementos of Childhood'.

28      *Official Catalogue of the U.S. International Exhibition 1876*.

29      C. M. Muelle, 'The History of Kindergarten: From Germany to the United States', paper for South Florida Education Research Conference, Florida International University, 2013.

30      The Fröbel 'gifts' were made available, to those that could afford them, from the early 1870s. Milton Bradley, a Boston-based toy manufacturer, had seen Elizabeth Peabody's Kindergarten in action and had been impressed, to the extent that he published his own book on the subject in 1869, *The Paradise of Childhood*. This was the first publication to illustrate all of the 'gifts'.

31      Kaufmann, 'Form Became Feeling'. The quotes within the quote are from Richard MacCormac, the distinguished English architect, who devoted a significant amount of effort into 'proving' the influence of the Fröbel Gifts on Frank Lloyd Wright's architecture.

32      Johnson, *Frank Lloyd Wright: Early Years: Progressivism: Aesthetics: Cities*, p. 46.

33      F. L. Wright, *An Autobiography (Edition 1)*, pp. 12-13.

34      Thomas D. Snyder (ed.), *120 Years of American Education – A Statistical Portrait* (Washington, DC: National Centre for Education Statistics, 1993), p. 27.

35      Mary J. Hamilton and David V. Mollenhoff, *Frank Lloyd Wright's Monona Terrace: The Enduring Power of a Civic Vision* (Madison: University of Wisconsin Press, 1999), p. 50.

36      Robert Lamp, born 1867, Wisconsin State Census 1905.

37      Barney, *The Valley of the God Almighty Joneses*, p. 75.

38      F. L. Wright, *An Autobiography (Edition 1)*, p. 13.

39     This was almost certainly the 1811 Jonathan Scott English translation of Antoine Galland's 1717 French version, the first into a European language. Later English translations used the more correct title *One Thousand and One Nights*.

40     Published from 1877 by the Pictorial Printing Company of Chicago.

41     Wordsworth wrote enthusiastically about the *Arabian Nights* in the Fifth Book of *The Prelude*, published in 1805.

42     Heller, *The Story of My Life*.

43     F. L. Wright, *An Autobiography (Edition 1)*, p. 15.

44     Henry D. Thoreau, 'Walden', in J. W. Krutch (ed.), *Walden and Other Writings by Henry David Thoreau* (New York: Bantam Classic Edition, 1981), p. 301.

45     F. L. Wright, *An Autobiography (Edition 1)*, pp. 1–2.

46     Barney, *The Valley of the God Almighty Joneses*, p. 13.

# 8

# The Book of Creation

## Early Spring 1878. The Valley, Wyoming Township, Iowa County, Wisconsin

Two hours before dawn. In his attic space above the living room, eleven-year-old Frank was woken by a loud clanging on the stovepipe, then a muffled shout from his Uncle James (Pl. 39 and Pl. 40). Four o'clock, time to get up and see to the milking. Fifty years later, when he was dictating his autobiography, his memory of the routine that followed is clear. Unlike his 'Prelude' and many other episodes of his childhood memoir, it is also entirely convincing. Milking the cows until his hands

ached and learning quickly which of them will try to crush him against the side of the stall, then returning to the house for a breakfast of fried pork and potatoes. After breakfast, feeding the calves, then working in the sawmill. A heavy lunch of boiled beef and vegetables followed by a long afternoon of fence-building. Then at twilight a supper, which was the same as the breakfast he had eaten at daybreak, followed by the evening milking of the cows.

> In bed about half-past seven, too tired to move. Again the outrageous banging on the stovepipe, almost before he had really fallen asleep. It had begun – this business of 'adding tired to tired, and adding it again'.

Frank struggled during his first summer at The Valley. He was disgusted by his sweat-soiled clothes that, 'stayed stiff until he limbered them up by working in them'. He was appalled by the extremes, the smells of the animals, the relentless mucking-out, the bloodiness of calving and slaughter. At the same time he was thrilled by the dynamism and exuberance of his Uncle James, a man who, in every physical and emotional attribute, was almost mockingly divergent from his own father; a man who was so good at everything he did that 'others liked to stop and watch him do it'.

The Valley was not a place of unremitting toil. Sunday was a rest day, for the male family members at least. There were occasional picnics, led by Uncle Thomas, and at the close of August the great team effort of harvest was fuelled by extravagant outdoor feasting, followed in the evening by music and song:

> there would be 'Esteddvod' then and there ... All grown ups and children too would have something or other to speak or sing ... But the hymn singing was the most satisfying feature of the day.[1]

These occasions were bilingual, the younger generation, Frank included, was more likely to use English, and the adults just as likely to use Welsh. Even several years later, when Maginel began to spend summers in The Valley, she recalled that Welsh was often used by her mother, aunts and uncles. In Frank's first summer, and over the years that followed, it would have been a regular part of the soundscape. Frank must have had some engagement with the language himself, even if it would be lost to him later. In the evenings, at his Uncle James's home, the custom was to read aloud and be read to, just as it had been for the generation before. Based on the testimony of Maginel and Aunt Jane, this included remnants of folklore that had originally been passed on orally in Welsh by Mallie to her sons and daughters. The consolation of his uncles and aunts carried him through the months until September, and his return to the sophistication of Madison. But something important had changed for him in that first Valley summer of 1878. He'd been part of a powerful team, a large and tight-knit family, the Lloyd Jones *teulu*; he'd been given responsibility, a kind of tethered freedom that he had never known, and he'd been enraptured by the brilliance of nature, living with it as for the first time. When he returned to Madison he was still a young boy, but not quite a child any more.[2]

Frank's intuition was that his mother felt he should spend time away from the city because he was 'too much in the imaginative life of the mind ... he preferred to read to playing with other boys ... above all he liked to dream by himself.' In other words, his mother had been worried that he was 'getting soft', and she sent him away to the farm as an expedient solution. From what is known of Anna, though, it seems more likely that she believed it a necessary and valuable stage in his education, and had always intended that Frank should experience something of the world that she had grown up in, which had strengthened her own character in a way that she hoped her son's would develop, within a vigorous, spiritual community and a physical environment that were wholly good, natural and True.

Anna educated her son intensively following her own instincts, in his every waking hour from the day that he was born until he was six years old and ready for Elementary School. Even then, the evidence suggests, she remained his principal teacher, as his schooling was fragmentary until his family settled in Madison. Then, each year from the age of eleven to seventeen he led alternating lives of farming

Pl. 39. Uncle James's farmhouse and family, in The Valley, where Frank lived during his boyhood summers. Uncle James is leaning on the tree in the background.
Courtesy Jack Lenehan, AldebaranFarm.us.

summers and city winters. He would withdraw from school in April, before the final semester, and head west to The Valley. He would live and work there until his return in early September, when school was due to start again. Just as his mother's generation had done, he worked full days, six days a week. His Uncle James even paid him a wage. As he got older, stronger and more experienced, his duties on the farm became more challenging, but he rose to them all. The 1932 version of his autobiography has three sections. Book 1 is 'Family Fellowship', Book 2 is 'Work' and Book 3 'Freedom'. The majority of Book 1 is concerned with Frank's memories of life and family in The Valley, and how the experiences formed his personal philosophy:

*he was insatiably curious and venturesome. So he learned to know the woods from the trees above to the shrubs below and the grass beneath. And the millions of curious lives living hidden in the surface of the ground, among the roots, stems and mould. He was soon happy in such knowledge. As a listening ear, a seeing eye and a sensitive touch had been given naturally to him, his spirit was now becoming familiar with this marvellous book-of-books, experience, the only known reading, The Book of Creation.*[3]

'A listening ear, a seeing eye and a sensitive touch' has the unmistakable echo of a Druidic triad. Despite Frank's extended discourse on his revelatory childhood experience of The Valley, the few paragraphs in which he discusses the Fröbel gifts and his father's music have been treated to vastly more academic scrutiny and assigned many times the significance that has been allowed to the influence of his Welsh family. The explanation is simple: for the average architectural academic, American or otherwise, the influence of New England, Beethoven and Kindergarten can seem crystal clear. In comparison the Welsh language, Welsh culture and the Unitarianism of Ceredigion are murky waters indeed.

In Frank's words,

*The Unitarianism of the Lloyd-Joneses ... was an attempt to amplify, in the confusion of the creeds of the day, the idea of life as a gift from a divine source, one God omnipotent, all things at one with Him. UNITY was their watchword, the sign and symbol that thrilled them, the UNITY of all things ... and there was a warmth in them for truth, cut where it might! And cut, it did – this 'truth against the world'. Enough trouble in that for any one family – the beauty of TRUTH!*[4]

From this perspective every exertion on the farm contained the virtue of sacrament; every moment of rest admitted the healing breath of Nature. Prayer punctuated each day, and on Sundays the family convened, usually at grandfather Richard's house, for a service and singing.[5] The service was led in the early years by Richard, and later by Thomas, the eldest of Frank's uncles.[6] It was also Thomas who led the annual Grove Meetings. These took place each summer on the anniversary of grandmother Mallie's death among the pine trees on the floor of The Valley. The Grove Meetings were an occasion for the gathering of the whole family, and an opportunity for Frank's mother to reunite briefly and tearfully with her son (Pl. 40). In later years, when Uncle Jenkin shared the arrangements with Uncle Thomas, the Grove Meetings hosted many famous speakers and drew a large congregation from miles around. Thomas's role as the leader of the building work earned him particular respect. As the summer months were also the building months, it is inconceivable that Frank did not witness construction work, led by his Uncle Thomas (Pl. 41). It would seem likely that he would also have been called upon to help. If it did happen, Frank makes no mention of it. Other than through his mother, his narrative does not allow for the Joneses to be a direct influence on his architectural destiny. He needs us to believe that it was all his own work, despite everything that they did, intentionally or otherwise, to make him the man that he became:

*It had come to him self-consciously out of his daily endeavours as underlying sense of the essential balance of forces in nature. Something in the nature of an inner experience had come to him that was to make a sense of this supremacy of interior order like a religion to him. He was to take refuge in it. Besides ... for several years the youth had been doing a man's work. He had learned how to do much and to do much well, do most of it happily, feeling himself master where he would. That gave him a whip hand.*[7]

Frank turned eighteen in June 1885. His father had left their home in April of that year.[8]

After the divorce Frank didn't go back to school or to The Valley. Instead he stayed in Madison with his mother and sisters as they worked out how to reorganise their lives, and in June 1885 he started work at a newly opened architectural practice near Madison High School, belonging to Professor Allan D. Conover and his junior partner, Lew F. Porter. This was the beginning of Frank's architectural career.

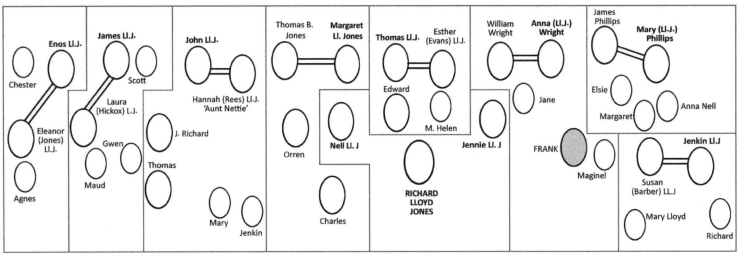

Pl. 40. The Lloyd Jones *teulu* gathered for the Grove Meeting of 1883. The empty seat next to Grandfather Richard is for the absent Mallie. The boxes on the key show the family groups. Daughters and sons of Richard and Mallie are named in bold text. In this picture the age difference between Anna and William Wright is strongly evident. William is the oldest person in the photograph, with the exception of Richard Lloyd Jones. Frank is in the middle row, towards the right. Wisconsin Historical Society WHS-63524.

Pl. 41. The home of John Lloyd Jones in The Valley. This house and that of Uncle James (Plate 39) were built by the family's first architect, Thomas Lloyd Jones. Wisconsin Historical Society WHS-03973.

Unlike Frank, Allan Conover was genuinely precocious. He had graduated with honours in engineering from Wisconsin University before his twentieth birthday, and by the time he was twenty-two, had been hired by the university as a tutor. Three years later he was appointed professor of Civil Engineering, a post that he held for the next eleven years. During his tenure he had been employed frequently by the city and county authority to advise on important public infrastructure works, including the sewer system. In 1884 county officials offered him a new brief. The new Dane County Court House had been designed by Henry Koch, an architect based in Milwaukee, at the eastern edge of the state. A supervising architect was needed to turn Koch's general arrangement drawings into a fully detailed design and then to procure and supervise its construction. It was a significant change of discipline for Conover, but one that he seemed to manage with some ease. Appreciating this, the university quickly offered him a similar brief for another Koch design, their new Science Hall.[9] Koch worked in the powerful Romanesque idiom of Henry Hobson Richardson, the most innovative American architect of the day. Conover was innovative himself: during restoration work in the 1970s, engineers were surprised to find that the structural frame of the Science Hall was fabricated substantially from steel. It was one of the first steel-framed buildings in America. Before either building was near completion Conover's impressive competence had attracted more commissions. He responded to the interest by setting up his architectural practice and in the early summer of 1885 he needed to recruit staff.

In his autobiography Frank recalls that his mother 'found a place for the budding architect' at the new practice. Disregarding the likelihood that William had already left the city, Wright's biographers have tended to doubt that Anna could have provided the connection to Conover, and have assumed that William must have facilitated it.[10] As professor of Civil Engineering, Conover also had oversight of the School of Mechanical Engineering, led by Professor Storm Bull. The two men were close colleagues and friends. Storm Bull, was a committed Unitarian, a recent migrant from Norway who had joined the First Unitarian Society of Madison as soon as he arrived. His Uncle Ole had been resident in the city for many years and was another member of the Unitarian Society.[11] Frank mentions in his autobiography that 'handsome Ole Bull' would sometimes come to the Wrights' house for musical evenings. Anna played a more active part in the social life of her church than her husband did. She taught in the Sunday School and was involved in the inception of Madison Ladies Society, 'organised by the Unitarians of [the] city for religious, social and literary purposes'. She served as Vice-President of the Society and as Secretary between 1884 and 1886.[12] It's reasonable to speculate that

Frank's opening at Conover's architectural office was indeed arranged by Anna with the help of her Unitarian friends, Ole and Storm Bull.

Frank was paid $35 a month as an 'office man', a general assistant to Conover's small professional team.[13] He joined the office without any useful experience, but he was eager, bright and attentive, and he was supremely confident. Conover's approach to training his staff was unusual. All his experience had been in teaching. Naturally he managed his office in the same way, by pressing the younger staff into taking on challenges and responsibilities that would stretch them, and by insisting that they spent as much time on site as they spent in the office.[14] Frank recalled a frozen winter day on which he was sent to the top of the Science Hall roof, when it was just a frame, to retrieve some misfitted steel joint-plates. This is exactly the type of dangerous job that a neophyte would be exposed to. Frank loved it. 'The office work with Professor Conover was a great good for him. As he realised then and since. Work that was truly educational.'[15] At Conover's office we get a glimpse for the first time of Frank on his own, free from school, free from the scrutiny and expectations of his family, becoming his independent self. He takes life in great gulps. His appetite for work seems insatiable and as he works he learns rapidly and learns well. Although there is no evidence of an interest in architecture before the summer of 1885, within a few months of joining Conover he had decided that architecture was to be his future career.

The Grove Meeting took place in The Valley as usual in mid-August of that year. Frank, for once, was there as a visitor, rather than as a farm hand. The gathering that summer was led by Uncle Jenkin, and in the course of his sermon he announced his ambition to build a church in the grove, a building which could be used as a chapel and a community hall and be the focus for Grove Meetings in years to come. It would be the realisation of a long-held ambition of Richard, the family patriarch who, at that time, was in steeply declining health.[16] In 1885 Jenkin Lloyd Jones was the leader of Unitarianism in the western states. He was a formidable fund-raiser: half of the target for the new chapel was already secured. Back at his Chicago base, at the same time, work was under way on his new headquarters, All Souls Church, the building inspired by Jenkin's memory of Pantydefaid Chapel. If Jenkin wanted a new church to be built in The Valley, everyone present must have known that it would surely happen. Frank, who by then had been working in Conover's office for barely two months, was alive to the opportunity. On 22 August, just a week after the Grove Meeting, he wrote to his Uncle Jenkin using Conover's headed paper:

*Dear Uncle, I have forwarded today my preliminary sketches for 'Unity Chapel'. I have simply made them in pencil on paper but the idea is my own and I have copied from nothing ... it can be built for 10 or 12 hundred. If necessary I will furnish you with more detailed drawings and working plans. Please let me know the faults and shortcomings and whether you can make use of them or not.[17]*

Sadly, Frank's drawings of his first architectural proposal have not survived. He wasn't to know, but Jenkin had already decided who would design the Jones family's Unity Chapel. It was to be Joseph Lyman Silsbee, the architect already engaged on the design of All Souls Church.

There is a line in Frank's letter to Jenkin that would stand out to anyone with an architectural background: 'the idea is my own and I have copied from nothing.' The typical novice architect does the opposite: they will be most concerned that the first thing they draw looks like a 'real building'. It becomes a case of how well the student can copy. Frank was different. From early childhood he was encouraged by his mother to see himself as exceptional, an idea that he completely embraced. By the time he was a young adult it was the core of his personality. It is not surprising, then, that from his very first efforts, it was so important to him that others should believe his work was entirely original. It is axiomatic that complete creative originality is impossible. Every idea has a source. But throughout his life Frank strenuously avoided any discussion of the sources that he drew from. As he wrote the letter to his uncle he was presumably thinking that he had not copied his design *in its entirety* from somewhere else, but of course that is not necessarily the way that the words might be interpreted.[18]

Professor Allan D. Conover was an astute judge of many things, but perhaps most of all he had a sense of the potential of young people. Frank had raw energy and a hunger to learn that Conover knew could take him far. Sometime in the late summer he suggested to Frank that he should enrol as a student at the University, and work his way towards the professional qualification that would set him up for a future career. Professor Conover could help him get around his lack of High School merits. He could support Frank's application to enrol as a 'special student'. It was an avenue usually made available by the university for applicants without schooling from the rural outlands of the state, and it was a compelling opportunity, one which must have seemed hard to refuse. Most parents in Anna's position would have been delighted: but was she? It was she who was responsible for his attitude to formal education. Much as she evidently loved the classroom, she seemed to expect Frank to transcend it. She was the one who had arranged for him to miss the last third of every school year since he was eleven years old, in the belief that he would learn more that was useful to him by working on her brother's farm. She knew that he had struggled in high school. She must have regarded the idea of university with a measure of ambivalence. For Frank, the attraction of university may not have been academic at all. The social opportunities seemed to excite him more. School had never worked for him. Would university be any different? In those days the academic year began in January, so it would be a while before he'd find out.

As winter closed in on The Valley Frank's grandfather Richard died. It was 6 December 1885. The Welsh Unitarian pioneer had suffered for many months with dementia: 'the near world was growing dim and distant to his eyes, but the Welsh village that he left forty years ago lay bright and clear as in the sunlight.'[19] He had been two days away from his eighty-seventh birthday. Richard and Mallie's farmhouse and land were bequeathed to the two American-born sisters, Jane and Ellen. This was the occasion for Jane to move back to The Valley from St Paul,

Minnesota. Ellen was also working in teacher training, now as Head of History at the State Normal School at River Falls, Wisconsin, a few miles across the state line from St Paul. She and Jane had always stayed close to each other. The following year, she too resigned her post to move back to The Valley. As the owners of the farm, they found themselves clients of the architect Joseph Silsbee, as the new Unity Chapel was being built on their land. Work had paused on its construction for the winter; only the stone base had been constructed.[20] Jane and Ellen soon announced their own plans for the building. It would be the family chapel of course, but they would also use it to house a new school of their own.

Frank's academic life, as a 'special student' in engineering, began on 7 January 1886. He took classes in the morning and worked in Conover's office in the afternoons. As a Madison resident he was not required to pay fees, but there were many other incidental expenses. His continuing employment provided an income to cover the costs. In effect the university was part-time for him, and this is reflected in the leanness of his first-year curriculum. University records show that he studied only mathematics, French, 'descriptive geometry' and technical drawing.

One of the most disarming stories in his autobiography concerns his student career. He explains that he had enrolled on a four-year course but that he felt increasingly disillusioned by the system as the years went by

> *There was something embarrassing in the competitive atmosphere. Something oppressive and threatening in the life of rules and regulations. Both hampered him, 'Education' meant nothing so much as a vague sort of emotional distress, a sickening sense of fear, of what he could not say.*[21]

At length, after wrestling with his conscience, after three and a half years' study and just two semesters before he was due to graduate, he resigned from the university and from

Conover's office, and struck out on his own. Could there be a more impressive demonstration of a forthright refusal to conform? A better expression of supreme individual will? Such were the questions that Frank trusted his readers to ask. It was not until the 1960s that it was finally established that Frank's story was another fabrication. He actually completed only two semesters of his first year before dropping out.[22]

The cost of student life could well have been a contributing factor. Although the income from his part-time job could sustain him, it did mean that there was almost nothing left to support his mother and sisters. At the same time, however, he kitted himself out with a gown and mortar-board, a fine suit and shoes. His impressive Unitarian connections opened the door to membership of the Phi Delta Theta Fraternity, the oldest on the campus. Membership cost only a little less than the money that he had saved on course fees.[23] The more likely reason for Frank's early abandonment of university was that he could not adapt to the formality of structured learning. His grades were poor to average in the few courses that he took,

> So the University training of one Frank Lloyd Wright ... was lost like some race run under a severe handicap, a race which you know in your heart you are foredoomed to lose ... It wasn't like the farm ... his 'classical' course, whenever he compared it to life on the farm, seemed to him to be the practice of the inappropriate.[24]

Feeling a failure in the classroom, he had come to the reasonable conclusion that the only effective way to learn, for him, was by working, by 'action', as he put it. He never did begin academic studies in engineering, still less architecture. The closest that he got to it was his geometry and drawing classes.

Remarkably, he kept three of his classroom drawings, which can still be seen in the Frank Lloyd Wright archive. They are proficient technical drawings and one in particular,

projecting the shadow cast by a parabolic form, was a difficult draughting exercise, well executed (Fig. 8.1).

But a more eye-catching feature of this particular drawing is his signature, F.LL.W. This is the earliest evidence of his decision to change his middle name, from Lincoln to Lloyd. His use of 'LL' is significant: he is aware that it is a single letter in the Welsh alphabet, another indication that the Welsh language was a meaningful presence at this stage in his life. His parents' divorce was the obvious catalyst for the change.[25]

For Frank, his new identity sat well with his sense of a crystallising architectural destiny, and the building of Unity Chapel, back at The Valley, offered a further crucial step towards it. His first university semester had ended in March 1886. In keeping with the habit of his lifetime, he was absent for the April to June session. It is not known whether he continued working with Conover during these months. It would surely have been awkward, given Conover's patronage of the student place that he had abandoned. It seems more probable that he made his way to The Valley, where he would be revitalised by the environment and meaningful work, and where he could help his Uncle Thomas supervise the construction of the new Unity Chapel (Pl. 42).

Many earlier Wright biographies identify Unity Chapel as the first known work of Frank Lloyd Wright. It is not his project at all, and Frank never claimed it to be, but he did help with its decoration. The chapel was completed in time for the annual Grove Meeting of 1886, just as Jenkin had promised the previous summer. In the 28 August issue of *Unity* magazine the Rev. William Channing Gannett reported on the dedication of the newly completed chapel:

> A cottage church, a gem of a church, the daintiest, cosiest nest of a church that ever lay on a meadow among the Wisconsin hills ... inside is a trinity of rooms which the modern church demands, an audience room, a parlour ... and a mite of a kitchen. In the first room eighty people can listen ... the parlour adds space for seventy seats more. Both are wood-ceiled, with pine in its own colour, one is calcimined in terracotta, one in olive-green. A boy architect belonging to the family looked after this interior.

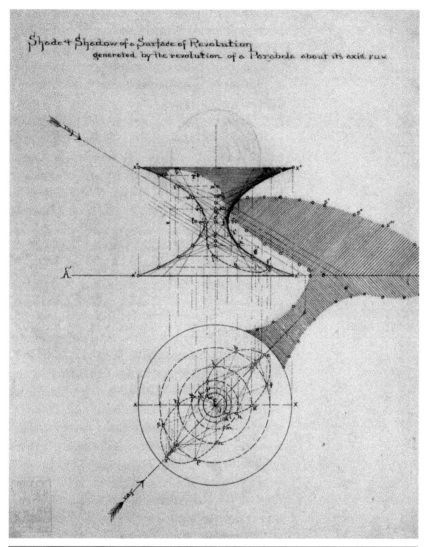

Shade + Shadow of a Surface of Revolution
generated by the revolution of a Parabola about its axis r.r.x

Fig. 8.1. Frank excelled at little during his short time as a university student, but his technical drawing was good. The drawing above is signed F.LL.W. This the first known occasion that he used 'Lloyd' in place of his original middle name, Lincoln.
FLWF/AAFAL.

The boy was Frank. Jenkin Lloyd Jones addressed the gathering with, 'special consecrating words', speaking first

in Welsh, 'for those that dwelt in it'. The Rev. Gannett's comment here is a rare reference to the fact that there were many in and around the Lloyd Jones *teulu* that preferred to use their mother tongue, even if they were highly literate in English. The American-born family members, Jane, Ellen, James and Enos, were all Welsh-speaking. They felt deeply and determinedly Welsh throughout their lives, as they had been raised to be. Their parents were both gone, but *Y Nod Cyfrin* was boldly engraved on the chapel gatepost to affirm their devotion to a remote motherland.

Joseph Lyman Silsbee was also in attendance at the dedication, where he would, undoubtedly, have encountered Frank. Later in the summer, presumably by arrangement with Uncle Jenkin, Frank travelled to Chicago to visit Silsbee's All Souls Church which, by then, was undergoing its final fitting out. Frank may even have worked in Silsbee's office for a few weeks.[26] That would have been Frank's first visit to the metropolis, a city that made Madison seem like a village. In early September Frank was back at the university in Madison, attempting to pick up his courses after missing the entire summer semester. The next transition in the young life of Frank Lloyd Wright is arguably the most significant. At some stage between the start and the end of his winter term at the University of Wisconsin it had been decided that the best move for his future, and perhaps for the welfare of his mother and sisters, was for Frank to take a permanent job in Chicago, and by the end of the year he had gone.

Frank Lloyd Wright's first published work appeared just a year later in the *All Souls Church Fourth Annual*. It was a drawing of Unity Chapel, not the finished building, but a copy of a drawing by Joseph Silsbee that had been printed the year before in Uncle Jenkin's *Unity* magazine. Like Silsbee's original, Frank's drawing is presented as a free-hand sketch in ink. Unlike Silsbee's, it shows the frailty of a novice struggling with an unfamiliar technique. It is almost certainly a transfer-tracing (Pl. 43). From the start of his time with Conover, Frank seems never to have doubted that he could express his own distinctive vision through the medium of building. But it is one thing to recognise the possibilities of the art form, and quite another to be able to fulfil them. In truth, few architects ever have, and when he joined Silsbee's practice there was nothing in Frank's architectural or artistic ability to suggest that he ever would either, certainly no hint of incipient 'genius'. He was in fact entirely average.

But there was a seed inside him with an extraordinary potential to flower. That potential came, to begin with, from propensities that he inherited in equal measures from his mother and father, and subsequently from his upbringing, which was, in the greatest part by far, the investment of his mother. Frank was, as his sister Maginel correctly observed, 'more than any other thing, a Lloyd-Jones'. This reality has been unacceptable to some of his biographers, for frankly unacceptable reasons, but it is, nonetheless a fact that can be authenticated, to a degree, by comparing the destinies of William Wright's children from his first marriage with those of his marriage to Anna. William and Permelia's son George became a lawyer, graduating from the University of Wisconsin in 1880; Charlie became a Baptist minister, after moving on from his early interest in mechanics. Lizzie married in 1881 and settled on a farm in Iowa.[27] Of his children with Anna, Maginel (Margaret-Ellen) became a professional illustrator, Jennie (Mary-Jane) an accomplished musician, and Frank became an architect. Anna's children were absorbed by creativity; Permelia's were not.

There is no obvious, equivalent correlation between Anna's preoccupations and the visual creativity of Frank and Maginel, but both recall that their mother's personal aesthetic was out of step with the norms of her time. She was deeply uncomfortable with the stultifying darkness, dense drapery and ornate clutter of the respectable middle-class homes of her Madison neighbours. Maginel remembered the great pride her mother took in a bright new polished maple floor: 'in time it was adorned with two Persian rugs [with] white backgrounds and brilliant patterns.'[28] There were two folding chairs upholstered in Brussels carpet, one was red and white, the other green and white. The windows were covered by translucent panels of fine white cloth, hung straight. 'And everywhere, books', Frank recalled, and 'simple vases were gracefully filled with dried leaves. A simplicity yes – but not of soul.'[29]

Pl. 42  Unity Chapel, built in 1885–86 to the design of Joseph Lyman Silsbee. Frank contributed to the decoration of its ceiling.

These descriptions convey an echo of the Nonconformist manner of the west Wales countryside, the aesthetic that the Jones family brought with them to America. Aunt Jennie was convinced that it was a visual sensibility that had originated with Anna's mother, Mallie. She once told Maginel that Mallie had, 'loved ... colour and rhythm of design. Whatever is associated with such things in her children and her grandchildren came straight from her.' Plain rooms, simply furnished; fabrics with abstract patterns and bold colours used sparingly. It's an aesthetic of necessity, limited resources and rural craft. Anna was highly attuned to her own emotions, as Transcendentalist philosophy encouraged her to be. She was only truly comfortable in surroundings that echoed those of her childhood, and which embodied the clarity and Truth of the Unitarian vision. Just as it seemed right and healthy to Anna, so it seemed to her children. In due course, as reinterpreted by Frank, it would come to seem 'modern' as well. But in those days, in urban Madison, it was considered strange.

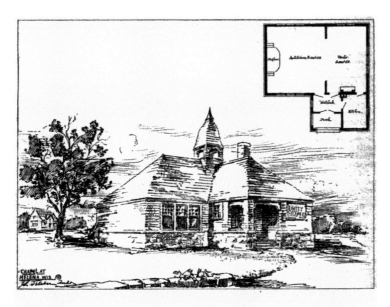

UNITY CHAPEL, HELENA, WIS.

Pl. 43. Joseph Silsbee's drawing of Unity Chapel, top, and Frank's traced copy, below. Frank's signature is below the rocks in the lower right corner of his drawing.
Unity XVI, 26 December 1885, above, and All Souls Church Annual 1887, below.

Frank Lloyd Wright's achievements were the expression of this unconventional aesthetic, spiritual and social environment. He was effectively home-schooled throughout his childhood, by his mother Anna, and by his Uncle James, by his aunts Ellen and Jennie, and by the rich cast of characters that made up the Lloyd Jones agricultural Welsh Unitarian family. From this background it is possible to discern the various strands that make up the colourful and abrasive fabric of his personality. He benefited from a remarkably progressive, free and natural education. He was widely read at a young age, but also encouraged to learn systematically and directly from the natural world. Yes, his father's music was a significant presence in his early life, but what he gained from it was a love of music, rather than an architectural impetus. It is a fact, also that Kindergarten was a preoccupation of his mother and of his two closest aunts, but the manipulation of the wooden blocks was just one small element of the Kindergarten system. Far more significant was Fröbel's foundational thesis, that Nature was the ultimate classroom.

With the encouragement of his family he was able to see and understand the presence of God around him, and within himself. From the Welsh folklore that entertained his family he came to believe in the three primary requisites of Genius – 'an eye that can see nature; a heart that can feel nature and boldness that dares to follow nature'. He came to understand that creativity was a divine gift and that he could be a vessel for its expression. In effect he was trained as a novice Druid, along lines that had been described by Iolo Morganwg a century before. Not in a magical or mystical way, but with a focus on self-discipline and self-awareness and on his own unlimited creative potential. Perhaps most significantly, he admired the resilience and bravado of his Welsh family, their conviction that they were possessors of TRUTH, and that everyone else was wrong. He had learned to despise convention and to distrust anyone who tried to constrain him to their own rules.

From his earliest years he was encouraged to believe that he had a unique gift and a message to convey to the world, and that he should let nothing and no one – even those closest to him – stand in his way ■

# 08    The Book of Creation
## *Notes*

1    Frank Lloyd Wright, *An Autobiography (Edition 1)* (New York: Longman, Green & Co., 1932), pp. 16–46. Frank's reference to 'Esteddvod' appears on p. 27. This is a misspelling of *Eisteddfod*. A festival of song and poetry, it is one of the most deeply cherished and established of Welsh traditions. The literal meaning of *Eisteddfod* is 'sitting together'.

2    F. L. Wright, *An Autobiography (Edition 1)*, pp. 16–46.

3    F. L. Wright, *An Autobiography (Edition 1)*, p. 23.

4    F. L. Wright, *An Autobiography (Edition 1)*, pp. 14–15.

5    Richard Lloyd Jones et al., *A Lloyd Jones Retrospective (Second Edition)* (Spring Green WI: Unity Chapel Inc., 1986), p. 57.

6    Thomas E Graham, *Unity Chapel Sermons 1984–2000* (Winnipeg: New Colgrove Press, 2002), p. 44.

7    F. L. Wright, *An Autobiography (Edition 1)*, p. 47.

8    William Wright kept up his restless lifestyle for the remaining nineteen years of his life, occasionally practising law but always preoccupied with his music. He did not serve as a minister again; his divorce almost certainly precluded it. His biography in the Colgate University Catalogue of 1914 lists the following: 'practiced law Wahoo Nebraska 1886–90; resided in Omaha 1890–92; director Central Conservancy of Music, Stromsburg, Nebraska 1892–95; resided St. Joseph, Montana 1895–96; Des Moines, Iowa 1896–97; Perry, Michigan 1897–1900; York, Nebraska 1900–02, retired Pittsburgh 1902–04. Died Pittsburgh 16 June 1904.' There is an account of this period in William Wright's life in Paul Hendrickson, *Plagued by Fire: The Dreams and Furies of Frank Lloyd Wright* (London: Bodley Head, 2019), pp. 450–6.

9    Andrew J. Aiken, *Men of Progress: Wisconsin* (Madison: The Evening Wisconsin Company, 1897), p. 867.

10    For example M. J. Hamilton and D. V Mollenhoff, *Frank Lloyd Wright's Monona Terrace: The Enduring Power of a Civic*

*Vision* (Madison: University of Wisconsin Press, 1999), p. 52; and Donald Leslie Johnson, *Frank Lloyd Wright: Early Years: Progressivism: Aesthetics: Cities* (Abingdon: Routledge, 2017), p. 72.

11    *Biographical Review of Dane County* (Chicago: Biographical Review Pub. Co., 1893), p. 169.

12    *Wisconsin State Journal* (23 June 1884). It is noteworthy that she held this role during the period of her divorce and its attendant embarrassment. It was evidently not something that her fellow Unitarians held against her.

13    This starting rate still exceeded the average wage of a school teacher. The large majority of school teachers were young, unmarried women.

14    Hamilton and Mollenhoff, *Frank Lloyd Wright's Monona Terrace*, p. 275.

15    Frank Lloyd Wright, *An Autobiography (Edition 2)* (London: Faber & Faber, 1946), p. 55.

16    J. Siry, 'Frank Lloyd Wright's Unity Temple and Architecture for Liberal Religion in Chicago, 1885–1909', *The Art Bulletin*, 73/2 (June 1991), 257–82.

17    Letter from Frank Lloyd Wright to Jenkin Lloyd Jones, 22 August 1885. The Frank Lloyd Wright Foundation archive, item reference J001A010000

18    Wright's sketch proposal for Unity Chapel has not survived. It is occasionally mistaken for his later sketch proposal for Sioux City Unitarian Chapel, which is discussed in the following chapter.

19    Meryl Secrest, *Frank Lloyd Wright: A Biography* (Chicago: University of Chicago Press, 1998), p. 6, quoting from George Eyre Evans (ed.), *Lloyd Letters 1754–1796* (Aberystwyth: William Jones, 1908).

20    *Unity* magazine (December 1885), quoted in Johnson, *Frank Lloyd Wright: Early Years: Progressivism: Aesthetics: Cities*, p. 73.

21    F. L. Wright, *An Autobiography (Edition 1)*, p. 56.

22    T. S. Hines Jr, 'Frank Lloyd Wright – The Madison Years: Records versus Recollections', *Journal of the Society of Architectural Historians*, 26/4 (December1967), 227–33.

23    Hamilton and Mollenhoff, *Frank Loyd Wright's Monona Terrace*, p. 55.

24    F. L. Wright, *An Autobiography (Edition 1)*, p. 56.

25    Members of the Jones family adopted Lloyd as a middle name at different times. Richard Jones seems to have been the first to do so. In the US Census of 1850 they were all named Jones. In 1860, for the next census, all of the male members of the family had become L. Jones, while all of the female family members are still recorded simply as Jones. In the Albion Academy archive for 1865 Frank's mother's name was recorded as Hannah L. Jones, and in 1870 both Ellen and Jane were recorded in the US census as L. Jones, as they completed their training at Platteville Normal College. As the years went by it was Frank, Anna and her American-born siblings who most conspicuously exercised the Lloyd name, to the extent that it became embedded in the surnames of the following generations.

26    Thomas A. Heinz, *The Vision of Frank Lloyd Wright* (Menai Bridge: S. Webb and Son, 2002), p. 16.

27    Elizabeth Wright Heller, *The Story of My Life* (unpublished, typed manuscript, *c.*1933).

28    Maginel Wright Barney, *The Valley of the God Almighty Joneses* (New York: Appleton Century, 1965), p. 59.

29    F. L. Wright, *An Autobiography (Edition 1)*, p. 30.

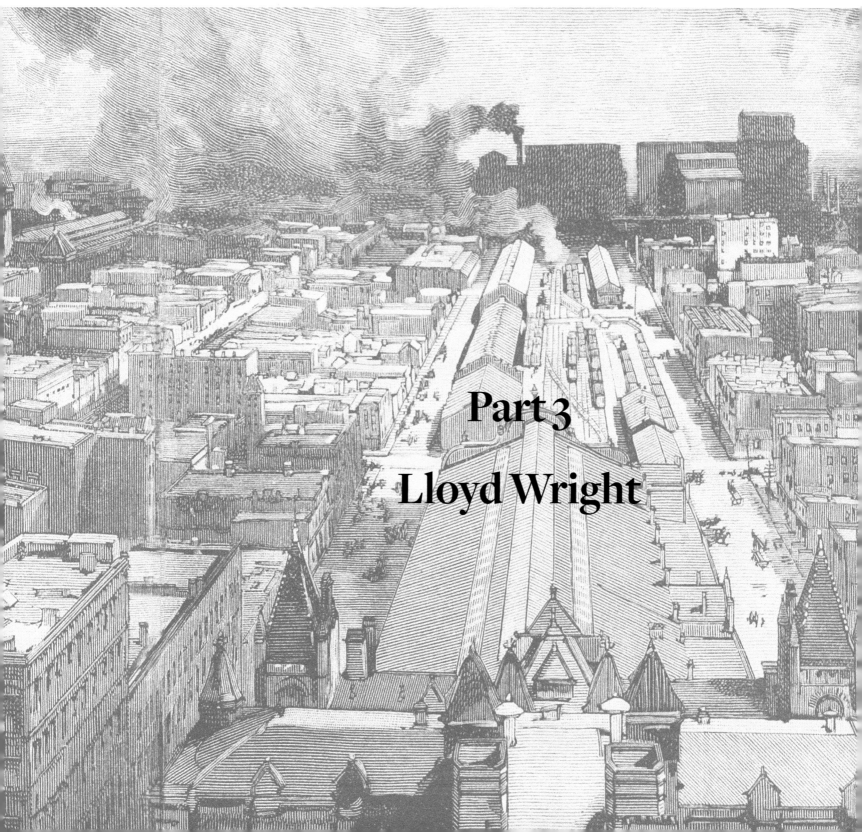

# Part 3

# Lloyd Wright

# 9

# The Grammar of Ornament

## 10 October 1871. Central Chicago

Smoke was beginning to disperse beneath a cloak of drizzle, the first rain that had fallen for over a week, and the last flames had died down. The heart of Chicago was gone, more than three square miles razed but for a few skeletal remnants. It had started in the south-west of the centre, raced northwards on the wind with such ferocity that it leaped 150 metres over the river to burn the whole of the central business district, including the entire northern lake front (Pl. 44). A headline in the *Chicago Tribune* the following morning exhorted the traumatised populace to 'CHEER UP. In the midst of a calamity without parallel in the world's history, looking upon the ashes of thirty years'

accumulations, the people of this once beautiful city have resolved that CHICAGO SHALL RISE AGAIN.'[1]

Until 1830 Chicago was barely more than a farm and a small military fort, either side of a river that fed Lake Michigan. A mile inland from the estuary the river split into two branches, one flowing in from the north and the other from the south. The watershed for the southern branch was not in an area of upland, but a mud lake. This was unusual, and what made it more so was that another river emerged from the same mud lake to flow westwards, into the Mississippi basin. The lake was a fulcrum between the vast central river system that fed the Mississippi, and the Great Lakes, which gathered the waters of the east. It was an unique conjunction, a funnel into the prosperous east for the unlimited future agricultural production of the west. Chicago was incorporated as a town in 1833. The completion of the Erie Canal, a few years before, provided the last chain in the pan-continental waterway. With a population of 350, it began as a typically sparse pioneer settlement.[2] By 1845, when the Jones family settled in Ixonia, it exceeded twelve thousand. The rate of growth from then to 1870 averaged almost 50 per cent per annum, it was the fastest-growing city in the world. The Great Fire of 1871 was witnessed by over 300,000 Chicagoans: Italians, Scandinavians, African-Americans, British, many Irish and, most numerous of all, Germans. A third of them lost their homes.

Rebuilding began within a week of the fire. Investment poured in from across America. There could be no more certain bet, Chicago's success was guaranteed by its location. There were stories of recycled bricks being laid before they had even cooled. By 1875 all of the debris had been cleared but there was still a large part of the 'burnt district' to rebuild. While there were impressive new shops and hotels on the main streets the majority of new structures had been cheaply erected on the same plots, and in much the same way as those that had vanished. City authorities demanded fireproof construction, but had no means of enforcing their ordinances, while the basics of welfare, law and order could barely be sustained. Homeless families had slept on the floor of City Hall during the winter of 1873, and in the summer that followed a second fire razed twelve city blocks in the south of the city, destroying over 800 properties, the majority of them newly built slums. The second blaze infuriated the city's powerful insurance industry which had been assured after the first fire that their risks would be reduced. Pressure from the insurers led to the introduction of new, more stringent building codes, and began a process of change from timber frame to steel that would open the way to an architectural revolution. Within a decade the world's first skyscrapers would be built on the congested, vastly expensive land of the central business district.

Upheavals, tumult, revolutions remained the Chicago condition through the whole period of the rebuilding. The city was stubbornly rough and unruly, much of it filthy, smoky and insanitary. The central streets were choked with carriages, and most routes south of the river were unpaved. For all its huge energy there was barely any space at street level to be at ease. Even the lake shore was beyond reach, cut off by a thick braid of rail tracks. The moneyed and the professional classes could withdraw to their new ballrooms, dining halls and palatial hotels. As for the poor, religion could offer hope, but for most the only escape lay in a cascade of new saloons, brothels and gambling houses. Only in the immediate aftermath of the fire had the city's people seemed like a single community. In the years that followed, encouraged by those who could take commercial advantage, it became increasingly aggressive, sectarian and suspicious. Vice underpinned the rebuilding and laid the groundwork for the city's distinctive gang culture. In the 1870s there was a saloon for every 150 inhabitants; disorderly clusters in 'Hell's Half Acre' and 'Dead Man's Alley'. South State Street became 'Satan's Mile'. During the summer of 1886 an alliance of socialist and anarchist groups called a rally in the city centre. Revolution was in the air. Police arrived to break up the gathering, and marched into an ambush. A bomb was thrown, hundreds of shots were fired. Many dozens were wounded, eleven were killed, seven of them policemen. The 'Haymarket Incident' made headlines around the world.

Trains from Wisconsin arrived at the Chicago and North Western Terminal, just a short walk from the scene

Pl. 44. Central Chicago after the Great Fire. *Chicago Tribune*, October 1871.

of the bombing. The heat of that febrile summer had given way to a cold winter as Frank Lloyd Wright stepped off the train from sleepy Madison into the heart of the seething metropolis. He recalled his disorientation, confronted by

*sputtering white arc-lights in the station and in the streets, dazzling and ugly ... the mysterious dark of the river with dim masts, hulks and funnels hung with lights, half smothered in gloom ... the brutal, hurrying crowd, trying hard not to see ... So cold, black, blue-white and wet ... the flood of hard city lights made the unseeing faces of the crowd in the drizzle, livid, ghastly.*[3]

This recollection seems vivid and real, but it sets the scene for a story of individual heroism that is otherwise entirely fantastical. He explains, in his autobiography, that he ran away to Chicago without telling his family; that he had gone

**Pl. 45.** All Souls Chicago, Jenkin Lloyd Jones's Church and home, designed by Joseph Lyman Silsbee. Jenkin Lloyd Jones lived in The Parsonage, on the upper floors of the church. Frank stayed with him there when he first moved to Chicago.
From *Abraham Lincoln Centre All Souls Church; Reports for 1912.*

work on All Souls Church for Frank's Uncle Jenkin (Pl. 45). How surprised his uncle was to find him there at Silsbee's office! The episode is presented as being the first occasion upon which he successfully exerted his will over adversity, the template for his many later triumphs. As a twenty-year-old, he may well have felt able to fend for himself, but beneath the fictional account of his first few days in the city is the truth that he was, at once, taken under the wing of his Uncle Jenkin, probably as he stepped off the train, and that there was a room ready for him at The Parsonage and, of course, his job at Joseph Silsbee's had been arranged well in advance.

Whether or not his mother was initially opposed to Frank's move, it is clear that when he left, it was with her full knowledge and that it had been planned with some care. Frank's name appears for the first time at a Chicago location in the *All Souls Church Third Annual*, dated 6 January 1887. He is listed there as a member of the church. As the *Annual* was published in the first week of January 1887, it is safe to presume that he was resident in the city in December 1886 at the latest. Silsbee's office was in the Lakeside Building, at the corner of Clark Street and Adams Street a few blocks south of the river. It was not actually on the lakeside, but in the heart of the Printer's Row neighbourhood. The building had been developed by a printing company, and the majority of its tenants were either publishers or printers. Given his own fascination with printing, it must have been a milieu that he enjoyed.[4] In the first few years of the 1880s, the electric trams, known as cable-cars, had evolved from being a novelty into the dominant mode of public transport in the city. Frank's commute from his Uncle's home in Oakwood to Printer's Row took him up South State Street, 'Satan's Mile':

> *the procession of saloons, food shops, barber shops, eating houses, saloons, restaurants, groceries, laundries – and saloons, saloons, tailors, dry goods, candy shops, bakeries and saloons became a chaos in a wilderness of Italian, German, Irish, Polak, Greek, English, Swedish, French, Chinese and Spanish names*[5] (Fig 9.1).

secretly to a Madison second-hand shop with a leather-bound copy of Plutarch's *Lives* and a set of Gibbon's *Decline and Fall*, books that his father had left behind. The money was enough to pay for his ticket to Chicago, leaving him with seven dollars to live on until he could find a job. With a slim folder of drawings beneath his arm, he made his way from one architect's office to another, offering his services and being turned away. A matinée provided a few hours of warmth before his return to the freezing streets, more entreaties and more rejections. He found a room at a hotel called 'Briggs House', which, although it sounds convincingly low-down, was actually one of the most expensive in the city. Somehow he eked out his funds and on the third day, as his last dollar dwindled, he was offered a trial by a sympathetic architect. As fate would have it, the architect was Joseph Silsbee, the designer of Unity Chapel, back in The Valley, who was in the process, just then, of completing

Stepping down from the cable car at Adams Street there was one other feature of the streetscape that would surely have been tremendously imposing to any young architect, and yet Frank makes no mention of it when recalling his time at Silsbee's. Directly across the street from the Lakeside Building stood what was reckoned at the time to be the tallest secular building in the world, William Le Baron Jenney's Home Insurance Building (Pl. 46). Fully ten storeys in height with a frame constructed entirely in steel, the world's first skyscraper had been completed just two years before.

Frank remembered his time at Silsbee's with great fondness for the friends that he made, and with frustration over the trivial nature of the work that was the mainstay of the business. He admired his employer, despite his concern that Silsbee was blind to his own talent. Silsbee lived at 79 Maple Street, on the northern edge of the central business district. It is likely that Frank occasionally visited, and that it was at Silsbee's house that he first encountered Japanese art. Silsbee's cousin, Ernest Fenollosa, was America's foremost expert on Japanese visual culture. He lived in Japan for most of his adult life, often sending collections of Japanese art back to America. One of Fenollosa's closest colleagues was Edward Morse, a zoologist and orientalist. In 1886 Morse published a book that was to become unexpectedly influential in American architectural circles, *Japanese Homes and their Surroundings*.[6] Given his connection to Fenollosa, and through him to Silsbee, it seems inevitable that Frank was exposed to the contents of this book early in his time at Silsbee's practice. Japanese art would become one of Frank's lifelong infatuations. Although it must also have been a significant part of Silsbee's cultural environment, its influence did not find its way into Silsbee's architecture, which remained resolutely picturesque, soft gothic combinations of 'gable, turret and hip with broad porches, quietly domestic'.[7]

As Frank gained confidence and understanding of the rudiments of middle-class residential design he seemed, simultaneously, to become uncomfortable with its constraints. Sensing that the stylistic rules had no practical basis, he began to resent them, although at that time, so

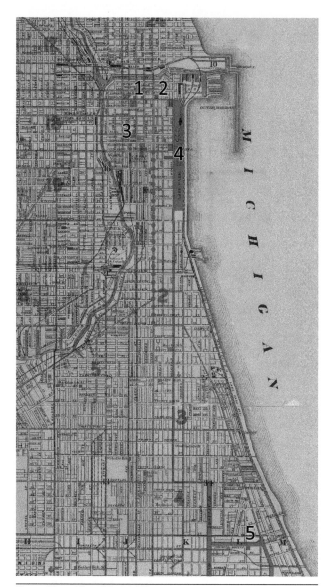

Fig. 9.1. Metropolitan Chicago, 1888.
1) The Lakeside Building, office of Joseph Silsbee.
2) Marshall Fields Warehouse, Henry Hobson Richardson's masterpiece.
3) The Borden Block, office of Adler and Sullivan.
4) The Auditorium, Adler and Sullivan's masterpiece, and their office after 1889.
5) All Souls Church, Chicago Southside. Frank's first residence in Chicago. The dotted line shows 'Satan's Mile', part of Frank's regular commute from home to work.
LOC.

Pl. 46. William Le Baron Jenney's Home Insurance Building of 1885 was the world's first steel-framed skyscraper. It was originally constructed with ten floors. Another two floors were added a few years later, as shown in this photograph. LOC.

Pl. 47. Frank with Cecil Corwin, his closest friend and colleague through Frank's early years in Chicago. FLWF/AAFAL.

early in his career, he had little notion of how he could work without them. In his reflections on his first year in Chicago it is possible, also, to detect a shift in his sense of autonomy. He had moved to the city at his mother's behest, to live under his Uncle Jenkin's protection and work for Silsbee, his uncle's friend. His mother would soon be fifty years old and his sisters were too young to earn a living. Before long it would be Frank's duty to support them. In all that he did and said at that time, there was urgency, suppressed impatience,

a yearning for change. At some point he would have to make a break, to prove to himself that he could thrive outside the embrace of his family, to become the provider, and no longer the provided-for.

Frank liked to think of himself as a man about town. He recalled contented evenings with his close friend and colleague Cecil Corwin, concerts at the Apollo Club or the Exposition Building on the lakefront, dinner at Madame Galle's 'Italian table d'hote' or the 'Tip Top Inn' at the

Pullman Building[8] (Pl. 47). In reality, though, he was still a country boy, still tethered tightly to his Welsh family and to his mother in particular. They corresponded weekly. Anna's letters overflowed with her worries for him, always urging him to stay true to himself and to his faith. Frank offered light-hearted reassurances in return, and a slice of his earnings to prove his mettle. He was fortunate to have the ready-made community of his Uncle Jenkin's church to ensure his security and to provide him with a rich domestic and social life:

> Evening events, lectures and meetings ... study classes of all kinds. All Souls had a circulating library, was a neighborhood-center in which were many activities, intellectual, social and literary ... The church was never closed. My Uncle's soul seemed a sort of spiritual dynamo that never rested.[9]

All Souls remained his cynosure well into the 1900s. Later in 1887, when he moved out of The Parsonage, it was not to move closer to his workplace, but around the corner from All Souls to Vincennes Avenue, to lodge at the house of the Waterman family, fellow members of the congregation. Harry Waterman, the son of the family, was another novice draughtsman at Silsbee's office.[10] The move was arranged, again, by his Uncle Jenkin. He grew particularly close to his cousin Richard, Uncle Jenkin's son, whom Frank recalled as being a worldly 'city guy', eager to enlighten Frank on the intrigues of the metropolis, this despite the fact that he was only fifteen years old at the time![11] 'Dickie' Lloyd Jones remained a close confidant and a robust interlocutor for Frank throughout his life. In 1928, it was Dickie, by then the wealthy proprietor of the *Tulsa Tribune*, who had paid the bond that enabled Frank to extricate himself from Hennepin County Jail.

Within a few months of arriving in Chicago Frank had firmly established himself in Silsbee's team, sufficiently, so he claimed, to have negotiated a pay rise that put him on a par with more experienced colleagues. For all that he lacked in finesse, he had self-belief in abundance. He had an effervescent charm, curiosity and a great appetite for learning-by-doing. He must have realised, also, that he was blessed with an intense visual and spatial acuity, an ability to visualise form and volume that was unusual, even among fellow architects. Early in May 1887 Frank, having already benefited from one pay rise, approached Silsbee for another, prompted by the fact that a new recruit had been taken on at eighteen dollars a week, six dollars more than he was earning. Although George Maher, the new man, was three years older and more experienced, Frank reckoned Maher's draughting skills were no better than his own. Silsbee disagreed, so Frank promptly quit and took his portfolio to the studio of Wheelock and Clay, on Dearborn Street, a few blocks to the north.[12] Their work, like Silsbee's, was almost entirely residential and designed in the Richardson manner. William Clay was impressed enough by Frank to take him on at the rate that Silsbee had refused him. Frank found out quickly that his own confidence had misled his new employer. He was set design tasks that were far beyond his limited capabilities, and after two weeks he had to resign. This was perhaps the one time in his professional life when he had, unwittingly, re-enacted the lifelong tendency of his father to quit in the face of adversity, brought on by his own ambition. He managed, still, to turn it to his advantage. He made his way back, apologetically, to Silsbee's office. According to Frank's memoir, Silsbee agreed not only to reappoint him, but to give him the further pay rise that he had originally asked for.

Silsbee's willingness to indulge Frank was, in part, pragmatic. Early in March, Frank had received an exciting letter from his Aunt Nell (Ellen). At that time she was still teaching at the college in River Falls, but busy planning for her return to The Valley. Unity Chapel was not yet a year old, but she and Aunt Jane were already working on a bold new project. More than a simple schoolhouse, it was to be a full-scale private boarding school. In the letter, Aunt Nell explained that she needed a copy of the plans of the original homestead, his grandfather's house, from Uncle Thomas.

Pl. 48. Staff and pupils in front of the new Hillside Home School, designed by Joseph Lyman Silsbee, 1887–88. FLWF/AAFAL.

They intended to dismantle the building and re-erect it on the opposite side of the road, where it would be enlarged to function as a residence for boarding pupils, to be called 'Home Cottage'.[13] Joseph Silsbee would then design a new main teaching building that would occupy the vacated homestead site. Together the buildings would be known as 'Hillside Home School'. It has, until recently, been assumed that Frank was involved in the design of the new teaching building. Most biographies identify it as his first built work. Frank is partly to blame for this. He invited credit for it by dismissing it as a juvenile mistake. However, from a careful reading of Aunt Nell's letter, and in particular the sketch that she provided, it is clear that she is asking for Frank's help with the re-purposing of the old homestead rather than the design of the new school itself. Aunt Nell was in a hurry: she wanted to be ready for men to start work as soon as the ground was soft enough, later in the spring. 'Do not take time

to make elegant drawings if you are busy but send a rough sketch of what you think the best plan as soon as you can.'[14]

The letter was Frank's first architectural commission, a challenging project handed to him barely two months after he had joined Silsbee's practice. There is a suggestion in the letter that Frank had been expecting it: 'I heard that you had been down to Hillside to look the ground over', Aunt Nell says. Her confidence in her nephew was touching, but he was some years away from being able to tackle such a brief on his own. She and Frank must both have known that the relocation of the old house was really another commission for Silsbee, albeit one in which she expected Frank to have a meaningful role.[15] Late nineteenth-century design and construction proceeded at a pace that seems inconceivable today. The new Hillside Home School was built under the supervision of Thomas Lloyd Jones, and ready for its first intake in the autumn of 1887 (Pl. 48). Barely six months had elapsed since Frank had received the letter from his Aunt Nell. The new school was archetypal Silsbee: heavy-set, sedately proportioned, comfortingly domestic in the manner that was referred to at the time as Queen Anne Style. It was Silsbee's project, but only because it gave his aunts the opportunity to boost the prospects of their beloved nephew. Frank had certainly played an important part, and from then on, as far as his aunts were concerned, he was the school's architect designate.

In the summer of 1887 Frank found out that the Unitarians of Sioux City, Iowa, were planning to build a chapel of their own. His Uncle Jenkin had inaugurated the Sioux City congregation two years before. Frank's design for the Sioux City Unitarian Chapel is the earliest surviving design that can be attributed to him. Perhaps, in his own mind, it was again an 'idea of his own, copied from nothing', but when he sat down to draw it he did so in a different environment from that of Allan Conover's office, his workplace of two years before. In Silsbee's studio he was surrounded by earnest young architects, every one of them, curiously, the son of a minister, and Silsbee himself was a graduate of Massachusetts Institute of Technology,

America's leading architectural school. Due deference was expected to the correct sources, and for all right-thinking progressive architects at that time, the pre-eminent source was Henry Hobson Richardson. Richardson was the doyen of the New England-based architectural establishment. He was particularly worthy of Unitarian respect: his great-grandfather was none other than Joseph Priestley.

The final section of Frank's 1932 autobiography is a fascinating selection of photographs, predominantly of family but also including significant colleagues. There is only one portrait of a man that Frank could never have met: that man is Richardson. His original expression of Romanesque resonated with the emerging themes of modern America: civic stability, reverence for nature, industrial power. He had been at the height of his creativity when he died, in the spring of 1886, aged only forty-eight. His work dominated the illustrated pages of the architectural journals, and, if that was not enough to make a strong impression on the mind of a novice architect, Richardson's most radical work, the austere, stately Marshall Field & Co. Warehouse of 1885 stood just two hundred yards east of Silsbee's office, looming massively over the streets, like the Pont du Gard extruded into a block (Pl. 49).

Silsbee's own work drew on Richardson's forms and his use of naturalistic textures and materials. Frank's design for the Sioux City Unitarian Chapel attempts to do the same (Pl. 50). Like Silsbee's design for the Unity Chapel, it has a masonry plinth that carries shingled walls and a steep hipped roof. The stonework is different; it is heavily rusticated and laid randomly like heaps of rough boulders. A house called Stonehurst was one of Richardson's last works, completed shortly after his death. Published in the journals in the months before Frank made his drawing, it has the same heavily rusticated features, including the low, craggy arch and slender, knobbly chimneys. Richardson arranged these elements to achieve the sophisticated visual harmony for which he was known. In Frank's design the elements are lumped together with an endearing clumsiness which, although it has been dismissed as 'puerile', is surprisingly confident.[16] There is a sense that its execution was not

Pl. 49. Henry Hobson Richardson's Marshall Fields Wholesale Store, Chicago 1887. Chicagology.com (May 2021).

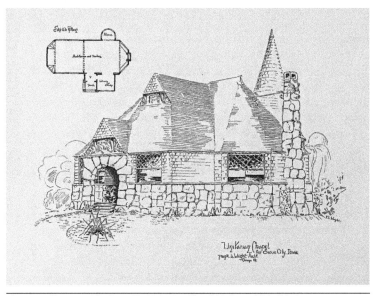

Pl. 50. Frank's proposal for Sioux City Unitarian Chapel, his first published design. *The Inland Architect and News Record*, vol. 9 no. 8 (June 1887), p. 86.

approached as a challenge, or, as lesser architects are so often inclined to declare, as a problem-solving process, but as a pure pleasure.

Frank must have been pleased with it at the time because he offered it to Chicago's most prestigious architectural magazine and, amazingly, they published it. It appears in a June 1887 edition of the fortnightly *Inland Architect and News Record*.[17] According to Grant Manson, the author of the first published biography of Frank Lloyd Wright, the architect later came to regret the publication, and would have preferred the Sioux City Unitarian Chapel to have been forgotten about. Manson referred to it as Frank's *bête noire*, perhaps because it displayed its influences so candidly.[18]

Frank must have come to appreciate, in the years that followed, that there was no more efficient way to learn the essentials of architecture than to design houses and to watch them being built, to understand what had to be drawn in detail and what could be left to the experienced builder to manage. Despite this, he was always disparaging about Silsbee's work. While he drew and listened, and watched and learned from the process of designing and constructing one middle-class shingled house after another, his imagination was fired, inevitably, by the prospect of working on bigger, more spectacular projects in the heart of the city. In this he was no different from the great majority of novice architects, then and now. At Silsbee's office in February 1888 Frank spoke with Walter Willcox, a technician from one of the electrical contractors they worked with. Willcox had recently been at the office of Adler and Sullivan, a practice that had been established five years before and had grown rapidly to become the most progressive and ambitious in the city. Willcox was looking for a chance to move into architecture. He'd worked occasionally for Silsbee, and had put himself forward for a vacancy as a draughtsman with Adler and Sullivan. He'd been told that he lacked the experience that they were looking for. He knew that Frank was restless. Perhaps if Frank moved on, it could open a permanent space for Willcox at Silsbee's? He had mentioned Frank Lloyd Wright's name at Adler and Sullivan. Frank needed no further encouragement.[19]

As a young man Louis Sullivan was one of very few Americans to be given a place at the École des Beaux-Arts in Paris, a testament to his superb draughting skills. Europe was a formative experience for him. He developed self-confidence, a taste for exquisite clothes, and he immersed himself in Transcendentalist literature and modern European music, all of which served to turn him against his academic training. At the École he 'vigorously rejected all he learned or might have learned except for the dicta of a mathematics tutor'.[20] He returned to Chicago in May 1875, his mind filled by a conception of architecture that had developed from the Beaux-Arts approach while still expressing his visceral aversion to the historicism of his French tutors. He had a clear vision of the work that he wanted to do. He set himself up as a freelance designer. In this capacity he provided his finishing services on the elevations and interiors for a host of Chicago's larger practices, steadily building a reputation for his arrestingly beautiful pattern making.[21]

One of the large practices that Sullivan served belonged to Dankmar Adler, an engineer by training and a specialist in complex public buildings. Adler had been impressed by the young designer's vision and creativity. In the spring of 1881 he employed Sullivan full-time, with a brief to provide graceful ornamentation for the practice's functional structures. Within two years he had been elevated to a full partnership, and the practice took a new name: Adler and Sullivan. It was a working relationship that yielded spectacular results. Adler's formal rigour and Sullivan's highly original, sensuous and intricate surface modelling were resolved so harmoniously that they seemed the work of one creative mind. When Frank Lloyd Wright arrived at the Borden Block with his portfolio, Adler and Sullivan's office already had a staff of twenty and was recruiting more to deal with a workload of around sixty projects including factories, office buildings and smaller jobs, houses, tombs and monuments. One of the projects was the colossal Auditorium Building, a structure so vast and complex that it had come to dominate the time and energy of both partners, pushing their other commissions to the margins.[22] Sullivan had given his first public speech in 1885, the year before the Auditorium commission, and had used it to position himself as a visionary outsider, a prophet in his own land with a mission to reshape society. The Auditorium project would be Sullivan's vindication, the means by which he would realise his mystical vision, but in order to fulfil his ambition he first had to work around his own occlusive personality.[23] He found it stressful to communicate directly with his own draughting team, as if the essential cohort of copiers and tracers occupied a more lowly realm. He preferred to work with a single assistant with whom he could share the intensity of his creative process and his deeper philosophical reflections. He needed an intermediary, an acolyte, someone who could be trusted to control the draughting team on his behalf and, ideally, also someone with artistic talent of his own.

Frank may not have fully appreciated the nature of the vacancy. According to his autobiography their first encounter was brief, as Sullivan was about to leave the office for a conference. Frank showed Sullivan some of the drawings he had made for Silsbee. 'These aren't the kind of drawings I would like to see, but I have no time now. I'll be back Friday morning. Make some drawings of ornament or ornamental details and bring them back in then.' Frank went away flushed with excitement, moved most of all by Sullivan's demeanour and his body language. He was, 'a small man, immaculately dressed. His outstanding feature his amazing big brown eyes. Took me in at a glance. Everything that I felt, even to my most secret thoughts ... He looked at me kindly, and saw *me*. I was sure of that much'[24] (Pl. 51). Perhaps Sullivan had recognised a kindred spirit in him, something in the incongruous flamboyance of Frank's attire, his long hair and his puppy-dog enthusiasm, a fellow outsider, but young and gregarious. It was the beginning of the most significant architectural relationship in the life of Frank Lloyd Wright. For the next three nights Frank worked his way through a sheaf of onionskin paper, tracing patterns from a book that he had borrowed from the All Souls library. The book was *The Grammar of Ornament*, an extraordinary source-book of historic ornamental design collected from cultures around the world. Why was this book, published only in London,

Pl. 51. Louis Sullivan.

to be found in the library of All Souls? Its multicultural content would have appealed to Jenkin Lloyd Jones, but there was another curious connection, or perhaps merely a synchronicity: its author, the architect Owen Jones, was the son of Owain Myfyr, erstwhile patron of Iolo Morganwg.

After Frank showed his new drawings Sullivan demonstrated his satisfaction with what he'd seen by removing a cover sheet from his own drawing board. Frank 'gasped with delight' at what he saw: 'if Silsbee's touch was like standing corn waving in the fields, Sullivan's was like the passion vine – in full bloom.' They agreed starting terms: $25 a week, a generous uplift from his wage at Silsbee's, on Sullivan's condition that Frank had to 'stick until the drawings for the Auditorium are finished'. He began work with Sullivan the following Monday.[25]

Frank's sudden appearance at Sullivan's side provoked resentment among Adler's long-serving German staff. Some had begrudged Sullivan's own rapid rise, and they now had to accept another callow youngster judging their execution of Sullivan's instructions. According to his autobiography, the simmering tensions were only resolved when Frank overpowered the most aggressive of his antagonists in an ugly brawl that spilled across the draughting room.[26] From then on the respect he acquired was earned doggedly, by his devotion to the work and his willingness to toil late into the night alongside his master. It was at Sullivan's side that he began properly to learn about architecture, to think analytically about the process of formal composition and about the countervailing forces; where the consensus dwelt and what the possibilities might be for a new American architecture. Sullivan spoke to him about architecture endlessly in philosophical and spiritual terms that seemed familiar to him, all the more effectively to entrance him. It must have been apparent to Frank, from early in their relationship, that Sullivan's passions and convictions had a distinctly Unitarian flavour.

Although he had been raised a Catholic, Sullivan's personal enlightenment had begun when he dropped out of Massachusetts Institute of Technology to take an apprenticeship with the great Philadelphian architect Frank Furness. It was Furness who planted the seeds of creative nonconformity in Sullivan's young mind. Where should an aspiring architectural student go for his education? Furness's advice: 'all schools are bad ... put him in an architect's office and let him work out his own salvation. Give him a chance to upset the rules' – words that might have been spoken by Frank Lloyd Wright himself.[27] Furness was an ardent Unitarian. His father, William Henry Furness, was the first ordained minister of Joseph Priestley's 'Unitarian Society of Philadelphia', itself the first church in America to identify itself as Unitarian. Ralph Emerson, Henry Thoreau and Walt Whitman were among William Furness's group of close friends. Frank Furness had grown up among the Transcendentalist giants, and it was he who introduced Sullivan to their philosophy. When Sullivan spoke to his young apprentice about Emerson he could not have anticipated that Frank had been nourished by Emerson from

infancy. From his reading of the Transcendentalists it had become clear to Sullivan that his instincts were his most reliable guide. The same insight had guided Frank's family for generations.

Over the many years that followed his time with Sullivan, Frank would always honour him as his one great mentor, the man who led him to the essential precepts of design. This has typically been understood as the relationship of an architectural teacher to a student, filling the gaps in Frank's tutelage. But for Frank the more significant revelation was that a Transcendentalist Unitarian sensibility need not just coexist with architectural practice, but that it could be directly and productively applied, that his contrarian instincts need not be reined in, but might in fact be his greatest asset. He was able to perceive for the first time that a single, clear and original architectural voice could indeed bring about a momentous change in all of society. He knew his own vigour was a crutch for Sullivan's frailties. He began to imagine that the voice of change could be his own, rather than Sullivan's.

Once he was settled at Adler and Sullivan, Frank felt sufficiently secure in his prospects to tell his mother that she could safely sell up in Madison and move to Chicago to join him. His mother's move seems to have been the next step in a carefully planned process of transition, a process, presumably, of Anna's devising, aided by his Uncle Jenkin. His sister Jane was eighteen years old and already teaching. Anna had been earning a modest living as a house mistress at her sisters' Hillside Home School; Maginel had been a pupil. She was ten years old and ready to start high school in the autumn. When she moved with her daughters, to Chicago, Anna had a useful cache of funds to draw upon. She had sold the remnants of her ex-husband's assets and she had a share of the inheritance from her father. She also had a share of the proceeds from the sale of their Madison house. The train from Madison to Chicago took them back through Ixonia, within yards of the little Welsh cemetery. Perhaps the log house was still there too, her childhood home, outgrown thirty years before. Although she was happy in Madison, Anna would never feel as comfortable in a town as she did in the country, and there was little prospect that she would be settled in the city of Chicago itself.

In 1888, Augusta Chapin was the Universalist Pastor of Oak Park, a genteel suburb twelve miles west of the city centre. Before moving there, she had led a church in the city centre, close to All Souls. She had shared in its busy social life and become acquainted with Jenkin Lloyd Jones. According to Frank, she was also a friend of his mother's, a connection that could have been made in Augusta Chapin's earlier life as an itinerant minister. In the autumn of 1888 Anna, Frank and his two sisters all moved in with the Rev. Chapin at what Maginel remembered as her 'big, ugly, red brick house' on Forest Avenue, in the centre of Oak Park village.[28] He described their neighbours as, 'good people, most of whom had taken asylum there to bring up their children in comparative peace, safe from the poison of the great city'.[29] It was one of the oldest suburbs of the city, and 'a favourite resort for literary and religious people'.[30] Among Chicagoans it was known as 'Saints' Rest', and the place where, 'the saloons end and the steeples begin', all of which would indeed be agreeable to Anna Lloyd Wright. It was equally agreeable to Frank. He was far more at home in the leafy suburb than he was in the city centre, and much as he enjoyed his occasional nights on the town, he would never be as comfortable there as his cousin Dickie seemed. Later in his life he would argue loudly for the eradication of metropolitan cities, and that diffuse suburbs were the natural habitat for Americans. Oak Park was safe, wholesome, spacious and verdant. He loved it, and it would be his home for the next twenty-two years (Pl. 52) ∎

Pl. 52 The View west from Oak Park along Madison Street. The township of River Forest can be seen through the trees on the right in the background. This photograph was taken in 1903 when the township was still surrounded by open fields and woods. The cable car connects the city of Chicago to its semi-rural hinterland. Courtesy of Oak Park Public Library.

# 09 The Grammar of Ornament
## *Notes*

1   *Chicago Tribune* (11 October 1871), 1.

2   Everett Chamberlain, *Chicago and its Suburbs* (Chicago: T. A. Hungerford & Co., 1874), pp. 19–29.

3   Frank Lloyd Wright, *An Autobiography (Edition 1)* (New York: Longman, Green & Co., 1932), p. 63.

4   See *www.chicagology.com/rebuilding* (April 2021) for extracts from *The Land Owner* (August 1872) and *The Inter Ocean* (20 July 1872).

5   F. L. Wright, *An Autobiography (Edition 1)*, p. 64.

6   Edward S. Morse, *Japanese Homes and their Surroundings* (Boston: Ticknor and Co., 1886).

7   Frank Lloyd Wright, *An Autobiography (Edition 2)* (London: Faber & Faber, 1946), p. 68.

8   F. L. Wright, *An Autobiography (Edition 1)*, p. 74

9   F. L. Wright, *An Autobiography (Edition 1)*, p. 72.

10  Donald Leslie Johnson, *Frank Lloyd Wright: Early Years: Progressivism: Aesthetics: Cities* (Abingdon: Routledge, 2017), p. 74.

11  F. L. Wright, *An Autobiography (Edition 1)*, p. 71.

12  *Lakeside Annual Directory 1885* (Chicago Directory Company), p. 324. [13]

13  Maginel Wright Barney, *The Valley of the God Almighty Joneses* (New York: Appleton Century, 1965), p. 114.

14  Letter, Ellen Lloyd Jones to Frank Lloyd Wright, 9 March 1887. Frank Lloyd Wright Foundation Ref. J001A030000. See also Johnson, *Frank Lloyd Wright: Early Years: Progressivism: Aesthetics: Cities*, p. 51.

15  Johnson, *Frank Lloyd Wright: Early Years: Progressivism: Aesthetics: Cities*, p. 75.

16      Johnson, *Frank Lloyd Wright: Early Years:
        Progressivism: Aesthetics: Cities*, p. 75.

17      *Inland Architect and News Record*, 9/8 (June 1887), xviii.

18      Grant Carpenter Manson, *Frank Lloyd Wright to 1910: The First
        Golden Age* (New York: Van Nostrand Reinhold Co.,1958), p. 17.
        See also, Brendan Gill, *Many Masks: A Life of Frank Lloyd Wright*
        (London: Heinemann, 1988), p. 58.

19      F. L. Wright, *An Autobiography (Edition 1)*, pp. 88–9.
        See also Johnson, *Frank Lloyd Wright: Early Years: Progressivism:
        Aesthetics: Cities*, p. 85.

20      H.-R. Hitchcock, 'Frank Lloyd Wright and the Academic Tradition
        of the Early Eighteen Nineties', *Journal of the Warburg and Courtauld
        Institutes*, 7 (1944), 48.

21      R. K. Williamson, *American Architects and the Mechanics of Fame*
        (Austin: University of Texas Press, 1991), p. 38.

22      R. B. Elstein, 'Adler & Sullivan: The End of the Partnership and
        its Aftermath', *Journal of Illinois State Historical Society*, 98/1–2
        (2005), 63.

23      Williamson, *American Architects and the Mechanics of Fame*, p. 38.

24      F. L. Wright, *An Autobiography (Edition 1)*, pp. 87–91.

25      F. L. Wright, *An Autobiography (Edition 1)*, p. 91.

26      There is corroboration of this story. See Paul Hendrickson, *Plagued
        by Fire: The Dreams and Furies of Frank Lloyd Wright* (London: Bodley
        Head, 2019), pp. 104–6.

27      George E. Thomas, *Frank Furness: The Complete Works*
        (New York: Princeton Architectural Press, 1991), p. 362, quoted in
        R. B. Elstein, 'Adler & Sullivan: The End of the Partnership and its
        Aftermath', p. 59.

28      Barney, *The Valley of the God Almighty Joneses*, p. 127.

29      F. L. Wright, *An Autobiography (Edition 1)*, p. 78.

30      Chamberlain, *Chicago and its Suburbs*, p. 426.

# 10

# Simplicity and Repose

## 1888. Oak Park, Illinois

Life at Augusta Chapin's house had its predictable stresses. She was a deeply serious and highly accomplished woman. While she led the Universalist church she also lectured in English literature at Lombard College in Galesburg, and was an active charter member of the American Woman Suffrage Association. She was exactly the kind of companion that Anna most valued, although the terms of their accommodation did not put them on an equal footing. Anna's job was to look after the household, Miss

Chapin included.[1] Frank recalled Augusta Chapin as a 'thick set woman's woman ... usually dressed in rustling black silk ... [wearing] alternately a very kind or a very severe expression'.[2] She was prone to occasional outbursts of rage, giving the unavoidable impression that, regardless of the size of her house, she would sometimes rather have it to herself. They all knew that they needed to find a home of their own, that staying at the Rev. Chapin's 'red brick' was not for the long term. But property in Oak Park was expensive. Even with Anna's savings, they still needed a mortgage, and Frank was the only one of them in a position, potentially, to get one.

The Auditorium Building filled the first two years of Frank's time with Adler and Sullivan. Its construction had caused excitement across the city and on its opening, in December 1889, the completed building was a nationwide sensation (Pl. 53). It was the largest single building in America and, at seventeen storeys, the tallest in the city. Its centrepiece was a 4,000-seat opera house, the ultimate showpiece for Sullivan's decorative design and for Adler's advanced acoustic engineering. Sullivan had depended heavily on Frank's support to complete the project, and had come to trust him apparently without reservation. At Frank's suggestion, he had recruited another of Silsbee's most talented young architects, a Scotsman named George Elmslie. When the Adler and Sullivan practice moved from the Borden Block, one of Adler's earlier buildings, to the top floor of the Auditorium tower, Frank and Elmslie were assigned a privileged corner office which adjoined Sullivan's own room and shared the view of the draughting studio.

As far as Sullivan and Frank were concerned, each was committed to their working relationship for the long term. Early in 1889, Frank persuaded Sullivan to advance him a $5,000 loan against his future earnings in exchange for a contract that would commit Frank to the practice for the next five years. At the same time they agreed a salary that, according to Sullivan, made Frank the highest-paid draughtsman in Chicago. With the borrowed money and with Anna's savings, the Wrights could afford, at last, to move out of Augusta Chapin's house and buy a house of their own. The property they settled on was only a short walk along

Forest Avenue at the corner with Chicago Avenue. It was a large plot, over a hundred metres long and around thirty in width, with a beautiful garden that had been laid out by its previous owner, a landscape designer. The house stood at the eastern end of the plot, away from the corner. It was a small house in the 'carpenter gothic' style. Maginel remembered it as being painted white and capped by 'scalloped eaves with a teardrop at each corner' (Pl. 54). It reminded her of Uncle Enos's house in The Valley.[3] To Frank's eyes it was depressingly ordinary, but he was content to bide his time there, living with his sisters and his mother, at least until he resolved his own domestic plans.[4] In the first months of 1889 those plans were the cause of turmoil in two households.

Frank had his first encounter with Kitty Tobin during the summer of 1887 at a *Les Misérables* costume party at All Souls Church. They collided on the dance floor, bumping heads.[5] She was only a few months past her sixteenth birthday while Frank had recently celebrated his twentieth. Their friendship grew slowly at first, and then gathered pace to the extent that, by the summer of 1888, everyone in the community of All Souls had begun to think of them as a couple.

Kitty's family was prosperous, middle-class, with a home on Kimbark Avenue in the fashionable Hyde Park neighbourhood, just a mile to the south of All Souls. They were devoted to Jenkin Lloyd Jones. While Kitty's parents were delighted to keep company with the minister's nephew, her father, at least, was distraught at the prospect that Frank's friendship with his daughter might lead to something more serious. Anna Lloyd Wright felt the same, and between them the parents of the young couple did all they could to disentangle them. In the summer of 1888 they conspired to send Kitty away to stay for three months with relatives, a move that provoked a furious outburst from Frank. The letter that he wrote to his mother has not survived, but Frank did keep Anna's apparently remorseful reply:

*Don't write or say a word to your Uncle of what I wrote to you. He is a friend of yours but he does not agree with your mode of living ... I begin to realise as never before how very disagreeable your mother and her relations are to you. I know they are humble people but thoroughly good*

Pl. 53.   The Auditorium Building. The windows of Louis Sullivan's office and Frank's office are one floor down from the top floor of the tower, between the light-coloured pillars.
LOC.

Pl. 54.   The house at 931 Chicago Avenue, Oak Park. Anna Lloyd Wright owned the house and Frank owned the large adjoining garden. Frank shared the house with his mother and sisters until he could move into the house that he built for himself on the garden.

*and respectable. Capable of being kind and true ... hate me as much as you are inclined to but love the truth and kindliness. Don't curse and use extravagant words. Try to walk on the genial side of life. Much love from your very sorrowful mother.*[6]

If she had been trying to make him feel guilty Anna must have known that it would be futile. She was, in effect, attempting to defy her own most fervent prescription, that above everything Frank should believe in himself unquestioningly. Frank was determined that he would marry Kitty, and Kitty felt the same about Frank. She was high-spirited, gregarious and full of fun. She was also devoted to him in a way that no woman, other than his mother, had ever been, and he seemed to take it for granted that Kitty would also, like his mother, subordinate herself unconditionally to his creative needs.

The wedding took place on 1 June 1889. By then it seems both families were reconciled to the inevitable as the ceremony was held at All Souls and led by his Uncle Jenkin. Kitty moved into the little white house with Frank's family. Maginel recalled that 'this was a most unhappy arrangement. Poor Kitty was scarcely more than a child and was bewildered and miserable at Mother's obvious antagonism.'[7] Despite her discomfort, before the end of June Kitty was pregnant. When they had bought their property, Frank and his mother had agreed to divide the plot. The house belonged to Anna and the garden was Frank's. As he was only buying a piece of empty land, Frank's financial contribution was smaller than his mother's. He had kept $3,500 of the money that he borrowed from Sullivan for his bigger plan. In the months leading up to the wedding he had begun to design his own house, to be built in the garden. Kitty's condition added urgency to the already pressing need, and in August builders began to clear the site for Frank Lloyd Wright's first building.

For many young architects, the first building presents a dilemma. There is always the concern that it could be the only building, not just the first, and the prospect that there might not be another leads the designers to find places to include as many of their particular ideas, likes and fancies as they possibly can, often at odds with each other and squeezed into a space too small to hold them. There are several extraordinary aspects to Frank's first building, but perhaps the most surprising is its utter self-confidence and calm maturity (Pl. 55). It conveys a clarity of purpose that is exceptional for a designer in his early twenties. Some might ask if this is only as it appears to the contemporary eye, but this seems not to be the case. It certainly stood out as unusual in 1890 because, with its modest, understated forms, it expressed a sense of serene and timeless integrity that diverged refreshingly from Oak Park's clutter of carpenter gothic. In its first form, it was no more than a cottage, with three rooms and a pantry on the lower floor, three rooms and a bathroom on the upper (Fig. 10.1). Only the front elevation could be seen clearly from the street. It had a simple outline: a tall triangle, almost equilateral, mounted on top of two projecting window bays. The whole house sat on a stone plinth, raised a few steps above the level of the garden. Six windows formed a

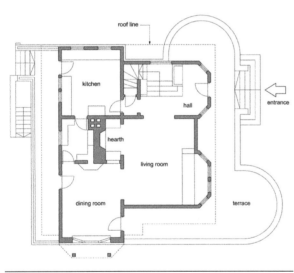

Fig. 10.1. Recreation of the early plan of the Oak Park Home and Studio, *circa* 1889.

Home School, a likeness that would certainly have pleased his mother. The symmetry was unexpectedly classical, the scale and the textures unmistakably domestic and the overall impression one of sombre solidity. Any sense of heaviness was dispelled immediately on crossing the threshold (Pl. 56).

Despite the lack of size it seemed remarkably spacious. There were no doors or even door frames between the rooms. The separating planes were equal parts solid and open so that there was always a clear perspective of adjoining rooms. With cream and pale honey-coloured distemper above the wainscot rail, and intermittent panels of warm grey and clear-varnished, blond oak panelling below, the bands of colour maintained their horizontals as they folded through the living rooms. It was a set of spaces and, at the same time,

Pl. 56. Oak Park Home and Studio. This is the space immediately inside the front door. The stairs, behind the timber balustrade, were made wide enough to serve as seats for a small audience to look into the sitting room; the landing wide enough to serve as a small stage, for an audience seated in the sitting room. Photograph James Caulfield/FLWT.

horizontal rectangular panel in the centre of the gable, and set above that, on the centre line, was a small lunette. The gable was shingled and painted with dark creosote, bringing to mind immediately the shingles of Unity Chapel and of Hillside

Pl. 57. Oak Park Home and Studio. The hearth at the centre of the house, with its motto 'Truth is Life', an affirmation of 'Truth Against the World'.
Photograph James Caulfield/FLWT.

limits: it was this property, emphasised by the continuous horizontal lines of the slender timber rails, that magnified the sense of space so unexpectedly. Some have identified it as the first deliberately 'open plan' house to be designed. It certainly embodies the characteristics of open planning but it cannot really be argued that Frank was led to this idea by pursuing an 'open-plan' spatial programme for its own sake, as would be the case for succeeding generations of architects. Frank seemed to do it as part of a broader set of ideas about familial cohesion and co-visibility which influenced another personal and perhaps more original aspect of the house. The spaces of the house were arrayed around a central fireplace, as if it was the fireplace that anchored the house to the earth (Pl. 57). Above the mantel there was a carved inscription that read, 'Truth is Life' and just below, 'Good Friend, Around These Hearth-Stones Speak No Evil Word of any Creature.' In the traditional Welsh farmhouse the life of the family was played out in the *cegin*, a combined kitchen and living room with a fireplace as its focus, the 'theatre of the Welsh farmer's domestic life', as Alfred Russell Wallace identified it.[8]

There are a few photographs that survive of the early houses in the Lloyd Jones Valley; all appear to have central chimneys, even Aunt Margaret's gambrel-roofed home. To Frank, the centrality of the fireplace took on a deep significance. The warmth and the light were metaphors for the love and spiritual purity of the family, a secure interdependence that bound the Lloyd Joneses tightly together, but which seemed elusive in his own childhood home. The symbolic central fireplace can be seen as an expression of his yearning to recreate the familial comradeship that he found in the *ceginau*, the traditional kitchen–living rooms, of his aunts and uncles during his blissful summers in the Lloyd Jones Valley.[9] Having settled on this notion, its significance seemed only to grow within Frank's conception of the ideal arrangement of living space. For the following two decades, almost without exception, when Frank sat down to plan a new house, one of his first moves would be to embed a substantial masonry fireplace at its heart.

The architectural scholar Henry Russell Hitchcock was the first to recognise a principal source of the design of

a single space. Although its floor area was modest, there was no position from which it was possible to perceive its overall

Frank's house. The bold triangular gable, its arrangement of glazing and the two bays at the base were replicated from two houses designed in 1885 and 1886 by the progressive New York architect Bruce Price. His Kent and Chandler residences had attracted the attention of the New York journals. Frank must have seen them; the images stayed with him. There is something more in the similarity. Following Hitchcock, Vincent Scully pointed out that the idea of open planning had also been explored by Bruce Price, McKim, Mead and White and a small coterie of east coast architects in the mid-1880s, and that it was, in fact, one of the defining characteristics of the emergent 'shingle style', as Scully named it.[10] Price's Kent and Chandler residences were both of this type. Some academics believe that Joseph Silsbee had himself begun to adopt this approach in the mid-1880s, as he had certainly embraced shingle cladding. Typically, however, the houses that Frank would have worked on with Silsbee were large, rambling structures for wealthy clients, and the application of open planning, such as it appeared, was intended to achieve a grandiose, baronial effect: wide, high and draughty with fireplaces at regular intervals around their perimeters. Although the provenance of the ideas is clear, Frank rethought them. His intentions were markedly different. Without an academic foundation, he drew from the most powerful architectural experiences of his own life, experiences that were entirely domestic and vernacular, life enfolded by welcoming spaces, a seat by the fire, a place at the table, a bed in the slope of the roof. As his knowledge of architecture accumulated Frank would develop an extraordinary capacity to gather, assimilate and syncretise images and forms from remote corners of the architectural world, and from sources outside architecture. He would acquire draughting skill and technical expertise to match any of his contemporaries. And yet the most powerful personal and lasting expression of his art is the one that came instinctively to him, an idea deeper than a theory, a Truth: that architecture was the materialisation of human spirituality, that an honest and simple existence, a life that matched the ideal he had been raised in, could only be lived within an honest and simple architecture. Like his mother,

Frank despised the darkness, gloomy drapery and cluttered bric-à-brac that distinguished the lifestyle of the American middle class. He was repulsed, not just by its intrinsic vulgarity, but by the suffocating, judgemental conformity it represented. Like the homes of the Lloyd Joneses in The Valley, like those of his ancestors in Cardiganshire, his Oak Park home was an expression of his uncluttered faith.

As Grant Manson noted, Frank had intuited 'a sense of decoration far in advance of its period', that was also 'somehow reminiscent of the interiors in [their] ... house in Madison and of the undeniable influence of his mother's taste upon him'.[11] Manson did not elaborate on this astute comment. He was the first to attempt an unravelling of Frank's influences. A tentative loosening of the knots was perhaps far enough to go; he can be forgiven for going no further. It is harder to be as lenient with the many later biographers who have sidestepped the essential issue of Anna's influence on her son. In his first public talk, delivered in 1894 to the University Guild at Evanston, Illinois, Frank advised his audience that 'Simplicity and repose are ideals to cleave to ... Simplicity', he said, was, 'something with graceful sense of beauty in its utility from which discord and all that is meaningless has been eliminated'. 'Repose' meant that any and every part would be 'perfectly adjusted in relation to the whole, in absolute poise, leaving nothing but a quiet sense of satisfaction with its sense of completeness'.[12] The spirit of simplicity and repose that was so powerfully present in the design of his own home did not come from Louis Sullivan, whose own work was intensely complex. Nor did it come from Silsbee or Allan Conover. It came from Anna Lloyd Jones, and she drew it from her religious asceticism, from her complete absorption in the ideas of Truth, of Unity and of the Godliness of Nature, ideas that were bred in her, as they were bred in Frank[13] (Pl. 58).

The house was completed in March 1890. Frank and Kitty made the 30 metre journey to move in just a few days before their son, Lloyd, was born.[14] Adler and Sullivan's successful delivery of the Auditorium Building brought more large commissions, but Frank's contributions to them were modest. He was considered sufficiently dependable to manage smaller commissions, in particular the houses

Pl. 58. At the entrance to the Oak Park Home and Studio, from left: Jenkin Lloyd Jones, his wife Sarah holding the tennis racquet, Jane Lloyd Wright, Kitty Wright holding baby Lloyd, Anna Lloyd Wright, Maginel, Frank and Mary, daughter of Jenkin and Sarah. Lloyd is very young, so the photograph must date from the summer of 1899. 'Dickie' Lloyd Jones is not in the picture; he was probably the photographer.
FLWT.

Street. To European eyes it is a house that appears to have originated from some centuries in the past. The massing, the small deep windows, the balcony and the overhang of the roof suggest that it was designed for a hot climate, perhaps that of central Italy, not for the cool and windy Midwest. The organisation of the elevation into three vertical sections, the subtle balance of projection and recess, and the horizontal overlay of modulated masonry are all characteristic of Louis Sullivan's approach.[17] It may have come to be recognised as one of a number of modest but charming neo-classical exercises in Sullivan's oeuvre, but it has assumed unexpected significance because, many years later, Frank claimed that it was he who had designed it, not Sullivan. The assertion was made first in Grant Manson's book of 1958,

> Although it is officially an Adler and Sullivan design it is, in reality, the first great monument of Frank Lloyd Wright's career ... It stands today clean and challenging among its outmoded neighbours, a ringing statement of belief in a new future for architecture. It owes no debt to anyone but its designer, much of whose coming development it forecasts, and it carries us in one amazing leap into the spirit of the next century.[18]

Since this claim was made, the authorship of the Charnley House has been contested between proponents of Wright and defenders of Sullivan. As is most often the case, the truth is surely in between. Frank's colleagues George Elmslie and Paul Mueller both recalled that Frank had worked on the drawings at home, and that the design was revealed to the office for the first time by Frank, but in both recollections it is unavoidably implied that Frank had merely developed a concept that had been given to him by Sullivan. This is exactly how architectural practices function: the principal produces the concept which, however rough, embodies the vast majority of the significant design decisions. The trusted junior adds the detail and 'makes it work'.[19] It seems unlikely that Frank could have designed it. The step from his own little cottage, with its happy mix of intuition and derivation, to the academic sophistication of the Charnley House is not one that could plausibly have been made within just a few

requested by important clients and families, which the partners would otherwise have preferred to turn away.[15] These included a summer house for Louis Sullivan himself, in Ocean Springs, Mississippi, and a Chicago townhouse for Sullivan's brother Albert.[16] The most noteworthy of the houses was designed for Sullivan's close friend, James Charnley (Pl. 59). It is a beautiful three-storey house, small by central Chicago standards, but overtly neo-classical with an emphatic symmetry that makes it appear much larger. It still stands in one of the most desirable quarters of the city, close to the lake at the corner of Astor Street and Schiller months, and the houses that Frank would go on to design in the following few years convincingly bear this out. The claims for its prescient modernity are no less dubious. The Charnley House may not be Beaux-Arts, but its classical pedigree is clear. Brendan Gill saw it as a conscious imitation of the French neo-classicist Claude Ledoux: 'Instead of carrying us "in one amazing leap into the spirit of the next century" it carries us in one amazing leap backward into the eighteenth century, a period that Wright was soon utterly to repudiate.'[20]

When he had agreed to make his generous loan, Louis Sullivan had warned Frank against extravagance. 'Now look out Wright! I know your tastes ... no "extras"!' By the time Frank had furnished his new home he had exceeded his budget by $1,200, quite an achievement for a project that was supposed to cost $3,500. He insisted that the rugs, the furniture and the few ceramics should be of the highest quality. Money spilled like water through his fingers. He wasn't sure why. 'The children that followed during those years made creditors a familiar sight – or was it the "tastes"?'[21] It was the first really troublesome manifestation of a careless regard for money and for debt that had begun in his adolescence and would burgeon outrageously in his later life. The solution seemed obvious. Although he was well rewarded by Adler and Sullivan, and already working long hours, he began to look for commissions of his own to boost his income. Remarkably, during the course of 1892, while clocking up his hours with Louis Sullivan, he also managed to design and deliver nine substantial homes for private clients, making it one of the most productive of his years in Chicago. He later referred to these projects as his 'bootlegged houses', built in breach of his restrictive contract with Adler and Sullivan.

The architecture of the bootlegged houses provides a succinct picture of the young architect's capabilities at the time. There is little to indicate the emergence of a distinctive style, but there is an abundance of the confident restraint and discipline that was evident in the design of his own house. Most of the bootlegged houses are competent exercises in the fashionable American Queen Anne style as it evolved into the shingle style.[22] This was the approach that he had assimilated in his time with Joseph Silsbee. Despite later claims by some to the contrary, Frank Lloyd

Pl. 59. James Charnley Residence, North Astor Street, Chicago. Adler and Sullivan 1892. Frank's role in the design has been contested for many decades. The building is now the headquarters of the American Society of Architectural Historians.

Wright was not superhuman. It was no more manageable in 1892 than it would be today for an architect to design and deliver nine different houses single-handedly while also working long hours for a commercial practice. Although he takes full credit for these projects in his autobiography, the workload was shared. His partner was Cecil Corwin, his closest friend from his time with Silsbee. It was Corwin who produced the construction drawings and supervised the building work, Silsbee's influence is doubly embedded. There is also a pragmatism in the repeated use of familiar forms. The builders knew the patterns, fewer drawings were needed, less supervision was required and costs were more predictable. There are, however, some deviations from the Silsbee style. The best-known is the house that Frank designed for George Blossom. It was a study in New

Pl. 60. Two of the 'bootlegged houses': George Blossom House and Warren McArthur House, South Kenwood Avenue, Chicago, 1892.

England Colonial Revival, with primrose and white painted clapboard, a large, semicircular colonnaded porch and Palladian windows. Later in the year he designed a house for the McArthur family in the Dutch Colonial style: dark, densely shingled and capped with a heavy gambrel roof. It was next door to the Blossom house, a space of just a few yards separated them (Pl. 60). The architect and the two neighbours must have found some enjoyment in the jarring contrast. The two houses still stand on South Kenwood Avenue in Chicago's Southside, just a short street away from the home of Frank's parents-in-law. The Tobins may have played a part in guiding the commissions from their neighbours towards their daughter's husband. Kitty, in the meantime, was expecting her second baby.

Distinguished American scholars have closely scrutinised Frank's bootlegged houses and, looking back across the full span of his remarkable career to its remote starting point, some have become convinced that these

early projects demonstrate Frank's precocious mastery of 'academic design', and even a gift for baroque planning, talents that he somehow acquired without formal training.[23] This perception is coloured by a true outlier in Frank's early portfolio: a competition design that he made in 1893 for Milwaukee Public Library. It was overtly Beaux-Arts classical. To understand his motivation for approaching the competition in this way it is only necessary to look at the winning design, the Milwaukee Public Library as it exists, designed by the city's leading practice, Ferry and Clas. It bears a close resemblance to Frank's proposal (Fig. 10.2). Both designs and, no doubt many of the other seventy-two submissions, replicated Charles Atwood's Arts Pavilion, which was, at the time, the favourite of the critics at Chicago's great Columbian Exposition (Pl. 61). Frank was simply playing to the known preconceptions of the adjudicators, hoping the roulette ball would drop onto his number and deliver him a life-changing opportunity. Had he been successful his career would have taken a different path. He might now be no better known than Ferry and Clas.

Frank's Milwaukee Public Library design and the bootlegged houses do tell us that, among his other talents, he was a proficient copyist. He was comfortable to apply any style that suited his audience, because it would appear that he was not so much interested in appearances at this stage in his development as he was in the more basic matter of how the occupants of his buildings might behave; how they would interact, what they would experience, what they would feel within the spaces that he created. Unitarianism was concerned, as a matter of course, with personal spiritual development as expressed through the individual's relationship with other people, in particular those closest to them. Whereas Louis Sullivan had thought in more abstract terms about the 'democratisation' of architectural space, Frank Lloyd Wright was fascinated by the influence of his architecture on human behaviour and emotions at the most direct, practical level. It was this preoccupation in the early days that most clearly differentiated him from his contemporaries. It is possible to see him working almost scientifically, testing forms and spatial arrangements, observing their varying consequences, trying things out.

It was an approach that would soon lead him away from stylistic convention and into new architectural territory, but that was still to come. If he had turned away from architecture in late 1892 – if, for example, he had gone into the ministry, as his mother had originally hoped – there is not much that would have drawn attention to this early body of work. Not much. But among the bootlegged houses there is one that really does seem as if it could have been a signpost to Frank's extraordinary future. Had he indeed come to nothing as an architect, the house that he designed for Dr Allison Harlan could still have stood out as a prescient aberration (Pl. 62). The only reason that it might not have done is that Dr Harlan and several subsequent owners altered it to such an extent that it was almost unrecognisable when, in 1963, it was finally destroyed by fire. The one project that marked Frank out, early on, as a truly progressive artist was just too strange to be lived in or to be lived with.

Dr Harlan was another near neighbour of the Tobin family. Whereas the Blossoms and the McArthurs had apparently directed their architect towards their stylistic preference, Dr Harlan must have offered him *carte blanche*. As if to dispel any uncertainty about his neo-classical tendencies the front elevation of the Harlan House is divided into six structural bays at ground level and seven at the upper level. Why would anyone do such a thing in defiance of structural common sense? In part the answer could be simply that there was an architectural convention that was so complacent in its inevitability that it just had to be broken. There is no theory, social, behavioural or aesthetic, behind this notion; it is purely contrarian, and this was just one of its oddnesses. At pavement level the house was shielded by a solid wall, rising above head height. The main entrance door was half way down the side, so that the front face of the house could be presented as an unbroken geometric pattern. The south-west corner, the left corner, if you were standing in front of the house, was supported by a free-standing column that carried the portal to the arcade that led around the side to the entrance. The column at the corner, almost disconnected from the body of the house, provides a glimpse of the structural expressionism that would become a defining feature of modernist architecture in later decades. Frank was keen to point out in his

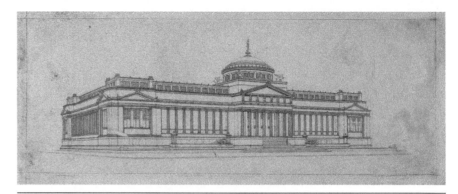

Fig. 10.2. Frank's entry for the Milwaukee Public Library competition of 1893. FLWF/AAFAL.

Pl. 61. Charles Atwood's 'Fine Arts Pavilion' at the Chicago World's Fair of 1893, evidently the inspiration for Frank's Milwaukee Public Library proposal.
From *Official Views of the World's Columbian Exposition*, 1893.

later years, that he was the one who had first worked with this idea, and Dr Harlan's house supports his case. It had a low-slung, hipped roof with wide, overhanging eaves, more like the roof of an 1890s railway station than that of any house, covering a confluence of living areas, carefully articulated but barely defined by structural division. Notwithstanding his playful treatment of the external envelope, the layout of the rooms recalls the fluidity of the spaces within his own home

Pl. 62. The Dr Allison Harlan House of 1893. Unlike the other bootlegged houses, it owed nothing to established styles. It was, in many ways, unprecedentedly strange.
From *Inland Architect and News Record* vol. 29 no. 6 (July 1897).

in Oak Park, and confirms again that it was the experience of space that most interested him. Unmoulded by architectural academia, he was by instinct an architect of space, a modern architect before modernism.

At the front of the Harlan House, on the upper floor, there was a full-width projecting veranda, an echo of the Charnley House, with an ornate fascia that paid homage to the curvaceous pattern-making of Louis Sullivan. Within a few years many of the strange ingredients of the Harlan House would be distilled into the radical spirit of Frank Lloyd Wright's 'Prairie Style', but the Sullivanesque ornament would be left behind. According to Frank it was the Harlan House that led to his break from Louis Sullivan. None of the other

bootlegged houses attracted attention, but Sullivan came to hear about the daringly strange new residence. At that time Louis Sullivan was living in the house that he had designed for his brother Albert. It was on South Lake Park Avenue, only half a mile from Dr Harlan's Greenwood Avenue home. When Sullivan saw the Harlan House, he realised that it could only have been designed by Frank. Taken to task by his employer for his disloyalty, Frank immediately resigned. Twelve years would go by before he saw Louis Sullivan again. There is a detail in Frank's story that gives credence to his memory of an emotional schism. He recalled that Sullivan angrily refused to hand over the deeds to Frank's house in Oak Park, even though his loan had been repaid, and that the document had later been posted to him by Dankmar Adler. This seems too curious an embellishment to have been invented. Furthermore, after the publication of his autobiography, George Elmslie, Frank's close colleague in the early days, made some remarks that implied that the relationship between Sullivan and Frank had indeed ended bitterly, but for less noble reasons than those that Frank had claimed. Biographers have made their guesses; the full story may never be known. What has become clear, however, is the fact that Frank's departure from Adler and Sullivan was part of a much larger upheaval.

Early in 1893 American banks were presented with increasing demands from foreign investors to take back their US dollars in exchange for exportable gold. This soon led to a run on the banks. The root causes of the 'Panic of '93' were obscure, but the consequences were rapid and devastating. As investment bubbles burst, hundreds of small banks, many in the west, were swept away in the backwash. Several major railroads and thousands of other businesses were bankrupted. In Chicago the commercial development, which Adler and Sullivan had come to depend upon, was rapidly disinvested. The work of the practice came to an abrupt standstill. Within weeks, the flourishing studio was reduced to a team of three, two of whom were the partners. The third, in the seat that Frank had once occupied, was George Elmslie. Frank was gone, pushed out to find his own way just as America slid into depression.

## Late 1860s. The Valley, Iowa County, Wisconsin

In the early years of Frank's childhood Native Americans would still occasionally find their way to the Helena valley. As Chester Lloyd Jones put it, 'They came usually in wandering groups, drawn back to their former hunting grounds by the nostalgia so strong among all primitive peoples.'[24] Richard Lloyd Jones thought of himself as a man of innate goodness, a Welshman with ancient roots that he cherished. When he encountered Native Americans on his land Richard would appraise them through sympathetic eyes. On one early winter evening, as he made his way back to The Valley from Helena, his horses stopped abruptly, unsettled by something on the ground in front of them blocking the track. The man was unconscious, stupefied by 'firewater'. Richard knew that the cold would kill him. He hoisted the lifeless figure onto his wagon, took him home and set him down on a mat with a blanket in front of the fireplace. Mallie and the children had already gone to bed. By the time they rose again in the morning their guest had gone. A few weeks later, as the Wisconsin winter tightened its grip, Richard stepped out one morning to find the front door blocked by a large, newly killed prairie antelope, a 'four prong buck'. More than enough good meat to see them through to the following spring.[25] Like his grandfather, Frank did not simply admire the pure instincts and the nobility of the 'savage', as the Romantic poets did. He felt those virtues within his being, and they stirred in him as he gazed up at the ancient, weathered remnants of the Mayan Gateway Arch of Labna.

## Early Summer 1893. Jackson Park, Chicago

Frank was not on the Yucatan peninsula, but on the lake shore of Chicago's Southside. A large section of a temple from Uxmal stood behind the Labna arch, and near it, across the path, the massive frontage of the House of Nuns, from Chichen Itza (Pl. 63). The replicas looked impressively real, but were made from timber, stucco and papier-mâché.[26] He had seen pictures of similar Mayan relics before, but the

Pl. 63. The Mayan exhibit at the Chicago World's Columbian Exposition of 1893. The life-sized replicas were built from timber and *papier maché*.
From *Official Views of the World's Columbian Exposition*, 1893.

imposing replicas seem to have made a profound impression on Frank, one that would stay with him.[27] They were the highlight of an ethnographic installation, which in itself was a minor diversion within the vast, sprawling, fantastical city-within-a-city of the World's Columbian Exposition. Entirely insulated from the economic panic, the exhibition had been in the planning for years, with the bold intention that it would re-establish Chicago as the capital of modern America, the reborn city, bigger, better and incomparably more beautiful than the city that had been consumed by flames twenty years before.

Daniel Burnham, the principal of Burnham and Root, the city's biggest practice, was chosen to be the Director of Works. Frederick Olmstead, the revered designer of New York Central Park, mapped out a lavish waterpark landscape. It was Burnham's privilege to devise the architectural master plan and to choose architects for the major buildings. Members of the Chicago architectural community justifiably expected that opportunities would come their way, but they were disappointed when the first five major commissions were awarded to east coast firms, all recognised leaders

Pl. 64. The 'Court of Honour', better known as the 'White City', the centrepiece of the World's Columbian Exposition, with the Grand Basin at centre.
From *Official Views of the World's Columbian Exposition*, 1893.

Pl. 65. A postcard showing 'The Golden Arch' of Adler and Sullivan's Transportation Building, the only large pavilion to defy the Beaux-Arts domination of the World's Fair.

in the Beaux-Arts style. Those first projects framed an ornamental lake, the Grand Basin. They were the centrepiece of the exhibition, the Court of Honour (Pl. 64).

There was only one building among the great pavilions that did not conform to the Beaux-Arts template, and that was the Transportation Building, designed, inevitably, by Louis Sullivan (Pl. 65). It was set back on the western edge of the park between the lagoon and the utility buildings, where it would not upset the prevailing classical harmony. It had a memorable, central feature, a monumental arched entrance rimmed by receding haloes of gilded ornamental relief. It became a popular attraction, but the building behind it was regarded with ambivalence. The Golden Doorway was 'a beautiful feature in an ensemble that is purposely devoid of entertainment and delight'.[28] Sullivan must have known, then, that the progressive path that he had hoped to carve out was closing quickly behind him. He was bitter to the end. Three decades later he ended his own memoir with a reflection on the impact of the World's Fair, 'the damage wrought will last for half a century from its date, if not longer. It has penetrated deep into the constitution of the American mind effecting there lesions significant of dementia.'[29]

Frank, on his own now, had no need to share Sullivan's neuroses. He could survey the battle of styles, the ascendancy of neo-classicism, as if from an elevated viewpoint. He could dabble in it, as he did when he entered the Milwaukee Public Library competition, or he could disdain it. It didn't really matter, because none of the established styles would ever be *his*. At some point during the watershed year of 1893, it became clear to him that if he was to properly differentiate himself as the self-reliant, true individual he felt he was destined to be, he needed to devise a new type of architecture, befitting modern America. He needed to succeed where Sullivan had stumbled. The most remarkable aspect of Frank's personal aesthetic was that it was a deliberate synthesis of disparate, heterodox sources with aspects of his own lived experience and his inherited Welsh Unitarian culture, a synthesis contrived with the specific purpose of producing original, radically modern artistic ideas. From the outset, as in the design of his own home, he was able to give free expression to his radical spirituality in his approach to the organisation of living space. Then his design for the Harlan House showed his intent to pursue an original formal lexicon, an architecture that could give full, inward and outward expression to his ideals of 'simplicity and repose'. Seeking inspiration he had to look to novel sources. His architecture would be drawn from images and idioms that originated far outside the established canon of Western architecture, from places that, he hoped, other architects wouldn't think of or care to explore.

The World's Fair set a new standard for architectural and commercial overindulgence. The 'great buildings' and the multitude of state pavilions exemplified everything that Frank would aim to avoid, but the 'national pavilions' were different. Every World Expo is defined, today, by its collection of national pavilions, each one designed by a native architect and built by native craftsmen to showcase the creative brilliance of the nation of origin. At least that is the idea. Often they are revealing in ways that were not intended. The Chicago World's Fair of 1893 was the first to include national pavilions (Fig 10.3). There were nineteen of them. Brazil, Germany and Sweden built spectacular structures. Norway's was outlandish. Great Britain's pavilion was expensive but dull. The few buildings from Asia were more intriguing. Turkey's was an ornamental box, beautifully assembled from shimmering geometrically patterned panels. Its most prominent feature was a low, hipped roof with very wide, overhanging eaves. Just below the roof there was a band of deeply recessed windows that ran around the perimeter. The effect was to make the roof appear as if it was floating above the building (Pl. 66). It was one of the first buildings to be completed on the exhibition site.[30] Frank worked on Sullivan's Transportation Building, so he made regular visits during the construction and after the opening of the exhibition. There was every opportunity for him to observe and to contemplate the exotic and novel forms.[31]

It's not difficult to see some echoes of the Turkish pavilion in Frank's design for Dr Harlan's house, just two miles north of the park, but of everything that he encountered in the exhibition park, nothing made a more profound impression upon him than the buildings from Japan. The Japanese government had moved quickly to claim a place at the heart of the exhibition. Astutely, they took a site at the north end of the 'Wooded Island' in the centre of a naturalistic water feature known as the Lagoon. There were no other buildings on the island, only lush landscaping of which several acres were designed in the Japanese manner. It was part of the fair but detached from it, a world within a world, within a world. Frank was aware of Japanese art and building. Silsbee had shown him prints, and had led him to the work of Edward Morse and Ernest Fenollosa. Those few images had been enough for him to sense the intense aesthetic richness behind the sparse and simple countenance. Three linked pavilions formed the Hō-ō-den Palace, each of the structures replicating a different period of historic Japanese design, although to Western eyes the differences were hard to distinguish (Pl. 67).

This was the first time that Frank had been able properly to experience the open, fluid nature of Japanese planning, the interweaving of building and landscape that he had previously only read about and seen in pictures. He was enchanted by the precision and the rhythm of the structure, expressed equally outside and within, the way that the lines of the supporting timbers formed a continuous, three-dimensional grid that flowed from floor to walls, then to converge in the ceiling as a simple grid of beams, the squares between them filled with iridescent mother-of-pearl. There was virtually no furniture, no clutter, everything needed for comfortable use seemed to be integrated into the building. There were no windows, but there was an abundance of light, filtered through slender translucent screens.[32] The Hō-ō-den seemed small and impossibly delicate among the colossi. Its apparent primitiveness attracted some ridicule, and Japanese visitors were embarrassed by its modesty, but to Frank it was a revelation, the living reality of a form of design that encapsulated the reverence for nature, for truth and for refined simplicity that he had been raised always to cherish, but which, until then, he had struggled to imagine in built form.[33]

Academics and biographers concur that Frank's encounter with Japanese and Mayan design at the World's Fair marks the beginning of the process from which his personal architectural vision was to emerge. The influence of the Turkish exhibit is more elusive, as there is scant

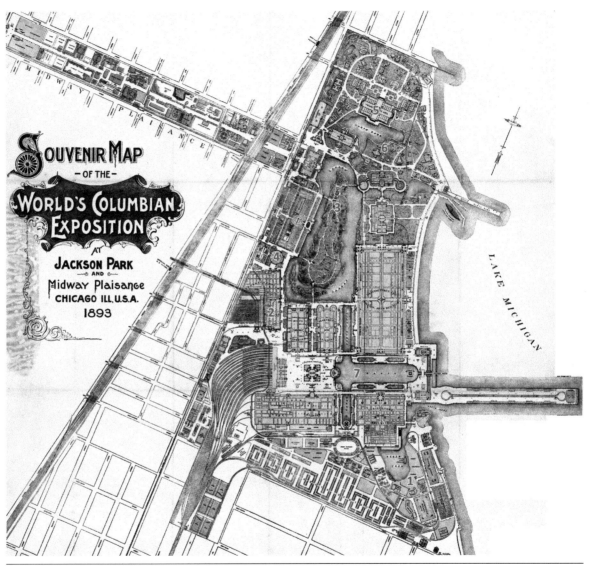

Fig. 10.3. Map of the 'World's Columbian Exposition', better known as the Chicago World's Fair of 1893.
  (1) The Mayan exhibit.
  (2) Adler and Sullivan's Transportation Building, with its 'Golden Arch'.
  (3) The Hooden Palace, the Japanese exhibit.
  (4) The Festival Hall (or Choral Hall) venue for the Chicago Eisteddfod.
  (5) Charles Atwood's Fine Arts Pavilion.
  (6) The Turkish Pavilion.
  (7) The Grand Basin, the water feature at the centre of Daniel Burnham's Beaux-Arts 'White City'.
  LOC.

evidence of the building, just a few, faint but compelling photographs. He wasn't drawn to these artefacts simply because they were strange, for there were many stranger things to be found at the fair. He was drawn to them because they reverberated in the taut strands of his identity: his American optimism, his Welsh Romanticism, his Unitarian admiration for the primitive and the universal It is probably a good thing, given Frank's sensitivities, that there was almost nothing among the physical exhibits at the fair to represent Wales or the Welsh, certainly nothing like the unfortunate caricatures that were supposed to speak for Ireland. In the Transportation Building, sent from Merthyr Tydfil, there were two of Trevithick's historic railway carriages mounted on a length of Penydarren track,[34] and if he had summoned the willpower to step inside Great Britain's pavilion he might have noticed the ceiling of the entrance hall, which was a reproduction of one of the ceilings at Plas Mawr, Conwy's famous Elizabethan manor house.[35] But the Welsh community of Chicago would not be overlooked. Over four days in early September the circular Choral Hall was the venue for the largest Eisteddfod, until then, to be convened beyond the borders of Wales. Two years earlier a 'Call and Invitation' had been sent to Wales, decorated with the mottos of the *Gorsedd*, *Y Gwir yn Erbyn y Byd* (Truth Against the World) and, naturally also /|\, *Y Nod Cyfrin:*

*The NATIONAL CYMRODORION SOCIETY, in the name of all the Welsh People of the New World, send their most earnest INVITATION to the Welsh People of Great Britain, and especially to the managers and promoters of the NATIONAL EISTEDDFOD, to come to their aid, and cooperate with them in holding conjointly, on an imposing scale, with BARDIC and MUSICAL dignity worthy of the Antiquity, Literature and Music of the CYMRY, a GRAND INTERNATIONAL EISTEDDVOD in Chicago in 1893, during the WORLD'S COLUMBIAN EXPOSITION.*[36]

It was signed by the members of the organising committee. Prominent among them was the name of the Rev. Jenkin Lloyd Jones. The Choral Hall,[37] which could seat 2,500, was well filled for the greater part of the four-day festival.[38]

Pl. 66. The Turkish Pavilion at the Chicago World's Fair was evidently a source of inspiration for Frank. He was working on the design of his first independent commission, the Winslow House, during 1893. Its front elevation appears to have been influenced by the front elevation of the Turkish Pavilion.
From *Shepp's World's Fair Photographed*, Globe Bible Publishing Co. Chicago (1893), p. 483.

Pl. 67. The *Hō-ō-den*, seen across the water of The Lagoon.
From Okakura Kakudzo, *Illustrated Description of the Hō-ō-den (Phoenix Hall) at the World's Columbian Exposition* (Tokyo: K. Ogawa, 1893), p. 25.

Jenkin Lloyd Jones even had a role in the proceedings as adjudicator of the novels submitted for competition, although his lengthy discourse on their merits was brought to a premature conclusion by the arrival from Wales of a famous choirmaster, igniting a spontaneous mass rendition of the national anthem, *Hen Wlad fy Nhadau*, an outbreak of harmonious anarchy that dispelled any doubt that Chicago's Eisteddfod was not the genuine article[39] (Pl. 68).

What might Frank have made of it? By his mid-twenties he had developed a bitter-sweet relationship with his Uncle Jenkin. He found his uncle's attentions stifling, and he bridled at his moralising. He also resented the way that Jenkin was deferred to in any family dispute. But at the same time Frank admired his uncle and respected him as a mentor, proof that a Lloyd Jones could pull himself to the top by his intelligence, charm and native wits. He also depended on him and his church community for support and for

Pl. 68. The Choral competition at the Chicago Eisteddfod, 1893.
Courtesy of the Church of Latterday Saints.

introductions to influential people and potential clients. To his mother and aunts, Jenkin was the shining figurehead of the family. They would certainly have been in the crowd at the Eisteddfod. It's likely that Frank was there too, to share in the awkwardness when his uncle's address was cut short, but Jenkin was not the sort to have been bothered by the rowdiness at all; he would probably have enjoyed it. For him and for the Lloyd Jones family the main event of the festival summer was to come the following week.

The World's Parliament of Religions was an extraordinary gathering of leaders of all major faiths, brought to Chicago from every part of the world. It was an event many times the size of the Eisteddfod, with a dense programme that ran for sixteen full days. Jenkin had been deeply involved in the planning, a responsibility that had brought him into close contact with many other American and foreign religious leaders.[40] Some of the visiting dignitaries stayed as guests with Jenkin at The Parsonage, where Frank often had the chance to meet them. It was there, for example, that he first encountered Jane Addams, the Nobel Prize-winning founder of Hull House, America's first 'settlement house' for the advancement of the working class and the poor. For Frank, these occasions were more than educational. It was inspirational to be among others who shared his radical instincts, and who had developed the clear philosophy and the cogent arguments that could persuade a conformist to throw off his chains. They were abilities that Frank needed to master. What he learned at All Souls would be just as significant as anything that he took from Sullivan or Silsbee. Hull House in particular would provide an important stepping stone in his career. The Parliament of Religions was also a turning point in Jenkin's career. The leader of the city's Liberal Christians found himself on the congress platform, sharing the limelight with the most prominent religious leaders of the day. His belief in the equivalence of all faiths epitomised the spirit of the whole event, and his fame and his following both blossomed as a result. Frank could not have wished for a more effective bulwark in a time of economic gloom. In the autumn of 1893, as the World's Fair eventually closed its gates, Frank took out a lease on an office at the top floor of Adler and Sullivan's Schiller Building. Business for the new practice of Frank Lloyd Wright, Architect, was already looking good ∎

# 10    Simplicity and Repose
## *Notes*

1    Dictionary of Unitarian Universalist Biography, *www.uua.org/uuhs/ duub/articles/augustajanechapin.html* (April 2021).

2    Frank Lloyd Wright, *An Autobiography (Edition 1)* (New York: Longman, Green & Co., 1932), p. 78.

3    Maginel Wright Barney, *The Valley of the God Almighty Joneses* (New York: Appleton Century, 1965), p. 128.

4    At the time of writing, the house still exists and appears much as it did in 1889. However, it is at risk. A proposal has been made to demolish it to make space for a visitor centre associated with Frank Lloyd Wright's Home and Studio next door.

5    F. L. Wright, *An Autobiography (Edition 1)*, p. 76.

6    Letter from Anna Lloyd Wright to Frank Lloyd Wright, Madison, August 1888. Frank Lloyd Wright Foundation Ref. W025B010000.

7    Barney, *The Valley of the God Almighty Joneses*, p. 130.

8    Alfred Russell Wallace, 'The South Wales Farmer', in *My Life*, vol. 1 (London: Chapman and Hall, 1905), p. 211.

9    Robert C. Twombley, *Frank Lloyd Wright: An Interpretive Biography* (New York: Harper Colophon, 1974), p. 71.

10   Henry-Russell Hitchcock, *Architecture: Nineteenth and Twentieth Centuries* (London: Penguin Books, 1958), p. 270; Vincent Scully, *The Stick Style and the Shingle Style (Revised Edition)* (New Haven: Yale University Press, 1971), p. 159.

11   Grant Carpenter Manson, *Frank Lloyd Wright to 1910: The First Golden Age* (New York: Van Nostrand Reinhold Co., 1958), p. 46.

12   F. L. Wright, 'The Architect and the Machine' (1900), in B. B. Pfeiffer (ed.), *Collected Writings*, vol. 1: *1894–1930* (New York: Random House, 1992), p. 23.

13    It may be the case that Frank's enthusiasm for Japanese architecture contributed to his thinking about 'simplicity and repose'. However, it was his sensitivity to these qualities that drew him to Japanese architecture in the first place. They were present in the asceticism that is synonymous with Welsh Nonconformism. In his influential book *Japanese Homes and Their Surroundings* (1886), Edward Morse referred often to the quality of 'simplicity' in Japanese design and, in one case, to its 'severe, Quaker-like simplicity' (p. 309). These were the similarities that Frank also recognised.

14    Barney, *The Valley of the God Almighty Joneses*, p. 130.

15    Thomas A., Heinz, *The Vision of Frank Lloyd Wright* (Menai Bridge: S. Webb and Son, 2002), p. 21.

16    Louis Sullivan himself was the first occupant of this house. He lived in it for several years.

17    H. A. Brooks, 'Frank Lloyd Wright: Towards a Maturity of Style 1887–1893', *AA Files: Annals of the Architectural Association School of Architecture*, 2 (July 1982), 47.

18    Manson, *Frank Lloyd Wright: The First Golden Age*, p. 27.

19    Donald Leslie Johnson, *Frank Lloyd Wright: Early Years: Progressivism: Aesthetics: Cities* (Abingdon: Routledge, 2017), p. 179.

20    Brendan Gill, *Many Masks: A Life of Frank Lloyd Wright* (London: Heinemann, 1988), p. 95.

21    F. L. Wright, *An Autobiography (Edition 1)*, p. 103.

22    As distinct from the English Queen Anne revival style of Norman Shaw, from which the American iteration was apparently derived.

23    H. R. Hitchcock, 'Frank Lloyd Wright and the Academic Tradition of the Early Eighteen Nineties', *Journal of the Warburg and Courtauld Institutes*, 7 (1944), 46–63; and Brooks, 'Towards a Maturity of Style', 44–9.

24    Chester Lloyd Jones, *Youngest Son* (Madison WI: self-published, 1938), p. 72.

25    Jones, *Youngest Son*, p. 72.

26    Mauricio Tenorio-Trillo, *Mexico at the World's Fairs: Crafting a Modern Nation* (Berkeley California: University of California Press, 1996), p. 185.

27    D. Tselos, 'Frank Lloyd Wright and World Architecture', *Journal of the Society of Architectural Historians*, 28/1 (March 1969), 58–72.

28    Halsey C. Ives, *The Dream City: A Portfolio of Photographic Views of the World's Columbian Exposition* (St Louis: N. D. Thompson Publishing Co., 1893), p. 7.

29    Louis Sullivan, *The Autobiography of an Idea* (Washington, DC: The Press of the American Institute of Architects, 1924), p. 325.

30    J. W Shepp and D. B. Shepp, *Shepp's World's Fair Photographed* (Chicago: Globe Bible Publishing Co., 1893), pp. 482–3.

31    D. Gebhard, 'A Note on the Chicago Fair of 1893 and Frank Lloyd Wright', *Journal of the Society of Architectural Historians*, 18/2 (May 1959), 63–5.

32    Okakura Kakudzo, *The Hō-ō-den (Phoenix Hall): An Illustrated Description of the Buildings Erected by the Japanese Government at the World's Columbian Exposition, Jackson Park, Chicago* (Tokyo: K. Ogawa Tokyo, 1893).

33    'Elocution Society', *The Japan Weekly Mail* (January 1894), 6. Although he was not to know it, Frank was not the only young architect to be inspired by the Japanese Pavilion or by the research of Edward Morse. The Californian practice of Greene and Greene is often cited as counterpart, albeit that a Japanese influence is not evident in their work until after 1904, when it emerged in an overtly mimetic manner.

34    John J. Flinn, *Official Guide to the World's Columbian Exposition* (Chicago: The Columbian Guide Co., 1893), pp. 111–12.

35    C. E. Pascoe, *An Illustrated Souvenir of Victoria House, the Head Quarters of the Royal Commission for Great Britain at the World's Columbian Exposition, Chicago 1893* (London: Johnstone Norman and Co., 1893), pp. 24–5.

36    Dilys Rana, *The Welsh Who Built Chicago: 1833–1893* (self-published, 2016). The Welsh words appear here as they were printed on the invitation leaflet, with 'Eisteddfod' spelt in two

different ways. See also *http://welshwhobuiltchicago.com/* (April 2021).

37      Also known as the Festival Hall.

38      J. Monaghan's 'The Welsh People in Chicago', *Journal of the Illinois State Historical Society*, 32/4 (December 1939), 505.

39      *Weekly Mail* (Cardiff, 16 September 1893), 14.

40      Rev. John H. Barrows (ed.), *The World's Parliament of Religions: An Illustrated and Popular Story of the World's First Parliament of Religions, Held in Chicago in Connection with The Columbian Exposition of 1893* (Chicago: Parliament Publishing Co., 1893), p. 6.

# 11

## Spoiled, First by Birth

The 'Panic of '93' began a downturn that took four years to run its course, and yet somehow Frank seems to have been untouched by it. It was as if the world of ordinary men was playing out in parallel to his own. He was on an architectural mission that put him on the fringes of his profession. By rights, that should have made things even more difficult for him, but he nonetheless attracted a steady flow of clients and, without exception, they were delighted by what they were given. There is a letter that survives, written by one of his clients, which provides a glimpse of Frank's captivating personality, and also of the persuasive assistance that he could call upon:

*I have been – seen – talked to, admired, one of nature's* noblemen – *Mr. Frank Lloyd Wright ... A* splendid *type of manhood. He is not a* freak – *not a 'crank' – highly educated and polished, but* no dude – *a straightforward business-like man – with high ideals. I met his mother, a* beautiful *type of woman.*[1]

Frank also knew the type of client that he needed, 'American men of business with unspoiled instincts and untainted ideals'. In other words, wealthy clients without 'cultured' preconceptions or the burden of too much education.[2] Step forward William Winslow, the first real client of Frank's new practice.

Winslow was the president of an ornamental ironworks. He had a large plot, surrounded by trees, in River Forest, a wealthy, arboreal suburb close to Oak Park. It was a site that had much in common with the parkland setting of the World's Fair, and it seems inevitable that there is something pavilion-like about the presentation of the Winslow House (Pl. 69). The front elevation has a solid formal symmetry that seems to imply a civic purpose. The base is a plane of intense yellow-orange, small, immaculately bonded roman brickwork. There is a white string course, and above it a plane of deep darkness which, while it sits slightly proud of the brickwork, reads visually as a recess or even a void. It is made from black-glazed intricately ornamented clay tiles, directly from the Sullivan workbook, but the detail is often barely visible, obscured by the deep shadow of the massively overhanging eaves. The visual purpose of the dark surface is to separate the roof from the brickwork base, to invite the roof to be seen as a pure, detached geometric form. Then every other part of the elevation starts to be seen in the same way. The windows are not 'just' windows: their proportions are odd, they are wider than conventional windows, and they are set too far apart. The front door is low and wide, with square windows to each side, forming a vaguely figurative triptych, set into a white plaque. A decorative ribbon runs around the windows and over the door. The overall effect is of emphatic horizontality, as if it has been stretched sideways. The classicism is deceptive: each of the elements of the façade has been expressed, intensified or distorted so that nothing can easily be assimilated or taken for granted. Common features assume a significance that transcends their conventional meaning. It is both strange and familiar, and hence more effectively strange than the unshackled oddness of the Harlan House from the year before.

It is possible to see how the features of the Turkish building at the Worlds' Fair could have led Frank to the idea of the dark band of tiles below the roof. The roof itself has aspects of the roof of the Turkish building, and of the Japanese buildings. The arrangement of the oddly proportioned front door and the windows to each side bears the faint imprint of the ornamental entrance of a Mayan temple, perhaps Structure 2 at Chicanna, the 'House of the Serpent Mouth' (Pl. 70). The effect of the whole is, impressively, of 'simplicity and repose', gracefully synthesising and transcending all of the influences.

The arrangement of the rooms within the Winslow House echoes the layout of his own house at Oak Park. The theme, again, is the sanctity of domesticity. For many decades now architectural academics have analysed Frank's techniques and motives, attempting to understand how he was able to extend his imagination into such uncharted spaces. It is fascinating to trace the sources of his ideas, but his motivation is another question. It is very clear that he was compelled by his faith, by the spirituality that he inherited, and it was the extent to which he sought to express it through his own architecture that truly set him apart. Shortly after the completion of the Winslow House he collaborated with William Winslow, who also happened to be a hobby-printer, on the production of a slender, exquisitely illustrated book titled *The House Beautiful*. The text was taken from a sermon written by his Uncle Jenkin's great friend and fellow Unitarian leader, William Channing Gannett:

*Call the great power 'God', or by what name we will, that power dwells with us in so literal a fashion that every stone and rafter ... bears stamp and signature to eyes that read aright: 'The house in which we live is a building of God, a house not made with hands.'*

Pl. 69. The Winslow House, River Forest, Illinois, completed 1894.
Photograph Bilyan Belchev/CC BY-SA 4.0.

Frank was quite systematic in his determination to extract original architectural ideas from arcane sources, but without his faith this would have been merely a technical process.

The aura of charm and integrity that impressed his clients came to him naturally, but while he was engaging to his clients, he was also deeply engaged *by* them. His fascination with their lives and motivations, with the morality and desires of everyone that he dealt with was, likewise, an aspect of the spiritual culture of his people, discussed and scrutinised endlessly. As he formulated his design approach, it occurred to him that the people for whom he designed and, most importantly, the setting of each building would both always be unique, and that if he opened himself up to their distinctive qualities, if he began his design process there, then he would give himself a good chance of emerging with an architectural outcome that was just as specific and unprecedented. It was the stable block behind the Winslow House, for example, that he designed around the trunk of a large, living tree, so that the building and its setting were inextricably bound.

Pl. 70. Entrance frieze at the Winslow House and the entrance to the House of the Serpent's Mouth, Chicanna, Mexico.
Top: Arian Zwegers/CC-BY 2.0.

A few months later, and just a short distance from the Winslow House, Frank completed work on a house for a family friend, Chauncey Williams (Pl. 71). The Wrights and the Williamses knew each other from Madison. The Desplaines River, which flows through the centre of River Forest, was a favourite picnic spot for the two families. Over the course of the summer of 1895 they used their time by the river bank to collect a heap of substantial weathered boulders. They were formed into mounds and bonded into

the brickwork at each side of the front door of the new Williams House.[3] They were also arranged around the plinth as a symbolic connection with its fluvial landscape and, at the same time, a powerful token of the shared experience of the Williamses and their architect in the making of their home.

This adds up to a subtle and complex design approach, far more sophisticated than the superficial battle of styles that preoccupied the architectural communities of America and Europe. In its curatorial aspects, its mining of primitive source materials and memories, its concern with integrity and morality, it is unmistakably a proto-modernist approach. Frank was always unwilling to attempt an explanation of it, not, at least, in academic architectural terms. He felt that he had no need to, and he assumed that, because of his lack of formal learning, he might be disparaged if he did. He first referred to it as 'organic' in a lecture, 'The Architect and the Machine', that was delivered later in 1894, evidently for a non-academic audience:

> Go to Nature, thou builder of houses, consider her ways ... Let your home appear to grow easily from its site and shape it to sympathize with the surroundings, if Nature is manifest there; and if not, try and be as quiet, substantial and organic as she would have been if she had the chance.[4]

He continued to use the term 'organic architecture' throughout his long career. His reluctance to give it a clear definition left him space, also, to modify its meaning or, on occasions, to forgo it entirely. He felt beholden to no one, and gave his critics and his admirers as little as possible that would enable them to deprecate or to imitate except in simplistic and ineffective terms.

The Winslow House, the first independent commission, has many of the features that are associated with the fully developed 'prairie style' of the early 1900s. But the Williams House, and the majority of the projects of the following three years were disparate, as one might expect of any new practice seeking a broad client base. Silsbee's influence was more obviously evident in some of the other houses of the period. Then there was a competition-winning scheme, completed in 1894, for the Lake Mendota municipal boathouse, back in Madison: an Italianate reverie that speaks of his memories of the lakes as a place of escapist refuge. There were also three courtyard tenement developments, each restrained, functional, elegant and apparently years ahead of their time. There was even a mock-Tudor house, built for his near neighbour, Nathan Moore. In among these were a host of unbuilt projects, many funded by his friend Edward Waller, the original owner of the River Forest estate.

Waller was a great early supporter of Frank's, to such an extent that he once tried to bounce him into the upper tier of Chicago architecture. Waller's house was close to the Winslow House; it could be seen across the lawns. Frank and Kitty were frequent dinner guests. Arriving at the Wallers's one evening, Frank was surprised to find another guest had arrived ahead of them, Daniel Burnham, the pre-eminent architect in the city and lead designer of the World's Fair. Burnham had been elated by the success of his White City, and was now looking to recruit a first cohort of scholars to attend a new American School in Rome, preceded by four years of study in Paris at the École des Beaux-Arts. The Winslow House, Burnham said, was, 'a gentleman's house from grade to coping'. Frank's name was the first on Burnham's list. His family would be supported for the six-year duration, and Frank would take a partnership with Burnham and Root on his return. Waller and Burnham worked hard to persuade him, but without success, 'It's too late now, I'm afraid. I am spoiled already', Frank admitted.

*I've been too close to Mr. Sullivan. He has helped spoil the Beaux-Arts for me ... I guess he regrets the time he spent there himself ... I can't run away from what I see as mine ... what I see as ours in our country ... just because it means success ... I know how obstinate and egotistic you think me, but I'm going on as I started. I'm spoiled, first by birth, then by training, and by conviction for anything like that.*[5]

Frank wrote these words in the late 1920s, many years after the event recalled, and long after his mother's death.

Pl. 71. The Chauncey Williams House, River Forest, Illinois, with its plinth of field stones. 1895. Courtesy of Douglas M. Steiner, Edmonds, WA, USA.

Whether or not it is an accurate recollection, there can be no denying that he really did possess such self-awareness in his early career; otherwise he could not have taken the path that he did. It still seems remarkable that he could have seen himself in such exceptional terms: 'spoiled' for the conventional world by birth, by training and by conviction, like his mother and like her forebears.

By early 1895 Frank and Kitty had three children with a fourth on the way, and the family was outgrowing its home. The first extension of the house more than doubled its size, an indication of the promise of Frank's business. A spectacular barrel-vaulted playroom was added at the rear of the upper floor, above a new kitchen (Pl. 72). The playroom supplanted the living room as the fulcrum of the house. His son John recalled his

Pl. 72  The low, arched passage that leads into the Playroom. Oak Park Home and Studio 1895. The mural of the
Fisherman and the Genie can be seen above the fireplace.
Photograph James Caulfield/FLWT.

*first impression upon coming into the playroom from the
narrow, long, low-arched, dimly lighted passageway that
led to it was its great height and brilliant light. The ceiling
twenty feet high formed a perfect arch springing from the
heads of group windows which were recessed into Roman
brick walls ... The semi-circle panel above the fireplace was
covered by a mural of the allegorical 'Fisherman and the
Genie' ... It was Dad's desire that his children should grow
up with a recognition of what is good in the art of a house.
He believed that an instinct for the beautiful would be firmly
established by a room whose simple beauty and strength are
daily factors. And Dad was right.*[6]

The 'Fisherman and the Genie' came, of course, from that
favourite story book of his mother's, *The Thousand and One
Nights*. Teaching was still the vocation of the Lloyd Jones
women. Kitty had become interested too, the playroom
became her Kindergarten, for her own children and those
of her neighbours, applying the Fröbel method under her
mother-in-law's keen eye.

Hillside Home School, back at the Lloyd Jones
Valley, was thriving, Aunts Nell and Jennie presiding over a
household of fifty boys and girls. In 1897, the Aunts took steps
to upgrade the water supply 'in case of fire or for irrigation'.[7]
This required a small reservoir to be dug at the top of the hill
and a wind pump to draw water up to it from the river. They
asked Frank to design it. Despite all the other demands of
their farms and of the school, somehow, according to Frank,
the plans for the windmill became a bone of contention;
even Uncle Jenkin got involved. His uncles all insisted that a
conventional steel derrick would suffice. They sought advice
from a local builder, who dismissed Frank's design as a 'waste
of time and money' and said that it would be toppled by the
first storm. His aunts passed this on by telegram to Frank,
who responded, bluntly, 'Build it.' That was reassurance
enough for them. When told that Frank's design would cost
nearly four times as much as a conventional tower, Aunt Nell
said, 'Only six hundred and seventy five dollars for all that
difference ... of course we are going to build it.'[8]

## Autumn 1897. The Valley, Wyoming Township, Iowa County, Wisconsin

We are all familiar with the image of the traditional Midwest
wind-pump: a many-sailed wheel and projecting rudder
mounted on a broad-based, skeletal pylon, obviously
designed to allow the wind to blow through. Frank's design
defied common sense. The farmers knew the damage that
a storm would inflict on any vulnerable surface, but instead
of a spread frame he proposed a hollow timber tower,
parallel from top to bottom, almost as if he intended it to be

blown over (Fig. 11.1). Frank explained that he had taken the elements into account by planning the tower in the shape of a teardrop. The sharp edge would point into the wind and the air would simply flow around it. The plan of the windmill is more than a technical exercise; it is generated from the overlapping of two pure geometrical forms, an octagon and a rhombus – a diamond. Later in his career, his fascination with geometry, and in particular with the spiritual symbolism of the various pure figures, would find spectacular expression in some of his greatest works, but his instinct that geometry embodied sacred significance was present from the very beginning. It was how arithmetic had been taught and understood in Unitarian communities for generations.

The design was based on intuition and instinct. Frank was no engineer, still less a meteorologist. The original plan, a copy of which is reproduced in the 1932 edition of his autobiography, shows that the edge of the diamond should face south-east.[9] It must be presumed from this that Frank expected the strongest winds to come from that direction. In his autobiography he recalls that several months after its completion the windmill withstood the, 'first real sou'wester' without harm, to the amazement of his uncles. State weather data inform us that the prevailing winds come from the south throughout the year, switching often to westerly during the winter. Winds from anywhere east of south are minimal. Iowa County would be troubled by storm winds seven or eight times each decade on average;[10] these would usually be from the west, and indeed the windmill was built with its blade facing sixteen degrees south of *west*, contrary to Frank's design.[11] That correction would have helped the tower to perform as Frank intended. It is intriguing to wonder how the change was made, and by whom. The landscape of The Valley has also contributed to its endurance. This was no prairie windmill, set against a remote horizon, bearing the full brunt. High hills embrace The Valley to the west, south and east, and the top of the windmill is below them. Nature was on its side from the beginning, but Frank's structure was certainly inventive.

The wooden frames of the octagon and the intersecting rhombus were extended vertically and in

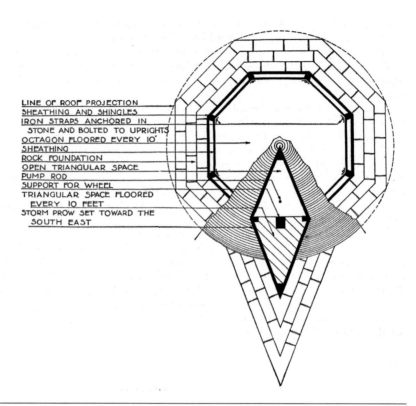

LINE OF ROOF PROJECTION
SHEATHING AND SHINGLES
IRON STRAPS ANCHORED IN
STONE AND BOLTED TO UPRIGHTS
OCTAGON FLOORED EVERY 10'
SHEATHING
ROCK FOUNDATION
OPEN TRIANGULAR SPACE
PUMP ROD
SUPPORT FOR WHEEL
TRIANGULAR SPACE FLOORED
EVERY 10 FEET
STORM PROW SET TOWARD THE
SOUTH EAST

Fig. 11.1.  Frank's plan for the Romeo and Juliet Windmill. Note that the 'storm prow' should be 'set toward the south east', an instruction not followed by the builders.
From *An Autobiography* (1932), p. 133.

parallel, up to within fifteen feet of the top, where the octagon terminated, allowing the diamond-shaped blade to continue up to a pinnacle. The wheel of the windmill itself is a modest embellishment above it. It was the two, mutually supporting, geometrical shapes that led Frank to name it 'Romeo and Juliet'. There were timber floors at intervals of ten feet all the way up, which braced the structure, and iron straps running vertically down the internal angles of the frame, which the builders compared to the straps of a barrel. The straps were extended deep into a heavy stone plinth at the base. The base had been built by the old Welsh mason

Pl. 73. The Fröbeltürm at Oberweissbach, 1890.

question has been overlooked. Why did he want to design the windmill as a solid tower in the first place?

There is an intriguing visual counterpart thousands of miles from Wisconsin, in Oberweissbach, southern Germany. Over the course of the late 1880s, a plea for funds was sent out from Friedrich Fröbel's birthplace to the worldwide Kindergarten community, accompanied by drawings of a tower, a monument for the great pedagogue to be built on a hilltop overlooking the town.[14] The Fröbelturm was inaugurated in July 1890 (Pl. 73). It is a stone tower, today surrounded by lower buildings, but originally an isolated form comprising two, merged volumes, the one projecting above the other. The taller structure is an extended octagon, and there are belvedere balconies wrapping part of the way around, midway up and near to the top. The octagon of 'Juliet' is also capped by a belvedere balcony. Frank's design is far more beautiful than Fröbel's tower; but the likeness is sufficiently compelling to conjure a scene in which Frank's aunts show him a grainy, indistinct image of an obscure building, from a distant country, a building that has real significance to them, and they say, 'What about something like this?'

The story of the windmill occupies several pages of Frank's autobiography. More space is given to it than he allows for many of his more celebrated works, and the reason for this is simply that he believed that he had proved himself, at last, to be worth something in the eyes of the Lloyd Jones uncles, who, he felt, had always doubted him. When that 'first sou'wester' blew over Frank was far away in Chicago, but he could envisage the morning's events:

*at sun up the anxious faces of five grey-bearded farmer brothers all came to as many farm-house doors, shading their eyes to peer over at the new tower. It was still there ... But the brothers kept on peering. For, 'what was one storm after all' ... Year after year this little drama of unfaith ... went on in the beloved Valley. Storm after storm swept over. But each storm only left all nearer the conviction that the next must be the last.*

David Timothy, and according to Frank, apart from his two aunts, it was only Timothy who had faith in his design, '"Trust the boy ... it will stand" Timothy insisted more than once, and he made the foundations even deeper and more solid than the specifications demanded.'[12] 'It was all simple enough', as Frank recalled in his autobiography, 'the wooden tower was rooted as the trees are. Unless uprooted it could not fall, for it would not break ... Try, sometime, to break a barrel.'[13] The windmill story is one of the most charming and frequently revisited episodes of Frank's early career, but it does seem, in all of the retellings, as if an important

Frank's story goes on to recount the sad passing of each of his uncles, one after the other to the grave, denied the satisfaction of seeing the windmill go first. How much of this was imagined is impossible to say, but there is no doubt that it was a formative experience for Frank, 'amateur engineering architecture – an idea of structure working itself out into architectural form – the future in embryo', as he recalled.[15] It was the first expression of his intuitive approach to structural engineering (Pl. 74). There was no calculation involved, he just seemed to know that it would stand up. The Romeo and Juliet windmill convinced him that it was an instinct that he could rely on. With his native gifts and resolute self-reliance he would continue to trust his structural instinct for the remainder of his architectural career. He would insist on doing so even when he shouldn't have.

## A Summer Morning in the Early 1950s. Bear Run Road, Pennsylvania

Edgar Kaufmann watched, relaxed, as his caretaker took the measuring rod across to the far side of the living room (Pl. 75). The windows swung out along the back of the long red sofa, and from below them, ever present, came the fizz of churning water. The caretaker stood the rod on the floor and held it up, plumb: the top just brushed the ceiling. No change there. The small ritual completed again, Kaufmann felt satisfied as the rod was returned to its cupboard. Then he glanced down at the varnished stone flags beneath his feet, gently undulating like the ripples on a pool, and he noticed that the joints between them had opened up a little in a few places again, and he knew, although his heart denied it, that the measuring rod was deceiving him. His caretaker had told him too. The floor that he stood on and the floor above him were both slowly descending at the same rate towards the waterfall below.[16] Kaufmann wouldn't worry; why should he worry? He didn't want to change a thing, because he was living in the most beautiful house in the world (Pl. 76).

Pl. 74. Romeo and Juliet Windmill, 1897.
Photograph Marco2001/CC BY-SA 2.0.

## 25th January 1937. Taliesin, The Valley, Wyoming Township, Iowa County, Wisconsin

Frank Lloyd Wright had a letter to dictate. It was addressed to Edgar Kaufmann:

> *I suppose there is nothing in your experience by which you might measure the disappointment and the chagrin which you have handed to me. I have put my best inspiration and effort into creating something rare and beautiful for you ... only to find that so far as you could add ruin to my work and reputation you did so behind my back ... The scare over the integrity of the structure is the usual exaggeration where such matters go. I have assured you time and again that the structure is sound.*[17]

It was not the first time that Frank had upbraided his client in these terms, and the crisis had arisen, as it had before, because Kaufmann had taken the precaution of consulting an independent firm of engineers. He'd asked them to check the structural design of his new house and to report on the cause of cracks that were appearing in the concrete terraces, even as they were being built (Pl. 77). The reports came to the consistent conclusions that the concrete beams that carried the projecting balconies were not deep enough and they were not adequately reinforced. The remedies were straightforward, and not particularly disruptive on a building that was being modified constantly, for other reasons, as work progressed. The beams could be made a few inches deeper and more steel reinforcing bars could be cast into them. The change would barely be noticeable, but Frank refused to pay heed. Even the company who supplied and installed the reinforcing bars got involved. Their foreman was alarmed to see how little was going into the floors. They raised their concern with Kaufmann, and received his permission to add more steel. It could be done without changing the shape of the beams at all, but it would still increase the strength of the floor. Frank's team informed him by telegram. His response was to demand, angrily, that the extra bars be removed.[18] As an argument about engineering, it makes no sense. But it was never really technology that was at issue: it was Frank's adamantine self-belief and his determination that his clients should share his unreserved trust in his own intuition.

He had lived off creative crumbs for years following the debacle of his divorce from his vengeful second wife, and then the Great Depression. He knew that Kaufmann's house had the potential to relaunch his career, so he had every reason to be conservative, just to get something solid off the ground. Instead, the project became a vessel for the release of all the years of suppressed creativity and all the resentment that he had harboured at being left on the margins, and even taunted: 'the greatest architect of the nineteenth century'.[19] It was important to him that its long, parallel balconies would be the most powerful formal

Pl. 76.  The sitting room windows can be seen in between the two concrete cantilevers, above the waterfall.
Photograph Christopher Little. Courtesy of West Pennsylvania Conservancy.

Pl. 77. The concrete cantilevers, propped while the concrete cures.
Courtesy of West Pennsylvania Conservancy.

that, he was convinced, could never have been conceived without his influence. He felt that he had to remind the public that these were his ideas; that they had been appropriated by others and it was about time he got the credit that he deserved. To do that, he believed that he had to push the structure further than anyone else would dare. He chose to do this not by making the balconies *appear* very thin – in fact the solid parapets of Fallingwater convey a powerful sense of mass – but he made them extremely thin regardless, and then argued insistently that they should be reinforced sparingly. The slow collapse of Edgar Kaufmann's house was eventually arrested in the late 1990s through a beautifully executed structural repair. By that time the outer edge of the living room had dropped by almost eighteen centimetres, a huge amount for a cantilever of only four and half metres. By most estimates it would have had, at best, a few more years before its inevitable collapse.[21] Like many of his predecessors, Edgar Kaufmann had become reconciled to Frank's irresistible nature. Being his client was a test of resolve, but nothing was more effective at putting the worries and the irritations into perspective than the magnificence of the end result.

Just as he had done to so many clients before, Frank had mesmerised Edgar Kaufmann at their first meeting. That was in November 1934. Frank's college, the Taliesin Fellowship, was struggling through its meagre early years, and architectural commissions were nowhere on the horizon. Kaufmann was a successful businessman, the owner of a Pittsburgh department store. His son, Edgar Junior, had signed up for a year at the Fellowship. His parents had come to Wisconsin for a visit. Over the course of the following year Kaufmann Senior found himself eased into the role of patron, persuaded to fund Fellowship exercises and to pay Frank generously to dream about grandiose projects that could never be realised. The notion of a summer house for the Kaufmann family seemed, initially, to be of little interest to the 67-year-old architect. Only a few weeks after they had first met, the Kaufmanns had taken Frank to the site at Bear Run, in the wilds of south-west Pennsylvania. But over the

expression of the house. The balconies are cantilevers that project out into the open space over the river while being anchored back into the rock at the rear. He wrote later: 'There, as in the branch of the tree, you may see the cantilever. The cantilever is the simplest ... structural resource now demanding new significance. It has yet had little attention in Architecture. It can do remarkable things to liberate space.'[20]

A structural cantilever really is a simple device. It will work effectively, provided it is stiff enough not to bend under its own weight or any load imposed upon it. Frank had worked with cantilever forms, roofs and terrace balconies, for decades. It annoyed him immensely that younger modernist architects were revelling in critical acclaim for using structures of this type to create forms winter, Frank's attention was focused on an exhibition in New York. Early in the new year he wrote to Kaufmann seeking funds for the exhibition, but asked, at the same time, for a contour map of the Bear Run site, a plan that would locate every significant rock feature, each boulder and each mature tree. It would be impossible during the winter. Kaufmann couldn't tell if it was an attempt to humour him, or a sign of genuine interest in the summer house idea. The survey drawing arrived at Taliesin late in March 1935 (Fig. 11.2). Kaufmann followed it up with a retainer fee, a prompt to get Frank started.

Then, in the early summer Frank had gone to Bear Run again with a small group from the Fellowship. Thereafter for weeks, and then months, there was nothing. Late in August Frank was informed that Kaufmann would soon be making a business trip to Milwaukee, just a few hours away, and that he hoped to visit Taliesin after his meeting. The scene was set for a legend to be made. In those days Frank typically worked with an audience around him, members of the Fellowship watching over his shoulder. There were plenty of witnesses, and they shared broadly the same recollection. The building now recognised by the American Institute of Architects as the 'Best All-Time Work of American Architecture' was designed, in its entirety, within the space of a few hours on the morning of Sunday 22 September 1935, just before Edgar Kaufmann's car arrived from Milwaukee.[22] It is this story that is put forward more than any other as evidence of Frank's true genius. It does seem miraculous that he could have summoned something so extraordinary from his imagination with such little apparent effort. As always, where Frank is concerned, there is more to the story than first appears. There really was genius of a sort at work, but not in an act of architectural conjuring. It was the genius that can inspire an exceptional artist: one with an eye that could see nature, with a heart that could feel nature, and with boundless courage to follow nature.

Because it is at the centre of the drawing, it is obvious from the site survey that Edgar Kaufmann expected

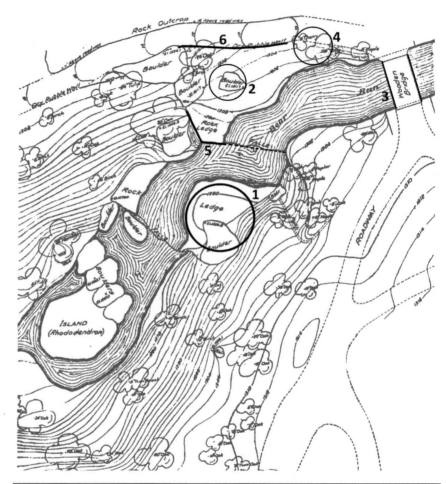

Fig. 11.2. The original survey of the Bear Run site, 1935, with details highlighted.
1) The waterside ledge believed to be the location that Kaufmann initially preferred for his summer house.
2) The tall boulder that Frank used as the spine of the house.
3) The bridge: the angle of the bridge was used to set up the structural grid of the house.
4) The two trees at the point where it was possible to step down off the road onto the rock ledge, which became the marker point for the door to the house.
5) The ledge of the waterfall, the base for the cantilever structures.
6) The old rubble wall along the track which provided the line for the back edge of the house.
Courtesy of West Pennsylvania Conservancy.

Pl. 78. The location of the entrance to Fallingwater was determined by two existing trees. One of the trees was retained to mark the entrance, shown in the centre of this picture. The parapet of the road bridge can be seen in the bottom left corner.
Photograph Ezra Stoller, courtesy of Esto Picture Library.

boulder would be its root into the rocks of Bear Run and the building would stretch its boughs out into the space above the waterfall. The rocky ground rose up steeply beyond the river. At some time in the forgotten past a rubble wall had been built along its contours to support a narrow trackway. Another few yards up there was an old timber bridge to carry the track across the river. The stone wall, the old bridge, the boulder, and lastly the slender trees that stood at the trackside at the north end of the bridge: each became a cardinal point in his thinking. To get onto the waterfall ledge you had to step down between the stems of the trees, so it was the trees that would mark the location of the entrance to Fallingwater (Pl. 78).

It is a building of intense richness, designed from simple beginnings: natural found features, and some that, although man-made, had become integral with the landscape. From these few fixed points Frank extended a planning grid of five-foot squares aligned with the bridge. He drew a heavy stone wall at the back of the house to reconcile the line of the old rubble wall with his new grid, and, inevitably, he fixed the position of the heart of the house, the living room fireplace, directly on the top of the jutting boulder at its core. Important features like the fireplace and the steps that lead down to the water, are located within the grid. In some places the walls face against the grid lines, in others the grid line is on the centre of the wall, and in a few places the walls aren't on the grid lines at all, but the grid and the natural features together provide the unique conceptual armature.[23] Once it was set down on the drawing sheet Frank knew that the design, as it emerged, would be no less exceptional. It would be a building that could only ever exist in that remarkable setting. The method by which the design then materialised was pragmatic, refined by decades of practice. It was certainly feasible for him to draft it in a few hours on a Sunday morning (Figs 11.3 and 11.4). What made the design process, and its outcome, so remarkable was not how it concluded but how it began.

Frank to position the house near a ledge on the river bank, around fifty yards downriver from the waterfall. From there, Kaufmann assumed, the house would give him a view up to the waterfall. This would be challenging enough for any architect, but Frank would never fall into line with the preconceptions of a client. When he'd made his second visit, early in the summer, his students had built a campfire against a prominent boulder, just a few yards from the edge of the cascade. Seated at his desk at Taliesin, he absorbed the details on the survey plan and he thought back to his impressions of the site. The boulder became steadily more significant, as if it contained the spirit of the site, its *omphalos*. He began to imagine a building growing up from it. The

# 1899. Oak Park, Illinois

Looking back over the first five productive years of his architectural practice, Frank must have reflected on the fact that the Winslow House was still his outstanding achievement. Other Chicago architects had even begun to copy it, but of all the houses he had built since, in the city or in the suburbs, none had given him the freedom he had been allowed by William Winslow. Budgets were too tight, plots too small, clients had ideas of their own: the familiar symptoms of an architect's discontent. Most of his clients came from connections he had made in the building trade or through the Unitarian Church. Helen Husser probably came to hear of him through her congregation. She was a devout Christian Scientist, sharing the fringes of Christianity with the Unitarians and the Universalists, and often mixing with them. Her father, John Marshall Williams, was a millionaire who raised a family of religious and political radicals.[24] Helen's husband, Joseph Husser, was a senior executive in her father's property development business, but before their marriage he had been her father's butler. Radical, egalitarian and very wealthy, they were the ideal clients for Frank Lloyd Wright.

The Hussers had acquired a large empty plot, just over half an acre, in the rural neighbourhood of Buena Park, six miles up the lakeshore from the city centre. Theirs would be the first house on the street, with an open view across meadows to Lake Michigan, just a minute's walk away. Despite having a roughly square site to work with, Frank gave the Husser House a linear plan that extended from the rear boundary almost to the roadside, and he aligned it against the eastern boundary of the plot. This provided all the windows and terraces on the long, west side of the house with a view across the breadth of their garden and beyond to the lake. A year earlier he had completed another house in the centre of Chicago southside, near to his in-laws, for Isidore Heller, an industrial designer. That was on a typically narrow city plot, and the house was necessarily also long and narrow, but it gave him a reason to think about ways of organising rooms that could make a virtue of a linear plan. Rooms could have windows on two

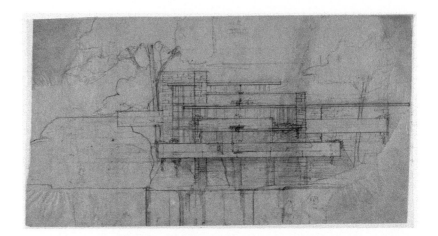

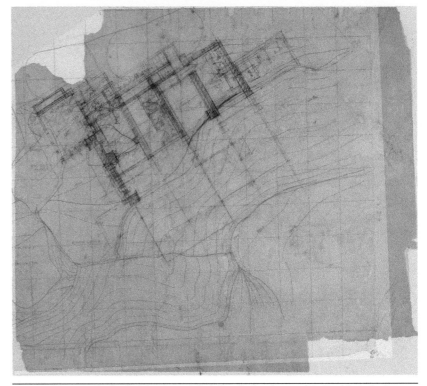

Fig. 11.3 and Fig. 11.4.  The sketched elevation and plan believed to have been made by Frank in the few hours before his first presentation to Edgar Kaufmann.
FLWF/AAFAL.

sides; they could be opened up to provide long internal vistas; they could be more effectively compartmentalised to allow the living and service spaces to operate smoothly, and the staff could also have bright, well-ventilated rooms in which to live and work. In the minds of some, this would be close to transgressive, but it was essential to Frank's spiritual purpose,

*Treat your servants as you treat your friends – with consideration. Give them good sleeping rooms ... and a pleasant little dining room or sitting room, for you gain in more ways than one by doing so.*[25]

The front entrance to the Husser House was half way along its east side, turned away from the road, so that the entrance hall could be located centrally, with the living spaces spreading out in wings to each side. The body of the building took the form of a long, narrow block with two prominent masses cutting across it, projecting outwards, perpendicular to the main body (Fig. 11.5). The larger of these projections, on the east side, contained the spacious, elevated dining room, with an octagonal end bay and a panoramic view of the water. The projection on the west side enclosed the main staircase. The two projections appear, in the plan, as if each is reacting to the other, not quite balancing but creating a sense of rotation, like the arms of a windmill. In the Husser House this innovation seems tentative, but Frank was enthralled by it. There was an energetic impulse in the volumes pushing outwards from the centre. The outline of the building seemed to shift as if branching into the landscape. However the thought had occurred to him, this apparently simple, geometrical manipulation had a profound effect: the building defied all familiar interpretation, it resisted being thought of as merely a house. Frank recognised that he had come to a threshold. Beyond it there was the prospect of a true, modern American architecture, taking shape, within his reach, and apparently tangible only to him (Pl. 79).

Good fortune, excellent connections and unshakeable self-belief had taken Frank a long way in a few short years.

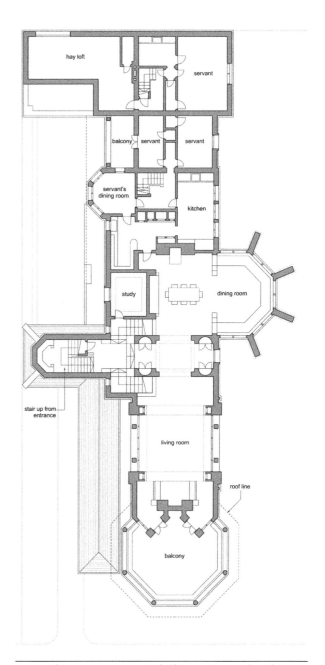

Fig. 11.5. The Husser House, Buena Park, Chicago, 1899. Main Floor Plan. Note the staff accommodation at the north (top) end of the house, on the same floor level as the family.

Although he was still in his early thirties, Chicago society had begun to take an interest in him, in what he was doing and why. To take the next, revolutionary steps he could not afford to wait years again for another opportunity like the one that the Hussers had given him. He needed to raise his profile, broaden his reach, but in this, as in every other aspect of his practice, he adopted a novel approach. He delivered a lecture on landscape architecture to his mother's Fellowship Club in Oak Park and submitted articles to the *Ladies' Home Journal* illustrated with his ideas for 'A Home in a Prairie Town' and 'A Small House with "Lots of Room in it"'. He even invited a journalist from the new *House Beautiful* magazine to review his own house, which he did in the most complimentary terms.[26] When he took his turn to address fellow members of the Architectural League or the Chicago Architecture Club he used the platform to disparage the established profession in the most scathing terms. Younger colleagues enjoyed his reckless attitude. He acquired a small, supportive following, the core of which shared an office suite in the attic of Steinway Hall on Van Buren Street, behind the Auditorium Building. Frank had quit his office in the Schiller Building in 1896, after Cecil Corwin moved back to New York, feeling that the place 'seemed nothing at all without him'.[27] For the following two years he had an office next door to his client, William Winslow, in Burnham and Root's Rookery Building. It was a prestigious address, but the attractions of a like-minded community were hard to resist and in 1898 he had moved again to join his friends at Steinway Hall.

Each of the architects in the Steinway Hall group had his own drawing board, and each used the shared office as his practice, with the exception of Frank. Frank would only design at his house back in Oak Park, and by the late 1890s he had a small, intensely loyal team working there for him. Steinway Hall was intended to be his office frontage, a meeting room for the convenience of city clients, but he came to cherish the camaraderie he felt there, and the time it gave him to talk and think away from the drawing board. Most of all he enjoyed the tacit acknowledgement

Pl. 79.  The west side of the Husser House. The low pergola that runs along the base at the right leads to the front door, at the foot of the stair tower.
From *The Architectural Record* vol. 23 no 3 (March 1908), p. 196.

of his pre-eminence among his colleagues, as they bonded intellectually around his progressive vision. Some were willing, even, to put their own time and effort into promoting him, in return for which Frank was prepared to swallow his disdain for their imitations of his work.[28] One of the group, Robert C. Spencer, an MIT graduate, made use of his Boston connections to get a richly illustrated article published in the *Architectural Review* of June 1900. It is credited to Spencer but might have been written by Frank himself:

*the architect shows his sympathy with nature, a natural sympathy developed by early training, with wise accentuation of early tastes and tendencies by his mother, and seasons of young manhood spent at Hillside farm among the woods and fields of Wisconsin ... You do not feel that these buildings have been dropped accidentally upon the ground ... The artificial structure reaches out and fraternizes with the natural environment ... There is no painfully hard and fast line between nature and art, there is no mutilation of the one to bring it into forced correspondence with the other. The architect has followed his own ideals rather than precedent ... and his success ought to give an added confidence in our ability to create an architecture of our own.*[29]

For those biographers who have assumed that Anna Lloyd Jones's influence on his aesthetics was contrived by Frank to add lustre to his mother's reputation for his much later autobiography, the reference here, from as early as 1900, to Anna's 'wise accentuation of tastes and tendencies' stands as a challenge ∎

# 11

## Spoiled, First by Birth
### *Notes*

1   Letter from W. E. Martin to D. D. Martin, 2 October 1902. Archives of State University of New York, Buffalo. Quoted in Brendan Gill, *Many Masks: A Life of Frank Lloyd Wright* (London: Heinemann, 1988), p. 141.

2   F. L. Wright, 'In the Cause of Architecture' (1900), in B. B. Pfeiffer (ed.), *Collected Writings*, vol. 1: *1894-1930* (New York: Random House, 1992), p. 89.

3   Grant Carpenter Manson, *Frank Lloyd Wright to 1910: The First Golden Age* (New York: Van Nostrand Reinhold Co., 1958), p. 72.

4   F. L. Wright, 'The Architect and the Machine', in B. B. Pfeiffer (ed.), *Collected Writings*, vol. 1: *1894-1930*, p. 23.

5   Frank Lloyd Wright, *An Autobiography (Edition 1)* (New York: Longman, Green & Co., 1932), p. 125.

6   John Lloyd Wright, *My Father Who Is On Earth* (New York: Putnam, 1946), p. 16.

7   *Weekly Home News* (Spring Green, Wisconsin, 23 September 1897), 3.

8   Frank Lloyd Wright, *An Autobiography (Edition 2)* (London: Faber & Faber, 1946), p. 122.

9   The plan of the windmill is shown on p. 133 of F. L. Wright, *An Autobiography (Edition 1)*. It has been reproduced many times. A clear reproduction is in Robert McCarter, *Frank Lloyd Wright* (New York: Phaidon, 1997), p. 187.

10  National Weather Office data for Iowa County, Wisconsin, record 128 severe storms with winds in excess of 57 mph over the years 1844-2014.

11  Confirmed in author's correspondence with Louis Wiehle, erstwhile member of the Taliesin Fellowship and architect for the 1992 restoration of the Romeo and Juliet Windmill.

12    Maginel Wright Barney, *The Valley of the God Almighty Joneses* (New York: Appleton Century, 1965), p. 86.

13    F. L. Wright, *An Autobiography (Edition 1)*, p. 131.

14    For the story of the building of the Fröbel tower see *www.gasthaus-froebelturm.de/common/pdf-gemeindebote/der-turm/* (April 2021).

15    F. L. Wright, *An Autobiography (Edition 1)*, pp. 129–36.

16    Robert Silman, 'Preserving Falling Water – An American Icon'. Lecture, *Master Builder Dialogues: Preserving America* (The Carpenters Company, 2011), *https://www.youtube.com/watch?v=yp_o2dMssa4*.

17    Donald Hoffman, *Frank Lloyd Wright's Fallingwater: The House and its History* (New York: Dover, 1978), p. 55.

18    Hoffman, *Frank Lloyd Wright's Fallingwater*, pp. 55–70. In the process of major repair works in the late 1990s a scan of the reinforcing revealed that the suppliers of the reinforcing bars probably did put additional steel into the living room floor, regardless of Frank's instructions. This intervention, for which they were not paid, could well have saved the house from later collapse. See Silman, 'Preserving Falling Water – An American Icon'.

19    Quote from the early 1930s, attributed to the architect and critic Philip Johnson.

20    F. L. Wright, *An Autobiography (Edition 2)*, p. 341.

21    Silman, 'Preserving Falling Water – An American Icon'.

22    Hoffman, *Frank Lloyd Wright's Fallingwater*, pp. 11–21.

23    Simon Unwin, *Twenty-Five Buildings Every Architect Should Understand* (Abingdon: Routledge, 2015), pp. 124–31.

24    Helen's sister, Isabella Blaney, was a prominent women's suffrage campaigner and one of America's first active female politicians.

25    F. L. Wright, 'The Architect and the Machine', in *Collected Writings*, vol. 1: *1894–1930*, p. 22.

26    *The House Beautiful*, 1/3 (February 1897), 64–9.

27    F. L. Wright, *An Autobiography (Edition 2)*, p. 131.

28    H. A. Brooks, 'Steinway Hall, Architects and Dreams', *Journal of the Society of Architectural Historians*, 22/3 (October 1963), 171–5.

29    R. C. Spencer, 'The Work of Frank Lloyd Wright', *The Architectural Review* (Boston), 7/6 (June 1900), 61–72.

# 12

# Art and Craft of the Machine

Frank was desperate to be seen as a complete original, but his insistence that his work was free of formal or theoretical influence could only go so far, particularly as it began to be discussed by colleagues like Robert C. Spencer, who had the catholic perspective that came from an academic training. The English Arts and Crafts movement provided a convenient touchstone. It shared his concern with the integrity of materials and craftsmanship, and it exalted the spirituality of nature and organic forms. It even had a social mission that aligned with the progressive aspects of Unitarianism, to champion the rights of ordinary working men and women. George Elmslie once recalled that the young architects of the Adler and Sullivan office were more excited by the arrival each month of the English periodical *The Studio* than they were about any other journal, because of its coverage of the English movement.[1] In 1896 Frank had his first meeting with the celebrated Arts and Crafts designer Charles Robert Ashbee.[2] The founder of the Guild of Handicrafts was on a tour of America, looking for modern ideas and for the signs of a new American idiom. When he visited Frank at his home in Oak Park he recognised, in the presence of the intensely charismatic young architect, that he had found what he'd been hoping for.

Buoyed by Ashbee's endorsement, Frank took up the Arts and Crafts cause more purposefully. In October 1897 he became one of the founders of the Chicago Arts and Crafts Society, based at Hull House. The location was apposite: Jane Addams had resolved to establish her 'social settlement house' in one of Chicago's poorest ghettos after making a visit to the very first welfare settlement house, Toynbee Hall, in London. In the late 1880s Toynbee Hall had been the home of Ashbee's Guild of Handicrafts. By the summer of 1898 the Chicago Arts and Crafts Society had over 120 members, many of whom were young architects, and Frank had begun to find its popularity irksome. His disillusion deepened as he recognised that, for most of his fellow members, Arts and Crafts was just another style to be copied. Worse still, being typically and conventionally white-collar and middle-class, they rejected the socialist philosophy on which the movement was based.[3] Frank's next meeting with C. R. Ashbee was in 1900, shortly after the great house on Buena Avenue was completed. It was a highlight of Ashbee's visit: 'He not only has ideas, but the power of expressing them and his Husser House, over which he took me, showing me every detail with the keenest delight, is one of the most beautiful and most individual of creations that I have seen in America.'[4]

Ashbee had been impressed by Frank when they first met. Now, four years later, he was in awe of him, and it was clear to Ashbee that 'the movement', Arts and Crafts, was something that Frank no longer needed or wanted. Frank had come to appreciate that Arts and Crafts in England meant something that it could never mean in America. The Industrial Revolution had transformed Britain half a century before industrialisation had begun to have any impact on America, and even then it was limited to the east. Although industry had changed the lives of almost every British citizen, including those of his Welsh grandparents, America was still an agrarian society. The vast majority of American lives were untouched by industry. The English Arts and Crafts movement was intended to resist the dehumanising effect of industrialisation, but Frank realised it was not a crisis that Americans shared, and that in fact the advent of the machine could represent a promise of greater creative freedom. In March 1901 Frank delivered a lecture at Hull House entitled *The Art and Craft of the Machine*, regarded by many Wright scholars as his 'first great manifesto':

the medium of artistic expression itself has broadened and changed until a new definition and new direction must be given the art activity of the future, and the Machine has finally made for the artist, whether he will yet own it or not, a splendid distinction between the art of the old and the art to come.[5]

The houses of the English Arts and Crafts were hand-built, every component wrought from natural materials in a deliberate effort to reach back to an imagined Arcadia. The Husser House, with rooms ten metres wide, could not have been built without a significant tonnage of Chicago's favourite material – mass produced, industrial steel.

Setting aside the Arts and Crafts banner so publicly left Frank with a dilemma. He found it easy to identify what he saw as being wrong in the work of his contemporaries, but more difficult to spell out in precise terms the design principles that he *did* believe in. He could speak persuasively to an audience of lay people about the qualities of a well-designed house, but when he addressed a professional or academic audience he seemed only to do so in lofty, rhetorical terms. *The Art and Craft of the Machine* is one of the more extreme examples, at times sounding more like an expressionist prose poem than a manifesto. But he was surrounded by eager, and better-educated acolytes at Steinway Hall, young architects who savoured academic theory and who pressed him to show them his way. Around the turn of the century there came a point when he could defer no longer.

He set out his design principles in the form of nine 'motives and inclinations'. Exactly when and how he did this is unclear, but he recalled, wistfully, in his autobiography that, 'I enjoyed them all ... and still enjoy them.'

First ... to reduce the number of necessary parts of the house or the separate rooms to a minimum, and make them all come together as free space ...

Second ... to associate the building as a whole with its site by extension and emphasis of the planes parallel to the ground...

Third ... to eliminate the rooms as boxes and the house itself as another boxing of the boxes ... ceilings and walls to flow ... eliminate waste space ... the whole made more sensible and liveable. Liberal is the best word ...

Fourth ... to get the unwholesome basement up out of the ground, entirely above it ...

Fifth ... To harmonise all necessary openings to outside or inside with good human proportions and make them occur naturally ... no holes cut in walls anywhere ... as holes are cut into a box ...

Sixth ... eliminate combinations of materials in favour of mono-material ... to use none that did not come out of the nature of materials ...

Seventh ... to incorporate all heating, lighting, plumbing that these mechanical systems become constituent parts of the building itself ...

Eighth ... to incorporate as organic architecture ... (the) furnishings, making them all one with the building ...

Ninth ... eliminate the [interior] decorator ... Inorganic.[6]

Six of the points, all but the fourth, fifth and seventh, are paraphrased from 'An Ideal Suburban House', an article written by a leading architect of the English Arts and Crafts movement, M. H. Ballie Scott, and published in *The Studio* magazine in 1895.[7] Though he appropriated some of them, Frank adhered to these guidelines, and they mark a decisive transition in his work, the crossing of the architectural threshold to which the Husser House had brought him. After 1900 there would be no more shingles, no classical columns, and no vestige of Sullivan's ornament.

## Summer 1892. Adler and Sullivan Office, Auditorium Building, Chicago

Louis Sullivan could not make small talk. He found it hard to relate to his clients and he had no time for the draughting-room staff. All the contractors, tradesmen, manufacturers Frank could deal with. Through the glazed screens of his corner booth, Frank looked out over the ranks of tilted drawing boards. Shafts of afternoon sunlight glared across stark walls, making dusty haloes over the cranked shoulders of the draughtsmen as they ground out sheet after sheet of construction details. Much as he admired Sullivan, their office was no different from the others: a 'plan factory', a machine that had to be fed.[8] When he had a practice of his own, he resolved, it would be nothing like that. In fact he couldn't imagine working in a 'practice' at all. What he needed was a more creative and more sociable working environment, a comfortable space that would be there for him whenever he needed it, something more like an artist's studio. That meant it would have to be part of his own house. Right as that felt, it seemed impractical, if not impossible. Why incur the huge cost of building a workplace of his own when office space was so cheap to rent in the city? But it was what he felt he had to do.

## 1897. Frank Lloyd Wright Home and Studio, Forest Avenue, Oak Park, Illinois

The windfall that enabled him to build his studio came from an unexpected source. In 1896, while he was based

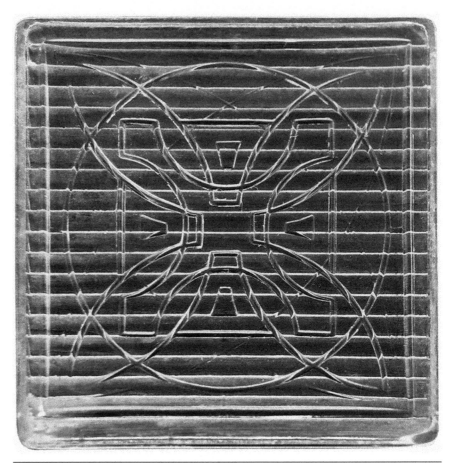

Pl. 80.  The only one of Frank's patterns for the Luxfer Prisms which is known to have gone into production. Courtesy of Douglas M. Steiner, Edmonds, WA, USA..

at The Rookery, Frank's client and friend, William Winslow, introduced him to an impressive new building product, the Luxfer Prism glazing system. Winslow was its co-inventor. He had perfected a method of joining small, prismatic glass tiles into large, apparently frameless panels. The back face of each glass tile was ribbed, so that daylight was captured by internal reflection and projected horizontally into any room behind. In Chicago, where shops and offices were typically

Pl. 81.  Grid-like panels of Luxfer prism tiles incorporated by Louis Sullivan into his ornamented façade for the Schlesinger & Mayer department store, Chicago, 1903.
From *Architectural Record* vol. 16 no. 1 (July 1904), p. 58.

narrow and deep, the redirected daylight could make a valuable difference (Pl. 80).

Within a few years the advent of affordable mains electricity would render it obsolete, but when Luxfer was launched with a vigorous newspaper campaign in the summer of 1897 and with Frank Lloyd Wright, the daring young architect, on board as a consultant designer, it was a resounding commercial success (Pl. 81). Before the year was out Frank had designed and patented forty-one new patterns for the tiles. Although only one of them, the 'flower pattern', went into production, his efforts were so amply rewarded that this one curious small piece of work gave him the boost to his funds that he needed, quite suddenly and with little apparent effort, to build his new studio exactly as he had dreamed it. He had been raised with the conviction that self-belief and willpower were reliable levers for providence. In his Oak Park heyday events seemed to prove it so.[9]

The new studio extension stretched from the north side of his house to the pavement of Chicago Avenue (Fig. 12.1). It had an entrance of its own directly from the avenue, through a compact loggia that made a statement of classical sobriety at a domestic scale, in much the same way that his house seemed to. The draughting room was a precisely composed square, overlooked by an octagonal balcony (Pl. 82). The library, to the right of the entrance, was another pure octagon, connected to the studio by a low narrow passage. It was this room that was used for client presentations, the drawings spread over the heavy oak table at its centre. In common with all his studio work spaces, the library was lit by high-level windows and skylights, so that the walls could be used for cupboards and shelves, and for hanging drawings. All the furniture was built to Frank's design in dark stained oak, much of it integrated with the structure. The books and draughting equipment shared shelf space with exquisite antique *objets*. His son John recalled *'scattered vases filled with leaves and wild flowers ... here and there a Yourdes of rare beauty covered a floor. A Persian lantern, samovars, windows which met and*

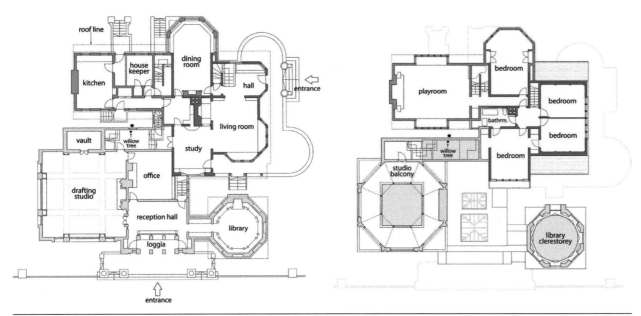

Fig. 12.1. Oak Park Home and Studio 1898. Ground level at left, upper level, right. The remnants of the original house are shown in red; the 1895 extension is shown in green and the 1898 additions in yellow.

*turned the corners, lights filtering through fret-sawed ceiling grilles, sunshine and shadows.'*[10] The studio was far removed from the plan factories of his competitors (Pl. 83). Exotic luxury and chiaroscuro lighting more suggestive of an arts club than a draughting room, set the scene perfectly for acts of architectural transgression.

The completion of the studio wing coincided with the arrival of Frances, the fifth child born to Kitty and Frank. Their caretaker and their cook made it a household of eight; then there was the Kindergarten in the playroom, the frequent attendance of Frank's mother and his sisters and the many other visitors drawn to Frank's light. At the back of the draughting room, a low door in the corner led to the passage, bisected by the large, living willow tree, that joined the workspace to the house. Just as Frank had intended, the life of the house flowed irresistibly into the studio, and the studio team became, inevitably, part of the family's life. As the historian Norris K. Smith observed, Frank's architectural staff

*formed a quasi-familial group of devoted followers ... their relationship to him marked by loyalty and a devotion to certain ideas. They were taken on as members, not as hirelings. They were not members of his family but they belonged to his household – an entity that had somehow to embrace within its pattern of order all that was socially meaningful.*[11]

Grant Manson, another of his important biographers, was more candidly perplexed:

*There was the 'Studio', workshop proper, with its carefully planned professional facilities, apart but connected. There were the apprentices, or draftsmen, working more-or-less en famille, taking lunch daily with the patron and his family. It is life in a Continental vein - paternalistic, imperious, strangely alien to American custom. Where did it come from? It is only one of many things about Wright's mode of living ... which was established at the same early date, that defy explanation.*[12]

Pl. 82.  The drafting room, Oak Park Studio 1898, following the superb restoration work of the Frank Lloyd Wright
Trust.
Photograph James Caulfield/FLWT.

at The Valley. It was the right way to live: paternalistic, but also wholesome, egalitarian and communal, as they brought it with them from Wales and as it had been practised by their ancestors for countless generations before.

Frank found his first recruit at Steinway Hall. Marion Mahony was the first registered female architect in Illinois, and only the second woman to graduate from Massachusetts Institute of Technology. She was a talented, open-minded designer and a superb draughtsman, the kind of exceptional talent that Frank was always drawn to. She took comfortably to the boisterous, bohemian milieu at Oak Park and became a close friend to Kitty. Walter Burley Griffin and Isabel Roberts were soon added to the studio team. During his time in Frank's studio, Griffin emerged as the senior designer, only to leave in 1906 when his hopes of a partnership were denied. A few years later Griffin and Mahony would marry and, while on their honeymoon, design the competition-winning proposal for the civic centre of Canberra. Isabel Roberts, like Marion Mahony, would stay at the studio, loyal to the family and the practice as long as it needed her. She was a designer, draughtsman, book-keeper, manager, nanny and personal assistant to Frank, and uniquely also a proxy client. It was the house that she and Frank designed for her mother that ended up with a large tree growing through its entrance hall.[13]

Maginel, at seventeen, was beginning her own career as an illustrator. Frank encouraged her to use the studio balcony as her workspace. The presence of Maginel and of the other women in the studio is remarkable. Roberts and Mahony would have been among very few female architects in the city, possibly the only two, and yet they both held vital roles in Frank's Oak Park team which, at its largest, numbered only eight. Without strong women around him, Frank felt rudderless. Roberts, Mahony, Kitty his wife and his sisters and, above all, Anna his mother knew this and responded to it. They worked in unison, purposefully, to support him, console him, steer him and inspire him through the most creative period of his life.

In unanimity, Frank's biographers have allowed us to infer that, at the beginning of the twentieth century, thoughts

It can, in fact, be quite easily explained. Among the words of Smith and Manson there is, almost perfectly expressed, the definition of *teulu*, the ancient form of Welsh household. It was the way of life that Frank had found among the Lloyd Joneses of Wales, the nation, his heritage, had no part to play in his creative thinking. But this is to deny Anna's continuing influence upon him. By 1901 Maginel had been working professionally for three years. She was a talented illustrator, earning as much in her first job as a teenager as Frank had managed only near his peak with Adler and Sullivan.[14] After those first three years she had saved enough to fulfil a desire that had haunted her mother for decades: to go back to the house and the chapels in Cardiganshire that she had last seen over half a century before.[15]

## Summer 1901. South Cardiganshire, Wales

Anna and Maginel travelled by steamship from New York to Liverpool, back along the route of the tortuous migration voyage. From there they rode by train into Wales through the 'tourist-ridden' north and then, within a few hours, into a landscape that, 'seemed suddenly familiar: the wooded hills, the streams and waterfalls and fields' – the image of The Valley. They were met off the train at Llandysul by a distant cousin, John Thomas, their host for the duration of their visit.[16]

Maginel recalled that, on the first morning of their stay, they were taken to church, which involved a ride up a hill so steep that the horses baulked. They had to get off the carriage and walk. From the churchyard there was a view of a 'toy-like' town below the hill. Her account seems to merge aspects of John Thomas's local Unitarian chapel on Graig Road in Llandysul, perched on a short but steep rise off the high street, and of the Anglican church at Llanwenog on its hilltop, where the remains of Anna's grandfather, John Enoch, lay alongside the graves of their older ancestors, the Unitarian pioneers of south Cardiganshire. The old chapel at Llwynrhydowen would have looked just as it did when Anna had last seen it. At Pantydefaid, however, there was an imposing new building that was very different from the one at which Jenkin had preached nineteen years before (Pl. 84). It was tall and almost perfectly square with a roof like a pyramid. Unitarianism was ascendant, the community more confident than it had ever been. Searching for her remote childhood past, Anna must have gone to Blaenralltddu, perhaps still swallowed by ivy as Jenkin had found it. Her father's birthplace, Pantstreimon, would have looked much as it had done in her childhood. Her mother's

Pl. 83. Oak Park Home and Studio (1898), seen from Chicago Avenue. The entrance loggia is at the centre, the octagonal library to the right and the drafting room to the left. The triangular roofs of the original house are to the rear.
Photograph James Caulfield/FLWT.

Pl. 84. Members of Pantydefaid Chapel in the village square with the 1898 chapel building behind. Photograph *circa* 1900. It is likely that Anna and Maginel met some of these people in the course of their visit to Wales.
Photograph John Thomas. NLW/Flickr Commons.

first home, Pen-y-Wern, perhaps the place that meant most to her, was dilapidated and soon to be replaced by the solid Victorian villa that still stands on the hillside looking across the marshy fields towards the great house at Alltyrodyn.[17]

## 1901. Kankakee, Illinois, Seventy Miles South of Chicago

Kankakee was characterised by rows of solid, traditional houses, Queen Anne, colonial and carpenter gothic. It had been transformed in 1895, when the giant David Bradley Manufacturing business, moved to the north of the town from its historic base in the centre of Chicago.[18] It was David Bradley's grandson, Byron Harley Bradley, who brought Frank Lloyd Wright to the town. His brother-in-law, Warren Hickox Jr, himself the heir of a local property baron, had sold Bradley an acre of delightful, flat land on the north bank of the tranquil Kankakee River, at the edge of Riverview, the town's most prosperous neighbourhood. The commission was for two houses, the larger for Bradley and his wife, and a smaller house next door, on a portion of the site that Warren Hickox Jr had retained, for himself. There is a general consensus among architectural historians that the two houses mark the advent of Frank Lloyd Wright's 'Mature Prairie Style', the breakthrough to which the preceding years of eclectic experiment had been leading. Grant C. Manson listed the definitive attributes:

Pl. 85.  B. Harley Bradley House, Kankakee, Illinois. 1901, considered the first of Frank's 'Prairie Houses'.
Photograph Robert Bohiman, courtesy of Wright in Kankakee.

*the flowing plan, the directional or centrifugal lines [of the plan], the generous, low roofs with pronounced overhang, the broad chimneys, the reduced floor-heights, the suppression of sills, the ribbons of casements, the geometrical ornamentation, the intimate liaison of house and site.*[19]

The Bradley House, the more opulent of the two, is extravagantly elongated at the rear and to the sides (Pl. 85). Before any of the detail claims attention, it is this intense expression of dynamic horizontality that is most powerfully affecting. In his autobiography Frank gave his account of 'Building the New House':

*the planes of the building parallel to the ground were all stressed – I like to 'stress' them – to grip the whole to Earth. This parallel plane I called, from the beginning, – the plane of the third dimension. The term came naturally enough: really a spiritual interpretation of that dimension.*[20]

A 'spiritual interpretation' of the third dimension: a striking notion. Both supporters and critics saw an evocation, in the extreme horizontality, of the wide horizons of the Midwest prairies, hence the term 'Prairie Style'. It was not a term that Frank was comfortable with. The more important association, for him, was with a higher realm. He wanted there to be more to 'The New House' than merely a new style, but it could not be denied that his new forms and lines were exhilarating. When Frank had been given the freedom to express himself previously, he had tended to favour low, hipped roofs. Given the same licence with the two Kankakee houses, he chose instead to give them deep, oversailing gables. The front edges of the gables lean very slightly upwards and more obviously outwards so that their overhang is deeper at the ridge than it is at the verges.

Earlier in 1900 Frank had completed a house for a lawyer in the West Pullman district of Chicago, around fifteen miles south of the city centre. Although contemporaneous, the Stephen A. Foster Residence bears little resemblance to the two Kankakee Houses, other than in the design of its roof. The Foster house is an oddity, a hybrid of shingle style and Japonism. Its gable roof, with angled overhang and pronounced upward slants, is unashamedly oriental.[21] In the *Ladies' Home Journal* of July 1901, Frank introduced his *Small House with 'Lots of Room in it'* by explaining,

> The average homemaker is partial to the gable roof. This house has been designed with a thorough, somewhat new treatment of the gable with gently flaring eaves and pediments, slightly lifted at the peaks, accentuating the perspective, slightly modelling the roof surfaces, and making the outlines 'crisp'.

The design of the 'Small House' was modelled closely on the Hickox House. Frank's rationale for the roof makes no mention of its obvious Japanese provenance, and so the cheerful imitation in the Foster house, sublimated in the Bradley and Hickox houses, is now accepted as another original and distinctive marker of the early Prairie Style.

The B. Harley Bradley House has another, less visible, link to an ancient foreign culture. Work on the house came to its conclusion late in 1901, a few months after Frank's mother and sister returned from their visit to Wales. In abstruse homage to his ancestors, when invited by the Bradleys to dignify their new house with a name, he presented them with 'Glenlloyd'. This was not an isolated case. During the busy year of 1900 Frank also designed a large summerhouse and a group of outbuildings for Frederick B. Jones, vice-president of Adams and Westlake, a huge manufacturing company that made hardware for railroads, steamships and streetcars. The Frederick Jones property was on the south side of Delavan Lake, a beautiful resort eighty miles north of Chicago, just across the Illinois-Wisconsin state boundary. The house shares the low-lying gable forms of the Kankakee houses, but in other respects it is more light-hearted, suited to its holiday purpose, with variegated timber shiplap boarding and a plinth course of large pebbles embedded in concrete. In 1836 a first full survey recorded

large areas of marsh on each side of the rivers that fed and drained the small lake.[22] There is no evidence that Frank ever visited the site, but he must have looked at survey plans, and perhaps noticed the indications of marsh. Or perhaps the presence nearby of marshland is a coincidence, regardless of his reasoning, when he was permitted by Frederick B. Jones to give a name to the summerhouse, Frank chose 'Penwern', 'above the marsh', the name of his grandmother's birthplace[23] (Pl. 86).

Frederick Jones's Penwern was built during the spring and early summer of 1901. It was designed for entertaining and used for its leisurely purpose for the first time later that year. Jones ran it like a gentleman's club. Each summer was punctuated by parties for his business associates and colleagues. Among the first visitors was Jones's immediate superior in the executive of Adams and Westlake, Ward W. Willits. Willits must have been impressed by Penwern, for within a few months Frank was working on the design of another new house, this time for the Willits family, which

Pl. 86. The Gate Lodge, Penwern, Delavan Lake, Wisconsin. 1901
Postcard from the collection of John Hime.

was to be built in dense woodland in the sparsely populated north Chicago suburb of Highland Park. The Ward Willits house was designed in 1902 and completed early in the following year (Pl. 87). It may not have been the first in the prairie style, but it so clearly crystallises the spatial and aesthetic intentions to which Frank was aspiring that it has been regarded ever since as the archetype.

Many years later Frank himself would agree that the Ward Willits house was 'the first great Prairie House'. The centrifugal room arrangement, still tentative in the two Kankakee houses, flowers into a pronounced cruciform, anchored at its intersection by a massive, multi-hearthed fireplace. Wide open family rooms fill three of the wings, and generous staff quarters occupy the fourth. The super-structure is expressed in the counterpoint of dark, bold timber framing and pale stucco infill, with a symmetry that is yet more faithful to Japanese precedent. The central block, facing the street, has the balanced repose of the Winslow House, but by relocating the main entrance to the side, almost concealed below the porte-cochère, Frank was free to arrange the principal elevation as a purely abstract grid of windows and structural framing. The pattern of the framing extends through the interior. In the words of Vincent Scully,

'the interior trim, interweaving around the central core, completely carries the spatial motif and, in a curious way, turns space and building fabric into one interwoven whole.'[24]

Frank often used the term 'plasticity' to describe the quality of continuity that he was searching for, in which walls, ceilings and floors seemed all to be aspects of the one, frequently folded plane. In his 1949 memoir of Louis Sullivan, *Genius and the Mobocracy*, Frank reflected on the differences between Sullivan's superficial grasp of architectural integrity, which he seemed only to express through surface ornament, and Frank's own desire for a more complete, holistic expression: 'I wanted to see … a building continuously plastic from inside to outside … I longed to see the thing go through and "button at the back", become *genuinely Unitarian*.'[25]

## 1902. Frank Lloyd Wright Home and Studio, Forest Avenue, Oak Park, Illinois

John Lloyd Wright had another colourful memory of his childhood, from the prodigious year of 1902:

*Papa kept a naked woman on his drafting room balcony. I saw her through the high windows opening over the flat gravel roof. She was pretty and had freckles … Dickie Bock, the sculptor, squinted his eyes in her direction, then pressed the clay into curves like those she was made of. Papa came to the balcony and scrutinized Dickie's work. All of a sudden he ripped it apart. Dickie watched him with big tears streaming down his face.*[26]

The sculpture that John had seen through the window was *Flower in the Crannied Wall*. Originally inspired by lines from Tennyson, which are inscribed on its back, it is a female figure reaching towards a tapering, abstractly patterned monolith, perhaps a model of a skyscraper. Both the figure and the model emerge from a tall, prismatic base (Pl. 88). The proportions seem misjudged, it is flimsily modelled, but it manages, still, to be a powerful expression of the torment of an artist, an architect, trying with every breath of his creative being, and entirely immune to embarrassment or

Pl. 87 Ward Willits House, Highland Park, Chicago, 1902.
From *Frank Lloyd Wright, Chicago: Sonderheft der Architektur des XX Jahrhunderts No. 8* (Berlin: Ernst Wasmuth, 1911), p. 50.

the risk of failure, to grasp at something completely new; in which natural and abstract geometric forms would emerge from the same, earthen base material, each to give a heightened expression to the other.

## 1902. South 3rd Street, Springfield, Sangamon County, Illinois

The sculpture was made to sit in the centre of the entrance hall to the palatial house that Frank had designed for Susan Lawrence Dana, a young widow, a campaigning progressive socialite, who had inherited her father's fortune and his property in Springfield, two hundred miles to the south-west of Chicago (Pl. 89). The Dana house was twice the size of the Bradley House and the Ward Willits House. It was by far the largest that Frank had designed to that date. Susan Dana asked for the house to be built around the parlour of her father's old home, so that it could be retained as a memorial. The remnants are there, but entirely subsumed in the luxurious brilliance of Frank's creation. Over three principal floor levels it contained thirty-five rooms, arranged over sixteen split floor planes. Frank resolved the complex arrangement of rooms to flow, one to the next, without corridors (Fig. 12.2).

Susan shared Frank's fascination with oriental art. Her house has prominent gable roofs like those of the two Kankakee houses. For the Dana House they were designed with sculpted copper verges, evoking unreservedly the roofs of a Japanese temple (Pl. 90). The body of the house is built in extremely fine roman brickwork that extends from the outside throughout the interior. It has over 450 superb stained-glass windows in dozens of different patterns, all abstract designs based on the distinctive leaves and fruit of the sumac tree (Pl. 91). The same motifs are embossed into the copperwork of the roof, woven into floor coverings and in the metalwork of the hanging lamps. He designed every piece of furniture, of which there are many dozens, every door, every hanging, rug or carpet. There is nothing in the house that he did not either design or select. He even designed clothes for his client, to ensure that she would feel at home in her surroundings.[27] Despite the enormous effort put into it, there are suggestions that, over the course

Pl. 88. *Flower in the Crannied Wall*, Richard Bock's sculpture in the entrance hall of the Susan Lawrence Dana House.
Photograph by Ron Frazier/CC BY-2.0.

of the three years that it took to build, Frank gradually lost some of his enthusiasm for the project. Perhaps he felt some discomfort in the lack of constraint; more likely, such was

Pl. 89.  The sculpture seen through the front doorway of the Susan Lawrence Dana House.
Photograph Doug Carr. Courtesy of the Dana Thomas House Foundation.

Pl. 90.  Susan Lawrence Dana House. 1902.
Photograph Randy von Liski/CC BY 2.0.

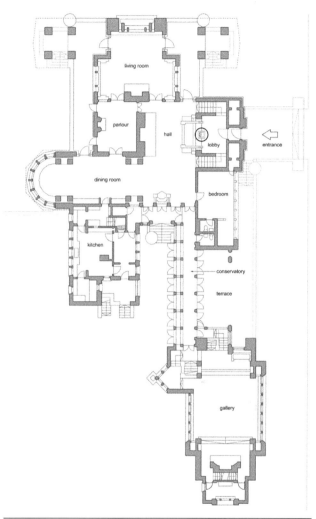

Fig. 12.2.  Ground Level Plan, Susan Lawrence Dana House, Springfield Illinois,
1904. The sculpture is circled in the entrance lobby.

the rate of his creative progress, he felt simply that he had
moved on.

Susan Lawrence Dana may not have noticed or
much cared if he did, because the house was everything
that she had hoped it would be. In 1904, when it was

formally opened, she hosted two receptions for a total of over a thousand guests, and in the years that followed it was used frequently as a venue for concerts, exhibitions and seminars, and later for political and religious meetings. But in time, much as Frank's design had swallowed the remains of her father's house, Susan herself was subsumed by the lifestyle that the house seemed to demand of her. When it became clear that she could no longer manage either the building or her debts, a court order was made to remove her from her home so that it could be sold. She spent her last years destitute, living in a small cottage directly across the rail tracks that still run along the side of her magnificent house.[28]

In 2017 a collection of Susan Lawrence Dana's financial records was uncovered in the archive of a law firm in Springfield. It included receipts for many of the special items that Frank had designed for her house, light fittings, fabrics and artworks, and another intriguing document: a note of a $4,615 loan made to Frank in 1903, equivalent to over $130,000 dollars today. The repayment date was given as August 1906, but Susan Dana cancelled the debt.[29] The circumstances of this loan are not known, but the dating could be significant. It suggests a link to another project which, although more modest, undoubtedly meant more to Frank.

Pl. 91.  The large 'sumac window' in the gable of the master bedroom of the Susan Lawrence Dana House.
Photograph copyright Doug Carr. Courtesy of the Dana Thomas House Foundation.

## February 1903. The Valley, Wyoming Township, Iowa County, Wisconsin

A team of local builders, led by Frank's Uncle Thomas, were hard at work on the final stages of a new building for Hillside Home School (Pl. 92). There was nothing like it in Iowa County, or even in Sauk. It was the first building in the area to aspire to true civic stature, and more modern than anything in southern Wisconsin. The initial plans were already ambitious: a long south-facing classroom block, set into the slope, with a tall assembly hall at its eastern end, balanced by a gymnasium block at the west. Then a covered bridge was added, springing outward to the north to connect to an annex containing an art studio, the Roberts Room for Arts, and a science laboratory, the Lawrence Gallery for Science

Pl. 92.  Postcard of the Hillside Home School new building, The Valley, Iowa County, Wisconsin, completed 1904.
Wisconsin Historical Society WHS-10204.

(Fig. 12.3). The art studio was paid for by a $9,000 loan from Charles Roberts, a prominent Oak Park Unitarian and one of Frank's earliest clients. Susan Lawrence Dana paid for the laboratory. She also made a generous contribution to the completion of the main building, gifts that eventually exceeded $27,000.[30]

The thirty-year history of Hillside Home School is as remarkable as any of the stories of the Lloyd Jones family. After the death of their father, having spent years teaching in urban centres, both Ellen and Jane (Nell and Jennie) Lloyd Jones returned to The Valley with the conviction that children grew up healthier and happier if raised in the open countryside (Pl. 93). Their early promotional booklets were aimed at middle-class urban parents, offering a 'Family and Farm school ... it has a group of six buildings located on a farm of a hundred acres ... situated in one of the beautiful side valleys that open out into the Wisconsin River ... with neighbours that are friendly to the institution.'[31]

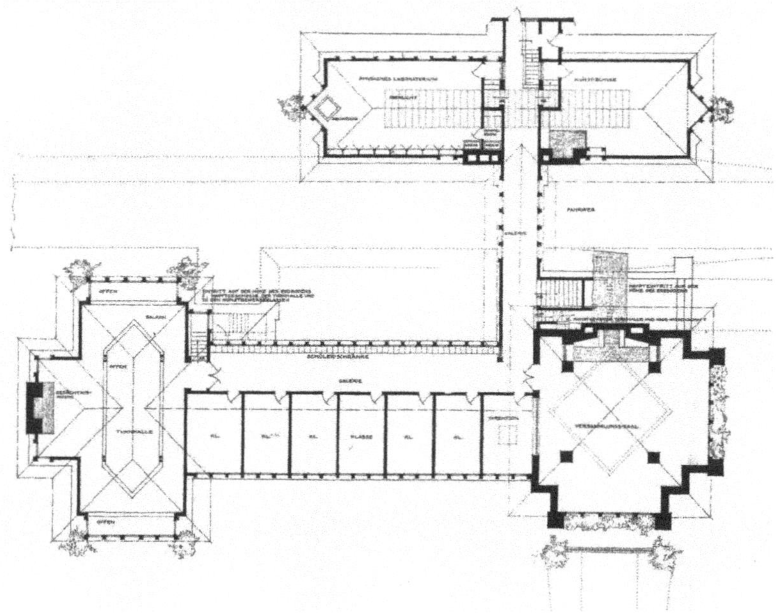

The most evocative and complete account of the school was published in 1939. *A Goodly Fellowship* is the memoir of the distinguished educationalist Mary Ellen Chase. She found her first teaching job at the school in 1909.

*Hillside was a school as well as a farm and a home. Indeed it was the best school for children of all sorts that I have ever known ... For three years I lived and worked at Hillside; yet no inadequate words of mine can catch or record its atmosphere or accurately explain just what it was to both teachers and children.*

*The well-defined boundaries of the valley, the uniformity, simplicity and stability of its people were naturally responsible ... for the triumph of Hillside; and yet these values might have lain undiscovered and useless ... had the founders of that school been other than they were ... The Lloyd Joneses one and all had within themselves, in their appearance and speech, in their humour and insight, in the simplicity and strength of their thinking, all the abundant*

Fig. 12.3. Hillside Home School, Ground Plan. The Assembly Hall is at bottom right and the Gymnasium at bottom left. There are classrooms between. The block to the rear contains the Lawrence Dana Room for Science and the Roberts Gallery for Arts.
Plate 10, *Ausgeführte Bauten und Entwurfe von Frank Lloyd Wright*, Berlin, Ernst Wasmuth (1910).

Pl. 93. Nell and Jennie Lloyd Jones, founders and leaders of Hillside Home School. Wisconsin Historical Society WHS-87747.

*riches of their own environment, and these riches they gave to every child.*

Mary Ellen Chase came to appreciate that Ellen and Jane's approach to teaching had been years ahead of its time,

*Ten years before Mr. John Dewey 'ignited the flame of the current educational revolution', fourteen years before Colonel Francis Parker lent his name to what he termed child-centred education, and a full quarter of a century before the progressive school as we know it was springing up from Massachusetts to California, this school in a remote Wisconsin valley was looking upon each child as an individual and centring all its efforts on his reasonable growth, activity and self-expression ... They were utilising these virtues of sympathy, understanding, patience, wisdom and humour simply because they were sympathetic, understanding, patient, wise and understanding women.*

It certainly didn't follow from this that the two headmistresses were tolerant of slackness, particularly among their teachers: 'They had a way of bursting into stormy Welsh to each other when some one of us had displeased them ... and the very fact that no one save themselves understood their vituperations rendered them all the more effective.'[32]

At its largest the school provided for a community of over one hundred children, teachers and staff, two-thirds of whom lived there, some throughout the year. A page from the census of 1900 lists resident pupils from twelve different states, from California to New York. The remaining third were day pupils, the children of neighbouring farms. Boys and girls had their rooms on separate floors of the houses, but were otherwise encouraged to live and learn together. It has been said that Hillside may have been the first co-educational boarding school in America. Neither was there a rigid segregation of age groups. Pupils were aged between five and eighteen, and the older pupils took an active part in raising the young. The children came from a variety of religious

Pl. 94. Hillside Home School: Senior girls in a chemistry lesson circa 1895. In 1924 Florence Fifer Bohrer became the first female State Senator to be elected to the Illinois General Assembly. The girl second from right is probably Florence: the resemblance is strong. The African American girl on her left must be Mabel Wheeler, Florence's close friend and roommate. (See Florence F. Bohrer, 'The Unitarian Hillside Home School', from *The Wisconsin Magazine of History*, 38/3 (Spring 1955), pp. 151–155). Wisconsin Historical Society WHS-25556.

backgrounds. The school was advertised as non-sectarian, but the approach to teaching was, 'strongly Unitarian both in conviction and splendid practice', as Mary Ellen Chase put it (Pl. 94). The mix of classics, foreign languages, practical skills, art and science followed the template of David Davis's Castell Hywel school, along with the conviction that Nature itself was the supreme classroom.

Frank played his small part in the creation of the first school in 1887. He designed the windmill ten years

Pl. 95. Tan-y-Deri, designed in 1907 by Frank for his sister Jane and her husband Andrew Porter, the financial manager of the school.
Photograph George Hall.

later, and the beautiful new school in 1901. Those were his own contributions, but over the same timescale Hillside was the most significant preoccupation of all of his closest family, so that it remained a constant presence in his life. His mother had been a housemistress there before her move to Oak Park. His sister Maginel had completed her own education there. His beloved Uncle James was Farm Superintendent, a role that required him to supervise the activities of all the children in the school while they worked with the livestock and cultivated the crops that formed the entirety of every school meal. His Uncle Thomas was the Head of Manual Training into his old age. His cousin Nell was the senior modern language teacher, and her sister, Frank's cousin Elsie, taught physical education. His cousin Tom, one of his Uncle John's sons, was a pupil himself before returning later to serve as Assistant Principal. Uncle Jenkin was frequently there in person, and a constant, guiding presence in spirit. Frank's sister Jane later joined the teaching staff, having moved back to The Valley in 1907 with her husband, Andrew Porter, when Andrew took

on the financial management of the school. Frank designed the house for them that was called 'Tan-y-Deri'[33] (Pl. 95). Frank's younger cousins attended Hillside, along with his and Kitty's own children, and the children of their cousins. The majority of their classmates came from middle-class families and farming families, but amongst them there were also, occasionally, the children of prominent public figures. Robert LaFollette was a Wisconsin Senator when he enrolled his son, Phillip, at Hillside.[34] He had already been a Member of the House of Representatives and served as state Governor. In 1924 he even ran for the Presidency, under the banner of his own Progressive Party. Phillip studied law after leaving Hillside, and in due course he also served as Governor of Wisconsin, but before that he was to play a decisive role in sustaining the career of Frank Lloyd Wright. It was Phillip LaFollette who, in 1927, led the effort of friends and supporters to establish 'Frank Lloyd Wright Incorporated', and it was his strategic engagement with the Bank of Wisconsin that saved the architect and his home, Taliesin, from bankruptcy and foreclosure in the aftermath of the disastrous episode of the Mann Act trial and Frank's imprisonment in Minnesota.

His Aunts Jane and Ellen had allowed Frank to design his windmill just as he wanted it, and they were prepared to build it just as it was designed. They allowed him the same freedom to design their school. He set to work with the experience of nearly fifty completed projects behind him. Of those, all were residential buildings, or their outbuildings, apart from the boathouse in Madison, a yacht club at Delavan Lake, a small golf clubhouse in River Forest – and the windmill.[35] There was nothing else to prepare him for the task of designing a school. At the turn of the century the majority of American children still attended archaic rural one-room schoolhouses. New urban schools were 'factory-like, dark and dank' utilitarian blocks containing rooms made as large as they could be, to hold as many children as possible at their small desks in tight rows.[36] Frank *needed* nothing to prepare him, other than to recall how much he had despised the schools that he had attended, and the certainty in his mind that all that was considered conventional must be fundamentally wrong. The pedagogy of Frank's aunts was strongly informed by their instincts, and from the principles of their inherited culture, as if they were regrowing education from its roots. Frank designed Hillside in the same way: to serve their unique approach to teaching efficiently, as if it was the first school ever built. Its technology was simple. Like the other buildings in The Valley it was constructed in load-bearing stone and timber frame. Stone quarried locally was cut into rusticated blocks for the plinth and outer walls. The timber structures of the assembly hall and the gymnasium, at each end, were couched between the massive stone flanks. The classroom windows were set into a heavy timber framing that projected over the top edge of the stonework, resembling the *hourdes* of a medieval castle. In later years, Frank would often write of his admiration for the French philosopher-architect Eugène Viollet-le-Duc, who had been brought to Frank's attention by Louis Sullivan. Viollet-le-Duc was an anti-classicist, a radical moderniser who was, nonetheless, bewitched by medieval architecture. Hillside Home School has the same duality: subtle historical vestiges giving character to an exceptionally modern countenance. It appears more modern now than any of the projects that preceded it. It was David Timothy, the old mason, who led the construction of the stonework. He had built nothing like it in The Valley before. It seems likely that he would have taken work in the cities on occasions, for his skills were valuable, but he was building the school for his adopted family, his *teulu*. It must have meant more. The last important Unitarian building that he had contributed to was the new chapel in Rhydowen, just a year or so before he had said 'hwyl fawr' to his homeland. That chapel and the new school have identical masonry, the same blocks, the same coursing, the same soul.

The heart of the new school was the assembly hall. It was the only room in which the whole school community could gather. Mary Ellen Chase recalled that the 'great common-room at school had been designed as much for family gathering as for study. A huge fireplace was at one end, and on cold winter days logs were always burning. Upon the wide long stone above it was carved in Welsh, *The Truth*

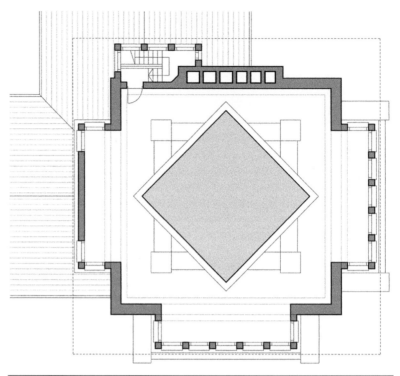

Fig. 12.4. The plan of the upper level of the Assembly Hall at Hillside Home School. Frank's approach to architectural geometry shares its roots with the domestic pattern making of Welsh Nonconformism. Compare this plan to the quilt pattern in Plate 96.

*against the World.*[37] The assembly hall is an extraordinary room. Its floor is a precise square, each corner defined by a massive, stone right-angle. Continuous windows fill the spaces between the corners on the south and east sides, and the monumental fireplace spans the north. It is overlooked by a gallery floor, which is also a precise square (Fig. 12.4). But the gallery is rotated by forty-five degrees relative to the main floor below - a square within a square. It was a motif that expressed 'unity', and this is generally taken to be its intention in the design of the hall, but it also recalls a more homely image, the rotated square within a square that was a quilt pattern familiar to the women of west Wales, spread

Pl. 96. A nineteenth century quilt from Carmarthenshire.
Courtesy of Jen Jones, the Welsh Quilt Centre.

Hillside Home school was a triumph, celebrated by local commentators and by journalists who had followed the construction process with exhilaration. The school was 'something out of the ordinary ... a beautiful and ideal building ... a great joy' to experience.[39] Anyone searching today for early photographs of the school will find that the majority are from picture postcards. Visitors came from far around to see it for themselves. Few went away without feeling that they had encountered something transformational. Awareness of the school, of its extraordinary new building and its unique culture, was raised to a new level. Demand for places surged. Despite dauntingly large construction debts, with its beautiful new building, the future of the school must have seemed assured.

Events soon to unfold would change everything. Although there is still unmistakable pride in their achievement, Aunt Jennie's 1916 memoir yields to a melancholy conclusion:

> When they built this building the sisters fondly hoped and fully expected that some one of the grandchildren of Richard and Mary would be willing to take the school when Ellen and Jane would cease from their labours, and would perpetuate the memory of their grandparents ... Hence the memorial room.[40]

over generations of childhood beds (Pl. 96). The open edge of the gallery is secured behind a deep parapet, clad in dark oak boards. The upper gallery is a library. The parapet serves as a bookcase, its outer face deeply inscribed with biblical texts and a scattering of *Nod Cyfrin* symbols. The stone above the fireplace is also inscribed, but not with *Y Gwir yn erbyn a Byd*, as Mary Ellen Chase recalled, but with that verse, in English, from Gray's 'Elegy' (see Pl. 10 and Pl. 11). This is the room that Jennie recalled in 1916, 'a memorial Assembly room which was also to serve as a chapel ... with a Welsh feel'.[38]

Frank found himself the owner of the school and its liabilities when it closed in 1915. It would be another sixteen years before he eventually restored and reopened the building for the Taliesin Fellowship, his own, very different kind of school. In 1917, at the time of Jane's death, it was an empty shell ∎

# 12    Art and Craft of the Machine
## *Notes*

1       D. Gebhard, 'C. F. A. Vosey – To and From America', *Journal of the Society of Architectural Historians*, 30/4 (December 1971), 307.

2       The meeting in 1896 has been recalled only by Frank's son Lloyd who would have been six years old at the time. Ashbee did visit America for the first time in 1896, but made no record himself of being in Chicago.

3       H. A. Brooks, 'Chicago Architecture – Its Debt to Arts and Crafts', *Journal of the Society of Architectural Historians*, 30/4 (December 1971), 312–17.

4       A. Crawford, 'Ten Letters from Frank Lloyd Wright to Charles Robert Ashbee', *Architectural History*, 13 (1970), 64. From Ashbee's *Journal* (December 1900).

5       F. L. Wright, 'Art and Craft of the Machine' (1901) in B. B. Pfeiffer (ed.), *Collected Writings*, vol. 1: *1894–1930* (New York: Random House, 1992), p. 58

6       Frank Lloyd Wright, *An Autobiography (Edition 1)* (New York: Longman, Green & Co., 1932), p. 142.

7       M. H. Baillie Scott, 'An Ideal Suburban House', *The Studio*, 4/1 (January 1895), 127–32.

        See also Meryl Secrest, *Frank Lloyd Wright: A Biography* (Chicago: University of Chicago Press, 1998), p. 154.

8       F. L. Wright, 'The Architect' (1900) in B. B. Pfeiffer (ed.), *Collected Writings*, vol. 1: *1894–1930* (New York: Random House, 1992), p. 46.

9       D. Neumann, 'The Century's Triumph in Lighting: The Luxfer Prism Companies and their Contribution to Early Modem Architecture', *Journal of the Society of Architectural Historians*, 54/1 (March 1995), 24–53.

10    John Lloyd Wright, *My Father Who Is On Earth* (New York: Putnam, 1946), p. 15. A Yourdes is a type of 'Persian rug' – see the *House Beautiful* article (February 1897) from which John Lloyd Wright took some of his words.

11    Norris K. Smith, *Frank Lloyd Wright A Study in Architectural Content* (Englewood Cliffs, NJ: Prentice Hall Inc., 1966), p. 67.

12    Grant Carpenter Manson, *Frank Lloyd Wright to 1910: The First Golden Age* (New York: Van Nostrand Reinhold Co., 1958), p. 46.

13    A short biography of Isabel Roberts can be found at *https://pioneeri ngwomen.bwaf.org/isabel-roberts/* (April 2021).

14    Maginel was paid $50 a week in her first job. Maginel Wright Barney, *The Valley of the God Almighty Joneses* (New York: Appleton Century, 1965), p. 136.

15    The 1901 date for Anna and Maginel's visit to Wales is based on the following: that Maginel started work after one year at art college, 1897–8, and that the trip took place the year after her sister Jane's marriage, which was in June 1900. Other sources have derived different dates, the latest being 1903.

16    John Thomas was a great-grandson of the Rev. David Lloyd, from his first marriage to the daughter of the legendary Jenkin Jones. Anna's eldest brother, Thomas, the builder, had kept up a correspondence with him.

17    Pen-y-Wern translates as 'above the marsh' or, more literally, 'top or head of the marsh'. Gwern/wern is also the Welsh name of the alder tree, which sometimes causes confusion.

18    *The National Rural and Family Magazine* (Chicago), 57/10 (9 March 1899), 314.

19    Manson, *Frank Lloyd Wright to 1910: The First Golden Age*, p. 108.

20    F. L. Wright, *An Autobiography (Edition 1)*, p. 140.

21    William A. Storrer, *The Architecture of Frank Lloyd Wright: A Complete Catalogue (Third Edition)* (Chicago: University of Chicago Press, 2002), p. 50.

22    William Tans et al., *Environmental Impact Statement on the Delavan Lake Rehabilitation Project* (Madison: State of Wisconsin Department of Natural Resources, 1989), p. 165.

23    Mark Hertzberg, *Frank Lloyd Wright's Penwern: A Summer Estate* (Madison, Wisconsin Historical Society Press, 2019), pp xxxi–xxxiv, 1–27.

24    Vincent Scully, *Frank Lloyd Wright* (New York: George Braziller Inc., 1960), p. 17.

25    Frank Lloyd Wright, *Genius and the Mobocracy* (New York: Duell, Sloane and Pearce, 1949), pp. 59–60. My italics.

26    J. L. Wright, *My Father Who Is On Earth,* p. 27.

27    This was a privilege that he would also offer to several later female clients, but which was not extended to any of the men. See C. R. Gorman, 'Fitting Rooms: The Dress Designs of Frank Lloyd Wright', *Winterthur Portfolio*, 30/4 (Winter 1995), 259–77.

28    Secrest, *Frank Lloyd Wright: A Biography* (University of Chicago Press, pp. 481–2. See also Roberta Volkmann, *Susan Lawrence: The Enigma in the Wright House* (Morgan Hill, CA: self-published/ Bookstand Publishing, 2011), p. 97.

29    C. Klickna, 'Dana-Thomas House: Documents Add to Rich History', *Illinois Times* (14 February 2018), *https://www.illinoistimes. com/springfield/dana-thomas-house-documents-add-to-rich-history/ Content?oid=11435728*.

30    Donald Leslie Johnson, *Frank Lloyd Wright: Early Years: Progressivism: Aesthetics: Cities* (Abingdon: Routledge, 2017), p. 58.

31    Hillside Home School Brochures 1890–1 and 1892–3.

32    Mary Ellen Chase, *A Goodly Fellowship* (New York: The Macmillan Co., 1939), pp. 87–121.

33    'Tan-y-Deri' translates as 'Under the Oaks'.

34    Johnson, *Frank Lloyd Wright: Early Years: Progressivism: Aesthetics: Cities*, p. 56.

35    From Storrer, *Frank Lloyd Wright: A Complete Catalogue (Third Edition)*.

36    Lindsay Baker, *A History of School Design and its Indoor Environmental Standards, 1900 to Today* (Washington, DC: National Clearing House for Educational Facilities, 2012), pp. 4–5.

37    Chase, *A Goodly Fellowship*, p. 113.

38    Thomas Graham (ed.), *Trilogy: Through Their Eyes* (Spring Green,
      WI: Unity Chapel Publications, 1986), p. 39.

39    *Weekly Home News* (Spring Green, WI, 6 November 1902), quoted
      in Robert C Twombley, *Frank Lloyd Wright: An Interpretive Biography*
      (New York: Harper Colophon, 1974), p. 79.

40    Graham, *Trilogy: Through Their Eyes*, pp. 39–40.

# 13

# The Protestant

## January 1902. Frank Lloyd Wright Home and Studio, Forest Avenue, Oak Park, Illinois

A letter from his Uncle Jenkin had made his heart sink. Frank had been labouring on the design of his uncle's 'twentieth century cathedral' for five frustrating years. It had seemed such an exciting prospect: the site was directly across the road from Silsbee's All Souls Church, and the new building, if it lived up to his uncle's ambition, would tower over it. Jenkin imagined a non-sectarian church that would also function as a 'social settlement', like the admirable Hull House. He called it 'The Abraham Lincoln Centre'.

Frank's first proposal had the character of a grand, corporate monument: a grid of masonry piers, deeply recessed windows, ornamented capitals and prominent cornice belts. With constant reference to his building committee, Jenkin had been prepared to endorse the internal arrangements, all of the social spaces, and the ample auditorium, but he seemed unwilling to accept that Frank's ideas for the outer form were right for the new type of religious building that he had in mind. They were too ornamental, too pretentious, an unnecessary expense. In an effort to separate their personal feelings from the professional relationship, Frank agreed to work on the project in partnership with Dwight Perkins, another of the Steinway Hall group and a member of All Souls Church. This may have reassured the trustees, but the correspondence between uncle and nephew suggests that family dynamics were always at play: 'humour me', Uncle Jenkin's letter began:

> just for a pencil experiment, throw away those short pillars ... that give the loggia effect to the upper storey and bring the windows out flush. The fine belt of plain wall which you have given them above and below will mean the more when you get those meaningless pillars that hold nothing up, out of the way. [1]

Frank replied in beseeching terms: 'the loggia is essential to the life and character of the building, the feature calculated to "lend verisimilitude to an otherwise bald and uninteresting narrative" ... I know and would stake my life that you will like it.'[2] Frank's response seemed to give Jenkin pause for a few months, but then came a decisive instruction:

> There must be radical revision ... I beg of you to throw to the wind once and forever all thoughts about 'monumental' construction effects and the like ... throw away as much of the present exterior as you possibly can ... I have pled for simple lines, plain exterior, for artistic and ethical reasons as well as economic. If the first reasons did not carry with you, the last must. [3]

There are fragments of evidence that shed light on the resolution of the design of the Abraham Lincoln Centre. The full picture remains unclear, but we do know that Frank was not involved. During the spring of 1903, as the final work was being done on Hillside Home School, Jenkin Lloyd Jones appointed Dwight Perkins alone as architect of the Abraham Lincoln Centre. Jenkin told Perkins that he thought that Frank was already too busy, that the work could not 'be done by him with sufficient promptness'.[4]

Frank certainly had plenty to work on at the time, but it is clear that he felt aggrieved by what had happened. His relationship with his Uncle Jenkin was at the heart of it. In his autobiography Uncle James embodies Frank's paternal ideal, but it was really Jenkin who became his proxy father. It was always Jenkin that his mother turned to and always Jenkin who made sure they were provided for. Frank knew that there was no better way of pleasing his mother than by winning Uncle Jenkin's approval, but hard as he tried there was always something in Jenkin's attitude that led Frank to feel that his uncle couldn't fully trust him, that something would go wrong. Jenkin always seemed more inclined to see his weaknesses where others saw his virtues, because there was some part of Frank that always reminded Jenkin of his absent father. It seems most likely that Jenkin eased the project away from Frank because he was concerned, perhaps convinced, that with Frank in charge the cost would soar, and furthermore, that he would not get the building that he wanted. Frank wasn't ready, at that time, to design something as utterly plain as a Cardiganshire chapel, however firmly Jenkin pushed him in that direction. Grant Manson offered his own explanation: 'uncle and nephew were too closely bound, not only by common patterns of thought but also by their common inheritance of Welsh temperament. The whole Lincoln Centre project was marked by one clash after another.'[5]

As it transpired, even Dwight Perkins became dismayed by Jenkin's insistence on architectural abstinence, insisting at one stage that each drawing should be stamped with the words, 'Designed in accordance with specific directions given by Jenkin Lloyd Jones against the protest of D. H. Perkins'.[6] In a later conversation with Grant Manson, Perkins recalled that Jenkin had personally taken 'pencil in hand to bring the building in line' with his demand for the, 'severest simplicity'.[7] There are a few of Frank's early projects

that are consistently claimed by architectural historians to be 'the first modern building', although there is no agreement about which of them it should be. It is an awkward fact, therefore, that the one building of Frank's Chicago period that stands out as the most modernist in form and in artistic intention is the Abraham Lincoln Centre, a building which owes its prescient qualities not to Frank Lloyd Wright, but to the design talents of his uncle, a Welsh Unitarian minister. It is often overlooked by architectural historians, so Donald Leslie Johnson deserves credit for identifying it, rightly, as 'one of the more important buildings of the twentieth century'[8] (Pl. 97).

## The Last Weeks of Winter 1904. Frank Lloyd Wright Home and Studio, Forest Avenue, Oak Park, Illinois.

The beautiful assembly hall at Hillside Home School had assumed its shape organically. There was as much of his aunts' spirit in it as there was of his own, but there was something unexpectedly powerful in its resolution, the way that the mass of it was drawn back to its corners. Frank looked hard at a different plan on the board in front of him. An office block, surrounded by factories and railways, rectangular, two hundred feet long and a hundred feet wide, seven storeys high. It was not a building type that he was used to. His client, Darwin D. Martin, chief executive of the Larkin Company, 'the world's largest manufacturer of soap', was a man of vision, of faith and of democratic principles. He believed that a contented workforce was a productive workforce, and he insisted on fresh air, good lighting, excellent welfare facilities, cleanliness: ideals that resonated with Frank's understanding of the sacrament of honest toil, the spiritual discipline that had driven him since his youth on the farm in the Lloyd Jones Valley.

Darwin Martin had offered kindness and candour, Frank had given him flagrant embroidery in return, claiming that it was he who was really responsible for the design of Adler and Sullivan's Wainwright and Schiller Buildings and a host of other large, unbuilt Adler and Sullivan office blocks. He was determined to get the commission to design the new building for the Larkin Company, and he wasn't prepared to let his inexperience deprive him of the chance. It could be the biggest break of his career, his largest building by far, to be built in Buffalo, New York, within the critical purview of the American architectural establishment. Until then he had felt that his lack of experience was an advantage. It had enabled him to think the unthought-of. He had been confident that it would work for him again. But when he looked at the

Pl. 97. Abraham Lincoln Centre, with its exterior largely to Jenkin Lloyd Jones's design. All Souls Church is at the right. Jenkin is at the centre of the group wearing a light coloured suit.
From *The Abraham Lincoln Centre and All Souls Church Annual Reports of 1909* (Chicago: The Abraham Lincoln Centre, 1910), frontispiece.

design, the product of weeks of effort, he was deflated. As he thought about his uncle's 'New Cathedral', the shell of which was almost complete, he must have acknowledged that it was more radical, more progressive than anything that he had dared to propose himself until then. There were those barbed words in the letter from his uncle: 'I have pled for simple lines ... for artistic and ethical reasons as well as economic. *If the first reasons did not carry with you, the last must.*' He started to draw the Larkin building again, stripping off all of the ornament, aiming for the plainness of expression that Uncle Jenkin had insisted on, but trying, at the same time to retain poetic expression in its starkness.

This was where the four-square pattern of the Hillside assembly hall resurfaced in his thinking. His original rectangular plan for the Larkin Building had stair towers at each of its four corners, and next to each staircase, a rectangular flue that carried fresh air through the height of the building. He separated the stair towers so that they stood out at each corner, and with that move, suddenly, the organic nature of the building became its most powerful characteristic. The parts of the building that gave it shape, the parts that made it work, and the parts that filled it with life were all different, but also contiguous, parts of an organic whole: 'The solution ... came in a flash. And I took the next train to Buffalo to try and get the Larkin Company to see that it was worth thirty thousand dollars more to build the stair towers free of the central block.'[9] A few years after its completion (Pl. 98), Frank prepared a brief description of the building for publication in his first monograph, the legendary *Wasmuth Portfolio*:

*The building is a simple working out of certain utilitarian conditions, its exterior a simple cliff of brick whose only ornamental feature is the exterior expression of the central aisle ... The pipe shafts, the heating and ventilating air intakes, and the stairways ... are quartered in plan and placed outside the main building at the four outer corners so that the entire area might be free for working purposes (Pl. 99) ... Here again, most of the critic's architecture has been left out. Therefore the work may have the same claim to consideration as a work of art as an ocean liner, a locomotive or a battle ship.*

The east coast critics did come to see the Larkin Building. The *Architectural Record* of New York advised its readers that

> The lover of architecture who looks, perhaps for the first time, at a building so entirely removed from the traditional styles and schools feels a shock of surprise – which is the reverse of pleasure. This monument is an extremely ugly building. It is, in fact, a monster of awkwardness.[10]

Frank responded in a letter to the magazine, which the editors declined to publish,

> It may be ugly but it has integrity and its high character is prophecy. The building is a group of bare, square edged, forms – uncompromising in their geometrical precision – fitted to one another organically with aesthetic intent, and with utter contempt for the fetish so long worshipped that architecture consists in loading surfaces with irrelevant sensualities or in frittering away their substance on behalf of the parasitic imagination of the slave of 'styles'. It is a bold buccaneer, acknowledging a native god in a native land with

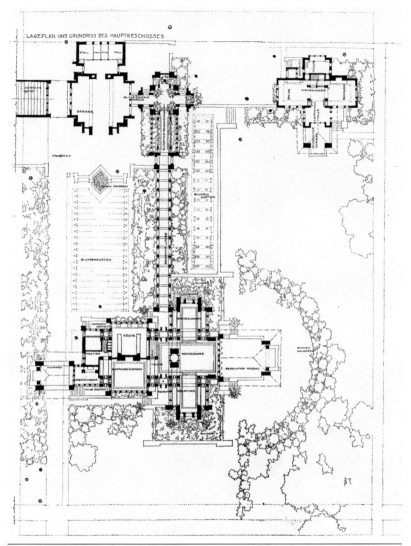

LAGEPLAN UND GRUNDRISS DES HAUPTGESCHOSSES

Fig. 13.1. Ground Plan of the Darwin Martin Residence and estate. The main house is the block at the
bottom, connected by a covered arbour to the other buildings on the estate.
From *Frank Lloyd Wright, Chicago: Sonderheft der Architektur des XX Jahrhunderts No. 8* (Berlin:
Ernst Wasmuth, 1911), p. 28.

*an ideal seemingly lost to modern life – that because beauty
is in itself the highest and finest kind of morality, so in its
essence – it must be true.*[11]

It was, he claimed, 'the first emphatic protestant in
architecture'.[12] Truth against the World, once more.

Darwin Martin had been introduced to Frank by
his brother William. The brothers were partners in another
business, the 'E-Z Polish Company', which had its base in
Chicago. William Martin lived in Oak Park, and in 1902 Frank
had built a house for him, a house of pale yellow stucco and
bold timber framing typical of his prairie style. It was William
Martin who had written that effusive letter describing Frank
as, 'one of nature's *noblemen*'. He had been writing to Darwin
who, at that time, was searching for an architect to design
the new Larkin Building. Frank was indeed the architect that
Darwin had been looking for, and he became more than that.
Frank's relationship with Darwin Martin was one of the few
that endured. Each was equally devoted to the other, each
equally candid, although Frank had more to confide and far
more to ask. Darwin offered his advice, and his money, with
unstinting generosity.

While Frank was still working on the design of the
Larkin Building, Martin commissioned him to design a house.
He had bought a large plot on Buffalo's northern fringe,
next to Delaware Park, five miles from the grimy canal-side
precinct of the Larkin factory. In faraway Springfield, Illinois,
the finishing touches were being applied to Susan Lawrence
Dana's palatial home. Frank had completed another seven
houses of more conventional proportions since work on
the Dana house had begun. Darwin Martin's brief was for
a house that would *exceed* Susan Lawrence Dana's in scale,
ambition and in its unlimited cost.[13] It was designed with
a contiguous conservatory, pergola and carriage house,
alongside annex dwellings for the family of Martin's sister and
for his gardener, the whole complex set into a meticulously
structured landscape garden (Fig. 13.1). The buildings were,
altogether, more than twice the size of the Dana residence,
but conceptually more concise, assimilated more comfortably
by the senses (Pl. 100). The difference between the two
great houses echoes the transition in Frank's design of the

Larkin Building, from its initial, self-consciously ornamented beginning to its rigorous, simplified resolution. The wide open floor spaces of the Darwin Martin House are punctuated at regular intervals by square clusters of brickwork columns. Each of the brick columns is also a square, a microcosm of the four-cornered wings of the cruciform plan of the house (Fig. 13.2). The column clusters are separated by voids that contain radiators, pipes and cables, an immediate reworking of the idea of 'articulation' that he applied for the first time in the design of the Larkin Building, and which he would continue to apply through the remainder of his career.

Every space in the Darwin Martin house is experienced as a variation on a recurring theme. More so than in any of his previous houses, Frank set out to control the consistency of structural rhythm and surface texture, to achieve a sculptural unity (Pl. 101). It is a vast house, spreading from the great, mosaic fireplace at its heart, far outwards to the boundaries of the site, but never sprawling; open at its many edges to gardens that were reciprocal to the internal volumes. Despite its great scale, the palette of materials is tightly controlled. The precise roman brickwork of the exterior continues throughout the interior; only the colour changes from red to buff. Then hardwood, painted plaster and, unexpectedly, immaculate, smooth concrete for important details: steps, lintels and planters. Windows and internal openings are filled with spectacular stained-glass panels, all variations on an abstract floral motif that has since become known as the 'tree of life'.[14] In the words of the academic biographer, Robert McCarter, it is 'a highly complex, rich and powerfully articulated series of interlocked symmetrical spaces, and the individual sets of elements have a purity, precision and balance rarely achieved in architecture'. McCarter also observed that Frank kept a plan of the house displayed prominently on the wall of his draughting room for the next fifty years: 'we may safely assume that this plan represented ... a kind of perfection to be sought after in all his designs.'[15]

For decades after, Darwin remained vigilant on Frank's behalf, always admiring of his talent, never asking much in return. In 1926 he was one of the first to invest in Frank Lloyd Wright Incorporated, and as Frank's career plunged to its nadir, Darwin rescued him with another commission, this time for a sumptuous holiday mansion, 'Graycliff', on the lake edge close

Pl. 100.  The Darwin Martin Residence and Estate, Buffalo. New York, 1904.
Photograph by Sabel/CC BY-NC-SA 2.0.

to Niagara Falls. Just three years later the Wall Street Crash took everything from the Martin family. Darwin died in 1935 at the age of seventy, having supported Frank emotionally and financially through his every crisis. He ended up penniless, with Frank owing him over seventy thousand dollars.

## Late April 1905. Nikko, Tochigi, Japan

Frank and Kitty would be heading back to America soon. They were in the last few weeks of a long tour of Japan that had taken them down the historic Tokaido Road from Tokyo to Kyoto, stopping at the landmarks and tourist sites that were familiar from Hiroshige's prints, and on to Takamatsu, far to the west. They had then turned back east for the long journey by rail to Nikko, followed by a slow climb into the mountains that were the seat of the shrine and temple complex, one of the largest concentrations of Shinto and Buddhist monuments in all Japan. Up in Nikko there was still snow on the ground, but, as they had planned, they were there for the arrival of the cherry blossom. Frank had been paid handsomely for his work

Pl. 101. The view between the column clusters, from the dining room, through the living room and into the library, of the Darwin Martin Residence.
Courtesy of Frank Lloyd Wright's Darwin Martin House.

by the Martins, enough to fund the two-month break and the luxurious voyage. He had, 'gone there to rest after building the Larkin building and the Martin residence, all but tired out'.[16] He had also gone with a business plan in mind. In the course of their travels he had bought hundreds of antique woodblock prints, often at minimal cost, from people who had little idea of their worth to American collectors. He also went there for the same reason that American architects routinely made the grand tour of Europe, to collect ideas, inspiration from sources which, he hoped, would be elusive to other architects and to his critics. He had taken a bulky quarter-plate camera with him that he used, when weather permitted, to record the buildings and landscapes that had most appealed to him. The trip left a profound impression. His interest in Japanese art grew to become an abiding obsession.

Like the Unitarians, the followers of Shinto saw the natural landscape as the realm of their spirituality. His admiration for the simplicity and cleanliness of Shinto living developed into a design principle to which he would always revert when overcomplication cluttered his thinking. At

Nikko the most important structures were the Tōshō-gū and the Taiyū-in Reibyō (Pl. 102). These were the seventeenth-century mausoleums of the first Tokugawa shogun, the unifier of Japan, Ieyasu, and of his grandson, the third shogun, Iemitsu. Each was lavishly decorated with layers of elaborate ornament and figurative carving, richly painted and gilded with an extravagance which, as was often said, seemed untypical of Japanese sacred architecture.[17] A few months after his return from Japan, Frank began to plan an important new project, another religious building, an opportunity to redeem the missed chance of the Abraham Lincoln Centre, and it would be built in the heart of his own Oak Park neighbourhood. He began with a simple square to enclose an auditorium, then a rectangle set apart from it with the same central axis. That would be the church hall. The two simple figures were then connected by a third, smaller rectangle, like a neck joining the two larger blocks. The Trustees of Unity Church would have no idea, and never did have, that the first lines of his pencil quite precisely followed the distinctive footprint of Iemitsu's mausoleum, the Taiyū-in Reibyō (Fig. 13.3).

## 4 June 1905. Oak Park, Illinois

The start of the Illinois summer had been hot. It gave way to a terrific thunderstorm that moved directly over the neighbourhood. Like everyone in Oak Park, residents at the top of Wisconsin Avenue were awakened by the racket as dawn broke, and then, between the thunder claps, heard a sound like the cascading of water. One of them remembered 'thinking what a violent rain it must have been ... Suddenly my mother called to me "Unity Church is on fire!" The noise which I supposed to have been made by falling water was the crackling of the flames.'[18]

The Wrights had been back at Oak Park for three weeks, still thrilled by their experience of Japan. Unity Church was their regular spiritual rendezvous. They were members of Uncle Jenkin's church too, but the Oak Park church was only a ten-minute walk away, and its community had become a source of friendship and of valuable commissions.[19] Services were shared by Unitarians and Universalists. When they had first settled in Oak Park, Augusta Chapin, their host and landlady, was its pastor. The building had been raised in 1872, built of timber 'board and batten', with a spire that 'burned like a torch' after drawing down the lightning bolt on that stormy morning.

Half the cost of the old church had been met by one of the founders, Edwin O. Gale. The same Edwin Gale had been Frank's client for three of his 'bootlegged houses'. Charles Roberts was another senior member and a trustee of the church. It was he whose donation had paid for the Hillside Home School art studios. Before that he had commissioned two residences from Frank, both in Oak Park. The trustees needed to find the right architect for their new church. They went through the earnest motions of a selection process before settling, inevitably, on Frank. The shadow of the Abraham Lincoln Centre loomed large in everyone's mind, for varying reasons. Jenkin's modern cathedral had been inaugurated just a few days before Unity Church burned. As the Lincoln Centre had risen above the Southside rooftops, the congregation in Oak Park had begun to feel dissatisfied with their own church anyway: it was too old-fashioned, too 'New England'. They had even begun

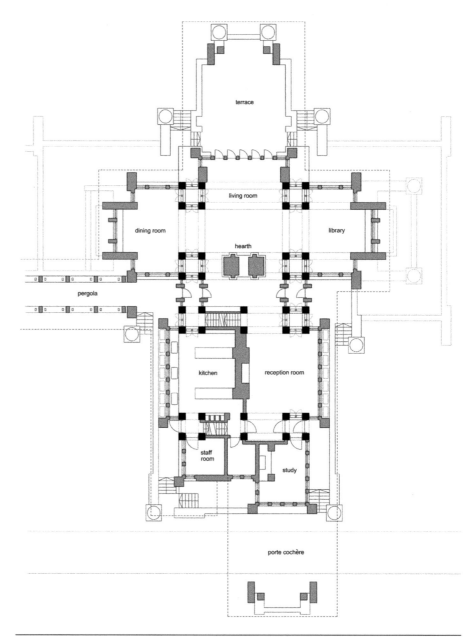

Fig. 13.2. Darwin Martin Residence ground floor plan. The column clusters are highlighted.

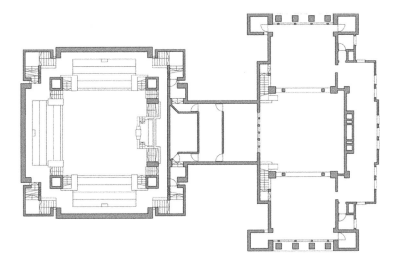

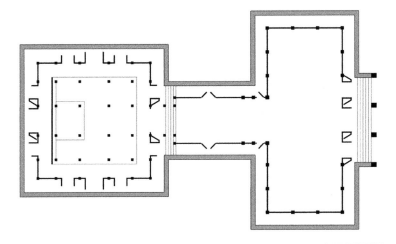

Fig. 13.3. Auditorium level plan of Unity Temple, top, and the plan of the Taiyū-in Reibyō shrine at Nikko, below. In both cases the sacred space is the square form on the left and the rectangular space on the right is a gathering hall. (After Kevin Nute).

to raise money for a more modern replacement, before Nature expedited the process. For Frank the new Unity Church would be a chance to show that he could create a building that embodied the artistic and ethical expression

of spiritual simplicity that his uncle seemed to suggest was beyond his understanding, and he could do it economically, without reducing it to something as spartan as the building that the tradesmen called the 'All Souls Cold Storage and Warehouse'.[20]

Frank's great insight was that he could generate his modern American architecture by weaving ideas together from obscure and widely divergent sources. The skill was in the syncretising of the sources, the integration of disparate formal elements to the point where they would seem quite naturally to flow together, where their individual identities would be subsumed into Frank's original vision. It was not until the 1990s that the scholar Kevin Nute recognised that Frank's idea for the arrangement of the three connected blocks of the new Unity Church had an ancient Japanese provenance.[21] Before Nute pointed this out, the curious block form of the new church was assumed to be entirely Frank's invention. The external appearance of the church, according to scholarly consensus, owes more to meso-American forms. There is no specific Mayan precedent, just a familiar density, the concentration of mass on the ground relieved by small, dark apertures, high up under the roof edge. The most audacious innovation of the new church is in its construction. The entire superstructure, inside and out, is cast as a single, contiguous volume of reinforced concrete (Pl. 103). There is one other point of general agreement among scholars: Unity Temple, as the new church became known, is one of the greatest, if not *the* greatest, of Frank's early works, the most radical, the most daring and the most brilliantly resolved. As late as 1952 Frank still thought of it as a pivotal moment: 'Unity Temple makes an entirely new architecture ... when I finished Unity Temple, I had it. I knew I had the beginning of a great thing, a great truth in architecture. Now architecture could be free.'[22]

In the 1932 version of his autobiography Frank devoted more space to Unity Temple than he did to any other project, recalling the intense effort that he demanded of himself to achieve an appropriate balance in the relationship between the three rectangular volumes, and when he had the arrangement of the volumes resolved to his satisfaction, he moved on to develop the more intricate detail:

*These studies seem never to end, and in this sense, no organic building may ever be 'finished'. The complete goal of the ideal of organic architecture is never reached ... But we have enough now on paper to make a perspective drawing to go with the plan.*[23]

The perspective drawing to which he referred showed the inside of the auditorium, the 'sanctuary'. A series of these perspectives survives, each represents a stage in Frank's laborious design process. At each corner box-like columns, set in from the walls, support the galleries and roof above, conveying the 'four-square' character of the room. There are no windows other than the high clerestory, but there is another source of daylight overhead. The central square of the ceiling is a dense grid of intersecting beams – the distinctive pattern of the Japanese *Go-Tenjo*.[24] In prestigious buildings, like the Hō-ō-den pavilion at the World's Fair, the squares between the intersecting beams were filled with lacquer or ceramic decoration (Pl. 104). In Unity Temple they are skylights, the daylight filtered through suspended screens of translucent coloured glass (Pl. 105). This is how the design of Unity Temple has been understood by scholars and enthusiasts for over a century: an intense intellectual endeavour focused on the manipulation of abstract geometric volumes, albeit with some recondite aesthetic sources, perhaps Mayan, probably Japanese (Pl. 106). However, one of the earliest of the interior perspective drawings offers a prominent clue that there was another influence on Frank's creative thinking, an inscription cut into the face of the parapet that runs around the upper gallery (Pl. 107). It is verse 8 of Isaiah, chapter 40: 'The grass withereth, the flower fadeth, but the word of our God shall stand for ever', the biblical passage that was particularly cherished by his grandfather, Richard Lloyd Jones.[25]

This perspective must have been one of the first drawings of Unity Temple that Frank showed to the members of the Building Committee, made at the stage when he was still thinking of it as a brick building, rather than as the concrete edifice it became. It revealed, at that early stage at least, that he was attempting to incorporate ideas that were not simply Unitarian but derived explicitly from his own experience of the faith, and from the history of his Welsh

Pl. 102. Taiyū-in Reibyō, the mausoleum of Iemitsu at the Nikko Temple Complex. Tochigi, Japan. Photograph by Andrea Moscato.

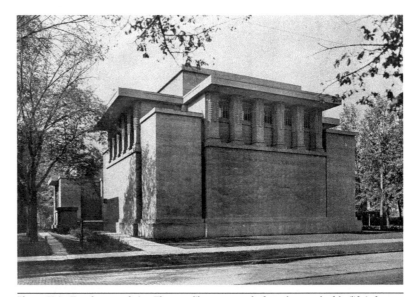

Pl. 103. Unity Temple at completion. The wave-like pattern on the front shows each of the 'lifts' of concrete poured successively into the mould.
From *Frank Lloyd Wright, Chicago: Sonderheft der Architektur des XX Jahrhunderts No. 8* (Berlin: Ernst Wasmuth, 1911), p. 12.

Pl. 104. *Jodan-No-Ma*, the central hall of the Hō-ō-den. The ceiling is built in a form that is known as 'Go-Tenjo': it resembles the grid pattern of the board that is used for playing the game 'go'.
From Okakura Kakudzo, *Illustrated Description of the Hō-ō-den (Phoenix Hall) at the World's Columbian Exposition* (Tokyo: K. Ogawa, 1893), p. 25.

Pl. 105. A view directly up to the spectacular ceiling structure of the Unity Temple with skylights in the manner of the Japanese *Go-Tenjo*.
Photograph by Nicholas James.

Pl. 106. The west elevation of Unity Temple, following its recent, magnificent restoration. The sanctuary is the larger block on the left, Unity Hall is the lower block on the right. The main entrance is located behind the screen wall, between the two blocks.
Photograph Tom Rossiter, courtesy of Harboe Architects, Chicago.

family. The inscription did not appear in the next perspective drawing. So is there anything else that could indicate that his family's story is embodied in the design? If we look again at the early perspective drawing there is something else that, at first, is easily overlooked but which would emerge to become one of Unity Temple's most celebrated and singular features. The interior is drawn from the viewpoint of the pulpit, the auditorium arrayed as the pastor would see it. But the seats facing him form an unbroken bank (Pl. 108). There is no aisle or nave through the centre, no indication of how the congregation would enter or leave the room. In his autobiography Frank gave an account of his thinking:

> Should the pulpit be put towards the street and let the congregation come in and go out at the rear in the usual, disrespectful church fashion, so the pastor missed contact with his flock? ... No. Why not put the pulpit at the entrance side, at the rear of the square temple, entirely cut off from the street and bring the congregation into the room at the sides? ... And when the congregation rose to disperse here was the opportunity to move forward towards their pastor and by swinging wide doors open beside the pulpit, let the flock pass out by the minister.[26]

Pl. 107. The first presentation drawing of the design for the sanctuary of Unity Temple, when Frank was thinking of it as a brick building. Richard Lloyd Jones's favourite Verse 8 of Isiah, Chapter 40 is inscribed in the band that runs around the base of the gallery parapet.
FLWF/AAFAL.

There would then be two doors into the sanctuary, rather than one, and they would not be facing the pulpit in the usual way, but to the sides of the pulpit instead. Writing a century after the opening of Unity Temple, Sidney K. Robinson echoed the uncertainty of generations of scholarly opinion,

> Wright makes much of the two 'hidden' exits ... because they allow the departing congregation not to turn their back

*on the speaker at the lectern. One can take him at his word and believe that the arrangement ... is a direct response to functional need, or one can take the position that it was initially a formal arrangement which Wright was creative enough to find a use for.*[27]

Actually, it is neither of these. The real explanation is more meaningful and far more personal.

Pl. 108. The view from the pulpit into the sanctuary of Unity Temple.
Photograph by James Caulfield, FLWF.

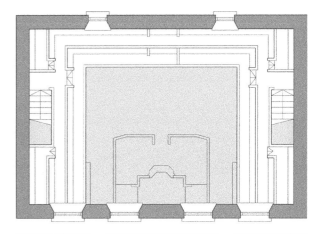
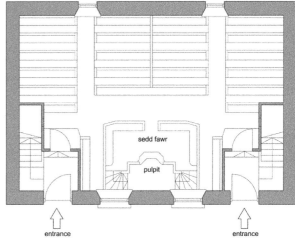

sedd fawr

pulpit

entrance                    entrance

Fig. 13.4. Ground plan (below) and gallery (top) of Llwynrhydowen Chapel. The space in the centre, within the gallery fronts, reads as a square void.

The earliest Nonconformist chapels built in Wales fall into three general categories. The most common type is like a traditional church, with a central entrance door facing the pulpit. These typically date from the mid-nineteenth century onwards. Then there are the two earlier forms, known as the 'long wall' chapel, and the 'square plan' chapel.[28] Of course, given the squareness of the Unity Temple sanctuary, the words 'square plan' seem significant immediately – and they are. The third Pantydefaid Chapel, the one that Frank's mother and sister saw in 1901, is an exemplary 'square plan' chapel. The ancient chapel at Llwynrhydowen, which had been visited by his mother, by both of his sisters, by his two educationalist aunts and by his Uncle Jenkin, who had preached there, is a 'long wall' chapel. The most distinctive feature of the 'long wall' chapel is that it has two doors, one at each side of the pulpit (Fig. 13.4). The sanctuary of Unity Temple bears a strong resemblance to the chapel at Llwynrhydowen, and, in its almost cubic squareness, it also evokes the chapel at Pantydefaid. Frank's design for Unity Temple was not influenced directly by the two Cardiganshire chapels; it was influenced by *the descriptions* of those two massively significant buildings that he had heard from his mother, his sisters and his aunts and uncles.

According to Welsh Nonconformist tradition, the 'long wall' chapel evolved from the days when Dissenters would meet secretly in converted barns, among the frames of the cattle stalls. The barns would typically have two doors, and the minister would have to stand with his back to the entrance wall.[29] The 'long wall' chapel did not migrate, with the Dissenters, to America. It was a form unknown to the New World, another item of arcane foreign vernacular that Frank could work with undetected.[30] Anyone who has visited both Llwynrhydowen and Unity Temple would also have noticed the similarity in the experience of entering the two chapel rooms (Pl. 109). At Llwynrhydowen the outer doors lead into small, low lobbies. You either climb a steep stair up to the gallery or pass through the inner lobby door, to find yourself below the overhanging gallery, the timber ceiling boards just inches above your head. The sanctuary at Unity Temple is very much larger, but the process of entering Unity Temple feels just as constricted. You are led along the low, dark passage with the gallery pressing down on you from above, before being allowed to turn and mount the steps that take you up into the central space, the room appearing all the more glorious as you rise from the shadowy cloister.

In the little Welsh chapel the galleries are so close to the pulpit that anyone who leaves has to pass directly to the side of the minister. Because Unity Temple is so much larger it was unsatisfactory for people leaving the sanctuary after the service to go back down into the cloisters at each side, through which they had entered. The galleries are set some way back from the pulpit and the route would lead them away from the pastor. For this reason Frank provided another set of doors – exit doors – which were directly to each side of the pulpit and which led straight back into the foyer. So the most important experiential aspects of both arriving and leaving, as recalled from Llwynrhydowen, were effectively recreated.

There are more similarities. Both rooms have simple, flat-fronted galleries around three sides. Earlier 'long wall' chapels were usually long, narrow rooms without galleries. Llwynrhydowen is more of a hybrid, having some of the aspects of a 'square-plan' chapel. Its length not much greater than its width, and, as at Unity Temple, the space between the galleries forms a precise square. Frank designed it as a square

Pl. 109.  Interior of the old Llwynrhydowen Chapel. The two entrances are to each side of the central pulpit, below the low gallery. The wooden enclosure in front of the pulpit is the *Sedd Fawr*, containing the long bench for the chapel deacons.
Photograph by Iain Wright. © Crown copyright: RCAHMW.

Pl. 110.  The sanctuary of Unity Temple.
(1) Entry steps from below the seating galleries to each side.
(2) Exit steps each side of the pulpit.
(3) The pulpit at the centre, with its enclosure and long bench, designed to resemble the traditional *Sedd Fawr*, a pulpit arrangement unique to Welsh speaking, nonconformist chapels.
Photograph by Tom Rossiter, courtesy of Harboe Architects, Chicago..

Pl. 111. The New Chapel at Llwynrhydowen, 1879, with masonry by David Timothy, before he migrated to join the Lloyd Jones *teulu* in Wisconsin.

because the multiple symmetries embody spiritual purity, as it was evident in the Shogun's mausoleum in Nikko, and more importantly, as it was invoked repeatedly in the Old Testament: 'And the altar shall be twelve cubits long, twelve broad, square in the four squares thereof' (Ezekiel 43:16). The square hall at Hillside Home School had been designed in that form for the same spiritual reasons. It was the same sacred, square geometry that provided the spiritual armature for the long-remembered chapels back in the land of his mother's birth.

For those still inclined to see these resemblances as coincidental, there is another affirmation of the opposite. While the 'long wall' form and simple quadrate geometry are common aspects of protestant chapels all around Britain, there is one feature that was unique to chapels in Wales, particularly to those chapels in which the Welsh language was used. This is the *Sedd Fawr* (the Great Seat), a long bench or a row of chairs, arranged behind a timber balustrade and located in front of the pulpit. The seats were occupied by the deacons who would stand and face the congregation for hymn singing, while the minister stood above them.[31] There is so much about

the sanctuary of Unity Temple that is unprecedented that the peculiar arrangement of the structure around the pulpit is often overlooked, or at best understood to be a simple abstract arrangement of parapets and furniture. To anyone familiar with the design of the old Welsh chapels, the pulpit of Unity Temple is strangely familiar. It has all of the features of a *Sedd Fawr* although, as with every vernacular idea that Frank adapted, its elements have been reworked. In a conventional chapel the organist would be much higher up, or on one side away from the pulpit, but at Unity Temple the organ seat is directly behind, and above, the parapet which is the back wall of the pulpit. The pulpit itself has the 'great seat', a long, upholstered bench, contained within its own enclosure, and there is a communion table on the floor at the front (Pl. 110). It is as if the organist sits where the pastor should be, and the pastor where the deacons should be. The Oak Park church had a board of trustees, senior members, but no deacons.[32] A conventional *Sedd Fawr* would have made no sense. So instead Unity Temple has a pulpit in the unmistakable guise of a *Sedd Fawr*.

In the great monograph of 1910, the *Wasmuth Portfolio*, Frank described Unity Temple as 'a frank revival of the old temple form'. It has always been assumed that he was referring to the 'four-square' figure of Old Testament record. It may just be a coincidence that the chapel at Llwynrhydowen had been known since 1879 as 'Yr Hen Gapel' (The Old Chapel). But it may also be a cloaked acknowledgement, for the benefit of those closest to him, that Unity Temple was indeed designed in homage to their Unitarian 'mother chapel'. It became known as 'The Old Chapel' in the course of a heroic episode in the history of the 'Black Spot' Unitarians. In 1876, because of their radical anti-Tory views, the members of Llwynrhydowen were locked out of the chapel by John Davies-Lloyd, the extravagant young landlord of Alltyrodyn. Davies-Lloyd spent most of his time travelling the world, hunting and speculating for diamonds and gold. He had only returned to Cardiganshire in 1876 because he was in poor health. The Unitarians, led at that time by the Rev. Gwilym Marles, were forced to hold their services in the road outside the chapel.[33] News of the outrage spread quickly across Wales, and certainly reached the Lloyd Joneses in Wisconsin. Dissenters came in their thousands to hear Marles preach and to support the Llwynrhydowen cause. The funds raised provided for the building of another Llwynrhydowen chapel.[34] This would be the 'New Chapel', the one built by the beloved stonemason, David Timothy, who decamped to Wisconsin shortly after (Pl. 111). As it transpired, John Davies-Lloyd died from tuberculosis at the age of twenty-eight, barely two years after he began the lock-out. His death prompted mass celebration in the Llandysul area, with marching bands and fireworks. The estate was inherited by his sister, who quickly returned the Old Chapel to the Unitarians. She was the last of her lineage to own Alltyrodyn. Within a few years the estate was broken up and sold to repay her brother's debts.[35] But the story of the *Troad Allan* (the 'lock out'), had already become a modern Unitarian parable, a revival of their foundation stories of resistance and ultimate vindication; of Truth Against the World.

## An Early Evening in Mid-October, 1907. The Valley, Wyoming Township, Wisconsin

It was the height of the small-grain harvest. A procession crawled steadily homeward through the twilight, returning from fields owned by James Lloyd Jones, a mile to the south of the family chapel. At the rear were the trailers heaped with grain, drawn by horses. Another team towed the water tank. At the head was the many-wheeled traction engine that had powered the threshing all day. The tender, now almost empty, bumped along behind and, hooked onto it, the long threshing machine itself. The steam engine had a cast iron seat on each side for the two men who drove it.[36] George Smith and George Culver, both exhausted, had to hold their concentration for just a short while longer to steer it up the track. They came to the old wooden bridge over the culvert next to Lawton's farm, getting the alignment right, slowing right down. The sound of any warning cracks would have been drowned in the racket of the engine. As it crossed the old bridge, the rear wheels, with all the weight of the furnace on the axle, broke through the main beam. The engine toppled back into the culvert, the tender, hooked at the rear, heaved forward on top of it, heavy machinery crashed onto heavy machine. The two drivers were caught between. Word was sent immediately to James Lloyd Jones. He had just returned from a meeting of the Regents at the university in

Pl. 112. Avery Coonley Residence, Riverside, Illinois, 1912. The west side of the house. Avery Coonley and Queene Ferry Coonley are at the corner of the pond, on the right.
From *Frank Lloyd Wright, Chicago: Sonderheft der Architektur des XX Jahrhunderts No. 8* (Berlin: Ernst Wasmuth, 1911), p. 97.

Madison, and was preparing for bed. He dressed and rushed out to the scene of the accident. It was dark by the time he got there. Holding a lamp he climbed up onto the rim of one of the wheels to get a view down into the wreckage. Then he saw the two drivers down below him, both dead, crushed by tons of steel. James recoiled from the shocking sight, lost his footing and fell down into the spokes of the wheel, trapping and snapping the bones in his leg. As Enos Lloyd Jones recalled, 'he was lifted into his buggy but soon fell into a coma from which he never recovered.'[37]

In the mid-1880s the prospects for farmers in the Midwest had seemed unlimited. Prices were good, labour easy to hire. The more a farm produced, the more profit it made. The Lloyd Joneses were commercially astute, all were good businessmen, but James was a real entrepreneur, with all the risk that that entailed. Through the late 1880s and into the 1890s, he repeatedly borrowed to buy up farms in their

Pl. 113. The Cheney Residence, Oak Park Illinois, 1904. Presentation drawing by Marion Mahony.
FLWF/AAFAL.

neighbourhood. The plat (boundary) maps of the time show James's property stretching miles to the east of Hillside, even into the neighbouring township. In order to borrow, he needed guarantors with collateral, and for that, naturally, he turned to his brothers and sisters, who, although hesitant at first, eventually obliged and signed their names, some several times over. Then came the 'Panic of '93'. Livestock, dairy, grains, vegetables, everything fell sharply in price. Corn, James's main crop, halved in value. Over the years of depression that followed, it rose only very slowly, never regaining its previous price. James worked on, harder than ever, just to cover costs and interest payments, unable to pay off his loans and holding on for 'the turn' that would never come.[38] He died on 22 October, at the age of fifty-seven, leaving a financial cataclysm behind him. 'It would take more than a broken leg to kill a man like Uncle James', Maginel said, 'Despair, I think, was the executioner.'[39]

It was the first time that Frank had lost someone so close to him. He went to The Valley, with his mother and sisters, to join the Lloyd Jones clan in laying his Uncle to rest in the yard behind Unity Chapel. Frank was forty years old, father to six children, unwitting creator and reluctant vanguard of the 'New School of the Midwest', able to look back at what could have seemed already to be a complete career. New clients kept coming to him for houses, and he could easily oblige. But was that all there was to be for him? In Buffalo, the Larkin Building was almost complete, and he had finished the great house for his friend Darwin. Unity Temple was half built, moving slowly, a real struggle with restless clients, doubters and antagonists among the trustees. He had been thinking about his life anyway. The joy seemed to have gone out of it, and the loss of his Uncle sharpened the sense of crisis. For Frank it must have been a great personal loss, but for others in his family the loss was multiplied. James's properties had to be sold in a hurry, for less than he had paid. Before the debts were cleared, Uncle John and Aunt Mary had to sell most of their own property too; Aunts Jennie and Nell had to reborrow on the school, and Uncle Enos was left only with his homestead.[40] Within months the once sweeping Lloyd Jones acreage had receded to a meagre footprint at the base of The Valley.

## December 1907. Frank Lloyd Wright Home and Studio, Oak Park, Illinois

A few weeks had passed since Uncle James's funeral. Frank wrote to Darwin Martin, sharing his melancholy, and his struggle to resolve the domestic troubles that had come in the 'aftermath of ruthless fate': 'Work seems to be at a standstill entirely and I guess for two years there is a hold-fast and hang-tight period ahead. I am ill prepared for it and what the outcome will be I can't say.'[41]

Earlier in the year he'd been commissioned by Harold McCormick, a member of the Rockefeller family, to design a vast house for a spectacular cliff-edge site on Lake Michigan. But it had come to nothing. McCormick's wife Edith had the last word, and she leaned firmly towards neo-classical. Some biographers have assumed, because of the timing, that it was the failure of this project that marked the turning point in Frank's outlook. But he was always sanguine about such setbacks. It was the loss of Uncle James that triggered his introspection. During the course of the same year, 1907, he had designed another of the greatest of his Prairie Houses for an industrialist, Avery Coonley and his young wife Queene Ferry, herself the heir to a huge fortune. The Avery Coonley House was the third, and final, large private estate development of Frank's Prairie House era, equivalent in its ambition and quality to the homes he had built for Susan Dana and Darwin Martin (Pl. 112). It was enough on its own to keep an architect busy for many months, and he'd had a dozen or more other large houses to work on at the same time. Frank recalled his first meeting with the Coonleys:

*Unknown to me they had gone to see nearly everything they could learn I had done ... The day they finally came to the workshop Mrs. Coonley said they had come because, it seemed to them, they saw in my houses 'the countenances of principle'. This was to me a great and sincere compliment. So I put the best in me into the Coonley House. I feel now, looking back upon it, that ... was the best I could do then in the way of a house.*

It was, he said, 'the most successful of my houses, from my standpoint'.[42]

The following Christmas, while the Coonley House was being built, Charles and Janet Ashbee made another visit to their good friends, the Wrights. Ashbee sensed that something had changed:

*Lloyd Wright who 8 years ago with his school was full of fire and belief, and meantime has become famous and practically made 'the School of the Middle West' has grown bitter, has drawn in upon himself, it is the bitterness of an anarchic socialism.[43]*

'Anarchic socialism' is a pithy mislabelling of Frank's intractable Unitarian, Transcendentalist worldview. The bitterness that Ashbee observed was, he presumed, the resentment of a man who felt unable to live according to the rules that he believed were right and true. In this regard, Ashbee's observation was astute. Also in December 1908 Frank wrote to Darwin Martin, as always, looking for a commission and complaining of a lack of opportunities, but then slipping into unusual candour:

*In my own life there is much that is complex at least. Life is not the simple thing it should be, if within myself I could find the*

*harmony that you have found. It is difficult for me to square my life with myself, and I cannot rest until it is done, or I am dead.*

Frank's sense of foreboding had little to do with a shortage of work. The true nexus of his personal crisis resided at another home of his design, one that he had completed four years before, the Cheney Residence (Pl. 113).

Edwin Cheney and Mamah Borthwick had both been students at the University of Michigan in Ann Arbor, where, it is likely, they first met. Mamah was born and raised in Oak Park, while Edwin had grown up in Detroit. Mamah studied European literature. After graduating, she progressed to an MA in teaching, and from there she took a job as a librarian in Michigan. Edwin's discipline was electrical engineering. Although they had little in common intellectually, it seems that Edwin was infatuated with Mamah. When he completed his own degree, he didn't wait in Michigan for Mamah to complete her studies. Instead, he moved to Oak Park, Mamah's hometown, as if in anticipation of her return.[44] This seems to have been part of a determined effort to draw Mamah into his embrace. There were stories later that he had 'literally carried her off into matrimony'.[45] They married in Oak Park in 1899.

Mamah was thirty years old. Looking beyond her home for like-minded companionship, she soon found her way to the 'Nineteenth Century Club'. This was the pre-eminent women's society in Oak Park, set up in 1891 by a group of the wealthier women of the neighbourhood to promote social and cultural enlightenment. Anna Lloyd Wright had joined in the first year, and remained an active member for decades. She would come to be seen as one of its founding spirits. The club originally had three departments: education, social economics and literature. Anna was one of the first chairmen of the literature department.[46] By the time Mamah began to attend the literary department meetings Catherine Wright was also a regular contributor. The Oak Park newspapers carried frequent notices of either Anna or Catherine presenting their 'well prepared papers' to the club. Catherine and Mamah became friends, and through Catherine, Mamah came to know Frank. It seems likely that Edwin Cheney commissioned Frank to design a new house for them at Mamah's bidding.

The commission came in 1903. The Cheneys' first child, John, had been born the year before. Edwin bought a plot at the north-eastern edge of the suburb, where the woods were still dense. Frank designed their house to be set far back into the plot, away from the road, where it would be overhung by large, ancient trees. A brick wall surrounds the house, around two metres high, set back from the road like an inner line of protection. To contemporary eyes, it is bunker-like. It has often been suggested that the design reflected a defensive attitude, perhaps in the character of either Edwin or Mamah Cheney, or somehow in Frank's own attitude to his clients. This speculation is purely retrospective, because it has been seen by some to cast light on subsequent events. It is a mistaken interpretation. There are a number of earlier buildings that feature similar screen-walls, beginning in the earliest years with the Harlan House, but it is illustrative of how difficult many have found it, otherwise, to account for the circumstances that followed from Edwin Cheney's commission.

The Cheneys' new house was only a half mile from Frank's studio. While Edwin worked each day in the city, Frank would visit the Cheney Residence, often conspicuously in his bright yellow Stoddard Dayton automobile. He and Mamah were observed together in its twin leather arm chairs, scooting along the tree-lined avenues. People did speculate, but it was not until 1907, in the aftermath of Uncle James's demise, that the nature of their connection became troublesome. In the turmoil of his introspection, Frank interrogated his feelings and concluded that he really was in love with Mamah, and that it would be most truthful to his instincts to live the rest of his life with her, even if it meant that he had to walk away from Kitty and their six children. It was not an act of callous disregard, or of selfishness in the conventional sense. It would have been so much easier to follow middle-class convention, stay with his family and allow his relationship with Mamah to play out discreetly in the background. But for Frank to do that would be to betray his most deeply held principles. *'It is difficult for me to square my life with myself, and I cannot rest until it is done, or I am dead.'* A kind of death indeed.

Mamah's academic achievement was rare for a woman of her time. She was an intellectual, widely read, and fluent in German. Frank's biographers have typically speculated that it was her intellect that fascinated Frank, that

he felt he could speak to her as an equal. There was, however, a deeper connection. Anna Lloyd Wright had achieved as much as Mamah Cheney, and had done so thirty-five years earlier, well before the University of Michigan would even admit female students, and she had overcome greater obstacles to do so. Like Mamah, Anna was most engaged by German and French literature. Like Anna, Mamah had a radically progressive outlook and was a committed advocate of women's rights. More so than any woman whom Frank had encountered so closely before, Mamah resembled his mother. Kitty had been very young when she and Frank married, but over the years of motherhood that followed she too had continued learning, to the extent that she could easily hold her own among the educated women of the Nineteenth Century Club. But for Frank, somehow, this was not enough. He seemed to have found it impossible to see her as more than a domestic archetype, committed more to the support of their children than she was to him. Mamah, on the other hand, had an ambivalent attitude to her own three children, as if they were more Edwin's than hers. Frank had cast her doubts about Edwin into the sharpest relief. She would find it easy to walk away from their marriage. She could give all of herself to Frank: Frank would expect nothing less.

Frank's desolate correspondence with Darwin Martin at the end of 1908 would lead anyone to presume that he was stuck in a creative trough, held fast there by domestic turmoil. The evidence suggests the opposite: that his fatalism, at that time, may have liberated his architectural imagination, as if he had nothing to lose. For Frank, the 'School of the Middle-West' had run its course, and he had no idea what would come next, or if he would have a career at all. If there was to be no more Prairie Style, then the last Prairie House would ideally be the apotheosis. And it was.

Fred Robie's father owned the Excelsior Supply Company, stamping out bicycles by the thousand. Fred was young, in his late twenties, but embedded in the business and already rich. He was thrilled by the new technologies of automobiles, aeroplanes and motorboats, anything to do with transportation. There was only one architect whose work really expressed the rush of modernity. He commissioned Frank to design his house in the early summer of 1908.[47] The site was in Hyde Park, in the Southside near to the university and with a clear view south across lawns and trees towards the Midway Plaisance, the western tail of the World's Fair park. It is not difficult to see the progression of the Prairie Style from its embryonic expression in the early 1890s to its mature definition through the sequence of Frank's many residential projects. The Robie House is a logical culmination, and yet the image of the Robie House, and the experience of it, still astonishes over a century after it was built. It is as if all of the formal innovations of the Prairie Style are amplified to their maximum effect, with a horizontal dynamism that pulls the eye so urgently that the house seems to slide past you on the pavement. It is structurally extreme. The brickwork parapet of the first floor balcony stretches twenty metres along the street, seemingly weightless, beneath chisel-blade, cantilevered roofs that glide far beyond the supporting walls (Pl. 114). A dense armature of structural steel was required to achieve such improbable effects, but none of the metalwork can be seen. When Frank spoke, as he often did, about the integrity of materials and structure his intention was to liberate their poetic potential. He had no interest in the concept of integrity that would later become central to the dogma of modernism. So it is, perhaps, ironic that of all his early work it was the Robie House that had the most decisive influence on the evolution of the modern style in Europe.[48]

Frank was always alive to the architectural potential of forms and structures in nature, and occasionally also to the suggestive qualities of man-made artefacts, ancient or modern, that had little to do with architecture; and he could weave those disparate conceptual strands into beautiful and harmonious patterns with marvellous dexterity. Frank spun the design of the Robie House from the character and the passions of his client. The arrangement of mass and void is boldly suggestive. The continuous glazing along the balcony terrace; the vast floating plane of brickwork below, and the smaller top floor with its chimney, projecting above the major volume of the house: all the vigorous elements of a ship, a sleek modern pleasure boat, like one of the many that skimmed over Lake Michigan. Few who saw it, from its first appearance, failed to see the resemblance. In the Germanic neighbourhood of Hyde Park it was popularly known as 'der Dampfer', the steamboat. It is certainly not an accidental resemblance. There

Pl. 114. The Robie House, Woodlawn Avenue, Chicago *circa* 1911. The clothing and the house seem to come from different eras.
FLWT.

are many subtle maritime references, the expression of a ribbed structure that runs the full length of the living area, the prow-shaped bay windows at each end of the same deck-like space, and the central fireplace that sits beneath its funnel-chimney (Pl. 115). The most striking evocation is the design of the entrance. Frank had often situated main entrances to the sides of his houses, but the entrance to the Robie House is at the back. It opens into a low, shadowy vestibule. The foot of a staircase projects forward from the right, inviting the visitor to ascend. As it climbs, the staircase doubles back. When you reach the top you emerge through a blaze of daylight

**Pl. 115.** The open-plan living space of the Robie House. The stair that leads up to it emerges behind the central brick core, which also contains the fireplace. The dining area is on the far side of the core. The room is glazed on both sides and open from one end to the other.

into a long chamber surrounded by windows. The transition closely replicates the experience of boarding a ship – the entry from the portside and the ascent to the open expanse of the passenger deck. The south elevation of the Robie House was its starboard side, open to the wide expanse of parkland. It was clearly conceived as a ship of the prairie.[49] In later years, Frank openly referred to it as his 'dampfer house', happy to admit to the origin of his ideas.[50] The living space of the Robie House really is one enormously long room (Fig. 13.5). The central fireplace provides a notional division, but the space flows around it and above it. It is not a room in which it is easy to imagine one could feel at peace. It seems a place of temporary repose, just like the deck of a ship or a railway carriage. It didn't feel like this to Fred Robie. Although he was only able to live in it for a little over a year, Fred Robie remembered it as, 'the most ideal place in the world'[51] (Pl. 116).

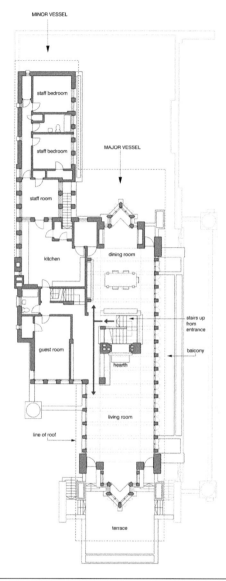

**Fig. 13.5.** Frederick Robie House, Woodlawn Avenue, Chicago 1910. Plan of the middle level (of three), the main living space. The plan comprises two connected blocks, which Frank referred to as the major and minor vessels. The minor vessel, to the rear (left of the drawing), contains service spaces and staff accommodation. At each end of the main living space there are triangular bay windows, which were referred to as 'prows'. Note the long balcony along the south (starboard) elevation. The arrows show the route from the entrance lobby up the stairs to the living space.

When Frank looked back at the latter years of his time in Oak Park it was always the Avery Coonley house that he recalled with most satisfaction, but it is the Robie House that tends to be measured as the greater achievement. Frank couldn't find it in himself to agree, and the reason for this was that he didn't feel that he could entirely own it. Although he had been in Chicago when its construction began, he had gone well before it was finished. Were there things that, had he been there, he might have changed? Or things that were changed despite him, in his absence? In 1908 Frank had been contacted by the Wasmuth Verlag, a publisher of art books based in Berlin. He was invited to travel to the German capital to work on a monograph, a portfolio of his most important projects. He was offered complete editorial freedom to chose the projects, produce the drawings and write the text. It had the potential to become a definitive manual for the new American architecture, the realisation of another ambition within his reach. It was an opportunity to visit a country that had intrigued him since his mother had introduced him to Goethe, and more than anything, it was his opportunity to break away, to change his life.[52]

As September 1909 drew to a close the congregation of Unity Temple convened for the long-delayed dedication of their beautiful new building. It was a triumph, but Frank wasn't with them. A few days earlier he had walked away from his family. Kitty was distraught, the children confused and upset. Lloyd, the eldest, thumped his father in the head, knocking him to the floor.[53] Frank asked Catherine for a divorce which she, understandably, refused. There must have been an uncomfortable resonance for Anna Wright, who had been glad to see the back of her own husband. Frank took the train from Oak Park to Chicago. He stopped there briefly to complete the formality of signing over his staff, his premises and his projects to Hermann von Holst, a young architect in the orbit of the 'Prairie School'. The arrangement ensured that Catherine and their children would be supported in his absence. Von Holst rehired Marion Mahony and Walter Griffin. It was Mahony who would take control of architectural matters, including the resolution of the Robie House. In Buffalo, Darwin Martin was dismayed by another letter from Oak Park: 'I am leaving the office to its own devices ... deserting my wife and children for one year, in search of

Pl. 116. Frederick Robie House, Woodlawn Avenue, Chicago 1910. Photograph by Tim Long/FLWT.

spiritual adventure ... you will probably not hear from me again.'[54] In his autobiography Frank recalled the emotional turning point and traced it back to his Wisconsin boyhood:

> *This absorbing phase of my experience as an architect ended about 1909 ... weary, I was losing my grip on my work and even interest in it. Every day of every week and far into the night of nearly every day, Sunday included, I had 'added tired to tired' and added it again and yet again, as I had been trained to do by Uncle James 'on the farm' as a boy ... I could see no way out. Because I did not know what I wanted, I wanted to go away. Why not go to Germany and prepare the material for the Wasmuth Monograph? ... I looked longingly in that direction.*[55]

He really did know what he wanted, in the short term at least. From Chicago he travelled to New York, where he met Mamah Cheney, and together they boarded a ship bound for Europe ∎

# 13 The Protestant
## *Notes*

1       Letter from Jenkin Lloyd Jones to Frank Lloyd Wright, 13 January 1902, *Jones Letter Book, 9 July 1901–18 June 1902*, pp. 334–6, Jones Collection, Meadville-Lombard Theological College. As quoted in J. Siry, 'Unity Temple and Architecture for Liberal Religion in Chicago 1885–1909', *The Art Bulletin*, 73/2 (June 1991), 265.

2       Letter from Frank Lloyd Wright to Jenkin Lloyd Jones, January 1902 (not dated). Frank Lloyd Wright Foundation archive reference J001C010000.

3       Letter from Jenkin Lloyd Jones to Frank Lloyd Wright and Dwight Perkins, 2 August 1902, *Jones Letter Book, 18 June 1902–17 June 1903*, pp. 66–99, Jones Collection, Meadville-Lombard Theological College. As quoted in Siry, 'Unity Temple', *The Arts Bulletin*, p. 265.

4       Siry, 'Unity Temple', *The Arts Bulletin*, 262–6.

5       Grant Carpenter Manson, *Frank Lloyd Wright to 1910: The First Golden Age* (New York: Van Nostrand Reinhold Co., 1958), pp. 156–8.

6       Donald Leslie Johnson, *Frank Lloyd Wright: Early Years: Progressivism: Aesthetics: Cities* (Abingdon: Routledge, 2017), p. 168.

7       Manson, *Frank Lloyd Wright to 1910: The First Golden Age*, pp. 156–8. See also Siry, 'Unity Temple', *The Arts Bulletin*, 266.

8       Johnson, *Frank Lloyd Wright: Early Years: Progressivism: Aesthetics: Cities*, p. 169.

9       Frank Lloyd Wright, *An Autobiography (Edition 1)* (New York: Longman, Green & Co., 1932), p. 151.

10      R. Sturgis, 'The Larkin Building in Buffalo', *Architectural Record* (April 1908), 312.

11      Jack Quinan, *Frank Lloyd Wright's Larkin Building: Myth and Fact* (Chicago: University of Chicago Press, 2006), pp. 113–15. Frank's reply was not printed in the *Architectural Record* because the critic, Russell Sturgis, had died a few days after his review was published.

12    F. L. Wright, *An Autobiography (Edition 1)*, p. 151.

13    According to the chronological record of B. B. Pfeiffer (ed.), *Frank Lloyd Wright: Complete Works*, vol. 1: *1885–1916* (Cologne: Taschen, 2008).

14    Website of Corning Museum of Glass, *www.cmog.org/artwork/tree-life* (April 2021).

15    Robert McCarter, *Frank Lloyd Wright* (New York: Phaidon Press, 1997), p. 58.

16    Frank Lloyd Wright, *An Autobiography (Edition 2)* (New York: Duell, Sloane and Pearce, 1943), p. 194.

17    Melanie Birk (ed.), *Frank Lloyd Wright's Fifty Views of Japan* (Chicago: Frank Lloyd Wright Preservation Trust, 1996), pp. 15–17.

18    Memoir of James Heald Jr, quoted in T. A Chulak, *A People Moving thru Time: A Brief History of the Unitarian Universalist Church in Oak Park, Illinois* (Chicago: The Unitarian Universalist Church in Oak Park, 1979), p. 9.

19    Manson, *Frank Lloyd Wright to 1910: The First Golden Age*, p. 158.

20    J. L. Wright, *My Father Who Is On Earth*, p. 21.

21    Kevin Nute, *Frank Lloyd Wright and Japan* (New York: Van Nostrand Reinhold, 1993), pp. 149–50.

22    B. B. Pfeiffer and G. Nordland, *Frank Lloyd Wright in the Realm of Ideas* (Carbondale: Southern Illinois University Press, 1988), p. 13. From a lecture delivered to students at Taliesin in August 1952.

23    F. L. Wright, *An Autobiography (Edition 1)*, p. 161.

24    'Go-Tenjo' is a ceiling that resembles the gridded board for playing 'go'.

25    Siry, 'Unity Temple', *The Arts Bulletin*, 276.

26    F. L. Wright, *An Autobiography (Edition 1)*, p. 156.

27    S. K. Robinson, foreword to David M. Sokol, *The Noble Room* (Chicago: Top Five Books, 2008), p. xix.

28    The second Pantydefaid Chapel, as pictured in the book *Youngest Son*, does not conform to any of these three types. It resembles a house.

29    K. Williams, 'The vernacular origins of Welsh Nonconformist chapels' (unpublished PhD thesis, Cardiff University, 2009). Kathryn Williams shows that the 'long wall' form, with its two doors, actually has it roots in the design of sixteenth-century Dutch Calvinist chapels.

30    Anne Kelly Knowles, *Calvinists Incorporated: Welsh Immigrants on Ohio's Industrial Frontier* (Chicago: University of Chicago Press, 1997), p. 148. Here is an exception that proves the rule: Welsh Calvinists at Jefferson Township, Jackson County, Ohio, built a timber 'long wall' chapel, Horeb, in 1838 that was a replica of their hometown chapel at Mynydd Bach, near Swansea. 'Chapel Carreg', built by Welsh Calvinists in 1831, in the town of Remsen, Oneida County, New York, is a hybrid with long-wall doors in its gable end.

31    S. Hughes, 'International Significance of Welsh Chapels', Addoldai Cymru/Welsh Religious Buildings Trust, *http://www.welshchapels.org/welsh-chapels/international-significance-of-welsh-chapels/* (April 2021).

32    Sokol, *The Noble Room*, p. 7.

33    H. R. Evans, 'A Village Worthy', *Ceredigion: Journal of the Cardiganshire Antiquarian Society*, 4/2 (1961), 174–80.

34    Gwilym Marles, was the bardic name of William Thomas, the great-uncle of the poet Dylan Thomas. Dylan Thomas's middle name, Marlais, was given to him in honour of his famous great-uncle.

35    D. Elwyn Davies, *They Thought for Themselves: A Brief Look at the History of Unitarianism in Wales and the Tradition of Liberal Religion* (Llandysul: Gomer Press, 1982), pp. 38–9.

36    In a letter to his son Chester Lloyd Jones, which is quoted in Chester's book *Youngest Son* (p. 100), Enos Lloyd Jones remarked that the traction engine had a vertical boiler, in which case it was almost certainly a David June & Co. 'Champion Agricultural Engine', as it was the only 'vertical' type in common use. See James H. Stephenson, *Farm Engines and How to Run Them* (Chicago: Drake and Co., 1903), p. 837.

37    Jones, *Youngest Son*, p. 100.

38    Jones, *Youngest Son*, pp. 97–102.

39      Maginel Wright Barney, *The Valley of the God Almighty Joneses* (New York: Appleton Century, 1965), p. 111.

40      Mary Lloyd Jones's land was in the legal ownership of her Scottish husband, James Phillip. He was known to the family as Uncle Phillip to avoid confusion with Uncle James.

41      Meryl Secrest, *Frank Lloyd Wright: A Biography* (Chicago: University of Chicago Press, 1998), p. 198.

42      F. L. Wright, *An Autobiography (Edition 1)*, p. 164.

43      Secrest, *Frank Lloyd Wright: A Biography*, p. 198. Quote from C. R. Ashbee's *Journal* (December 1908).

44      Edwin Cheney is first listed as a resident in the *Oak Park Directory 1894*. His family is recorded as resident in Oak Park with him from 1898.

45      Anthony Alofsin, *Frank Lloyd Wright The Lost Years, 1910–1922: A Study of Influence* (Chicago: University of Chicago Press, 1993), p. 26. Quote from *Chicago Daily Tribune* (8 October 1909), 7.

46      See, for example, *Oak Park Vindicator* (23 September 1898), 1.

47      This date is assumed from the fact that Robie acquired the site in May 1908.

48      John Fabian Kienitz, 'Fifty-Two Years of Frank Lloyd Wright's Progressivism', *The Wisconsin Magazine of History*, 29/1 (September 1945), 64.

49      Donald Hoffman, *Frank Lloyd Wright's Robie House: The Illustrated Story of an Architectural Masterpiece* (Mineola, NY: Dover Publications, 2012), p. 15.

50      F. L. Wright, *An Autobiography (Edition 2)*, p. 252.

51      Robert McCarter, *Frank Lloyd Wright* (New York: Phaidon, 1997), p. 101. Quote from *Chicago Sun Times* (18 November 1958).

52      Alofsin, *Frank Lloyd Wright: The Lost Years*, p. 4.

53      Roger Friedland, and Harold Zellman, *The Fellowship: The Untold Story of Frank Lloyd Wright and the Taliesin Fellowship* (New York: HarperCollins, 2006), p. 29.

54      Friedland and Zellman, *The Fellowship*, p. 30.

55      F. L. Wright, *An Autobiography (Edition 1)*, p. 165.

# 14

# The Shape-Shifter

### December 1909. Tuscany, Italy

Early in his career Frank, enjoyed provoking his contemporaries with his disdain for Renaissance architecture. In his first manifesto, *The Art and Craft of the Machine*, he had bemoaned 'the decadence which we call the Renaissance. It is the setting sun that we mistake for dawn.'[1] In the last month of 1909, and for the remainder of that winter, Frank's home was an apartment in an ancient Florentine villa, less than a mile from the Piazzale Michelangelo. When he had set off for Europe there was nothing to suggest that his objective was to reach the heartland of the Renaissance. He and Mamah had arrived in Berlin in late October, but had been discovered there within days by an agent of the *Chicago Tribune*. They fled the city as soon as Frank had completed arrangements with

Wasmuth for his publications. Their next known destination was Paris, home of the École des Beaux-Arts, a city which, for that reason, Frank had always disdained. From there, he and Mamah went separate ways. She travelled back to Germany, to Leipzig, where she found work teaching English. Frank went south to Tuscany and found so much there that delighted him that he realised he had to stay. In his Preface to the *Wasmuth Portfolio*, written in Tuscany, Frank admitted that

*of joy in living there is a greater proof in Italy than elsewhere. Buildings, pictures and sculptures seem to be born, like the flowers by the roadside, to sing themselves into being. Approached in the spirit of their conception, they inspire us with the very music of life.*

He also wrote freely, for the first time, of his admiration for vernacular architecture, untutored architecture, the Romantic principle that he had always followed, in words that might have come from the pen of Iolo Morganwg a century before. In Italy

*as elsewhere the true basis for any serious study of the art of architecture is in those indigenous structures, the more humble buildings everywhere which are, to architecture, what folklore is to literature or folksongs are to music, and with which architects were seldom concerned.*

Before the end of 1909 two of his draughtsmen came from Oak Park to join him at the Florence apartment. Working on plain timber boards, on tracing paper with crow-feather quills, they began work on the drawings to fill the one hundred loose pages of the *Wasmuth Portfolio*.[2] One of the draughtsmen was Frank's nineteen-year-old son Lloyd, his anger somehow assuaged, and the other, a young Mormon named Taylor Woolley. During February, Frank moved his studio to a small villa in the hill town of Fiesole, just to the north of Florence. The Villino Belvedere had a walled garden and a superb view of the ancient city to the south; it would

Pl. 117. The small, single storey house up the sloping side-street is the Villino Belvedere, in Fiesole, the house that Frank and Mamah Cheney shared during the summer of 1910.
© Google 2020 / Google Earth.

newspapers claimed; that he had in fact, 'declared openly' to her and to Catherine, over a year before his departure 'that I was going to take her away with me as soon as I could'. He had said the same to Edwin Cheney. But he admitted to his mother that he knew his time in Europe was running out, that he had to return to Oak Park, to be

*welcomed by my friends with open rejoicing and secret contempt ... The basis of this whole struggle was the desire for a fuller measure of life and truth at any cost, and as such, an act wholly sincere and respectable within. This, by my return, I discredit ... This bitter draught seems to me almost more than I can bear. I turn from it in disgust.*[5]

He felt trapped; he viewed the future with dread, but there was the beginning of an idea that he needed to share with her. He wanted to leave Oak Park, to move well away, to start again. There was only one place that he could imagine being truly content, one place to which he belonged, and that was the Lloyd Jones Valley. He had in mind a piece of land that adjoined the farm of his sister Jane and her husband, Andrew Porter, the tenacious manager of Hillside Home School. 'I would like to farm it beside him with that tract of Reider's and Uncle Thomas's farm joined together.' Thomas had died in 1894, bequeathing his farm to his sisters Jennie and Nell. Several new families moved into The Valley after Uncle James's death, picking up properties that the Lloyd Joneses had urgently sold. A family named Michels had bought the land first farmed by Uncle Thomas. The Reiders acquired all the land on the east of The Valley, wrapping north around the Porters' farm and extending to the bank of the Wisconsin River. Frank seemed to be talking about an area of some two hundred acres, enough for a change in career from architecture to agriculture. But he then went on to list his financial burdens: school fees for his children, Kitty's household expenses, and how little he had left when his dues were paid: 'my situation is too discouraging to contemplate such luxury ... this doesn't look much like a farm to me.'[6] The seeds of an idea had been planted, however.

be Frank's home for the remainder of his 'spiritual adventure' (Pl. 117). Lloyd returned to America in March, so that there would be no awkwardness when Mamah arrived. She joined Frank just as spring was coming in, and stayed with him in Fiesole through to the end of an enchanting summer.[3]

There were times of great happiness at Fiesole, but both Mamah and Frank also felt on occasion as if they were blown along in a gale of social and emotional confusion, sometimes consumed by guilt and regret while also being convinced, always, of the morality of their actions. They were told consistently by friends that the right thing to do was to give up the venture and go back to their families.[4] They listened to the advice; they thought hard about it, and they rejected it. Despite the difficulties ahead they were determined to plan a future in which they could be together. Early in July 1910, Frank wrote to his mother. His family were being humiliated by sensational press coverage. Frank reminded her that it was untrue that he and Mamah had abandoned their marriages without warning, as the

## Summer 1908. Tower Hill, Old Helena, Iowa County, Wisconsin

Jenkin Lloyd Jones was supervising the construction of an unusual building:

*I was getting ready for at least two years for the building of this barn ... The first storey was built of stone that had to be brought from the quarry three miles away ... The upper storey was to be frame but suitable siding and shingles were priced too high ... so after the solid 'sheeting' in rough boards ... this barn was roofed and sided with felt paper – an innovation which awakened the distrust of neighbours. But my barn was small and was to be a preacher's barn; I could afford to experiment – nay the missionary opportunity tempted – and so I ventured on the 'paper barn'.[7]*

For Jenkin, as for Frank, 'the missionary opportunity' always tempted. Jenkin had purchased the derelict land at Tower Hill in 1889 with the support of his brothers and some fellow ministers. Each summer, from 1890 onwards, he hosted a summer camp there, which he promoted as the Tower Hill School of Religion and Ethics. He attracted a host of notable writers, theologians, scientists and politicians to deliver lectures on progressive themes. Large crowds attended from the locality and from Chicago, many of them camping through the summer. Jenkin approached the building of the barn as he did everything else, entirely in his own way. In one important aspect, however, the barn was true to a Valley tradition: the stone foundations and walls were built by the 'good Welsh mason', David Timothy. It was to be Timothy's last monument; he died the following summer at the age of sixty-nine. Jenkin delivered his eulogy in Unity Chapel:

*perhaps the last piece of work to which he gave his heart was the little barn on Tower Hill last summer. He was then feeble and could not do much ... often he would drop his hammer and slowly, laboriously come to our Westhope Cottage ... with some anecdote or noble passage, with an 'englyn' on his lip.[8]*

The building of his barn also provided the theme for one of the most popular of Jenkin's sermons, in which he marvelled at the advent of technology in farming, and which concluded with a pointed comparison of the intense care that was brought to the husbandry of farm animals with the apparent carelessness that some 'up-to-date men and women' felt for their own children. It was obvious who he was thinking of when he concluded his sermon with the words: 'It behoves the favoured citizens of the country to hear and heed the voice of God speaking through the anguish of little ones, through the cry of the orphaned whose parents are still alive, of the widows with unburied husbands and the widowers with undivorced wives.'[9]

## October 1910. Wright Family Residence, Forest Avenue, Oak Park, Illinois

Frank returned on his own from Europe, leaving Mamah in Germany. On his way back he made his long-promised visit to C. R. Ashbee, who was living then at Chipping Campden in Gloucestershire. His first visit to Britain took him to within forty miles of the Welsh border. Before his visit he had written to Ashbee to explain his predicament, calling again on his rebellious ancestry: 'I am cast by nature for the role of the iconoclast. I must strike – tear down – before I can build.'[10] Once back in America his progress followed the pattern that he had predicted to his mother with such wretched self-pity. He had no alternative, other than to move back to Oak Park and try to revive his practice in a community which now thought of him, above all, as a notorious adulterer. The beautiful house and studio was brutally subdivided; the studio converted into a home for Catherine and the younger children, and the house separated so that it could be let to tenants, to provide Catherine with an income. Frank moved back into his mother's house, at the bottom of the garden and rented a small office at Orchestra Hall in the centre of Chicago. He took any small project that he could find, trying hard to give the impression that his relationship with Mamah was over.[11]

Then, in January, he made a return voyage to Germany, where he said he needed to resolve some final details of his publishing contract. Wasmuth's original intention had been to print a simple soft-cover book on Frank's work, a *Sonderheft*, a 'special edition' of their regular *Architecture of the Twentieth Century* magazine. It was Frank who had persuaded them also to print the spectacular large monograph. For this Wasmuth required a substantial financial contribution. Frank borrowed from Darwin Martin to fund his voyage and to settle the publishing deal. It was money that Martin would certainly not have provided if he had known that the primary purpose of Frank's voyage was a reunion with Mamah.

Leaving Mamah behind him in Europe again, Frank returned to Oak Park in late March 1911. On 10 April he was almost two hundred miles away, in Spring Green with his mother, at the office of Thomas King, a young lawyer and notary.[12] They were there to complete Anna Lloyd Wright's purchase of thirty-one and half acres of land from the Reider family. It cost nearly $2,300, a small part of which had been provided by Anna.[13] The remainder was money that Frank had kept aside from Darwin Martin's loan.[14] The Reiders must have been perplexed by the transaction. They had sold a tract of rough, stony land that was of minimal use for farming. It was the ridge of a hill, with its north side sloping down towards the Wisconsin River bank and the south side, topped by a rocky escarpment, facing down The Valley towards Hillside Home School. The Lloyd Joneses had never bothered to acquire it, but it was a hilltop that Frank knew well, a precisely remembered landmark and a vantage point that he had climbed frequently as a boy.[15] He remembered it well enough to begin the design of a house, which he called, at first, a 'Cottage for Mrs. Anna Lloyd Wright'.[16]

*So when family life in Oak Park ... conspired against the freedom to which I had come to feel every soul entitled ... I turned to the hill in The Valley as my Grandfather before me had turned to America – as a hope and a haven ... And it was unthinkable that any house should be put on that beloved hill ... It should be of the hill, belonging to it, so hill and house could live together each the happier for the other ... There must be some kind of house that would belong to that hill, as trees and the ledges of rock did; as Grandfather and Grandmother had belonged to it ... [if only] there was a house that [the] hill might marry and live happily with ever after. I fully intended to find it.[17]*

It is obvious from Frank's earliest plan of the 'cottage' that it was never intended to be a residence for his mother. Anna's ownership was a practical necessity: if Frank possessed the title his wife would have claim to half of it. The earliest drawing shows a building, roughly a crucifix in plan, aligned just below, and parallel with the ridge, divided at the crossway by a covered courtyard in the form of a loggia. To the east of the loggia were large living spaces, two bedrooms on the ground floor and smaller guest rooms on a lower level. Work areas extended to the west of the loggia, the largest of them a draughting studio. As the plans developed, during the summer of 1911, they grew to include staff bedrooms, stabling for horses, a barn and a milking parlour with a belvedere dovecote. The building extended from the foot of the initial crucifix to wrap around and along the curves of the hill (Fig. 14.1). In some places rugged retaining walls branched out to support terrace gardens, in others the rooflines merged into the original stony contours. It was conceived in the image of the ancient hilltop farmsteads that had impressed him so deeply during his months in Tuscany, buildings that seemed to have grown from their ground 'like the flowers by the roadside' (Pl. 118). The preface that he had written for his *Wasmuth Portfolio*, with its paean to the Tuscan vernacular, was Frank's brief to himself, and from it came his poetic vision of

*a garden and a farm behind a workshop and a home ... an architect's workshop, a dwelling as well for young workers who came to assist ... a complete living unit, genuine in point of comfort and beauty ... [a] recreation ground for my children and for their children perhaps for many generations more.[18]*

## May 1953. NBC Affiliate TV Studio, Chicago

Hugh Downs, then a young staff announcer, was conducting a filmed interview with Frank Lloyd Wright.[19] Frank was eighty-six years old and at the height of his fame. After a discussion of the meaning of organic architecture, Downs turned to the subject of the architect's own house, 'Where did the name "Taliesin" come from?' 'My people were Welsh,' Frank replied:

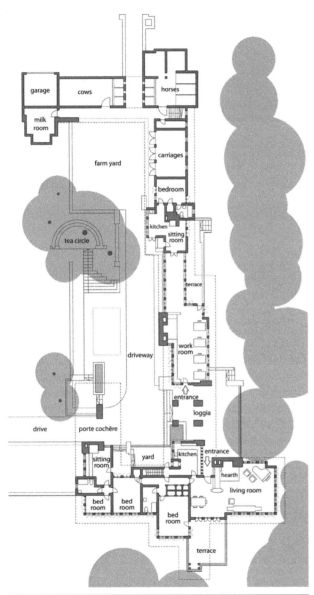

Fig. 14.1. Main floor level of Taliesin, 1911. The hill rises toward the left of the drawing. The 'work' area is above the loggia, and the 'living' area below.

Pl. 118. The first Taliesin, soon after completion in the winter 1911–12.
Photograph by Taylor Woolley / J. Willard Marriot Library, University of Utah.

*My mother's people were Welsh immigrants. My old grandfather was a hatter and a preacher and they were the cultivated element in the county. They all had Welsh names for their places. So I chose a Welsh name for mine, and it was Taliesin, a member of King Arthur's Round Table who sang the glories of fine art. I guess he was about the only Britisher who ever did.*[20]

## Summer 1911. The Valley, Iowa County, Wisconsin

Frank's immersion in the experience of Europe was instrumental to his own renaissance. His architecture did change: it became naturalistic, more ambiguous, more expressionistic. Among his hundreds of completed works there are only a few that can be thought of as stone buildings. Hillside Home School was one, Taliesin another. It had to be built of stone, and the stone had to seem like an upward tumbling of the limestone beds on which it stood, as if it had grown from the hillside. David Timothy now lay in the yard of Unity Chapel. Had he lived longer, he might have baulked at Frank's request to lay the slabs in rough strata, with alternate courses projecting in ragged shelves. The stone came in 'great flakes' from the quarry, which was on land belonging to Aunt Mary and Uncle Phillip, south-west of the site, around a mile away.[21]

*The stone went down for pavements of terraces and courts. Stone was sent along the slopes into great walls. Stone stepped up like ledges on the hill, and flung long arms in any direction that brought the house to the ground. The ground! My Grandfather's ground.*

The internal structural walls, columns, chimneys and fireplaces were all built from the same stratified stone, inside and outside treated the same[22] (Pl. 119). It was a

*combination of stone and wood as they met in the aspect of the hills around about. The lines of the hills were the lines of the roofs. The slopes of the hills their slopes, the plastered surfaces of the light wood walls, set back into the shade beneath broad eaves, were like the flat stretches of sand in the river below and the same in colour, for that is where the material that covered them came from.*

The sand from the river was mixed with plaster and raw sienna for the internal walls, 'natural, drying out tawny gold'. The same sand was mixed with cement to make a warm grey stucco for the outside of the upper walls, framed in timber. 'The finished wood outside was the colour of grey tree-trunks in violet light. The shingles of the roof surfaces were left to weather, silver-grey like the tree branches spreading below them.'[23] On the slopes below the house Frank planted hundreds of fruit trees in loose grids, like the olive plantation of a Florentine farmstead. Even as it was being built, Taliesin had the character of a house from another age and another continent, a house that had held its site for centuries.

Frank's clearest memories of the inside of Taliesin were of the ribbon windows that skirted the perimeter, the sensation of floating within the treetops; the continuous shelves of rough limestone; the underside of the roofs, pitched without trusses or ties, like tents over the open prospects of the living rooms, the furniture, loose or integral, all built to his design. Japanese screens, oriental vessels and figures, rugs and tapestries 'overflowed into the rooms'. His collection was spectacular in size and in quality. In his autobiography he imagined a spiritual dialogue:

*Hovering over these messengers to Taliesin from other civilizations and thousands of years ago must have been spirits of peace and goodwill ... For the story of Taliesin, after all, is old: old as the human spirit. These ancient figures were traces of that spirit ... and they now came forward to find rest and feel at home ... But they were only the story within the story: ancient comment on the New.[24]*

Taliesin was certainly unprecedented in America, 'new' in that respect, but it is different in its intentions from the architecture that Frank had produced before 1910. Not starkly provocative, not 'protestant': new, but attuned to consensual ideas of architectural beauty. Few photographs survive to show the original Taliesin. Those that do, provide testament to its extraordinary elegance.

Mamah returned to America during the summer of 1911. She met Edwin Cheney to settle the terms of their divorce, and by August she was living at The Valley, a guest of the Porters at 'Tan-y-Deri', while builders rushed to complete the new house. From then on she would be Mamah Borthwick. She moved into the new house, with Frank, just as winter came in, and enjoyed a few weeks of discreet happiness before the *Chicago Tribune* found them again. Their first Christmas was that one blighted by newspaper frenzy, the humiliating public 'trial' of their morality throughout which they believed they held the high ground. There are glimpses in the newspaper coverage of how unconventional the house appeared. Taliesin was a 'limestone grotto, or cave', a 'Castle of Love', a 'Love Bungalow'.[25] It still girdles the hilltop at the north end of The Valley, but very little of the original exquisite Taliesin remains. Within three years it was almost completely destroyed.

## February 1938. Western Edge of the McDowell Mountains, Sonoran Desert, Arizona

Outside the shelter, the view to the west was 'a look over the rim of the world', but at that moment Frank was concentrating on his drawing. Rough pencil, smudged on brown butcher's paper, used to reduce the sun's glare off the surface.[26] The plan showed a long, skeletal draughting room and, at each end, block-like chambers, some set askew to the dominant grid. One of the blocks would contain his office, another housed a workshop. Then there were living spaces, the garden apartment that he would share with Olgivanna, dormitories for the apprentices and a small, cave-like cinema. Frank flipped the plan, rotated it a few degrees at a time until the principal axis aligned with the prominent cone of Granite Reef Mountain, around seven miles to the south-east (Pl. 120). As he slid the footprint towards the central quadrant of his land he realised that he could also align its transverse grid with Camelback Mountain, rising up at the edge of Phoenix, nine miles to the south-west. With no other anchor, nothing in the untouched desert to constrain, the pristine intersection of the two sightlines, meeting at right-angles, splitting the compass points, was the natural place to start.[27]

Frank had brought the apprentices to Arizona before, to escape the Wisconsin winter. They had occasionally lodged there or camped on land owned by Alex Chandler,

Pl. 120. Taliesin West *circa* 1950. The mountain peak at the top right-hand corner is Granite Reef Mountain, with which the principal axis of the campus is aligned.
FLWF/AAFAL.

Frank's client for 'San-Marcos-in-the-Desert', the wonderful resort project that had foundered with the Wall Street Crash. By 1938 the prospects had changed. Frank had backed up the triumph of Fallingwater with the astonishing Johnson Wax Administration Building. For the first time in decades he had a full order book, and money to spend.

*There was plenty of room and plenty of superb sites ... With sleeping bags we went to and fro like the possessed from one famous place to another. Finally I learned of a site twenty-six miles from Phoenix, across the desert of the vast Paradise Valley ... On the mesa just below McDowell Peak we stopped, turned, and looked around. The top of the world! Magnificent – beyond words to describe!*[28]

In December 1937 he bought a quarter-section of the mesa and leased another adjacent to it. Three hundred

Pl. 121.  Apprentices of the Taliesin Fellowship, building the 'desert masonry' walls of Taliesin West, *circa* 1937.
Photograph by Pedro Guerrero, courtesy of Dixie Guerrero.

healthy, they were, for the most part, unskilled. The design took this into account, made it a virtue. Everything applied in its most basic form, by the simplest of means. In this paucity he found creative liberty, an unbounded profusion that he had never found before or would seek in the same way again.

Frank wanted the buildings to emerge out of the landscape, like a crystallisation of the desert floor. The desert boulders were a distinctive red quartzite, igneous, unworkable, so the apprentices were sent out to harvest them and set them just as they were found, into heavy timber box-forms.[30] Lean cement grout was tipped and tamped into the gaps between the boulders. The forms that emerged were not recognisably walls, but rugged angled plinths, pedestals, abutments, elevated in places to become abstract sculptures, dappled with dense, rusty boulders. The structures of the sunscreens and roofs were slender timber cages built off the masonry base. White canvas was stretched across, some sheets mounted in secondary panels that could slide back to reduce glare or increase air movement (Pl. 122). Like the limestone strata of Taliesin, the 'desert masonry' possessed an ancient, immutable solidity. The roof covering, striking a delicate counterpoint, could hardly have been more ephemeral. At the end of each winter season the canvas top was dismantled, and at the start of the following winter Frank rebuilt it, always to a different design, at the same time adding new structures in desert masonry, new pools, gardens, routes and roadways spreading out across the desert. With its most basic ingredients, without pretension or preconception, the winter camp evolved within a few years to become one of the most charming and uplifting places that a visitor could hope to experience. It is no less special or memorable today (Pl. 123).

For the first few years Frank and his Fellowship referred to it simply as 'The Camp'. It was not until 1941, when the first phase of building was complete, that they eventually settled the matter: 'we arrived at it after many more romantic names were set up and knocked down. The circumstances were so picturesque that names ran wild.'[31] The more pragmatic were happy to stick with 'Desert Camp'. 'Rockledge' was a poetic suggestion. Frank was tempted, for a while, by 'Aladdin', the name of his childhood hero.

and twenty barren acres for less than a thousand dollars. There was no guarantee that he would ever find water, but Frank had somehow known it was there. He spent another ten thousand dollars to tap a deep spring and recovered the whole of his investment in the process.[29] The winter studio took shape over the next three years. The process was familiar: only local materials, simple construction, fidelity to the natural character of the site. Timber, canvas, steel rod and cement had to be brought up from the town. Water was abundant, rock and sand lay all around. For Taliesin Frank had imposed the constraints that would yield his new vernacular; he had chosen deliberately to hold back from refinement. In the desert there was no choice. The camp had to be built by the apprentices (Pl. 121). Although eager and

Eventually 'we settled sensibly to the one we already had', and the desert camp became 'Taliesin West'. As Neil Levine has pointed out, 'Wright ultimately chose the name that linked him and the Fellowship to the place ... Taliesin West is Taliesin, moved west.'[32]

## 1954. Plaza Hotel, 5th Avenue, New York

After eleven years of effort, Frank could sense that the Solomon R. Guggenheim Museum, Manhattan's most controversial building project, was nearly ready to move from the drawing board onto the building site. Since the start of the decade he and Olgivanna had stayed at the Plaza Hotel, often for weeks at a time, while he steered the project around endless obstructions and, by force of will, prevailed over what he perceived as the modernist architectural establishment of the city – the younger, Eurocentric generation who would have revelled in his failure.[33] The Plaza was an opulent playground for the city's most privileged, an eighteen-storey extravagance in the French château style and a propitious corner-piece at the south-east elbow of Central Park. Given everything that he had said about his distaste for the 'eclectic', Frank's was an unlikely affection, but he had been a guest of the Plaza since its earliest days. It was there, in 1909, that he had stayed with Mamah Cheney for the few nights before their voyage to Europe. It had also been a favoured haunt during the fugitive years of the early 1920s, when he and Olgivanna were banished from Taliesin by debtors and pursued by the law.

In the spring of 1954, almost a half century after his first visit, he approached the Plaza management to take out a lease on two combined suites, numbers 223 and 225, at the north-east corner of the second floor.[34] The suite had been decorated and furnished by Christian Dior. Frank stripped it back to the skin. He mounted timber frames on the walls to divide them into screens, which were then lined with handmade Japanese paper, rich cream flecked with gold leaf. Dark red velvet curtains dropped the full four metres from ceiling to floor and circular mirrors were hung in the centres of the arched window-reveals, high enough to reflect only the ceiling.[35] The suite was large, but compared to his homes in Wisconsin and Arizona it was extremely confined. The mirrors

Pl. 122. The Drafting Room of Taliesin West, 1959.
Photograph by Pedro Guerrero, courtesy of Dixie Guerrero.

did, at least, create the illusion of space. The apprentices built lacquered shelves to display precious items from Frank's oriental collection and hung some of the best of his woodblock prints. Then the other essentials, without which it would not be a home – the heavily stacked bookcases, the Steinway and a large portrait photograph of Anna, his mother.[36]

Since the Oak Park years, Frank's home and work life were deeply intertwined. His suite at the Plaza was the same. Work continued there alongside social visits, media interviews, parties and client conferences on the Guggenheim and on many of his remarkable late projects: the Price Tower at Bartlesville, Oklahoma (Pl. 124); Beth Sholom Synagogue, designed for the Philadelphia suburb of Elkins Park (Pl. 125), and the proto-space-age Annunciation Greek Orthodox Church at Wauwatosa, back in his native Wisconsin. The suite was Frank's New York base for five years. He checked out, for the last time, in January 1959 to make the customary trip to Taliesin West,

Pl. 123.  Taliesin West, near Scottsdale Arizona, commenced 1937.

where he would, as always, wait with relish for the advent of the desert spring.[37] Soon after he made his Plaza suite into a home he, and everyone close to him, his apprentices, his family, his *teulu,* all came to refer to it as 'Taliesin East'. Once again, unavoidably, the name linked Frank to the place.

When Frank explained to the millions of viewers who watched his 1953 television interview that Taliesin, 'sang the glories of fine art', before offering the breezy aside that he was 'about the only Britisher that ever did', it became easy to infer that his identification with Taliesin was no more than superficial. Perhaps, after all, it was just the name of a house. But this is certainly not the full picture. The medieval Welsh poet and the modern American architect were more closely enmeshed than Frank implied. The Welshness of Taliesin was crucial, but Frank cloaked the importance of the idea of Taliesin, just as he had habitually concealed the sources of his architectural ideas.

Encouraged by his mother, Frank, as a child, had sought literary heroes, archetypes to inspire him. He assumed the persona of Aladdin, a boy of humble origin blessed with acute native brilliance, destined for magical greatness. In his late teens he occasionally imagined himself as Goethe's Wilhelm Meister, escaping the bourgeois world to find spiritual enlightenment, or as Alcibiades, the Athenian statesman celebrated for his flamboyance, vanity and military brilliance.[38] Taliesin was different: he existed in myth but also in fact, both mortal and eternal. In our time, and in Frank's time, Taliesin could still be present. He is defined by his very persistence, slipping from form to form, through age to age. The significance of Frank's comment in the 1953 television interview changes when it becomes apparent that the entire conversation, including the remark about Taliesin, was scripted in advance. When he said that Taliesin was, '*about the only Britisher that ever did*' sing the praises of fine art, it was not the spontaneous dig at the old world that it might appear. Taliesin was a great poet, beloved and honoured, and more importantly, according to Frank, prepared to stand out as a lone voice in defence of a precious culture. The figure of the lone defender is, perhaps, not Taliesin at all, but that of Iolo Morganwg, the revered poet-architect who had retrieved Taliesin from history. In Frank's understanding of his inherited mythology, it is as if Taliesin and Iolo had merged into one. Frank had been raised to aspire to Iolo's heroism, to Taliesin's heroism. He moulded himself in their image: creator and defender of the only true American architecture.[39] It was almost a bloodline.[40] Perhaps Frank really was Taliesin. In his autobiography he declared that, 'Taliesin lived wherever I stood'.[41] There could be no doubting the resemblance: the artistic brilliance, endurance, the ability to evolve, adapt, always to stay ahead of the game by way of staying aside

Pl. 124. Price Tower, Bartlesville, Oklahoma 1956. Photograph Carol Highsmith / LOC.

and, regardless of the most harrowing blows, always to come back, always to prevail. When Frank spoke about Taliesin he was really describing himself.[42]

Pl. 125. Beth Sholom Synagogue, Elkins Park, Philadelphia, 1959.
Photograph courtesy of Laszlo Regos Photography.

## 1912. Taliesin, The Valley, Iowa County, Wisconsin

As he and Mamah settled into Taliesin the prospect of the future that they had dreamed of together began to take tangible form: 'Gradually creative desire and faith came creeping back to me again. Taliesin was there to come alive and I to settle down to work.'[43] He designed a beautiful small Kindergarten for the grounds of Avery Coonley's mansion, as bright and joyful as a young child could wish for (Pl. 126). The 'Playhouse' was crowned by a triptych of coloured glass, a frieze of confetti, balloons and American flags, pure pop art, decades before its time.[44] For Francis Little, another of his old clients, he designed a long, sleek country house overlooking Robinson Bay at Lake Minnetonka. It had prairie-style aspects, arranged

loosely, with the natural informality he had expressed for the first time in the design of Taliesin. But the flow of unsolicited domestic commissions, the new names and introductions that had always supported his practice, was gone, sacrificed to his transgressive instincts. In its place he reached for commercial clients and worked speculatively on projects of which barely any could progress beyond the concept stage: ideas for shops, banks, railway stations and office buildings. In truth there was little of substance to detain him. In January 1913 Frank left America, with Mamah, for a print-collecting excursion to Japan. At that time his art dealing was more profitable than his architecture, but there was another tantalising prospect in his sights. He had been told confidentially, by a fellow orientalist, that plans were being made for a huge international hotel to be built in the heart of Tokyo, and that Frank's name had been mentioned to the Emperor.

## January 1913. Tokyo, Japan

The first Imperial Hotel had been opened in 1890. Designed in the Beaux-Arts manner, it was seen as a symbol of Japan's entry into the international community. Barely two decades passed before it came to seem outdated and undersized. The new Imperial had to be larger, more modern, more remarkable in every way. The Japanese authorities made discreet inquiries about potential architects. Frank's name was put forward long before he was aware of it. His admiration for Japan and its culture was well known. The power of his imagination and his ability to deliver were undeniable, but it was just as obvious that he carried an unpredictable edge. He knew there was a long way to go before the opportunity could become reality. Frank and Mamah spent four months in Japan, devoting most of their efforts, as they had planned, to the accumulation of woodblock prints. They stayed at the old Imperial Hotel and socialised, when they had the chance, with senior managers and important officials. Frank was as charming as ever, establishing and consolidating mutual trust. The fact of his presence was, as he had anticipated, deeply appreciated in itself. There was a visit to the site, and a presentation of some initial architectural thoughts, ideas that demonstrated a unique vision, more than equal to the

Imperial's expectations.[45] Frank had been desperate for the propitious relaunch project. The Imperial was ambitious enough to confound the scandal-mongers and the sceptics, to show that he was back in business and bolder than ever. He returned to Taliesin in the late spring, convinced the commission was imminent. While he waited, he arranged a new team, youngsters including his sons John and Lloyd, prepared to be on stand-by for a short while, alongside him. He then spent the summer helping Mamah with her writing, and trading prints from his newly expanded collection. But as months went by there was no word from Tokyo.[46]

A new and extraordinary inquiry came suddenly, in the autumn, to dispel the clouds of frustration. Edward Waller Jr had been known to Frank since his boyhood. Waller senior was his old client, the developer of River Forest. It was at the Waller residence, across the street from the Winslow House, seemingly a lifetime before, that Daniel Burnham had tempted Frank, unsuccessfully, with the promise of a rich Beaux-Arts future. Yet again, it was a lifeline from a trusted friend. Waller Jr had a sparkling proposition:

*Frank, in all this black old town there's no place to go ... that isn't bare and ugly, unless its cheap and nasty. I want to put a garden in this wilderness of smoky dens, car tracks and saloons ... Chicago would appreciate a beautiful garden resort. Our people would go there, listen to good music, eat and drink ... something like those little parks round Munich where German families go.*

Frank had been in Munich the year before, with Mamah. As he recalled the exuberance of social life in Germany and Austria he thought, also, of the vigorous new art movements, the strange art of the Secession and the Jugendstil, both primitive and bracingly modern. There was a greater logic to the German connection: Waller's site was at the western end of the Midway Plaisance, close to the university and its prosperous German community. They would defy the Chicago climate, Waller explained, by, 'putting a winter garden on one side for diners with a big dancing floor in

Pl. 126. The Coonley Playhouse, 1912.

the middle'. There would be an orchestra shell of concert standard, garden terraces, dining rooms, a casino, lounges and bars, all served by industrial-scale underground kitchens. Max Bendix, the original concertmaster of the Chicago Symphony, was already booked with his own orchestra to provide the music for the first season, and the catering would be controlled by the famous restaurateur John Vogelsang, another prominent Chicago German. High art would be woven through popular culture; the whole thing would be, 'a high class entertainment on a grand scale'.[47]

## January 1914. Midway Plaisance, Chicago Southside

The Imperial Hotel was soon forgotten; it was Midway Gardens that would consolidate Frank's new beginning! A fantastic brief, a young and adventurous client and a building that would spread over an entire block in the heart of the city. John Lloyd Wright recalled that his 'Dad's spirit soared'. The urgency of the enterprise only added to Frank's gleeful excitement. Waller's borrowing was as grand as his vision. There could be no delay. 'It was a rush job', John recalled; 'we were to have our working drawings ready for contract in thirty days and the construction completed ninety days thereafter.' An impossible target, but they came close. One day in early January 1914 John watched as his father draughted plans, elevations and perspectives, apparently without preparation – the essence of an extraordinary, futuristic design from nothing in a matter of hours. ' "There it is" he said. "Now get into it. Get it out!" '[48]

Midway Gardens was a vast design exercise, the only concession to expediency was in its symmetry. In every other respect it was innovative, structurally daring, architecturally radical. He used familiar materials, brick and concrete, arranged with the planar austerity that he had originated a decade before, but the surfaces at Midway were pulled apart, flipped and extended into precarious cantilevers and delicate picture-frame towers (Pl. 127). Walls became openings, windows became walkways, surfaces were densely patterned and pierced. His work, before Taliesin, had seemed always to aspire to a sense of resolution, the elegant tying-up of planes and lines, a skill for which he was justly admired. At Midway Gardens the energy of line and plane was released, unconstrained, to slice like searchlights through Chicago's evening sky. 'I meant to get back to first principles', Frank recalled,

> *pure form in everything; weave a masonry fabric in beautiful pattern in genuine materials and good construction, bring painting and sculpture in to heighten and carry all still further ... A synthesis of all the arts.*

His 'pure form' was the greater part of the risk:

> *Would Chicago respond to adventure into the realm of the abstract in the sense that I wanted to go into it? Did Chicago know what 'abstraction' meant anyway? ... the straight line, square, triangle and circle ... were set to work in this developing sense of abstraction, by now my habit.[49]*

These were very new ideas to America. The sensational 'Armory Show' exhibition of 'cubist and futurist' art had

visited Chicago in the spring of 1913, prompting a flurry of outrage that Frank might have envied, being wary, always, that he might fall behind a younger avant-garde. A year later, while the Gardens were taking shape, a journalist challenged him: 'Hasn't your work rather cubistic sympathies?' 'What do you mean by "cubistic"?' Frank replied, 'If you refer to the fact that the work is a form of natural design rather than nature imitation, I might plead guilty.'[50]

The unprecedented artistic programme included relief castings, mosaic, murals and, most unexpectedly, rows of semi-abstract figurative sculptures lining parapet tops and marking prominent corners (Pl. 128). Frank had been impressed by the early Expressionist sculpture he had seen in Germany with Mamah. There was no hint of the saccharine comeliness of Art Nouveau, still the mode in Chicago. Frank's 'sprites' emerged from prisms of spiritual geometry, part human, part crystal. The expression of sacred geometry was unambiguous. There were female figures titled 'Sphere' and 'Triangle'; male figures, 'Octagon' and 'Cube'. Antony Alfosin, the eminent Wright scholar, has observed that these figures 'had deeper and more universal meanings recalling Wright's symbolic interpretations in which the circle stood for infinity, the triangle for structural unity, the square for integrity'. This was a Unitarian line of thought, a primal spirituality that lay behind every natural form and every sacred truth.[51]

Perhaps Frank's only real concern, at that time when everything seemed possible, was that Taliesin and Mamah were so far away. It was late in the spring of 1914. The project had consumed his mind and his time since the beginning of the year. He went back to The Valley, occasionally, for a few days at a time, leaving John to supervise the works, but their separation still troubled him. Mamah's children, Martha and John, would be joining their mother at The Valley for the summer. She was not alone at Taliesin. Frank had two draughtsmen, Emil Brodelle and Herb Fritz, both of whom worked and lodged at the house, and there was always a small crew of workmen tending to the building and its gardens. They, and the draughtsmen, generally occupied the business quarters at the west end of the house, while Mamah made her home at the opposite end. Frank asked John Vogelsang if there were staff he could recommend, a cook and a housemaid to make sure that Mamah and the children were well looked after. Julian Carlton and his wife Gertrude had both worked for Vogelsang's own family, who found them discreet, likeable and trustworthy. Frank met them and found them agreeable too. They moved to Taliesin and began work there in the middle of June. Frank had been struck by Julian's intelligence. He seemed well educated for a worker of his standing. There was nothing to suggest that he might be seriously ill.[52]

The 'realm of the abstract' rose rapidly above the treetops of the Midway Plaisance. Construction had started in early April and, astonishingly, Midway Gardens was ready for a gala opening on 27 June. Five hundred builders still worked around the clock as the Bendix orchestra attempted to rehearse over the noise. It was far from complete, but close enough. Several thousand visitors came for the triumphant inauguration, thousands more were turned away. It was a magical occasion and, for John Lloyd Wright, a moment of transcendent wonder:

> *Midway Gardens were phantom gardens to me from the beginning ... I could hear the music ... I could see Pavlova dancing in the open air ... surrounded by balconies, terraces, urns overflowing with flowers. I could see the acrobats ... running over the many roof levels ... I could hear the tinkle of iced glasses coming from Vogelsang's underground kitchen, mingling with the exclamations of delight from the crowd. Later Dad and I sat alone in the Architect's Box, a sculptural finial at the corner – a needle of light ran up into the sky. This romantic building, like the expression he bore, was the mask of a great inner love.*[53]

The city's appetite for 'abstraction' was more healthy than Frank could have hoped. He had been raised to admire the spiritual purity of the ancients, ancestors who drew their own creativity directly from Nature. His career had been nourished by ancient cultural sources from the beginning, but it had never suited him, until then, to concede his influences. The artistic world around him was changing. He

Pl. 127.   The entrance to Midway Gardens, on Cottage Grove Avenue, viewed from the north-east. September 1914. Photograph by Clarence Fuermann.

had made huge sacrifices; stripped his own life back to a state of personal clarity from which he hoped to seize the entirety of his creative potential. At Midway Gardens, for the first time, he revealed his primitive soul:

> *And this scene came upon the beholders as a magical spell. All there moved and spoke as if in a dream. They believed it must be one. Yes Chicago marvelled, acclaimed, approved. And Chicago came back and did the same marvelling again and again and again. To many it was all Egyptian. Mayan to some, very Japanese to others.*[54]

The visitor numbers in those first few weeks were 'almost frightening', according to the *Chicago Tribune* (Pl. 129). There had been over 17,000 on just one July weekend. As revelry

Pl. 128. The 'Queen of the Gardens' holding aloft a cube: one of the semi-abstract figures created by Alfonso Ianelli under the direction of Frank Lloyd Wright. Midway Gardens, 1914. Photograph by Clarence Fuermann.

Pl. 129. A postcard from Midway Gardens showing the vast crowds that attended the opening season.

bubbled around them, Frank and his team of artists, pressed on to complete the details, content that they had already succeeded beyond expectations.[55] People were happy. America was prospering; the horizons were bright and clear. Two days later the front page of the *Chicago Tribune* carried news from Serbia of the killing of Archduke Franz Ferdinand. What had seemed to be a dawn would turn out to be a setting sun.

## Saturday 15 August 1914. Taliesin, The Valley, Iowa County, Wisconsin

It was a typical summer afternoon, peaceful and warm. Frank had gone back to Chicago the Tuesday before, after the Grove Meeting, the annual celebration of his grandmother Mallie's memory. He was at Midway Gardens, working on his murals. At the Tower Hill camp, a mile away to the east, Jenkin Lloyd Jones was leading his community in uplifting spiritual debate. Mamah (Pl. 130), eight-year-old Martha and her brother John, three years older, were at their lunch table on the terrace at the high, eastern prominence of Taliesin (Pl. 131). It was a delightful vantage point, the whole valley was laid out below them in late summer splendour. There may have been a slight awkwardness: Julian and Gertrude would be leaving the next day. Frank had already put an advert in the State journal, looking for new staff.[56] Julian had never really seemed settled at Taliesin. On occasions he would seem sullen, unsociable, but on his last day he attended to the table with courtesy. He moved quietly from the terrace, through the living room and back to the kitchen, clearing plates, and then returned as if to refresh their glasses but carrying a short-handled tool. It was a shingling axe, with a stout blade designed for splitting hardwood. He struck Mamah first, a single fatal blow. He killed John in the same way, immediately, before the boy could move from his seat. Martha managed to run past him, back into the wide living room, but he caught her quickly and cut her down. It must be supposed that this all happened so quickly and quietly that the men, who were gathered for their own lunch at the working end of the house, were oblivious.[57]

Their dining room was small, and connected to its own small kitchen. The two draughtsmen, Herb Fritz and Emil Brodelle, were at the table with David Lindblom, the gardener, and Tom Brunker, an odd-job man, getting on in years. Billy Weston, the foreman, was also with them. He was at the house to keep an eye on things, with Ernie, his thirteen-year-old son. The men would have known that Julian's priority was at the other end of the house, but as they ate, the butler came in to ask Billy Weston for permission to draw a can of petrol. He said that he needed it to clean a carpet. Minutes later Herb Fritz noticed a stream of liquid – he assumed it must be dishwater – trickling into the dining room beneath the kitchen door, but it was petrol that immediately exploded into flame. Fuel vapour filled the room and in an instant the men found their clothes ablaze. As each of them fought the flames the butler swung his axe. Emil Brodelle, Tom Brunker and young Ernie Weston all sustained mortal wounds. Herb Fritz escaped. He threw himself through a low window and fell heavily onto rocks below. His arm was broken but he was able to roll down the bank and smother his burning clothes. Billy Weston and David Lindblom both had severe burns and axe wounds but were able, somehow, to escape Carlton's trap. They ran half a mile to the Reiders' house. After raising the alarm Weston left Lindblom to be cared for and went back to Taliesin. Men from the Reider and Sliter farms soon arrived. They found Billy Weston with the garden hose, struggling on his own to hold back the flames. Before he had set fire to the workers' dining room, it seemed that Julian Carlton had taken the petrol to the scene of his first attack. He had drenched the bodies of Mamah and her children and set them alight. The eastern end of the house was well ablaze. Billy Weston's efforts with the garden hose saved most of the 'working end', but the rest of the house was lost (Pl. 132).

Within two hours of the first attack hundreds of helpers and onlookers crowded the grounds of Taliesin. Jenkin Lloyd Jones brought his calming presence and took charge of the recovery efforts. Finding Julian Carlton was one priority, saving him from lynching was another. Carlton had come close to killing the entire household. Earlier in the day he had told Gertrude to pack her things and leave. She supposed that he was intending to follow her, and she was waiting at the edge of a nearby field, from where, it is presumed, she must have seen the smoke. Frank arrived back at The Valley in the late evening. He

Pl. 130.  Mamah Bouton Borthwick. Mamah had this photograph taken in June 1914 as a gift for Frank on his forty-seventh birthday.
Courtesy of Ellen Keys Strand.

had taken the only train out of Chicago for Madison. It was to be expected that Edwin Cheney would do the same. He joined the train as it passed through Oak Park.

Pl. 131. Taliesin, summer 1912. The studio and work quarters are to the left of the central, open loggia, and the living quarters are to the right. At the end of the carriage drive a girl on horse is leaning down to speak to a boy. They are probably John and Martha Cheney, Mamah's children.
Wisconsin Historical Society WHS-83123.

Pl. 132. The same view after the fire and murders in August 1914. The man in the white shirt and dark waistcoat has been identified as Frank.
Wisconsin Historical Society WHS-55871.

The two men sat together, for hours, in silence. John Lloyd Wright stayed close, to shield them from the journalists. The news already filled the late editions. Lurid headlines; judgemental relish. Frank's Aunts Jennie and Nell were waiting at Madison to join him on the connecting train to Spring Green. Richard Lloyd Jones was there too.[58] John's memories of that evening were vivid and traumatic:

*Dad was growing weaker every moment, he was about to collapse. Cousin Richard grabbed him by the coat collar, pounded him on the back, shook him vigorously and thundered: 'Stand up, Frank! It couldn't be worse, get hold of yourself!' Some of Richard's rugged strength seemed to flow to him.[59]*

The car from Spring Green took them to Tan-y-Deri where the dead and dying were laid out in the parlour under white sheets. Four of them had been killed almost instantly, or within a few minutes of Carlton's assaults. Young Ernie Weston and the gardener David Lindblom both died of their burns within three days of the attack. Most appallingly, eight-year-old Martha Cheney was not only alive, but conscious for a few dreadful hours after she had been struck three times by Carlton's axe and then set on fire. Only Herb Fritz and Billy Weston survived.

Julian Carlton was found, two days later, hiding inside the boiler furnace in the basement of Taliesin. He had swallowed a bottle of hydrochloric acid, enough to mutilate his mouth and oesophagus but not enough to kill him directly. He and Gertrude were both held in prison at Dodgeville, the capital of Iowa County. Gertrude told her own story, the only useful account of Julian's psychological decline. At times she had felt threatened herself. Julian had become convinced that he was being persecuted; there were explosions of fury out of nothing. He had started to sleep with the axe by his side, but she could never have imagined what he would do. Gertrude was released with seven dollars in her purse and the clothes she was wearing. No one knows what became of her. Julian had no appetite left for life. He could barely eat anyway. He was cared for, humanely, in the Dodgeville jail until his death by starvation on 7 October.[60]

The years since 1910 had been fraught with upheavals. Frank had pulled the structure of his own life apart, battering his family in the process, before attempting to rebuild it in a new form, according to radical, progressive morals that he regarded as unimpeachable. By Frank's own frequent admission, it had been tortuous and damaging, but he had always felt that he was following the most honourable path. The break had been necessary, and by 1914 it was complete. There had been many hard moments along the way, but he had seized his own destiny; he had forced his own will to prevail.

In the dark wreckage of Taliesin he was confronted by the collapse of his conceit: 'All I had left to show for the struggle for freedom of the past five years, that had swept most of my life away, had now been swept away.' For the first time in his life he faced the possibility of his insignificance. The shock was profound:

> *Something strange had happened to me. Instead of feeling that she, whose life had joined mine there at Taliesin, was a spirit near, she was utterly gone ... a kind of black despair seemed to paralyze my imagination in her direction and numbed my sensibilities. The blow was too severe ... I got no relief in any faith nor yet in any hope. Except repulsion.*[61]

For a few days, while the funerals took place, Frank stayed in a small bedroom next to Taliesin's workroom, unaware of Julian Carlton in his iron coffer, just a few feet below. With the consent of Uncle Enos, and helped by his son John and by Enos's boys, Ralph and Orren, Frank laid Mamah to rest in an unmarked grave at Unity Chapel. He had lost her, and he had lost Taliesin, but what haunted him most was the implication that he had lost the moral argument: that God had listened to his justifications, his insistence that his union with Mamah Borthwick was spiritually pure, and that He had passed His judgement. The bigots and the blinkered who had persecuted him were on God's side after all. The press and the pulpits fizzed with judgemental glee, they had him just where they

wanted him. They assumed that he was broken, that he would never recover. Now he had to prove them wrong again.

Maginel arrived presently from New York, to help him through his nightmare. They went riding together, 'farther than we would have ridden in a happier time', in virtual silence, for days at a time. Thinking back, years later, Maginel said that she felt that Frank 'would have been glad ... to leave the place and never face its terrible memories again'.[62] But that was not a realistic prospect. Frank had no choice but to rebuild himself, and he could only rebuild himself by rebuilding Taliesin:

> *I believe that the equivalent of years passed within my consciousness in the course of weeks. Time, never very present to me, ceased to exist. As days passed into nights I was numb to all but the automatic steps towards rebuilding ... I could get relief only by looking towards rebuilding – get relief from a kind of continuous nausea, by work.*[63]

Rebuilding began spontaneously, an adjunct to the clearing of debris, and driven at pace by Frank's sombre imperative. He moved back to Chicago, into the small house on East Cedar Street, in the Near North Side, that he was renting during the construction of Midway Gardens.[64] While they had been in Fiesole, Frank and Mamah had talked seriously about moving to Chicago. The Near North Side was upmarket and liberal, and it was her favourite neighbourhood. Frank had designed an exquisite small house for a site on Goethe Street, a few blocks from his rented rooms. It would have been the perfect address for them, but it was too expensive, unattainable.[65] Back at East Cedar Street, he was alone but for the company of a maid. She brought him three meals a day, which he ate 'by sheer force of habit', while he drew plans for the rebuilding and sent them back to The Valley. For the first time in his life he sought isolation. He was glad of the distance between him and the Southside, and the many people there who were familiar to him. With Mamah gone, Kitty encouraged the children to spend time with him, but he found their company hard to bear.[66]

*A horrible loneliness now began to clutch at me, but strange to say I longed for no-one I had ever loved or that I had ever known. My mother was deeply hurt by my refusal to have her with me. My children – I had welcomed them eagerly always – but I did not want them now ... strange faces were best and I walked among them.*[67]

Frank designed the new Taliesin around the limestone mainstays of the first house, the chimneys, plinths and cross-walls that had survived the fire, the stone in places turned from gold to pink by the heat of the flames. 'What could be used was used anew', Maginel recalled, 'even the shards of porcelains and statues were set like jewels in the cement.'[68] Hundreds of precious artworks had been lost. Almost every copy of the *Wasmuth Portfolio* was either burned or saturated. Frank's recourse was to add more space for more art, more fireplaces, courtyards and cliff-like walls. He stretched the house westward, back along the ridge, in two parallel wings. There were new, larger workrooms and farm enclosures, and, for the first time, an apartment for his mother. The second Taliesin would be more than twice the size of the first.

While the house grew again, Hillside Home School ebbed towards extinction. As Uncle Jenkin had feared, it was as if the two were linked by some rule of inversion. Nell and Jennie were both in their late sixties and tired of the struggle. Earlier in the year they had recruited a new principal from Chicago, but the events of mid-August had confounded their plans. When the doors were opened for the start of the academic year barely anyone came. They were closed for the last time before Christmas. Frank extended the Taliesin floorplan again, to add an apartment for his aunts. He agreed to provide them with 'bath and board', and a small allowance; and for the price of one dollar he became owner of the abandoned school.

Maginel went to The Valley again in May 1915. Work on Taliesin was well advanced, 'Jane ... had been working like a stevedore, and now I came to help her; she and I with a neighbour or two, daily fed the twenty-five men at work on the building ... the new Taliesin began slowly to take shape.'[69] Friends offered loans, others gave gifts. Some offered patronage. As the new Taliesin was resolved

Frank was himself reassembled, work became possible again. His attorney, Sherman Booth, pushed forward with his plan for a new house in the rustic hinterland of Ravine Bluffs, twenty miles north of Chicago. He asked Frank to design another five houses, for rent, at the same time, grouped into a small commune. There were new inquiries too, tentative approaches from unusual people, undeterred by Frank's recent history, like Arthur Richards, a Milwaukee entrepreneur, who had been so excited by Frank's vision of low-cost, prefabricated housing that he had set up a business to bring it to reality, and Aline Barnsdall, a political radical who dreamed of a new form of theatre and who was also, helpfully, the millionaire daughter of a Pennsylvania oilman. Both would become important clients. A small article appeared in the *Racine Journal Times* on 17 November 1915 under the heading 'Wright Love Bungalow is Rebuilt':

*Frank Lloyd Wright's bungalow at Hillside is about rebuilt and will soon be completed. The new building is similar to the one destroyed by the fire ... last summer: the only difference is that the structure is larger ... It will be fully equal, if not surpass, the beauty of the old building.*[70]

A restrained accolade, carefully offset by its reference to the 'love bungalow', but an accolade nonetheless. Taliesin was back; by God's will, Frank was back, and both were bigger, bolder and stronger than before. Frank had been right all along. He quit his lease at East Cedar Avenue, and was back living at Taliesin before Christmas. The great Welsh writer Emyr Humphreys reflected on the efforts made by English scholars to subordinate the ancient Taliesin, to make him part of their own spurious history, before Iolo Morganwg restored him. 'There were attempts to tame him', Humphreys said, 'but he wriggled free with a shapeshifter's ease.'[71] ∎

# 14 The Shape-Shifter
## *Notes*

1   F. L. Wright, 'Art and Craft of the Machine', *Catalogue of the Fourteenth Annual Exhibition of the Chicago Architectural Club* (Chicago, March 1901), 6.

2   Anthony Alofsin, *Frank Lloyd Wright: The Lost Years, 1910-1922: A Study of Influence* (Chicago: University of Chicago Press, 1993), p. 43.

3   Filippo Fici, 'Frank Lloyd Wright in Florence and Fiesole 1909–1910', *Frank Lloyd Wright Quarterly*, 22/4 (2011), 5-17.

4   Alofsin, *Frank Lloyd Wright: The Lost Years*, pp. 43-5.

5   Letter, Frank Lloyd Wright to Anna Lloyd Wright, 4 July 1910, quoted in Ron McCrea, *Building Taliesin: Frank Lloyd Wright's Home of Love and Loss* (Madison: Wisconsin Historical Society Press, 2012), p. 23.

6   McCrea, *Building Taliesin*, p. 23.

7   J. L. Jones, 'Barn Building', with notes by Thomas Graham, *Wisconsin Magazine of History* (Winter 1983-4), 127-33.

8   An *englyn* is an ancient form of short poem written in one of the strict bardic metres. There are several variations of *englynion*, each with its own rhyme and rhythmic pattern. Any successful *englyn* requires a precise effort in poetic engineering.

9   J. L. Jones, 'Barn Building', pp. 127-33.

10  Neil Levine, 'The Story of Taliesin: Wright's First Natural House', in N. G. Menocal (ed.), *Wright Studies*, vol. 1: *Taliesin 1911-1914* (Carbondale: Southern Illinois University Press, 1992), p. 24.

11  Alofsin, *Frank Lloyd Wright: The Lost Years*, pp. 64-9.

12  Thomas King's father was Owen King, a timber merchant who owned a farm on the east side of the Lloyd Jones Valley.

13  In some accounts of this period, for example in Neil Levine's excellent study *The Architecture of Frank Lloyd Wright*, Anna sold

her house in Oak Park to finance the land purchase in The Valley. This seems not to be the case, however. Anna and her daughter Jane maintained the address at 931 Chicago Avenue until Anna's death. See for example Anna's 1920 Passport Application.

14    A. Alofsin, 'Taliesin 1, a Catalogue of Drawings and Photographs' in N. G. Menocal (ed), *Wright Studies Vol. 1 Taliesin 1911–1914* (Carbondale: Southern Illinois University Press, 1992) pp. 98–9.

15    Frank Lloyd Wright, *An Autobiography (Edition 1)* (New York: Longman, Green & Co., 1932), p. 170.

16    One of these early drawings is reproduced in Alofsin, 'Taliesin 1, a Catalogue of Drawings and Photographs', p. 100.

17    F. L. Wright, *An Autobiography (Edition 1)*, p. 171.

18    F.L. Wright, *An Autobiography (Edition 1)*, pp. 172–3.

19    Debra Pickrel and Jane Hession, *Frank Lloyd Wright in New York: The Plaza Years 1954-59* (New York: Gibbs M. Smith Inc., 2007), p. 85.

20    Patrick. J. Meehan (ed.), *The Master Architect: Conversations with Frank Lloyd Wright* (New York: John Wiley and Sons, 1984), p. 44.

21    The quarry is shown on the US Geological Survey Map 1:65,000 Quadrangle for Spring Green, WI, 1960. It is near to the centre of Wyoming Township, subdivision No.36.

22    F. L. Wright, *An Autobiography (Edition 1)*, p. 173.

23    F. L. Wright, *An Autobiography (Edition 1)*, p. 175.

24    F. L. Wright, *An Autobiography (Edition 1)*, p. 177.

25    McCrea, *Building Taliesin*, pp. 123–7.

26    Neil Levine, *The Architecture of Frank Lloyd Wright* (Princeton: Princeton University Press, 1996), p. 264.

27    This can be derived from United States Geological Survey mapping. It is evident that there has been some confusion about the relationship of the building to prominent mountains. This could stem from an essay by Bruce Brooks Pfeiffer in a Japanese publication, *Frank Lloyd Wright Selected Houses 3: Taliesin West* (Tokyo: ADS Edita Co. Ltd., 1992), p. 12. Mr Brooks Pfeiffer refers to alignments with two mountains, both to the north of the site. He identifies these mountains as 'Black Mountain' and 'Granite Reef Mountain'. Neil Levine, in his important book *The Architecture of Frank Lloyd Wright*, pp. 268-9, repeats the same names.

However, the mountain to the north is 'Granite Mountain', not 'Granite Reef Mountain'. As Prof. Levine himself observes, both of these northern peaks are actually barely visible from the site. 'Granite Reef Mountain' is actually an alternative name for 'Sawik Mountain', which is much closer to the site, directly to the southeast and the most distinctive peak on the horizon. See *The National Gazetteer of the United States of America: Arizona 1986* (Denver: US Geological Survey, 1986), p. AZ251.

28    Frank Lloyd Wright, *An Autobiography (Edition 2)* (New York: Duell, Sloan & Pearce, 1943), p. 452.

29    Meryl Secrest, *Frank Lloyd Wright: A Biography* (Chicago: University of Chicago Press, 1998), p. 451.

30    Cornelia Brierly, *Tales of Taliesin: A Memoir of Fellowship* (Portland, OR: Pomegranate Communications Inc., 2000), p. 41.

31    F. L. Wright, *An Autobiography (Edition 2)*, p. 452.

32    Levine, *The Architecture of Frank Lloyd Wright*, p. 273.

33    Anthony Alofsin, *Wright and New York: The Making of America's Architect* (New Haven: Yale University Press, 2019), pp. 242-3.

34    In this instance it is also the second floor in British terms.

35    The windows themselves were simple rectangles with double hung sashes.

36    The exhibition 'Sixty Years of Living Architecture' had toured America before concluding in New York. The model Usonian House and the pavilion were seen by over eighty thousand visitors during the autumn of 1953. Frank believed that the popularity of the exhibition had played an important part in building public support for the Guggenheim Museum project.

37    Pickrel and Hession, *Frank Lloyd Wright in New York*, pp.19–24.

38    Roger Friedland, and Harold Zellman, *The Fellowship: The Untold Story of Frank Lloyd Wright and the Taliesin Fellowship* (New York: HarperCollins, 2006), p. 12.

39    Pickrel and Hession, *Frank Lloyd Wright in New York*, p. 85.

40    Gwyneth Lewis and Rowan Williams, *The Book of Taliesin: Poems of Warfare and Praise in an Enchanted Britain* (London: Penguin Classics, 2019), p. xxxv.

41    F. L. Wright, *An Autobiography (Edition 2)*, p. 262. Frank appears to attribute these words to Olgivanna, his wife, but the sentiment is his.

42    Alofsin, *Frank Lloyd Wright: The Lost Years*, p.125.

43     F. L. Wright, *An Autobiography (Edition 2)*, p. 175.

44     The Coonley Playhouse windows are among the most popular of all of Wright's creations, reproduced on key-fobs and place mats by the thousand.

45     K. Smith, 'Frank Lloyd Wright and the Imperial Hotel: A Postscript', *The Art Bulletin*, 67/2 (June 1985), 296–310.

46     Julia Meech, *Frank Lloyd Wright and the Art of Japan: The Architect's Other Passion* (New York: Harry. N. Abrams, 2001), p. 14.

47     F. L. Wright, *An Autobiography (Edition 2)*, pp. 175–84.

48     John Lloyd Wright, *My Father Who Is On Earth* (New York: Putnam, 1946), pp. 71–2.

49     F. L. Wright, *An Autobiography (Edition 2)*, p. 181.

50     H. Sell, 'Interpretation Not Imitation', *The International Studio*, 55/219 (May 1915), lxxix–lxxxiii.

51     Alofsin, *Frank Lloyd Wright: The Lost Years*, pp. 141–2.

52     McCrea, *Building Taliesin*, p. 192.

53     J. L. Wright, *My Father Who Is On Earth*, p. 72. Anna Pavlova, the world's greatest ballerina, did dance at Midway Gardens, but not on the opening night.

54     F. L. Wright, *An Autobiography (Edition 1)*, p. 214.

55     McCrea, *Building Taliesin*, p. 144.

56     Paul Hendrickson, *Plagued by Fire: The Dreams and Furies of Frank Lloyd Wright* (London: Bodley Head, 2019), p. 304.

57     None of the extant drawings of the first Taliesin appear to show an arrangement of rooms that is consistent with the survivors' account of the events of 15 August 1914. It is possible to see where the workers' dining room was located, and also to envisage how its setting would have allowed for the events to play out as the survivors recalled. It is well known that the layout of Taliesin was in constant flux, even before 1914. Wright scholars have conceded that it will never be possible to establish the sequence of changes, or when they were made.

58     Secrest, *Frank Lloyd Wright: A Biography*, p. 221.

59     J. L. Wright, *My Father Who Is On Earth*, p. 83.

60     There are many accounts of the murders. Paul Hendrickson's 2019 book *Plagued by Fire* is a good starting point for anyone with an interest. The author's primary research into Julian Carlton and his background is valuable. William R. Drennan's *Death in a Prairie House* (Madison: University of Wisconsin Press, 2008) intends to be a definitive account. Meryl Secrest provides an excellent concise summary in *Frank Lloyd Wright: A Biography* (Chicago: University of Chicago Press, 1992). The most engaging all-round discussion is to be found in McCrea, *Building Taliesin*.

61     F. L. Wright, *An Autobiography (Edition 2)*, p. 188.

62     Maginel Wright Barney, *The Valley of the God Almighty Joneses* (New York: Appleton Century, 1965), pp. 146–7.

63     F. L. Wright, *An Autobiography (Edition 2)*, p. 187.

64     Levine, *The Architecture of Frank Lloyd Wright*, p. 107.

65     By coincidence, presumably, 25 East Cedar Street was also less than a minute's walk from Joseph Silsbee's old Maple Street house.

66     Secrest, *Frank Lloyd Wright: A Biography*, p. 237.

67     F. L. Wright, *An Autobiography (Edition 2)*, p. 188.

68     Barney, *The Valley of the God Almighty Joneses*, p. 147.

69     Barney, *The Valley of the God Almighty Joneses*, p. 147.

70     McCrea, *Building Taliesin*, p. 206.

71     Emyr Humphreys, 'Taliesin and Frank Lloyd Wright', *Welsh Books and Writers* (October 1980).

# 15

# The Genius

## February 1920. Oak Park, Illinois

A short, dramatic report appeared in a local newspaper:

*Mrs. Anna Lloyd Wright and Dr. Emily Luff left on Thursday night for Vancouver and will sail from there to Tokio, Japan. Word was received several weeks ago that Frank Lloyd Wright, who is building the Royal Citadel in Tokio, was seriously ill of Japanese fever. No word has been received in the last two weeks on account of a broken cable.*[1]

Japanese fever, also known as Japanese encephalitis, is a mosquito-borne viral infection. In a few cases, as with Frank, it spreads to the brain and is life-threatening. He must have known this when he sent for his mother. As she boarded the *Empress of Japan*, Anna must have feared that he could already be dead.[2]

Frank had eventually been appointed to design the Imperial Hotel late in 1916. As he had anticipated, it consumed his working life. He spent three and a half of the following six years in Japan. Even when he was back at Taliesin, the hotel dominated his thoughts and efforts. The challenge, always, was to keep the trust and the confidence of his extremely sensitive Japanese clients. It had been a prolonged courtship.

His pursuit of Miriam Noel was very different, the work of a few heartbeats (Pl. 133). For many weeks after the Taliesin disaster Frank was encumbered by squalls of unsolicited mail. There was an occasional message of sympathy, but the majority were spiteful. The letters became less frequent as the months passed. This is, perhaps, why one letter caught his attention. He received it in early December 1914, just before he moved back from Chicago to Taliesin. 'One's sense of loss would be deeper as the holiday season approached', the writer advised him. She knew this well, as she had experienced a similar loss herself. She was appalled by the scale of the disaster he had endured, but she knew from her own experience that he could learn to forget, that he could take comfort from the certainty that the one he had lost had gone on to a place of bliss. It was signed 'Madame Noel'. He was intrigued. The letter had come from an address in Chicago. He replied with an invitation for Madame Noel to visit him at his small office in Orchestra Hall, and suddenly she was there, 'brilliant, sophisticated, as might be seen at a glance. She had evidently been very beautiful and was so distinguished by beauty still.' Frank was enraptured. ' "How do you like me?" she said .... "I've never seen anyone like you" I said honestly ... and here began the leading of the blind by the blind.'[3] Frank invited her to East Cedar Street for dinner. She was oblivious of the modesty of his little house, her eyes drawn to the oriental artworks that Frank had disposed, with his usual finesse, around his space. She thought it 'as rare and lovely as a miniature Palace of Baghdad!'[4] By Christmas Day they were a couple (Pl. 134).

Miriam was a woman of means. Her grandfather had been one of the wealthiest plantation owners in western Tennessee. She had been only fifteen years old when she married Emil Noel, the scion of another southern dynasty. Noel had brought her to Chicago, where he worked as an executive for the prestigious department store Marshall Field. She was forty-five, with three adult children, when she met Frank for the first time. Her marriage had ended long before and she had lived for years later in Paris, in pursuit of a doomed love affair. She had found comfort in her sculpture and her poetry, making a modest name for herself before the outbreak of war had forced her to leave. Frank found her beautiful, exotic and alluring.

Anna Lloyd Wright had railed against Frank's marriage to Kitty, but she had come to accept her as family, and to cherish her for her uncomplicated soul. Anna had warmed to Mamah too, for her intellect and her spiritual courage. Provided they respected her, she could accept the company of either of them. Miriam Noel she despised. Anna had the measure of her in a moment, and could only bite back on her disappointment that Frank had been so easily seduced. He had been traumatised: he was vulnerable. It was an excuse of sorts, but that made it all the more difficult to accept. The more she saw Miriam, the more she knew of her, the deeper her loathing became. Frank worked diligently to make sure they stayed well apart.

## December 1919. Chiyoda Ward, Tokyo, Japan

Frank arrived, with Miriam, in mid-December 1919, for his third long sojourn in Tokyo, to be confronted with a disaster. The annex of the old Imperial Hotel had burned to the ground a few days before. As the hotel struggled to preserve its business he was thrown immediately into the task of designing a temporary replacement. He proposed a very simple, flat-roofed structure which appears now to be a work of genuine proto-functionalism, the sort of thing that would soon emerge from the Bauhaus. It was not a path that he was to pursue, but at that time there were few, if any, other architects in the world who could have done it. The drawings were complete enough for building to begin within ten days. It

Pl. 133. Miriam Noel and Frank. Photographs from their 1919 passport application, travelling as husband and wife although not yet married.
US National Archive..

Pl. 134. 25 East Cedar Street, Chicago. This was Frank's rented home during the construction of Midway Gardens, to which he returned while Taliesin was being rebuilt. The house was recently demolished.
Photograph by Paul John Higgins.

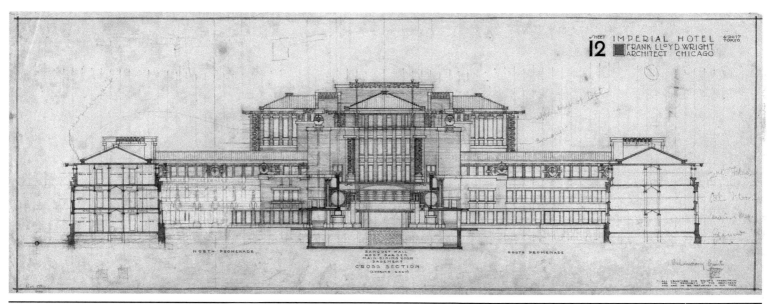

Fig. 15.1.   Imperial Hotel, Tokyo. Cross Section 1917. The tapering walls of the two wings added stability but also implied massive weight. FLWF/AAFAL.

was an exhausting achievement, which provoked unwelcome questions: why was it, then, that construction of the main hotel had itself only just begun, two years behind schedule?

Then came the onset of his fever, a heavy price for some relief from the scrutiny of his clients. After a two-week crossing, Anna arrived in Tokyo in early March to find Frank still badly debilitated, but apparently through the worst of it, sustained by the constant attention of hotel doctors. Miriam had found herself unable to support him and had responded only with afflictions of her own. As Frank observed later, Miriam

> had for many years been the victim of strange disturbances ... disabilities appeared to cling to her ... An unnatural exaggeration of emotional nature that grew more and more morbid ... something like a terrible struggle between two natures in her would seem to be going on within her all the time and tearing her to pieces.

The tremors, the pallor, self-pity, emotional torment: although he didn't quite spell it out, Frank was surely aware that Miriam was addicted to morphine. She was absent for the duration of Anna's visit. Her relationship with Frank may even have ended, temporarily.[5] It is easy to imagine her withdrawing into the shadows. Like anyone so afflicted, her addiction set the measure of her life. It might be said that Anna lived in similar bondage, in her case, a lifelong devotion to her son. There, in Tokyo, for a few precious weeks he could be dependent on his mother once again, a pleasure that they would both savour for the last time in their lives. By a remarkable effort, the new hotel annexe was complete before the end of April, to coincide with Frank's full recovery. He set up home in one of the bright corner suites. Anna returned to Oak Park in early June,[6] 'with a new lease on life', delighted to have received, 'many honours from [Frank's] distinguished Japanese friends'.[7]

The Imperial Hotel is an aberration, according to the critical and scholarly consensus (Fig. 15.1). A misjudgement, an extravagant expression of ideas that were barely current at its inception but which, in the course of a world war, became grossly anachronistic. It is true that time and events seemed to slip away from Frank's apprehension. His inherited pacifism accounts for part of it. He argued strenuously against America's participation in the war, and for the duration of the conflict his heart and his mind were invested in Japan, an ocean away from American preoccupations. He had been encouraged to 'retain the feeling and spirit of Japanese architecture and yet construct a building that would be comfortable according to the standards ... of travellers from around the world'. If he could do this, it would be 'an object lesson to Japanese and European and Americans alike.'[8]

There were other client expectations brought to bear. The design gives the unavoidable impression that Frank's clients believed that the proportions and forms of Beaux-Arts classicism still had international currency, which of course they did, and that the status of the hotel should be conveyed in that way, provided Frank gave it a suitably modern expression (Pl. 135). The Imperial was Frank's largest single building up to that time, and it is the one that appears most compromised.[9] Like Midway Gardens, it had a symmetrical plan that framed an ample rectangular site. Thereafter it is a challenge to identify the two as coeval works of the same designer. The Imperial seemed massively heavy, its masonry dense and furrowed. The steel and concrete frame was clad in dark orange brickwork, elaborate concrete façade details, and in sculptural features carved from a native stone known as *oya*. This stone was a compaction of volcanic ash and lava, more sponge-like than the coarsest travertine. Frank was attracted by its porous texture, and by the fact that local masons considered it worthless. The public spaces were engulfed in waves of *oya*-stone carving. Rhythm and pattern, Frank's touchstones, were all but lost within the elaborate folds of masonry, perhaps with intent to offset the neo-classical physiognomy of the whole (Pl. 136). As images began to appear in the American press critical reaction was ambivalent at best. In a few cases it was damning. An article entitled 'A Building That Is Wrong' in the journal *Architect and Engineer* described the hotel as a 'monstrous thing of

Pl. 135.   Imperial Hotel, Tokyo, completed 1923. This picture dates from the 1960s. The building was demolished in 1968.
From Film and Digital Times, courtesy of the Imperial Hotel, Tokyo.

Pl. 136.   Inside the lobby of the Imperial Hotel. This part of the hotel has been saved and reconstructed at the Meiji Mura open-air museum, Nagoya, Japan.

supposedly antique influence but really prehistoric in plan, design, structure, decoration and state of decay'. It was a structure that, 'should never have been built'.[10]

Frank appeared to have drifted away from his contemporaries, seemingly untethered from the certainties and securities that had bolstered him through his early career. Miriam's demands were destabilising. He was also, almost certainly still recovering from the trauma of 1914. He had never been further from his mother and from the Lloyd Joneses, so remote from his spiritual harbour, and he would never seem so lost again. Several pages of his autobiography are devoted to the story of the hotel, but there is barely a word to explain his architectural thinking. Instead, as his account has it, his entire approach to the design of the hotel was based on the avoidance of disaster, the violent disturbance of the earthquakes for which Tokyo was notorious, and the fires that would always follow. He devised a system of tapering shallow pile foundations and structural movement joints that, he believed, would enable the hotel to absorb ground movement and ride out tremors. He designed the structural frames of the bedroom wings so that all the floors were supported from the central corridor lines, cantilevered from the spine. He did this to ensure that the floors would not collapse if the outer walls were shifted by the heaving of the earth. The external walls themselves were tapered, made much thicker at the bottom, to improve their stability, which unavoidably contributed to the impression of heaviness. He took care that pipes and wires would not be broken in an earthquake by suspending them loosely within wide ducts that ran through the building. The large courtyard pools were also firefighting reservoirs. These innovations were expensive to develop and to build. The design of the foundations alone was a significant factor in the delays that led to the hotel being completed nearly three years behind schedule.

His years in Tokyo took a relentless toll. The combined strain of the project, the management of his team, his restless clients and Miriam, his turbulent partner, all contributing to the pressure. Early in 1921 he sent a poignant note to his daughter Catherine:

*It was a rather lonely Christmas and New Year ... of late years I rather dread it for lack of little children ... I am never very well here but my Welsh ire will wear through – never fear. My work is very hard – intense concentration and immense responsibility ... Once upon a time I could never strike the bottom of my physical resources – but now I find that every grey hair and fifty three years – indicate something that I will have to pay attention to.*[11]

The pressure was to get a great deal more intense, reaching its peak in April 1922, in the aftermath of a second fire, in which the whole of the old hotel itself burned to the ground, just as its annexe had done three years before. Only Frank's replacement annexe remained. The new hotel simply had to open, or the Imperial would go out of business. Eventually, in early July, the first guests were welcomed into their rooms in the north wing. Work on the south wing had been stalled to ensure that the north would be ready. Frank had had enough by then. He was assured that the south wing would be finished quickly. It was, after all, the mirror of the north. He was given a hero's send-off. Cheering workers lined the streets as he and Miriam were driven to their ship. They left Yokohama on 22 July 1922. Frank never saw Japan again, never saw his hotel complete.

The story of the Imperial Hotel has an extraordinary postscript. Completion of the south wing took over a year, not the few weeks that had been promised when Frank departed. The formal opening luncheon was arranged for 1 September, 1923. Just minutes before the function began, the ground began to shake.[12] The convulsions of The Great Kantō earthquake, over fifty aftershocks and the fires that followed destroyed almost the entire city (Pl. 137). Just a few structures prevailed, standing above the desolation. Most prominent among them was the Imperial Hotel. It became the centre for emergency relief, a shelter and canteen for thousands of desperate survivors. Many foreign embassies, whose buildings had been lost, decamped to the hotel, along with civil servants and newspaper companies, all struggling with the loss of communications. Several days passed before news of the earthquake reached America. Some of the first reports said that the hotel had been lost. Then, on 13 September he received a telegram from Baron Okura, the President of the hotel:

*HOTEL STANDS UNDAMAGED AS MONUMENT OF YOUR GENIUS. HUNDREDS OF HOMELESS PROVIDED BY PERFECTLY MAINTAINED SERVICE. CONGRATULATIONS. OKURA.*[13]

It was a remarkable story, one that seized the attention of the American press, bringing Frank's name to a wider audience than he had ever previously enjoyed. For once the reports put him in a positive light, without scandal or sarcasm, and, thanks to the Baron's telegram, the word 'genius' was liberally applied. A year before the earthquake Frank had written to Darwin Martin with a note of regret:

*My experience in building the great building in Japan has taught me how difficult [the] realisation of my ideal in Architecture is ... I realise now ... how rash I was to aim so high and how much my clients had to give in patience and forbearance to get things which, in the beginning, they did not really want.*

In the aftermath of the earthquake Frank began to see the whole, taxing experience in a different light. There were dividends that he had not anticipated. The arguments about style that had put him on the defensive seemed trivial compared to his technical accomplishment. It was the first indication that the American career, that he had virtually abandoned, might be revived. The scholar Kathryn Smith draws attention to a resonant episode from this time:

*After years of being ignored by the Chicagoan A. N. Marquis, the compiler of* Who's Who in America, *it was only a few months after the earthquake that Wright received notice*

Pl. 137. Destruction of the Great Kantō Earthquake of 1923, with the Imperial Hotel standing intact in the background.

*that he was to be included for the first time. On the form requesting information, in answer to the question 'What have you done that is worthy of special mention?' Wright wrote 'The Imperial Hotel of Tokyo, Japan and 176 other Buildings of Note.'*[14]

Frank's years of work on the Imperial Hotel bracketed a period of transformational events, and in the background the greatest of all transitions, the war in Europe. The *Wasmuth Portfolio* had been published in Berlin in 1911. In the few years before war broke out a generation of young European architects was exposed suddenly to Frank's work, to ideas that confounded their understanding of modern design. Le Corbusier recalled that he was 'totally unaware that there could be in America an architectural manifestation so purified and so innovative ... Although I knew almost nothing about Wright, I still remember clearly the shock that I felt at seeing these houses, spiritual and smiling.'[15] Another gifted young architect, the Viennese Richard Neutra, was equally impressed: 'whoever he was, Frank Lloyd Wright, the man far away, had done something momentous and rich in meaning.' Neutra and his countryman Rudolf Schindler both made their way to America, to work at Taliesin. Each would go on to write his own chapter in the history of American architecture, but it was Frank's vision that first inspired them. A young Czech, Antonin Raymond, arrived at Taliesin in the spring of 1916. He was astonished by the grandeur of the restored Taliesin, and perplexed by the fact that there seemed to be no building projects under way. With the Imperial Hotel commission still to be confirmed at that time, the only work in hand was the system-built housing for the Richards Company, a project that seemed to grow with the time that was available.[16]

Raymond walked across to Hillside, where he found the gracious school buildings in a ruinous state. Most of the windows were smashed and the library wrecked, books scattered across the floor.[17] It must have been hard for Frank's aunts to bear, a sadness sharpened by their nephew's inability to provide the modest pension that he had promised them. In May 1917, as Maginel recalled, just a few days after Frank returned to Taliesin from his first Imperial Hotel assignment, 'Aunt Jennie went back to the school, now desolate and deserted. She crept back into the great, echoing, empty building that had been her home, and up to her own old room. She died there, alone.'[18]

Without Jennie, Nell and Anna found it impossible to live with each other. Frank wrote to his sister Jane for her help to keep the two sisters apart. He complained that Aunt Nell's, 'misery pervades the whole house and her state is unbearable ... Mother herself is impossible to live with quietly but when Aunt Nell enters into the proposition then there is perfect hell.'[19] Frank's presence, and more so that of Miriam, exacerbated the tensions. Anna did move out of Taliesin to live with her daughter Jane, back at Anna's old house in Oak Park.[20] Nell died peacefully at Taliesin, in November 1919. Frank set off again, with Miriam, to Japan a

few weeks later, soon to be followed by his mother on her mercy trip.

It was an emptier Valley that Frank returned to in August 1922. All but two of Richard and Mallie's ten children, the Lloyd Joneses of the Valley, were gone. Thomas, John, Margaret, Mary and James had all died before 1914. The last years of Jenkin Lloyd Jones were consumed by the most worthy of his causes, the argument for peace. In 1915 he joined a large American delegation at an anti-war conference in neutral Stockholm. None of the warring nations was represented and the event was dismissed in the American press as a waste of time. Two years later, as America moved closer to joining the war, he went on a lecture tour, still making the case for peace in the face of increasing hostility. He used the pages of his journal Unity to encourage readers to join his campaign, without a care for the risk that he could be seen as a renegade. The postmaster of Chicago responded by blocking its distribution. Jenkin petitioned for the ban to be lifted, but for once in his life he had been silenced. He was at Tower Hill in September 1918 when the ban was eventually lifted. The war was approaching its end. Unity was free to be printed again. As Jenkin scanned the new edition he suffered a heart attack, and within a few hours he was gone.[21]

Uncle Enos, once the 'Youngest Son' was now the wary patriarch. He and his family still worked their small farm, just to the south-west of the empty school. Along The Valley at Taliesin, Frank's teulu dwindled in number as work on the hotel came to an end. Anna had moved back from Oak Park to Taliesin and had been comfortable there, running the household, but with Miriam's arrival emotions erupted again. Within days of their return Miriam fled to a hotel in Chicago. Frank wrote to his sister Jane, telling of his despair at Anna's insistence that she would not leave The Valley, nor ever live under the same roof as Miriam. He said that he had considered repairing Tan-y-Deri for Anna, so that she could live there, with a housemaid to care for her. Jane suggested, more pragmatically, that Anna would get better care at a good sanatorium. In this correspondence of late 1922, there is a mention again that Anna was struggling with 'falling sickness', epilepsy. Frank told his sister that their mother had 'just come through another [fit], sunk so low I thought she was dying and sent for Uncle Enos. Next day – yesterday – she sat up bright and dressed and snappy as ever.'[22]

Anna Lloyd Wright left Taliesin for the last time in September 1922. Miriam had forced an ultimatum and Frank had capitulated. She was transported, presumably against her will, to a care home on a lake shore in Oconomowoc, close to the mill where her beloved Uncle Jenkin had succumbed to malaria, when all she knew of America was forest and swamp.[23] She died there on 10 February 1923 (Pl. 138). Anna had always been radical, no less so than Frank. She was also always demanding and emotionally intense. She had been wounded by her experience of marriage, the injustice of the sacrifice that had been forced upon her. Even if her husband had been young and successful, she would still have despised his yoke. Separation saved her from despair. Although she could never be the woman she had once planned to become, she embraced her freedom and made the best of her time. Her obituary featured prominently in the *Oak Leaves* newspaper, affirmation that she was a more significant presence, a more impressive person in all respects, than has hitherto been acknowledged:

*Madame Wright lived almost half her eighty-four years in Oak Park and bore a prominent part in the social and intellectual life of the community. She was fortunate in her ancestry, for she came from a long line of teachers and preachers, leaders back in the Welsh homeland as well as in the new home in America ...[24] She herself possessed qualities of real leadership. Intellectually keen, independently critical but deeply appreciative of the best in literature, music, art and nature. Uncompromising in the search for truth, she found rare joy in sharing with others the treasures she found in books, in pictures, in melody and in her beloved outdoors ...*

*Her life was a busy one always and she found joyous reward for her early toil and sacrifice in the distinguished recognition which her talented children won later in the world of art. And she never failed them! ... If one seeks the underlying basis for*

Pl. 138. Anna's grave marker at Unity Chapel.
Photograph by Rob Barnett.

*this gallant spirit one finds what seems to be the keynote of her wonderful character – a faith so vivid, so rooted on a sense of God's nearness and His power ... that no burden could crush, no blow shatter that abiding faith.[25]*

Anna was buried in the yard of Unity Chapel two days after her death. Her coffin was carried to its resting place under the towering pine trees, 'by her nephews and her grandson',[26] while snow fell heavily over the gathering. Frank was two thousand miles away, in Los Angeles. He might have found it difficult to be a part of the ceremony anyway; it may have seemed too impersonal. A few years later, writing his autobiography, he cast his mind back to Mamah's burial, the complex emotions that he struggled with. Similar feelings surely resurfaced when he thought about his mother's interment. They would have helped to reconcile him with his absence: 'I felt that a funeral service could only be a mockery. The undertaker's offices – too, his vulgar casket – seemed to me profane ... I wanted them to leave me there alone ... to fill the grave myself.'

It was a time of transition. In November 1922, after a decade of hesitation, Catherine Wright had accepted a divorce. Robert, the youngest of Catherine and Frank's six children, was nineteen years old. It was time to get on with life. Exactly a year later, the minimum allowed by law, Frank and Miriam were married secretly, on a bridge above the Wisconsin River, close to Taliesin. Frank hoped that it might settle the disturbances, but then, before the end of spring, Miriam had fled, away from Taliesin, away from Frank. With half of Frank's assets now legally hers, she left him, as Anna had been sure she would. Frank found out later that she had gone to Los Angeles, but by then he had realised that life seemed easier without her.[27]

## Summer 1924. Griffiths Sub-Division, Los Angeles

Frank's eldest son, Lloyd, shaded by a canvas awning from the burning sun, surveyed a scene of biblical industry. Labourers toiled with grit from the barren slope, shovelled it through screens and sprinkled it with cement and water then packed the mix into moulds. Another group, close by, loosened the stiffened compound from boxes, filled minutes earlier, and set the fresh blocks out to cure in the sun (Pl. 139). Concrete blocks were approaching ubiquity in American building at the time, but it was still a novel technology.[28] Frank was determined to push it as far as it could go. His concrete 'textile-blocks' were slender, gorgeously patterned, perforated and designed to be stitched together within the grid of interwoven steel wires that gave them their name. His clients, Charles and Mabel Ennis, were wealthy, even by Los Angeles standards. Charles had made his fortune selling affordable menswear to legions of Hollywood arrivistes. From their ledge below Griffiths Park, the Ennises could look down on the sprawl of Hollywood, and just a mile to the south, rising above the suburbs, the prominence of Olive Hill and the faint outline of the neo-Mayan palace, the Hollyhock House, that Frank had built for Aline Barnsdall. It was something similar that they had in mind. They had

also seen the little houses that he was building for John Storer and Sam Freeman, both using the textile blocks. Frank had convinced them, on one of the few occasions they had actually met him, that he could give them a home as stately as the Hollyhock House, but made from the same patterned blocks. When the drawings came through they loved them (Pl. 140).

When Frank was young he'd had an abundance of certainty, the pathway to Truth had been clear to him. He needed to find a way back to it. He had repaired his friendship with Louis Sullivan, found his old master penniless and dying, and stayed with him until the end, in the spring of 1924. After Mamah, after his time in Japan; after Miriam, after the war, now with his mother gone, and his beloved mentor too, the world was a different place. In Los Angeles, Aline Barnsdall, the oil baron's daughter, had become resentful. There had been other clients who had lost faith in him, some who, he knew, disliked him. But she had deserved better. Her ideas were inspirational, an artistic commune, a bulwark of pure creativity in the heart of the gimcrack city. She had trusted him completely, allowed him absolute freedom; but he was distracted. Between Tokyo and Taliesin he couldn't bring his mind to bear on Hollywood, and in the end she had lost patience with him. She was so disillusioned that she soon moved out of her Hollyhock House, leaving Olive Hill as a gift to the city (Pl. 141).

After his time working on the Wasmuth publication with his father, Lloyd had roamed Europe and then America for a few years, switching between design companies. Then, in 1916, he started a landscape design business from an office in downtown Los Angeles. In the early 1920s, he worked hard to revive his father's fortunes. Despite the disappointment with Aline Barnsdall, Lloyd assured his father that there were still rich opportunities for him in southern California. The city had the freedom and creative energy of Chicago in the 1880s, and it was growing just as vigorously. Lloyd gravitated towards the bohemian community of the city, the creative milieu which fed the growing film industry. Like his father he was drawn to other artists, as they were to him, the more radical the better. One of them was Miriam Lerner, a charismatic organiser best known today as the muse of

Edward Weston, the great photographer. She was a writer and activist in the Young People's Socialist League, and she was private secretary to the millionaire Wisconsinite Edward Doheny, the first man to strike oil in Los Angeles. Lerner was adept at directing Doheny's patronage, often finding jobs on his estate for friends in need.[29]

Lloyd's encouragement was effective. In 1922, almost as soon as he had returned from Japan, Frank registered a downtown office, using Lloyd's address in the Homer Laughlin Building on South Broadway.[30] He then moved south-west to set up home at a run-down apartment on the corner of Fountain and Harper Avenues in West Hollywood, where he began to work on a spectacular residential development for Edward Doheny's estate at Franklin Canyon, north of Beverly Hills[31] The work was almost certainly speculative, but Lloyd's connection with Miriam Lerner meant there was a chance it could be seen by the famous oilman. Perhaps, more importantly, it gave Frank a platform from which to develop an idea which could re-establish him at the forefront of American architecture. It was an idea that had taken shape in his mind over several years, but which he now believed would be the basis of an American architecture for the twentieth century, rooted in the distinctive landscape of the Golden Coast.

The hillside at the Doheny Ranch was steep and sliced by deep arroyos. Frank's houses were set into the creases, bridging the gaps, bedded among treetops like a vision of Himalayan temples. These spectacular structures were built entirely out of his textile blocks, each house with its own unique pattern.[32] Frank had used patterned concrete slabs first at Midway Gardens, at a time of great optimism when new ideas flowed in torrents. In 1921 he had designed a warehouse for a wholesaler named A. D. German. It was built in Richland Center, Wisconsin, the unlikely town of Frank's birth. It seems apposite that it is among the most incongruous of his buildings (Pl. 142). Since his move to The Valley he had bought fuel and grain from German's company, but rarely paid for it. German had agreed to waive the debt in exchange for a design from Frank. The warehouse is an imposing brickwork box, crowned by a bulging frieze of

Pl. 139. Manufacturing the concrete blocks for the Charles Ennis House, Los Angeles 1924. FLWF/AAFAL.

patterned concrete blocks. The contrast of the two layers, plain below with patterned projections above, shows the influence of Mayan building forms as freely as they were expressed in the Hollyhock House, but much closer to Canada than to Mexico.[33]

It is not known if Edward Doheny ever did see Frank's visionary proposal for Franklin Canyon. Nothing seemed to come of it directly, other than the distillation of his new ideas. His first new project in Los Angeles came from another old client. He had built a house for George and Alice Millard in Highland Park, north of Chicago, in 1906. The Millards moved to California when George retired from his bookshop. George died in 1918, leaving Alice, who was much younger,

Pl. 140. One of Frank's early perspective drawings of the Ennis House. Griffiths Sub-Division, Los Angeles, 1924. FLWF/AAFAL.

to build her own rare book business in Pasadena. By the time she reconnected with Frank she was already established among the leading dealers in the region. 'I was proud', Frank wrote, 'now to have a client survive the first house and ask me to build a second.'[34] She had bought a flat plot of land. Frank persuaded her to sell it and instead purchase a wooded ravine in the Arroyo Seco neighbourhood of Pasadena. He designed her house to span the ravine. It was intricately designed, beautifully efficient in its organisation, deceptively simple, but in reality highly complex (Pl. 143). This was inevitable given the need for every surface, inside and out, to be assembled from a grid of sixteen-inch-square

blocks. It was while the Millard Residence, 'La Miniatura', was being built that Frank's enthusiasm for Los Angeles was at its brightest. For the first few months of construction he was on site every day, monitoring progress, supervising the concrete mix, and checking the quality of the blocks as they came out of the wooden moulds. He was elated to be able to 'take that despised outcast of the building industry – the concrete block [and] make it live as a thing of beauty'.[35]

Frank had been fascinated since the earliest stage of his career with the idea of the mass-produced house. He believed in the democratisation of his art; it was consistent with his radical ideals. Many of his wealthiest clients had made their fortunes from the manufacture of products that were designed just once. In the early days he had hoped to sell his low-cost house designs through the *Ladies Home Journal*. The 'American System Built Homes' that he had designed for Arthur Richards had resulted in only thirteen complete houses, not the thousands that they had expected. It's not difficult to see, now, that they were too far ahead of their time. The textile blocks had more promise as a construction system. Once it was perfected he could spread the system across the nation. Simple, small, low-cost homes, modern and suitable for mass production, that was where his future lay: 'Other buildings sprang full formed into my mind from this humble beginning. They arose in bewildering variety and peerless beauty ... Standardisation was the soul of the machine, and here I was, the Weaver, taking it as a principle and knitting a great future with it.'[36] At the same time, though, he could not help but become absorbed in the intricate spatial puzzle, the complexity of the volumes, all the qualities that made his architecture so special. 'La Miniatura' could never be simple or cost-effective. It was the opposite, something so novel and so complicated that, at times, it seemed unbuildable.

As work progressed he found that he had to limit his time on site, and in his absence progress faltered. In his autobiography Frank recalled, with familiar bitterness, the mendacity of the builder. It was the builder who was to blame for the delays and the punishing cost overruns. Frank had to put thousands of his own dollars in to make sure that his crucial relaunch project was properly completed. Builders came and went, the quality of the work suffered. Eventually it was finished, compromises grudgingly accepted by the architect, but with a relieved and happy client. Then within a few months of its overdue completion, the 'dry' arroyo beneath the house was flushed by floodwater which filled the basement. Fortunately Alice Millard stored her books on the top floor. Unfortunately, then the roof leaked. She went over Frank's head to get it fixed. Despite the setbacks Alice Millard was enraptured by her house, as were her many friends and clients. It became the bohemian salon that she had dreamed of. Before 'La Miniatura' was completed,

Pl. 141. Hollyhock House, Los Angeles, 1922, photographed soon after completion. Photograph by Julius Shulman, courtesy of the Getty Research Institute.

Pl. 142. A.D. German Warehouse, Richland Centre, Wisconsin, 1921. 'Mayan Revival' in the north west. Photograph by Lowell Boileau/CC-SA 3.0.

didn't prevent him from becoming more ambitious with the architecture. It was as if the lessons could not be learned. Costs overran, clients became agitated, Frank's enjoyment waned. He began to spend less time in Los Angeles and more at Taliesin, leaving Lloyd to deal with the crises. For Lloyd the experience became increasingly difficult and thankless as the clients lost faith in him, wanting only to deal with his absent father. The commission for the Charles Ennis House came while there were still major issues to resolve on the Freeman and Storer houses. The much larger scale of the Ennis brief, and the superb cliffside site, dispelled technical reservations. As Lloyd watched the block production on that hot afternoon in the summer of 1924, with the project already mired in problems, he must have known that his father's Los Angeles venture was coming to an end. Frank wrote to Lloyd from Taliesin on 15 September: 'work is not so far forward as I imagined. But I've no doubt you are doing your best and that is good ... The Ennis work looks backward. How is it possible that the surveys on that work and on Freeman should have been so far out?' Mrs Ennis had added to the disruption at the site, and Lloyd had tried to prevent her from visiting. Frank advised:

> *To stave her off would only arouse her suspicions and be bad for the result ... She and he are in the right spirit, I am sure. I shall write to them to stick close to you ... Freeman et al are the usual difficulties, no more. Do not chafe too much, the stake is high for which you are playing.*

Frank was commissioned to make two similar houses, like the first one, both small and ornate with grandiose ambitions. The houses for John Storer (Pl. 144) and Samuel Freeman (Pl. 145) were in the Hollywood Hills, built almost simultaneously, each with its own block pattern.

Frank had come to realise that the success of the process was entirely dependent on its precision: small dimensional slips would accumulate into irresolvable misalignments, and sometimes to major rebuilding, but this

He then revealed that his work prospects were meagre: 'there is nothing immediate – all is on long lines, with "cash" as scarce as ever, only more so ... I have less than none by forty-seven thousand dollars.' It was an enormous debt, made worse by his having to contribute to the cost of Alice Millard's house. His home life was equally impoverished: 'I am learning to be alone by degrees. It is a long time since anything warm and human has transpired in my life with M. [Miriam]. She left on May 5th but for years before that really.'[37]

By virtue of its many appearances in films, the Ennis house is the best known of the four Los Angeles textile-block houses (Pl. 146). At its completion it was derided by critics for promoting concrete as a suitable material for a prestigious residence. Others disparaged it for its conspicuous countenance, but it troubled critics most because it, and the other textile-block houses, seemed unrelated to anything in the continuum of mainstream western architecture. It is generally referred to now as an example of the 'Mayan Revival' style, a manner that was only identified retrospectively, years later, and which Frank, through these projects, was responsible for initiating. But while the block pattern of the Ennis house recalls Mayan stone patterns like those at Mitla in Oaxaca, for example, the overall massing of the house has a different meso-American provenance, in the forms of the adobe settlements of the Taos Pueblo Indians of New Mexico. The Ennis house can appear either ancient, contemporary or wildly futuristic, and does so in the various Hollywood films in which it has featured. It is flawed, but genuinely thrilling, a building that exerts an overpowering attractive force. It is impossible to be near to it without feeling a fierce desire to be inside, looking out, and when you are inside, it is everything that one can imagine it should be (Pl. 147).

Frank wrote to the Ennises as he promised Lloyd he would:

> *The time is approaching when things look darkest, in the building of a building. It is about now that you need your architect's counsel and moral support and I am sorry not to give it in person ... Don't let any influences or uneasiness of your own mind as to costs or conduct alienate you from Lloyd or Lloyd from you ... You see, the final result is going to stand on that hill a hundred years or more. Long after we are all gone, it will be pointed out as the Ennis house and pilgrimages will be made to it by lovers of the beautiful.*[38]

Pl. 144.  John Storer House, Los Angeles, 1923
Los Angeles/CC-SA 3.0.

Pl. 145.  Samuel Freeman House, Los Angeles 1923.
Photograph Julius Shulman, courtesy of the Getty Research Institute.

Pl. 146. Charles Ennis House, Los Angeles, 1924.

Pl. 147. Interior of the Charles Ennis House following its 2015 restoration.

The letter was not successful. Soon afterwards, once the windows were installed – the last stained-glass windows in any of Frank's buildings – the Ennises terminated Frank's services, and Lloyd's too. They brought other designers, 'inferior desecrators' as Frank, no doubt, thought of them, to complete the work.

Frank had thought that his first career had come to a close in 1910, when he had abandoned his family to be with Mamah Borthwick. Then, after the tragedy of August 1914, he endured what must have seemed a severe resetting of his commitment and his principles, the traumatic interlude that preceded his years in Japan. While he was committed to the Tokyo project, the western world experienced its own traumatic reset, leaving Frank, on his return to America, unsure of his next steps. The enterprise in Los Angeles had promised, at first, to be his way forward, but he had put all his energy into his experimental concrete block technique which, while being spectacularly beautiful, was ultimately too impractical and too strange for the market he had hoped to seduce. When he wrote to Lloyd in September 1924 he had complained that all his projects were 'on long lines', that there was 'nothing immediate' for him to look forward to. This was the real conclusion of his first architectural career. He was fifty-seven years old. Over the course of the next ten years he completed only two built projects for clients other than himself. The first, in 1926, was the lifeline from his most loyal supporter, Darwin Martin, the summerhouse 'Graycliff' on the Lake Erie shore. The second, was 'Westhope', a vast, textile block mansion situated outside Tulsa, Oklahoma, designed in 1929, at the depth of the Great Depression (Pl. 148).

The commission was a hand-out from his faithful cousin Richard Lloyd Jones, by then the wealthy proprietor of the *Tulsa Tribune*. It was the troublesome flat roof of Westhope that provided one of the best-known Frank Lloyd Wright anecdotes. When, after repeated relaying, water still found its way through the roof to drip into his study, Dickie made an angry telephone call to his cousin, 'Dammit Frank, it's leaking onto my desk!' Frank's solution: 'Richard, why don't you move your desk?'[39]

# 30 November 1924. Congress Hotel, Chicago

Frank had put his Los Angeles experiment behind him. He was in Chicago alone, to pursue a huge commission, his biggest yet, a towering office complex for the National Life Insurance Company (Fig 15.2). He had told the press that he intended to move back to the city and that commercial architecture was to be his future specialism. He had been staying at the Congress for a few weeks, so he would be seen about town. At the same time, he admitted later, he felt, 'lower down in my estimation than I had ever been'.[40] The cause of his anguish was loneliness. No woman at his side, no mother to protect him, he had never felt so vulnerable. The quiet of a Sunday afternoon was interrupted by a knock on the door. An old acquaintance, an artist named Jerry Blum, had arrived unexpectedly. They hadn't seen each other in ten years, not since Blum had worked on the murals at Midway Gardens. Blum was compelling and slightly dangerous – a firework of a man. At that moment he was just the company that Frank needed. Blum told Frank that they should go to the Eighth Street Theatre. It was only a few minutes' walk away, and he had two tickets for the matinée, a rare performance by the great dancer Tamara Karsavina. The show was sold out. Frank was intrigued when Blum, the struggling artist, led them to seats in a private box. The stage and the packed stalls were spread out below them. Frank took a seat at the end of the box. There was a third seat, unoccupied, at the other end, apparently the only free seat in the house. Karsavina's performance was the third piece in the show. She had just begun to dance when an usher quietly pulled back the box curtain and showed a young woman to the empty seat. Frank remembered the moment with vivid clarity, how he found himself 'losing all interest in the stage. Although I can perfectly see Karsavina poised on one toe as she stood when the gentle stranger entered the box and my life'.[41] The stranger was Olgivanna Hinzenberg (Pl. 149). Frank recalled that Jerry Blum tried to make small talk with her, drawing her into a whispered conversation about Karsavina's brilliance. Frank intended his retort to be

Pl. 148. 'Westhope', Tulsa, Oklahoma, the Richard Lloyd Jones residence. It was the last house to be built in textile block.

provocative, a bit of harmless bombast. He had no idea how much more meaningful it would seem to the mysterious woman, 'No, Karsavina won't do. She's dead. They are all dead', he added, looking down at the audience, 'the dead dancing to the dead.'

For seven years before her first meeting with Frank, Olgivanna's life had been devoted to the Armenian mystic, George Gurdjieff (Pl. 150). For most of those years she had lived with him in his Parisian commune. She was married with a young daughter, Svetlana, but estranged from her husband. Olgivanna was only twenty-six years old. Gurdjieff's message, delivered always with a punishing insistence, was that humanity was trapped in a state of semi-consciousness, and that its true, higher state could only be reached through arduous physical and mental discipline, a

Fig. 15.2. Frank's spectacular proposal for the National Life Insurance Building,
Chicago 1924.
FLWF/AAFAL.

*Starved – for poetry – that was it, the best in me for years
and years wasted – starved! This strange chance meeting,
was it … poetry?*

The meeting was more 'strange', and less 'chance', than
Frank imagined. Years later Olgivanna admitted she had
known Jerry Blum before that afternoon at the theatre, that
he had been part of Gurdjieff's circle in New York. This can
mean only one thing: that her meeting with Frank had been
orchestrated. The circumstances point to the possibility that
she and Blum were acting on Gurdjieff's behalf, and that their
objective was to deliver Taliesin to Gurdjieff, for it to become
his American base. When he had told the Chicago papers
that his future lay back in the city, Frank had, inadvertently,
given impetus to the mystic's property ambitions.[43] In
reality, Frank's public statement was made for one reason
only: to secure the National Life Insurance project. He hadn't
intended to give up Taliesin, and he never would. Fate –
'poetry' – made its intervention anyway, on Frank's behalf
that afternoon. Barely a month later Olgivanna was settled
with him at Taliesin. He would never be lonely again.

## 20 April 1925. Taliesin, The Valley, Wyoming Township, Wisconsin

Daylight had faded, the sky over The Valley was covered
by the thick cloud of a looming storm. Just a few months
into their new life, Frank and Olgivanna were dining
together in a small, detached pavilion that he had built on
the slope above Taliesin. His housekeeper excused herself
for the interruption, but told Frank that the call-buzzer
in his bedroom had been ringing for twenty minutes,
even though the room was empty. Frank went down to
investigate. He must have smelled smoke as he opened
the door: he shouted for buckets. He found the bed and
curtains smouldering and flames licking up from the switch
box on the wall. Help came quickly and the fire in the room
was soon extinguished. Then there was the baleful snap of
burning timbers overhead, somewhere in the void above the

'war against sleep'.[42] Frank's casual judgement of the dancer
and her audience had struck a deep chord,

*A quick comprehending glance from the young Frenchwoman
… The glance went home: a strange elation stole over me.
Suddenly in my unhappy state something cleared up …*

ceiling, and within a minute the roof of the house was well ablaze, fanned by a blustery wind.

Around twenty minutes after it started a cloudburst ended the fire. By then the whole of the 'living part' of the house had been burned to the ground, again. Mercifully, this time no one had been harmed. Frank noticed a portentous pattern: the first Taliesin had been built for Mamah and had died with her. The second had been Miriam's home. Now, for Olgivanna, he had to build it again. He wondered if higher forces were really at work.

*No doubt Isaiah still stood there in the storms that muttered, rolled and broke again ... The lightning often played and crashed above us ... [Was] Isaiah, with eyes aslant where the beautiful would show its face ... waiting there behind the hills to strike, should life at Taliesin rise from its ashes a third time?*

He imagined the two sages contesting his spirit:

*Isaiah is the vengeful prophet of an antique wrath. I say Taliesin is a nobler prophet, not afraid of him. The ancient Druid Bard sang and forever sings of merciful beauty. Wherever beauty is, there Taliesin is singing in praise of the flower that fadeth, the grass that withereth. Taliesin still loves and trusts ... man.*

Isaiah was the judgemental rigour of his grandfather, Richard Lloyd Jones, and of all of the Lloyd Joneses, while Taliesin embodied the inspirational, uplifting aspects of their Welshness and their Unitarianism. Frank felt the dual forces struggling to control his own spirit. There could be only one winner: 'Taliesin the Celt humbly declares ... an architecture on this soil for a conscious United States of America.'[44]

Frank was energised by the prospect of rebuilding again. On this occasion the house had been insured, sufficient to cover most of the rebuilding, but there was still a severe loss to endure. His fees from the Imperial

Pl. 149. Olgivanna Hinzenberg in 1924, the year that Frank met her. From the *Daily Independent* of Helena, Montana, 2 October 1926.

Hotel had been invested in a superb collection of sculpture, tapestry and painted screens, by his estimation worth half a million dollars. They had all been lost, uninsured. He had

Pl. 150.  Georges Gurdjieff, Olgivanna's ostensible puppet-master.

committed to his needs. Anna's death had left him adrift, but it was in Olgivanna's character to be both wife and guardian. She filled the void that Anna had left. She gave him new direction and purpose, and he began to feel, once again, that anything was possible. In the short term, however, Olgivanna's presence created only turmoil. The fire may have been a spiritual restitution, who could say? But her arrival certainly triggered the cascade of events that led them to the cells of Hennepin County Jail in the late summer of the following year, the episode with which this particular version of Frank's story began. The notoriety was damaging. His spirit may have been restored, but the architectural practice which he had worked so hard to rekindle seemed finally to sputter out.

## 29 March 1931. Taliesin, The Valley, Wyoming Township, Wisconsin

A letter arrived, sent by Frank's friend and ally, the architectural critic Lewis Mumford. Many artists would have received it with great pleasure, but Frank read it with increasing despondency. The Museum of Modern Art in New York was planning an exhibition on modern architecture, and they wanted Frank to be part of it. The exhibition would introduce America to the 'New Pioneers' of European design and to some of the young architects in America who were embracing their new, modern style. The curators were the young architectural critic, Henry-Russell Hitchcock, and a well-connected, even younger Harvard graduate named Philip Johnson. Frank knew of Hitchcock. His reputation was built on his first book, published two years before, an acclaimed survey of western architecture from the Romantic era to the modern day. It included an essay about Frank Lloyd Wright in which every acknowledgement of his importance seemed to be qualified by harsh critical judgement. It concluded in double-edged terms: 'Too much has been set down in negative criticism. It remains to be said ... that he is, without qualification ... the greatest American architect of the first quarter of the twentieth century.'[46] 'Yesterday's Man' in other words, and, to make matters worse, of those that now led the way 'the most important is surely the Austrian

been waiting for the right time to sell, knowing it would yield enough to clear his debts, in fact enough to set himself up for years to come. That comforting prospect was gone.[45] His future would not be easy, but with Olgivanna by his side he was ready for it. When he recalled the aftermath of the second fire, he declared his confidence in their future together in unexpectedly poetic terms, a Druidic Triad of his own making, posed as a challenge to himself:

> Any man has the right to three things if he
> is honest with all three. Had I been, could I
> be, honest with them all?
> Honest with the man's life?
> The man's work?
> The man's love?

In her time with Gurdjieff, Olgivanna had become accustomed to living a life of devotion. Now Frank had become the subject of her allegiance. Only Frank's mother had ever been so

R. J. Neutra in Los Angeles ... [whose work] displayed ... an integrity of aesthetic expression only found in the best work of Wright.'[47] Neutra had been his draughtsman only a few years before! Frank's first instinct was to have nothing to do with the exhibition, but it was clear that Lewis Mumford had worked hard on his behalf to persuade the young curators that he should not be left out.

It would be a moment of reckoning for Frank. He had enjoyed the reflective discourse of his Princeton lectures, but his plans for the Taliesin Fellowship were still nebulous. He was in the process of finalising the graphic design of his autobiography.[48] It could seem that he was putting his affairs in order, signing off his architectural career. He was sixty-four years old. He had, 'never thought of himself as anything other than the most advanced and accomplished architect in the world'.[49] But as one barren year followed another, he had to face up to the fact that a younger generation of European designers had taken the lead, and that he could soon be consigned to history. If his place in the forthcoming exhibition was to be that of a historic precursor it might as well be his swansong. In which case, wouldn't it be better to decline? But if he refused to take part, would that not also set him back?

In July 1931 he gave a talk to the Michigan Society of Architects in which he said: 'I believe that Le Corbusier and the group around him are extremely useful ... extremely valuable, especially, as an enemy.'[50] By the time he gave this talk he had begun working on a project that he called 'House on the Mesa', with the intention that it would be the centrepiece of his display at the Museum of Modern Art (Pl. 151). It was a conceptual design for a palatial house, set high on the Colorado Plateau. It bore features he was known for – textile block, spreading cantilevers – but within a formal arrangement that had no precedent in his previous work. White, orthogonal pavilions with flat roofs, linked to a spinal loggia 300 feet long. The distinctive Wrightian features were in the detail, but there was no mistaking the manner of the whole. It would be as 'modern' as anything that Hitchcock's 'New Pioneers' had to show.[51]

With only a month to go before the opening Frank was given the details of the other presentations. It was only

Pl. 151. 'House on the Mesa', 1932. The model used as the centrepiece of Frank's presentation at the 'Modern Architecture: International Exhibition'.
Photograph by Hedrich-Blessing, from *Architectural Forum* vol. 68 no. 1, January, 1938.

then, it appears, that he found out his work was to be mounted alongside projects by Richard Neutra and the New Yorker Raymond Hood.[52] Since Neutra had been championed by Hitchcock at Frank's expense, Frank couldn't help but think of his ex-draughtsman as another 'enemy'. Hood was worse: a year earlier he had been appointed as one of the architectural selectors for the Chicago World's Fair of 1933. Frank had every right to be involved, but Hood had rejected him for being 'too much of an individualist'.[53] Another enemy, and to make matters worse, anything good that either Hood or Neutra had done had been appropriated from him![54] He sent a telegram to Philip Johnson, announcing his intention to withdraw: 'My way has been too long and too lonely to make a belated bow as a modern architect in company with a self-advertising amateur and a high-powered salesman.' He was referring to Neutra and Hood.[55] Mumford was not prepared to let him go. He understood Frank as well as anyone did. His telegraphed reply was perfectly pitched, 'We need you and cannot do without you. Your withdrawal will be used by that low rascal Hood to his own glory and advantage. As for company, there is no more honourable position than to be crucified between two thieves.'

Frank relented.[56] He played his part in the exhibition, but the outcome justified his anxieties. According to the catalogue it was Neutra who had designed 'without question stylistically the most advanced house to be built in America since the war', and it was the young Austrian that received the acclaim of the press. As for Frank, Hitchcock's view was that 'America need not develop entirely in the footsteps of her great individual genius ... The day of the lone pioneer is past ... Throughout the world there are others beside Wright to lead the way toward the future.'[57]

The experience of the first 'Modern Architecture' exhibition may have been uncomfortable, but Frank emerged from it with an invigorated, more pragmatic spirit. Since his beginning he had scoured primitive sources for his ideas, returning repeatedly to Asian, meso-American and classical paradigms, drawing deeply from the wellspring of his ancestral faith. After 1932 he opened his imagination to new concepts, became more openly receptive to the shapes and lines of the late Machine Age, even to the stark abstraction of his modernist 'enemies'. He would dismiss them as thin imitators of his original ideas, he would denounce them for avoiding the meaningful aspects of nature and spirituality, but by engaging with their approach he believed that he would be able to steer 'modern architecture' back to his own, true course. As Vincent Scully observed, he 'never admitted such receptivity, quite the contrary, but it would seem to have existed in fact, and its effect was to help him – as he had helped the Europeans earlier – to clarify and redirect his design.'[58] Within four years Frank would confound them all. The late 1930s would become an era of great achievement, a high point to exceed the peak of his Oak Park years. His place, as an 'individual genius' at the vanguard of his profession, would not be questioned again.

## 4 June 1937. 16th and Howe Street, Racine South, Wisconsin

Frank had already won the day, there was a chance, now, for him to make a real event of it. To the reporter at the *Racine Journal Times* Frank was 'Wisconsin's famous architect'. He was not yet the 'Greatest in the World'; that would come just

Pl. 152. Testing of the column for the Johnson Wax Administration Building, June 1937. Frank in standing to the right. His client, Hib Johnson, is second from right.
Photograph courtesy of S. C. Johnson & Son Inc.

a year later, but he strode across the broken ground of the building site with the bearing of a champion, into the shade of the spreading column, and rapped the stem firmly with his cane. The concrete structure around which the crowd was gathered was like nothing any of them had seen. A slender pillar two storeys high that tapered slightly outwards towards its head, surmounted by a broad disc, almost as wide as the column was tall (Pl. 152). To the newspaper men it resembled a golf-tee, but Frank thought of it in botanical terms, with a stem, calyx and petal.[59] The petal was the delicate, spreading disc at the crown. He needed a building permit from the Wisconsin Industrial Commission: they were not inclined to give him one, and it was holding up progress. S. C. Johnson & Sons Incorporated – 'Johnson Wax' – was one of the largest employers in the city of Racine. There had been very few larger projects in Frank's long history. There was so much to lose, but still he took quite startling risks. He got on the wrong side of the Commissioners from the beginning. It was Wisconsin, so he proposed 'dry wall' foundations, the frost-proof substructure that he had learned from David Timothy. There was nothing like it in 'the code', and the plans were rejected. Frank's response was to propose empirical testing. He would build and test a mock-up of every novel element, and the Commissioners would be invited to witness the outcome.[60] 'Here is the fatal weakness of Democracy: the bureaucrat', Frank wrote later; '[it] does not lie in ... civil disobedience or anything like that. It lies in this dumb, sheep like submission to Authority.' Unitarian; Jacobin. Truth Against the World.[61]

The supremely elegant columns of the Johnson Wax Administration Building were only nine inches wide at the base. The code of the Wisconsin Industrial Commission insisted that a column of that width could be no more than six feet high. Frank's was four times that height and it was designed to carry six tons. The bureaucrats wanted to see it carry twelve. They expected the slender stem to buckle; they hoped to see it snap. The day had begun chilly and overcast. Olgivanna, Frank and his team from Taliesin sat with Hib Johnson, their client. The group from the Commission kept a distance as the sandbags were hoisted up. The sun was high by the time they had six tons in place. There was no hint of fragility, the first milestone had been reached with ease. The loading went on, the pile of sandbags grew wider and higher. Gradually a crowd had gathered to watch. At twelve tons the work ceased and a close inspection was made through field glasses for any sign of cracks. Nothing. It was for the pleasure of the onlookers that Frank made the show of striking it with his cane.[62] The Commissioners might have concealed a guilty wish that it would bury him, but the stem was quite sound. A decision was made to keep on with the loading until, after sundown, it had become impossible to

Pl. 153.  Gateway to the Johnson Wax Administration Building, Racine, Wisconsin, 1939.
Photograph Carol Highsmith / LOC.

add more without ballast tipping over the edge. 'The sight was incredible', Frank recalled, 'The police had taken charge and roped the populace from the vicinity of that heroic, slender stem, standing up there ... straight and true until sixty tons ... were on top.' It had to be brought to an end. Frank told the builders to pull one of the props away. As the column tipped the disc shattered and broke at the 'calyx'. The stem fell to the side, still intact. 'The commissioners, saying nothing, disappeared. Their silence gave consent.'[63]

Fleets of tourist coaches began to arrive at the new Administration Building months before its opening. Frank had been sure they would. The $200,000 office building he'd originally been asked for had become a model complex of work and welfare at fifteen times the price. He told his embarrassed client that the publicity would far outweigh the overspend. Johnson, before long, conceded the point. From a distance Johnson Wax has the squat mass of a block-house (Pl. 153). Skimming horizontals and curved edges soften the rigorous outline and sweep visitors, in their vehicles, into a low undercroft, an ethereal space with a ceiling sculpted in a pattern of deep concavities, lifted on tapering, ribbed columns. The car park alone is among the more remarkable modern structures in concrete. The entrance is a plane of clear glass, a concession to corporate modernism. Inside seems another world. Frank once said it was his 'most organic' building, which helps to clarify one of the more significant meanings of this elastic term. He meant that every part of it can be understood as both a functional element and as a piece of a complex, entirely integrated sculptural whole. It is the purest architecture, yet it seems as remote from a conventional building as a cave or a forest. The columns recall the forms of lily pads or trees, with their crowns almost touching overhead. Diffuse daylight floods into the room through prismatic glass in the spaces between. It is the quality of the light that is most arresting. The room is two storeys high, no more lofty than a school hall, but it has an extraordinary effect on the senses: you feel small but also elated. Your spirits soar, as if in the wilds of nature on a warm and peaceful day (Pl. 154).

Pl. 154.  The Great Workroom of the Johnson Wax Administration Building, Racine, Wisconsin, 1939.
Photograph courtesy of S. C. Johnson & Son Inc.

S. C. Johnson & Sons was proud of its standing as a enlightened company, 'bringing the employer and worker together', providing them with, 'proper wages and proper working conditions'.[64] Hib Johnson challenged his architect to provide an environment in which his workers would feel valued. To Frank this was familiar ground. It resonated with his Unitarian principles. Darwin Martin had set him the same test many years before. The Larkin Building had been designed in that spirit, a cathedral to work. It was the last large commercial building that Frank had completed before the Johnson commission. Although separated by a gulf of time he began to see the two projects as counterparts. Both were windowless, surrounded by industrial sprawl, and in each the joy and pleasure of employment would come entirely from the aesthetics of the workplace, 'Organic architecture designed this great building to be as inspiring a place to work in as any cathedral ever was in which to worship. It was meant to be a socio-architectural interpretation of modern business at its top and best.'[65] Hib Johnson's employees were dazzled by what they had been given and productivity soared. There was intense competition to be hired. It became a problem that staff preferred to stay there rather than go home at the end of the day.

Although similar in broad aspects to the Larkin Building, Frank had never built a space quite like it before, nor did he do so again. It's hard to resist the notion that, to some extent, its qualities are serendipitous. He had begun with the idea of an object rather than a space, the circular column as a repeated unit, a column which would also function as a roof. He had used a similar column form in 1931 in the design of a newspaper printing plant for the *Capital Journal* in Salem, Oregon, another on the long list of unbuilt projects of that era, and the source goes back a little further.[66] A different newspaper plant had been featured in *The Architectural Record* in late 1930. It was the work of the Finnish architect Alvar Aalto, an impressive exercise in functionalism that was also featured two years later in Hitchcock and Johnson's 'Modern Architecture' exhibition at the Museum of Modern Art, where Frank had obviously seen it. It had outward-tapering columns to carry the great weight of machinery and paper stock. Frank's 'mushroom columns' had a more greatly pronounced flaring at the capital than Aalto's, but he used them in the *Capital Journal* design for the same reason: the shape allows the heavy floor loading of the printing plant to flow gradually into the columns, avoiding concentrations of stress at the column heads. But at Johnson Wax the columns carried only their own weight and that of the delicate tubular glazing that filled the spaces between them. They were more slender, more graceful – as much containers of light as elements of structure. Another possible source-image comes to mind, the 'torchiere' floor lamps that were fashionable in Europe in the early 1930s. The Parisian Jean Perzel, for example, designed lights and furniture for luxury ocean liners. His catalogues circulated throughout Europe and America. The 1931-2 edition shows a floor lamp with familiar lines, a delicate stem that tapers down to a narrow foot; a shallow, dish-like lantern spinning out from the top, fringed with iridescent glass[67] (Pl. 155).

These and other 'streamline' forms evolved from the Art Deco of the mid-1920s as it converged with the broader modern style. This was at a time when 'streamline' clocks, radios and refrigerators were features of many American homes. Frank, who had always recoiled from anyone else's style, was surprisingly willing to describe Johnson Wax in these terms: 'it was high time to give our hungry American public something truly "streamlined", so swift, sure of itself and clean for its purpose ... that *anybody* could see the virtue of this thing called Modern.'[68]

For once, in these words, Frank undersells himself. The great architectural critic Kenneth Frampton described Johnson Wax as 'not only the greatest piece of twentieth century architecture realised in the United States ... but also possibly the most profound artwork that America has ever produced'.[69] This Frank did at the age of seventy while, at the same time, designing and constructing 'Fallingwater', possibly the only other artwork that might compete for Frampton's ultimate American tribute. In each case he had assimilated what he perceived to be a superficial contemporary idiom and transmuted it into a timeless expression of sublime, natural unity: beautiful, organic and True.

Pl. 155. 'Lampadaire No. 51', from the 1931–32 Catalogue of Ateliers Jean Perzel. Courtesy of Ateliers Jean Perzel, Paris.

## January 1938. Offices of Time Inc., East 42nd Street New York

The publishers of the *Architectural Forum* believed that the first edition of the year was, 'the most important architectural document ever published in America'. It was, they claimed, 'the first and only record in print of what we have come to call the Modern Movement'. It was devoted entirely to the work of Frank Lloyd Wright, 'architecture as thoroughly indigenous to America as the earth and rocks from which it springs'. The publisher of *Architectural Forum* was also the publisher of the two leading news journals: *Time* and the pictorial, *Life*. In the same January Frank stole headlines in both publications and even appeared, in portrait, on the cover of *Time*. Frank was particularly grateful to Howard Myers, the editor of the *Forum*: 'Howard Myers took me out of mothballs and put me in circulation again', he admitted.[70] Frank's ascent owed more, in fact, to the powerful influence of Henry Luce, the owner of Time Inc., publisher of the three journals. Luce was among an increasing number of corporate luminaries who had begun to question the growing influence of European ideas on American cultural life. New American leaders were needed, Luce believed, and so, after decades of mocking and judgemental newspaper coverage, it was from this moment, early in 1938, that Frank found himself elevated suddenly in the popular consciousness, to become the standard bearer for American architecture that he had always claimed to be. As the scholar Daniel Naegele incisively noted, 'Wright, the one-time renegade who so often had kneed the groin of polite America, now was heralded as its great hero.'[71]

Although neither was complete, Fallingwater and Johnson Wax were splendidly portrayed across the three magazines, but among his many bold statements there is one, apparently more modest, that also catches the eye:

> *Says Wright ... of the Small House: To give the little American family the benefit of industrial advantages of the era in which they live, something else must be done ... The house of moderate cost is not only America's major architectural problem, but the problem most difficult to her major architects. I would rather solve it with satisfaction to myself than anything I can think of.*[72]

Frank wrote these words late in 1937 as construction neared completion of a house that he had designed for Katherine Jacobs and her husband, Herb, a newspaper journalist in his old hometown of Madison. Their plot was only a mile from the university and, most remarkably, the house had been built fully to plan for just five thousand dollars.[73] The Jacobs House would become known as Frank's first 'Usonian House'. It was the ideal of a simple, modern low-cost home that could easily be replicated, and one that was indeed repeated in varying forms around sixty times by Frank himself, and then imitated a million times over in every 'ranch style' home built in

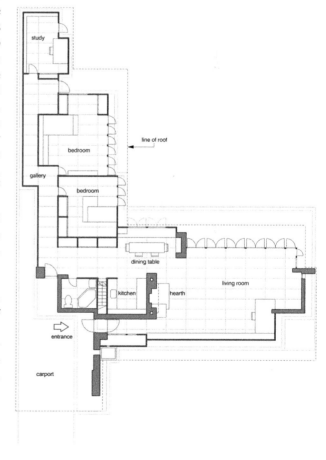

Fig. 15.3. Floor plan of the Jacobs House, Madison, Wisconsin, 1937. This was the first of Frank's Usonian Houses.

America over the following decades.[74] The Jacobs House more obviously occupies the conceptual space of the 'New Pioneer' architects than either of the two landmark projects that were its contemporaries. It is single-storey, an 'L' shape in plan, with an open-plan workspace at the cruck consisting of a combined kitchen and dining area that flowed into the living room (Fig. 15.3). It was designed to allow for Mrs Jacobs to sit at its fulcrum, with a clear view of everything her husband and her children might be doing.[75] This simple, space-efficient idea, at the literal and figurative heart of Frank's Usonian House, would influence the whole of later American domestic design.

The Jacobs House has a flat roof that overhangs; brick and timber walls to shield it from the road and a full height glazed screen along the inside of the 'L', open to the view of a large, landscaped garden (Pl. 156). It has no foundations, just a flat concrete slab threaded with pipes to deliver underfloor heating, a technology new to America. The walls of solid brickwork were the same inside and out. The remaining wall surfaces were prefabricated panels only 60 mm thick, triple layers of pine board. It had integrated tables and seats, illuminated by concealed indirect lighting, bookshelves built into the walls and, outside, a 'car port' canopy that extended from the roof of the house. At the same time there is an unmistakable organic repose in the tightly controlled use of primary materials, brick, timber, concrete, glass, the transparency of the sun-facing elevations and the free flow of the living space. Herb Jacobs recalled that the 'floor to ceiling windows on the garden side made nature a great part of the house, letting in the sun, the moon and the stars, adding the changing landscape as a permanent part of our daily life'.[76] In the best passage of his recent study *Plagued by Fire*, Paul Hendrickson makes two convincing observations. First, that the Jacobs House 'is as complete a work of art as what leans out over a waterfall at Bear Run, as what stands on the industrial southside of Racine … this supposedly simple home will always be the first among equals. And … her influence and implications seem vaster.' Hendrickson's second observation is more potent, that in the process of designing and building the Jacobs

Pl. 156. The Jacobs House, Madison, Wisconsin, 1937.
Photograph James Steakley, WC CC-BY 2.0.

House, Frank 'got back in touch with his true architectural and personal self. In Greek mythology the hero's journey is a journey of return.' Through the successful realisation of this project, the fulfilment of a lifelong goal, Frank had

> *found a way home to the small-town and common-man values from which he'd sprung … he'd again touched his roots, whether he exactly understood it that way or not. On some level … the deep touching gave him psychic strength for … a late life explosion of creative energy that no-one, doubtless not even he, saw coming.[77]*

By the decade's end Frank's stature in American architecture was fully restored, his pre-eminence acknowledged across the nation for the first time. There were others who would build more, others who would make more money from architecture, and still others who would be garlanded more generously by the establishment. But throughout what remained of his long lifetime, there was no one who could match his achievements, no one so blessed with his 'great individual genius', and there has been none to compare with him since ∎

# 15

## The Genius
### *Notes*

1    *Oak Park Oak Leaves* (14 February 1920).

2    Some sources state that Anna travelled on another Canadian Pacific steamer, the *Empress of Asia*. Online records from the port of Vancouver appear to contradict this. The *Empress of Japan* is also referred to in Anna's passport application.

3    Frank Lloyd Wright, *An Autobiography (Edition 2)* (New York: Duell, Sloan & Pearce, 1943), p. 202.

4    Miriam Noel's memoir, quoted in Meryl Secrest, *Frank Lloyd Wright: A Biography* (Chicago: University of Chicago Press, 1998), p. 240.

5    Secrest, *Frank Lloyd Wright: A Biography*, p. 276.

6    Vancouver Harbour records indicate that Anna travelled back on the *Empress of Japan*, arriving on 6 June.

7    Anna Lloyd Wright Obituary, *Oak Park Oak Leaves* (17 February 1923), 38.

8    K. Smith, 'Frank Lloyd Wright and the Imperial Hotel: A Postscript', *The Art Bulletin*, 67/2 (June 1985), 297. Quotation from F. W. Gookin, letter to Frank Lloyd Wright.

9    In his entire career it was only the Marin County Centre, a building that he didn't live to see, which was larger.

10   L. C. Mullgardt, 'A Building That Is Wrong', *Architect and Engineer*, 71 (November 1922), quoted in K. Smith, 'Frank Lloyd Wright and the Imperial Hotel', p. 309.

11   Frank Lloyd Wright to Catherine and Kenneth Baxter, 7 February 1921. Copy at Avery Architectural and Fine Arts Library, Columbia University. Quoted in K. Smith, 'Frank Lloyd Wright and the Imperial Hotel', p. 306.

12   The April 1922 earthquake is recorded as 6.8 on the Richter scale. The Great Kantō earthquake was a 7.9–8.3 magnitude event.

13   F. L. Wright, *An Autobiography (Edition 2)*, p. 222.

14   K. Smith, 'Frank Lloyd Wright and the Imperial Hotel', p. 310.

15   Letter from Le Corbusier to H. T. Wijdeveld, 5 August 1925, quoted in P. V. Turner, 'Frank Lloyd Wright and the Young Le Corbusier', *Journal of the Society of Architectural Historians*, 42/3 (December 1983), 351.

16   There are 960 drawings of the American System Build Houses in the Frank Lloyd Wright Archive, more than were produced for any other project.

17   Antonin Raymond, *An Autobiography* (Clarendon, VT: C. E. Tuttle, 1973), quoted in Secrest, *Frank Lloyd Wright: A Biography*, p. 253.

18   Maginel Wright Barney, *The Valley of the God Almighty Joneses* (New York: Appleton Century, 1965), p. 123.

19   Secrest, *Frank Lloyd Wright: A Biography*, p. 253.

20   In Anna's passport application there is an affidavit, provided by Jane, which records that both Anna and Jane were living at 931 Chicago Avenue, Oak Park.

21   *Dictionary of Unitarian and Universalist Biography*, www.uudb.org Unitarian and Universalist History and Heritage Society (April 2021).

22   Although it is sometimes linked to old age, epilepsy can affect people of any age. It seems, at least, possible that it could account for William Carey Wright's questioning of her sanity in the years before their divorce.

23   Secrest, *Frank Lloyd Wright: A Biography*, p. 278.

24   She used 'Madame' to distinguish herself from Catherine, who was 'Mrs Wright', and also, obviously, for her love of French literature.

25   Obituary, *Oak Park Oak Leaves* (17 February 1923), 36-7.

26   Obituary, *Oak Park Oak Leaves* (17 February 1923), 37.

27   Brendan Gill, *Many Masks: A Life of Frank Lloyd Wright* (London: Heinemann, 1988), p. 287.

28   James P. Hall, 'The early history of concrete block in America' (unpublished MSc thesis, Ball State University, Indiana, 2009), 55-7.

29   Mike Davis, *City of Quartz* (New York: Verso, 1990) p. 90, n. 20.

30   *Los Angeles City Directory 1923* (L.A. Directory Co.), p. 3311.

31   C. Lockwood, 'Searching Out Wright's Imprint in Los Angeles', *New York Times* (2 December 1984). In 1924 Lloyd moved his office to Hollywood Boulevard, and Frank relocated to one of the two small guest houses that he had designed alongside the Hollyhock House.

32   There is an echo in this of a project from many years before: the patterns that Frank had designed for the Luxfer glass blocks. In his role as their cutting-edge proponent, Frank had produced a design for an office building, the façade of which was made entirely from the Luxfer blocks, stacked in grids. This playful proposal stands out now as the one that is most ahead of its time, made almost thirty years before Mies van der Rohe's celebrated Friedrichstrasse office project.

33   The Nunnery and the Governor's House at Uxmal are well-known examples of this type.

34   F. L. Wright, *An Autobiography (Edition 2)*, p. 241.

35   F. L. Wright, *An Autobiography (Edition 2)*, p. 242.

36   F. L. Wright, *An Autobiography (Edition 2)*, p. 246.

37   Letter, Frank Lloyd Wright to Lloyd Wright, 15 September 1924, quoted in Gill, *Many Masks*, pp. 277-8.

38   Letter, Frank Lloyd Wright to Charles and Mabel Ennis (4 September 1924), quoted in Gill, *Many Masks*, p. 278. If the dates are correct as given in the notes in Gill's biography, Frank wrote to the Ennises *before* his letter to Lloyd. In his text Gill gives the opposite impression.

39   J. L. Jones, 'A House for a Cousin: The Richard Lloyd Jones House', *Frank Lloyd Wright Newsletter*, 2/4 (1979), 2.

40   F. L. Wright, *An Autobiography (Edition 2)*, p. 508.

41   F. L. Wright, *An Autobiography (Edition 2)*, p. 509.

42   Colin Wilson, *G. I. Gurdjieff: The War Against Sleep* (London: Aeon Books, 2005) is a good short summary of Gurdjieff's philosophy and life.

43   Roger Friedland, and Harold Zellman, *The Fellowship: The Untold Story of Frank Lloyd Wright and the Taliesin Fellowship* (New York: HarperCollins, 2006) pp. 96-9.

44   Wright, *An Autobiography (Edition 2)*, p. 274.

45 M. J. Hamilton, and D. V. Mollenhoff, *Frank Lloyd Wright's Monona Terrace: The Enduring Power of a Civic Vision* (Madison: University of Wisconsin Press, 1999), p. 75.

46 Henry-Russell Hitchcock, *Modern Architecture: Romanticism and Reintegration* (New York: Payson and Clarke Ltd, 1929), p. 118.

47 Hitchcock, *Modern Architecture*, p. 204.

48 Bruce Brooks Pfeiffer (ed.), *Wright Complete Works, 1917–1942* (Cologne: Taschen, 2010), p. 206.

49 Levine, *Architecture of Frank Lloyd Wright*, p. 219.

50 Levine, *Architecture of Frank Lloyd Wright*, p. 219. Extract from 'Highlights', *Architectural Forum*, 55 (October 1931), 409.

51 R. Wojtowicz, 'A Model House and a House's Model: Re-examining Frank Lloyd Wright's House on the Mesa Project', *Journal of the Society of Architectural Historians*, 64/4 (December 2005), 522–51.

52 Bruce Brooks Pfeiffer and Robert Wojtowicz (eds), *Frank Lloyd Wright and Lewis Mumford: Thirty Years of Correspondence* (Princeton: Princeton Architectural Press, 2001), p. 17.

53 Secrest, *Frank Lloyd Wright: A Biography*, p. 391.

54 Pfeiffer, *Wright Complete Works, 1917–1942*, p. 205.

55 Friedland and Zellman, *The Fellowship*, p. 167.

56 Pfeiffer and Wojtowicz, *Wright and Mumford Correspondence*, p. 131.

57 Henry-Russell Hitchcock, Phillip Johnson, Lewis Mumford and A. H. Barr, *Modern Architecture: International Exhibition*, catalogue (New York: Museum of Modern Art, 1932), pp. 158, 37.

58 Vincent Scully, *Frank Lloyd Wright* (New York: George Braziller Inc., 1960), p. 26.

59 *Racine Journal Times* (afternoon edn, 7 June 1937), 5.

60 Brian Carter, *Johnson Wax Administration Building and Research Tower – Architecture in Detail* (London: Phaidon,1998), pp. 10–12.

61 F. L. Wright, *An Autobiography (Edition 2)*, p. 480.

62 Friedland and Zellman, *The Fellowship*, p. 313.

63 F. L. Wright, *An Autobiography (Edition 2)*, pp. 480–1.

64 *Milwaukee Journal* (24 March 1946), quoted in J. Lipman, *Frank Lloyd Wright and the Johnson Wax Buildings* (New York: Rizzoli, 1986), p. 1.

65 F. L. Wright, *An Autobiography (Edition 2)*, p. 472.

66 Pfeiffer, *Wright Complete Works, 1917–1942*, p. 212.

67 'Lampadaire No. 51', *Atelier Jean Perzel Catalogue 1931–32*.

68 F. L. Wright, *An Autobiography (Edition 2)*, p. 471.

69 Lipman, *Frank Lloyd Wright and the Johnson Wax Buildings*, Kenneth Frampton's Introduction.

70 Edward Durell Stone, *Evolution of an Architect* (New York: Horizon Press, 1962), p. 31.

71 D. Naegele, 'Waiting for the Site to Show Up: Henry Luce Makes Frank Lloyd Wright America's Greatest Architect', *Histories of Post War Architecture* (Bologna), Issue 0 (2017).

72 *Life*, 4/3 (17 January 1938), inside front cover.

73 This would be equivalent to approximately £75,000 in the UK in 2020.

74 Frank used the term 'Usonia' to refer to the broad, liberal democracy of America, as he saw it, as distinct from the nation of dominant institutions and bureaucrats that he despised. Frank claimed, incorrectly, that he had taken the term from Samuel Butler. It appears to have been coined by the American writer James Duff Law, who gave it a different meaning from that applied by Frank.

75 The layout of the first Jacobs House is a reworking of Frank's unbuilt 1936 design for the Robert D. Lusk House, Huron, South Dakota.

76 Paul Hendrickson, *Plagued by Fire: The Dreams and Furies of Frank Lloyd Wright* (London: Bodley Head, 2019), p. 388. Unreferenced quote from Herbert Jacobs.

77 Hendrickson, *Plagued by Fire*, p. 389.

# 16

# The Unitarian

## January 1949. 'Solar Hemicycle', Off Old Sauk Road, West Madison, Wisconsin

Jennie Turner's letter held nothing back. Frank was 'unendurable, arrogant, artificial, brazen, cruel, recklessly extravagant, a publicity seeker, an exhibitionist, egotist, sensationalist, impatient, unscrupulous, untrustworthy, erratic and capricious'.[1] It had been sent to the pastor. He circulated copies to the members of the First Unitarian Society of Madison while they reflected on the momentous step that they had taken. The majority had been content to choose Frank to design their new church, content enough in some cases to have given their own labour freely to transport hundreds of tons of stone, for the walls from a quarry thirty

miles away (Pl. 157). Herb and Katherine Jacobs were among them. They were living, by this time, in the second house that Frank had designed for them, the Solar Hemicycle,[2] out in the country to the west of the city. Their architect had nothing to prove to them, but there were strong reservations among some in the society still to overcome.

Frank was a frequent irritation to the civic leaders of Madison. They had been embarrassed by the various scandals in the earlier years; and now the architect had exchanged notoriety for fame, they found themselves often having to mount a defence against Frank's public derision of their cherished civic buildings and of the ignorance of the city's favoured architects. In November 1938 his intervention at a Council meeting resulted in the cancellation of a major public development, a combined City and County Hall. Frank put forward a counter-proposal, a spectacular civic centre that he called 'Olin Terrace', overlapping the shore of Lake Monona. The result was that neither project gained approval, but he would never be forgiven by the businessmen and politicians whose plans he had derailed.[3]

Frank received forty new commissions in 1939, more work than he had ever been offered. His future had never looked brighter – until conflict broke out again in Europe. He was appalled at the collapse of morality, and dismayed at the threat of disruption to his work. He used his new public platform to make the nation aware of his forceful opinions on war, democracy and the bloody British Empire – convictions that had flowed through Lloyd Jones veins since the time of Iolo Morganwg. His pacifism was fortified by his affection for the antagonists, Japan and Germany, nations that had sometimes shown more kindness to him than his own. Then it became clear, after Pearl Harbor, that he was on the wrong side of American sentiment. He lost friends and saw loyal apprentices imprisoned for refusing the draft. The Madison judge who sentenced them encouraged the FBI to look into the root of the problem, Frank Lloyd Wright himself. J. Edgar Hoover took a personal interest.

As the progress of the war and the emergence of its horrific truths made ambivalence impossible, Frank found himself, for once, having to row back on some of

## November 1878. Assembly Chamber, State Capitol, Madison

Pl. 157. Members of the First Unitarian Society of Madison batching dolomite stone for the construction of the Meeting House, 1950.
Wisconsin Historical Society WHS-26547.

Jenkin Lloyd Jones was a youngster among venerable company at the Twenty-Fifth session of the Wisconsin Conference of Unitarian and Independent Societies.[4] He was the Missionary Secretary of the Western Conference, and a considerable source of vitality for the cause. Madison was delighted to welcome the prestigious gathering. On the Sunday that followed the convention, Jenkin led a congregation at the Assembly Chamber and invited prospective founders of the First Unitarian Society of Madison to make themselves known.[5] It was Jenkin's mission, at that time, to establish as many new societies as he could; he was exceptionally good at it. His base was Janesville, forty miles south of the state capital, but his missionary work took him around the whole of the Midwest. Could there be another reason why, in late 1878, his attention had turned to Madison? Might it be a coincidence that Anna Lloyd Jones and her family had moved to the city, from the Lloyd Jones Valley, just a month or two before?[6] In his eagerness to ensure his sister's welfare, Jenkin had promoted William Wright's election to a secretarial post in the Wisconsin Conference, because 'paying him for his services would have been much kinder than an outright subsidy to his family'.[7] In January 1879, in his secretarial capacity, it was William Wright, Frank's father, who presided at the inaugural meeting of the First Unitarian Society of Madison. Its original 'Bond of Union' has been preserved, and it is in William's hand. He was later elected to the Society's standing committee on music and, hoping always for a more prominent role, put himself forward twice for the pastorate, without success. He was still a newcomer to the city, not yet known or really trusted, and his Baptist background counted against him.[8] Anna was elected Vice-President of the Ladies' Society.[9] When Frank proclaimed later to the membership of the First Unitarian Society of Madison that he was 'a Unitarian, descended from Unitarian Ministers on both my father's and mother's

his early protestations. He was fortunate that the conflict itself became so much the larger story that he dropped from the headlines, and he was as relieved as any when the hostilities, domestic and military, came to an end. He was seventy-eight years old, desperate to get back to his architectural work, the creative impetus as strong as ever. It was, perhaps, only in south Wisconsin, among civic enemies, conservative neighbours and the many businesses and tradesmen to whom he once, or still, owed money, that he was still regarded with deep suspicion or, in some cases, with outright hostility. When Jennie Turner composed her vitriolic letter to her pastor she undoubtedly felt that she was speaking for many in the wider community. But she was too late. The war was in the past; optimism had returned. The 'dry stone' foundations of the First Unitarian Meeting House had already been laid, and the rugged dolomite walls were rising from the ground.

side of the family', he might have added that they had been there at the Society's very beginning.[10]

In the late 1930s the First Unitarian Society still held its services in a city centre church that had been dedicated in March 1886, the year after William and Anna Wright's divorce.[11] Frank had attended the church with his mother and sisters as a nineteen-year-old in the months before he made his fateful move to Chicago. He became an active member of his Uncle Jenkin's All Souls Church while he lived in Chicago, and when he moved to Oak Park, he joined the neighbourhood Unitarian and Universalist Society, for whom he later designed Unity Temple. After 1910 and his flight to Europe, membership of any society was impossible, and conventional habits were abandoned. He lived in spiritual independence, guided by the fluid credo that he apprehended in the philosophy of Emerson, Goethe, Thoreau and Ellen Key, the poetry of Whitman and the fierce contrarianism of the Lloyd Joneses.

Pl. 158. Monona Terrace, as constructed on the shore of Lake Monona, Madison, 1994–97.
Courtesy of Monona Terrace Community and Convention Center.

## Sunday, 4 December 1938.
## First Unitarian Church,
## East Dayton Street, Madison,
## Wisconsin

It seems possible that it was Herb Fritz's idea that Frank should make contact again, after an interlude of fifty years, with the First Unitarian Society of Madison. It was Herb Fritz, then a novice draughtsman, who had escaped the dreadful events at Taliesin in August 1914 by diving headlong through the dining room window. He had returned to Taliesin in 1937 to rejoin Frank's blossoming practice. Soon after, he and his wife signed up as members of the First Unitarian Society. They had joined for the company of fellow Unitarians, but for Frank the initial motivation was less to do with faith than his need for the Society's help. It hadn't been Frank's intention that his grandiose Olin Terrace proposal would be used as a political wrecking-ball. His ideas, however ambitious, were always well intentioned, so he'd been delighted when the Madison press had hailed his proposal as a masterstroke (Pl. 158). He needed support to move the project forward, to overcome his opponents in the city, and it seemed possible that the Unitarian Society might rally to the cause.

The church was full to hear Frank give a spirited presentation of his plans. He was received with a standing ovation, but the citizens' committee that he had urged them to form never did take shape. His struggle to realise Olin Terrace would go on for many more years. It was on that day, however, that Frank added his name to the membership roll and stepped back into the Unitarian fold.[12] From then onwards Frank, who tended to invoke a nebulous spirituality, began to refer more often to religious themes and to use more specifically Unitarian language in the communication of his ideas. This may reflect the increasing opportunities that he had to speak publicly, particularly to groups of young people, but it is evident also that his faith and his memories of the religion of his forebears became more important to him as his later years went by.

The Rev. Kenneth Patton joined the First Unitarian Society of Madison as pastor in 1941, at a time when the membership was in gradual decline. He was attracted by its progressive background, 'the last little feather on the tip of the left wing of left wing Unitarianism'.[13] Under Patton's energetic leadership the Society steadily grew in size until 1945, when he received a generous offer from a city-centre retailer to buy the site on which their old church stood. It came as a relief because the cost of its upkeep was by then beyond the means of the Society. The windfall appeared sufficient for them to build a new church, ideally to the west of the city centre, where land was easier to find and where most of the members lived. The pastor encouraged them to discuss the way forward, while gently steering them to the choice that he was sure to be the best for them: only Frank Lloyd Wright could give them what they needed and deserved. Sometime later the Rev. Patton wrote to Frank to explain his confidence in that decision:

> You have certainly suffered from the illiberalism and inanity of public judgement. I have already caught my share, for in religious viewpoint and practice my religion is just as extreme and innovational, and just as far from popular understanding, as is your architecture. That is why I am 'your boy' when it comes to matters in your field.[14]

Frank might have explained, in response, that the extremity of his architecture was a consequence of his upbringing in the same extreme and innovative religion, that they were two expressions of the same faith.

When he had designed Unity Temple, Frank had worked with square and cubic geometry because those forms were understood to symbolise Unity. He began the design of the First Unitarian Meeting House with a different form in mind. He had become interested in triangular geometry a few years before. He built an experimental house near San Francisco in 1937 for a young, academic couple, Paul and Jean Hanna, designed on a triangular grid (Fig. 16.1). For someone who had always been so devoted to orthogonal geometry it seemed an arbitrary move to make. The Hannas, and everyone who came to experience their house, were astonished by the spatial fluidity that was released by the omission of right-angled walls. In his early career Frank had often spoken of 'breaking the box', opening up the stifling, cellular packages of traditional domestic architecture. Triangular elements had begun to appear in some of his unbuilt designs from the late 1920s, but always within an orthogonal armature. Then, after pursuing his box-breaking ideal for half a century, it seemed to have occurred to him, apparently quite suddenly, that by starting with a hexagonal or triangular grid there need be no

'box' at all.' The plan of the Hanna House had been designed on a grid of triangles, but its walls had been projected vertically upwards to meet horizontal roof planes, so the cross-section of the house was still orthogonal. When he came to work on the Meeting House, he took the next logical step and projected the triangular geometry into the vertical plane too (Fig. 16.2). Frank explained that his concept took

> three customarily separate parts of a church and gathered them into one unit which serves as spire, chapel and parish hall in one … The plan you see is triangular and out of this … you get this expression of reverence without recourse to the steeple … the roof itself says what the steeple used to say, but says it with greater reverence.[15]

The roof of the Meeting House is its most distinctive aspect. At its lower, south end it extends beyond the line of the outer walls to form a low canopy (Pl. 159). At the north end it rakes spectacularly upwards, with its apex, a flying arrow-tip, above the enclosing glass screen of the auditorium. All the intersecting surfaces are generated from triangular geometry. 'The building is unity made evident, as a circumstance of life', Frank explained; 'its roof is itself a form of prayer … pointing upwards to God knows what.'[16] The thinness of the roof is illusory, but its delicacy is real. It is supported by a concealed structure, an elaborate mesh of slender, triangulated trusswork in which none of the timber pieces is larger than a domestic floor joist.[17] The trusses were so light that they were difficult to lift without snapping.

The structural design suggests the influence of another Unitarian, Richard Buckminster Fuller. Frank had met Fuller, then a relative unknown, in New York in the early 1930s.[18] In the years between, Fuller had become a regular feature in the national press with a procession of spectacular futuristic inventions. One of Fuller's maxims was to do more with less, to make structures as lightweight and as efficient as possible. It could even have been Fuller's early interest in the properties of triangles that sparked Frank's own exploration of the form.[19] In 1946, as Frank was developing his ideas for the Meeting House, Fuller first publicised his work on the 'geodesic dome', a structure based on the most efficient possible use

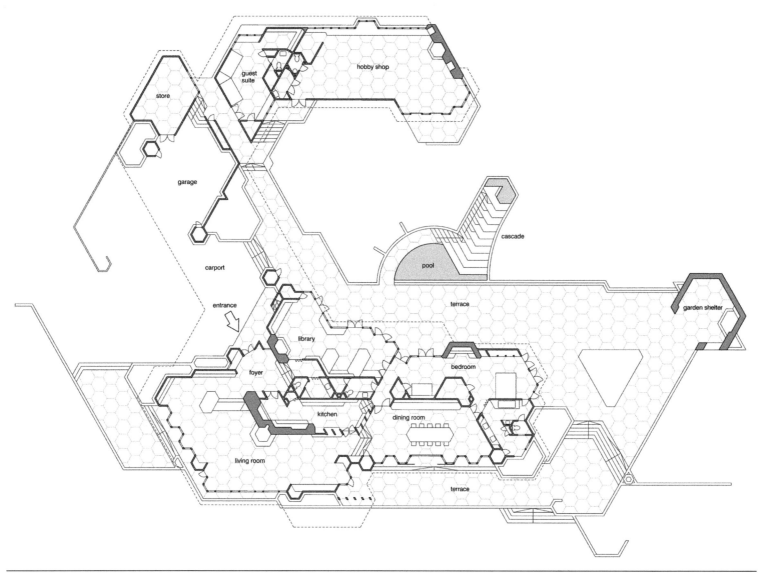

Labels in figure:
- guest suite
- hobby shop
- store
- garage
- cascade
- carport
- pool
- entrance
- terrace
- library
- garden shelter
- foyer
- bedroom
- kitchen
- dining room
- living room
- terrace

Fig. 16.1. The extraordinary plan of the Hanna House, also known as the Honeycomb House, in its most recent form. Stanford, California, 1937.

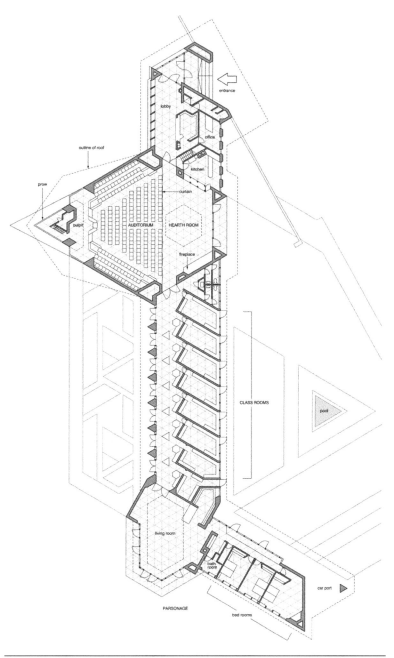

entrance

lobby

offices

outline of roof

kitchen

prow

curtain

pulpit

AUDITORIUM    HEARTH ROOM

fireplace

CLASS ROOMS

pool

living room

bath room

car port

PARSONAGE

bed rooms

Fig. 16.2. Plan of the First Unitarian Meeting House, Madison. 1951.

of triangulated frames. This must have made an impression on Frank. He had made a habit of stretching structure to its limits, but when he told his apprentices that he wanted to 'build that church with toothpicks',[20] he was, deliberately or otherwise, using a phrase that was synonymous with Fuller.[21] It suggests that he approached the design of the Meeting House roof with the veiled intention to prove, perhaps only to himself, that he was Fuller's equal in structural extremism.

The Meeting House can, in every other respect, be read as a hymn to Frank's lifelong creative principles and to the ancestors from whom they flowed. Consider the choice of the site: he urged the Society to move out of the city entirely, to find a truly rural site for the new Meeting House. This felt appropriate because, to Frank, Unitarianism was a *rural* faith. In reality in America, as in Britain, Unitarianism was the denomination of urban progressives. Back in Wales the rural enclave in Cardiganshire, origin of the Lloyd Joneses, was the exception, not the rule. There is another, more profound aspect to this duality in Frank's psychology. He had developed an acute sensitivity, during his adolescence, to the contrasts between urban and rural experience. He'd lived for half the year, each year, in The Valley and the other half in urban Madison. He was invigorated and enervated by turns by Chicago. He felt comfortable in Oak Park until the suburb was subsumed in the metropolis. When its social and spatial constraints became too much to bear, he fled to the country and settled again in The Valley. Frank felt compelled to solidify the sensations and the memories that chafed at him into a thesis of his own. In the early years of the Taliesin Fellowship, with no meaningful commissions to work on, he had time to turn his mind fully to the issue. His conclusion was that the metropolis was doomed to decline and that it had no part to play in the healthy and prosperous future of mankind.

The key word was 'decentralisation', and his vision of the future ideal was 'Broadacre City'. It was a sprawling settlement in which every home would be set on its own free acre of land, linked to neighbours and scattered amenities by a grid of highways, realising, for the first time, the full, liberating potential of the automobile. It was an idea that he had touched on during his 1930 lecture series at Princeton and then set down in 1932 in a book entitled *The Disappearing*

*City*. The apprentices built a spectacular model of Broadacre City which became the centrepiece of the exhibition that was funded by Edgar Kaufmann, in the year before Frank designed Fallingwater (Pl. 160). Over all of the years that followed, Frank held on to this vision of a decentralised future, the emptying of the cities into the countryside, even when he was comfortably settled in New York. It seems, now, to have been the most quixotic of his enterprises. When the *Capital Times of Wisconsin* asked for his initial thoughts on the Meeting House he told them: 'The little Unitarian Society at Madison is taking the courageous first step over the threshold of the new era's decentralisation.' Addressing the Society later he reminded them that 'The Unitarian faith is a faith in a living, growing Mankind. The growth of man is better told by his buildings than by anything else. No Unitarian would, if he could, neglect the more difficult tasks of decentralisation which face us now.' He reminded them of how he had pushed the trustees to move to a site outside the city, and of how they 'went out, but not far enough'.[22] The theory, the social rationale, all seemed plausible, but the urgency he felt, in his advancing age, was, in truth, to recreate an arcadian vision, the glowing apparition of the happiest and most fulfilled time of his life, the summers of his youth in The Valley. He wanted to believe that everyone could live that way.

Jenkin Lloyd Jones returned to Chicago from Wales in 1882 exhilarated by the experience of preaching at Pantydefaid, a chapel more like a house than a church. The Lloyd Joneses's Unity Chapel was designed in its image, with a curtain to divide its two meeting rooms (Fig. 16.3). The curtain could be drawn aside so that they were combined to become one larger hall, a room for all purposes. This was more than a concession to the small scale of the chapel. Jenkin used the same arrangement at All Souls in Chicago, a building many times the size but, again, much more like a house than a church. The First Unitarian Society of Madison operated in the traditional way, their old church and parish house were two separate buildings on the same street.[23] The Rev. Patton helped to persuade the members that the new Meeting House should be a new start, that the church and parish house should be combined into a single 'multiple-purpose room, like the modern living room ... usable for weekday

Pl. 159.  First Unitarian Society of Madison Meeting House. The Hearth Room canopy and chimney: triangular geometry in plan and elevation. Photograph Carol Highsmith, LOC.

Pl. 160.  Frank (wearing beret) and apprentices working on the model of Broadacre City at La Hacienda, Chandler Arizona, 1935.
From the *Chandler Republic* newspaper, courtesy of Chandler Museum Archives.

as well as Sunday activities, a building without its major auditorium limited to a special purpose, such as a worship space'. It would instead be 'the living room of the parish'. The local press was intrigued: 'a lounge type auditorium is being considered for the new church, a distinct departure from standard seating arrangements in houses of worship.'[24] So there is a direct lineage, through Frank and his Uncle Jenkin, that connects the First Unitarian Meeting House of Madison to the Pantydefaid Chapel of a century before.[25]

There was another youthful experience that Frank had always cherished, the physical process of construction, the communal effort, the harmony of craft and muscle-power that he had shared under the guidance of his Uncle Thomas, with the rest of the Lloyd Jones *teulu* in the raising of barns and the building of homes in The Valley. He designed the Meeting

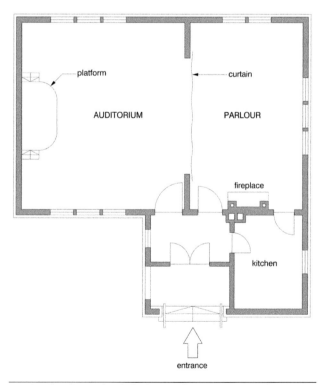

Fig. 16.3. Plan of Unity Chapel, Lloyd Jones Valley, Wisconsin, 1885. The room arrangement with the curtain divider was replicated in the First Unitarian Meeting House of 1951. Both were influenced by Jenkin Lloyd Jones's memory of the second Pantydefaid Chapel, as he saw it in 1882.

House to be made from stone and timber, like the buildings in The Valley, so that it could be built economically and built by hand. When the members of the First Unitarian Society volunteered to transport stone to the site from the quarry – eventually over a thousand tons of it – they did so initially to save money, but then came to feel the deeper involvement in the building process that made the Meeting House seem more truly their own. Where there were other opportunities to contribute directly, the members embraced them. Using looms borrowed from Taliesin, the Women's Alliance wove the curtains that Frank had designed to divide the two ends of the hall, having first dyed the yarn themselves and having taught themselves to weave (Pl. 161). One of the looms was at the Jacobs's house. Katherine Jacobs was responsible for enlarging Frank's small drawing into the full-scale patterns from which they wove each unique, gorgeously textured panel of a textile screen 3 metres high and 36 metres long.[26] Frank was in his early eighties by the time the Meeting House approached completion. It seemed to stretch out of reach; funds were exhausted, the budget long before exceeded. He couldn't bring his own physical effort to bear, so he did the next best thing, he sent his apprentices to the site to add their free labour to the cause. Then in 1951, when the end was in sight, he gave two public lectures in the almost complete Meeting House, donating the proceeds to the Society. It was just enough to complete the job.

The auditorium holds around 250 on its folding benches. When the curtain is opened the Hearth Room can provide for a hundred more. From the rear of the auditorium the line of sight is drawn irresistibly up along the centre-line of the ceiling which, at its lowest, directly overhead, is only slightly inclined. As the ridge rises higher, the sides of the ceiling pitch more and more steeply as if in the motion of closing. The surfaces are actually twisting planes, in Frank's words, 'like the underside of the wing of a bird' (Pl. 162). A visiting theologian saw the line of the rising internal fold as an 'active line ... inviting the eye to follow upward and outward into the unknown', and then, when the colourful rolls of the curtain were parted, 'one need only face in the opposite direction ... and focus on the low ceilinged Hearth Room where ... there is a home-like atmosphere, complete with welcoming fireplace and adjoining kitchen. Home

Pl. 161. The original textile panels that were stitched together to form the dividing curtain between the Auditorium and the Hearth Room of the First Unitarian Meeting House, Madison.
Photographs by Harry Carnes, First Unitarian Society, Madison.

Pl. 162. Interior of the Auditorium, showing the complex curvature of the ceiling.
Photograph Tapan Shah, First Unitarian Society Madison.

suggests stability and the comfort of familial love.'[27] As they relax in the warmth of the great fireplace members can gaze up into a softly lit hexagonal recess in the ceiling of the Hearth Room. It is framed by a belt of oak onto which Frank had inscribed the names of six prominent American Unitarians: the pioneering preacher William Ellery Channing, the educationalist Charles Eliot, the Transcendentalist minister Theodore Parker, then Thoreau and Emerson, the twin beacons of Frank's personal philosophy, and, properly placed among them, his own uncle, Jenkin Lloyd Jones. The pastor Max Gaebler recalled that Frank would visit the Meeting House, often on his way from Madison airport, before returning home to Taliesin,

> not on a tour of inspection but to experience the building yet again. He would sit quietly for a few moments on one of the benches, then go up to the prow and gaze out towards Lake Mendota ... At such moments there could be no question of his special attachment to the place. It was in every way his church.[28]

## July 1950. Brynmawr, Brecknockshire, Wales

As he took in the bleak surroundings, Frank must have thought, at least momentarily, about the familiar view through the ribbon windows of Taliesin, across the valley to the hill called Bryn Mawr, the high point on the horizon. He might even have thought of the salubrious enclave at Edgewater, Bryn Mawr, in the North Side of Chicago. Those grand houses, some of the first buildings that he'd worked on in his youth with Silsbee. Weather-beaten, high up on moorland, adrift between scant farmland and mountains: was he now looking at the original Bryn Mawr? If it was not for his exhilaration at being there, in Wales, the depleted coal town could have seemed a depressing counterpoint. The ironworks and the colliery around which it had coalesced were long gone. In their place was a cavernous new factory, a rubber plant, built, he had been told, in that remote setting to bring back the prosperity that Brynmawr had once enjoyed, decades before. The factory was a year from opening, but its superstructure was complete. It may have been the best time to see it. It had a spectacular cascade of concrete barrel vaults along its edges and a central production hall with a vast roof of ballooning handkerchief vaults, all cast in the thinnest concrete (Pl. 163). It had been designed by the young men who had brought him there, the principals of Architects Co-Partnership, all still in their thirties. It was, they had told him, the most advanced building in Britain, designed for a truly democratic workforce, following socialist principles. Decentralised, democratic, structurally expressive, truly poetic and, by his own terms, even organic. Frank was surely impressed, but he took care not to show it. Ken Capon, one of the young architects recalled that Frank offered, 'a mixture of encouraging and caustic remarks'.[29] He was observed later relieving himself against the factory's outside wall. It had been a long drive.[30]

Frank had travelled to Britain with Olgivanna at the invitation of Robert Furneaux Jordan, Principal of the Architectural Association School of Architecture in London. He had first written to Frank in May 1949, asking him to 'use [his] great influence to find not less than a million dollars' to secure the future of the AA School.[31] In the correspondence that followed, the proposition changed gradually until it was Jordan offering to pay Frank to make a visit to London. 'There is only one great architect in the world', he told Frank, 'and [the] students ought to see him.' There was more to it than a simple star turn. Furneaux Jordan saw Frank as role model for his students as they contemplated the task of post-war rebuilding:

> In the first half of this century he – in his way – went through just the same sort of fight with men and traditions that the young architects of today will – in their way – have to go through in the next half century … it is evident that if a new visual and physical environment is to be created in our cities that the same old battle against obscurantism, philistinism, commercialism and academicism will have to be fought all over again.[32]

Between dinners and prize-giving obligations Frank and his young audience made time to entertain each other. It appears that he left London only once, and that was for his visit to Wales. Ken Capon recalled: 'Just before the building was finished some of us took part in showing Frank Lloyd Wright the native country of his ancestors for the first time. We also slipped in a visit to the Brynmawr factory.' It is a striking recollection, suggesting that Frank's real interest was simply to set foot on his ancestral homeland. At eighty-three years old, it might have been his last chance. It doesn't seem likely that the trip could have been condensed into a single day. In 1950 the high road from London to Wales was the A48 – one lane in each direction for most of its length. The architects of the rubber factory had a routine of leaving London in the early evening, driving the first hundred miles as hard as they could, and then pausing for a good dinner in the Cotswolds. They would break again near to the Welsh border in Herefordshire because 'there was a good pub there' before going on to Abergavenny, where they would stay for the night.[33] They knew the south-east corner of Wales better than they did the rest of the country. Another two-hour drive could have brought them within reach of Cardiganshire, but it seems unlikely that they would have gone west of Cardiff. It is easier to picture them taking in the prospective capital, with its shining Beaux-Arts civic centre, before travelling north through the coalfield, and on up to the edge of the mountains. Civic Wales, industrial Wales, rural upland Wales, all conveniently close together. Then Brynmawr would be a small detour from the homeward route. Furneaux Jordan had shared the trip. He recalled Frank's reluctance to admire the picturesque charm of the Cotswolds, but that

> His excitement returned when … he went to see his ancestral Wales, and in Wales an industrial development area – new factories, new housing, new schools. This was real as well as romantic, and it belonged to the future, not to the past – it was more, it was his own decentralisation at work, getting men out of dead cities … here in the Welsh mountains where men had rotted in the 'thirties something was really happening … and F.L.W. was really excited at last.[34]

A lifetime of hearing, thinking and talking about the land of his fathers - his Uncle Jenkin, his aunts Nell and Jennie, his mother, his two sisters: they had all been there many years before. Now, at last Frank had set foot on the good earth of Wales for himself.

## July 1950. London, England

The few days that Frank spent in London are more fully accounted for. His hosts took him to another vast construction site, only a short ride away, on the south bank of the Thames. Work on the Festival of Britain was well advanced, on schedule for opening the following spring. Its two dominant structures were the Dome of Discovery, which showed the unmistakable influence of Buckminster Fuller, and the Royal Festival Hall, a large orchestral performance space and one of the few structures that were intended to be kept after the Festival's end. Frank had little interest in the site. They went on to the adjacent London County Hall where he met the architects of the Festival Hall (Pl. 164). He examined the plans and models before giving some worrying news to the young designers. The acoustics, he told them, were sure to be a disappointment, regardless of the fact that the acoustic design had been guided by cutting-edge science. Peter Moro, one of the architects at the gathering, recalled Frank's untimely advice, 'Boys, boys, it won't work; it's got to be in the section of a trumpet!' Someone else in the group responded: 'So you fear, Mr. Wright, that we might get a little too much reverberation?' 'Fear? I don't *fear*, I know!' Frank answered. It was only years later that it emerged that Frank had, in effect, been right. In 2007 many millions were spent to correct its acoustic weaknesses.[35] But regardless of acoustics, as a statement of humane and democratic modernism the Festival Hall had many admirable qualities. It hovered serenely over the south embankment, a cheerful montage of maritime curves and refined angles far removed from the flat austerity of the 'glass box boys' that Frank routinely disparaged. One of its most appealing features was a gently curving picture window that ran the length of the front elevation, two storeys high, north facing and robustly fenestrated to provide visitors with splendid, framed views along the winding Thames (Pl. 165).

Pl. 163. Brynmawr Rubber Factory, Brecknockshire, Wales, newly completed, 1951.
Photograph H. Tempest & Co/RIBA Collections.

## Late July 1950. University Bay Drive, Madison, Wisconsin

The walls and roof of the Meeting House were progressing well, the most difficult work was behind them. The last substantial part of the envelope to build was the high wall at the north end of the auditorium, the structure that was referred to as 'the prow'. Its central section was an intricate structure of patterned concrete block with insets of thick stained glass that Frank referred to as 'the steeple'. The prow was technically complex and quite different from the rest of the structure. The detailed drawings had all been made, and Marshall Erdman, the contractor, was ready to make a start when Frank arrived at the site, just back from his visit to Britain. He spent some time within the shell of the auditorium, looking out to the north, to Lake Mendota lacing the horizon. Curtis Besinger, the apprentice responsible for the working drawings, recalled the following morning, when Frank 'sat down at my desk and said that he had changed his mind, that he wanted to keep the effect of having the prow open, rather than blocked by the steeple. On the drawings I had laid out he quickly drew a section of the wall of glass as it now exists.'[36] The Wright scholar Joseph Siry has noted that he probably

Pl. 164  Frank, with his back to the camera with Robert Furneaux Jordan on his right, at County Hall surrounded by the young team of London County Council Architects, all working on the Festival of Britain.
Photograph by Sam Lambert/RIBA Collections..

Pl. 166.  The glass prow of the Meeting House auditorium.
Photograph by BeautifulCataya/CC BY-NC 2.0.

*wanted to change the prow because the interior would have looked much darker had the concrete block and stained glass not been changed to clear glass … [It] would allow a view out into the landscape from the auditorium, creating the 'broad prospect' that he wished for his ideal democratic church.*[37]

It's a curious fact that none of Frank's commercial or civic buildings before the Meeting House had been designed with a glass wall.[38] Some of his most celebrated projects were emphatically windowless, and he had spoken loudly and often of his aversion to the glass walls of the more minimal branch of modernism. He first conception of the Meeting House recalled the image of a rock-chapel, coarse stone and cleft ceiling, daylight glimpsed through small fissures. The change to glass was a significant conceptual volte-face at a very late stage in the project, justifiable surely, as it's hard to imagine that the Meeting House would have been better with its original concrete 'steeple'. The glass wall, with bold diagonals framing the view of the lake, seems the optimal resolution of the Meeting House, as if always intended, as if the rest of the building was designed around it (Pl. 166). If Frank had not gone to London when he did, and spent that time in good-humoured conversation with the designers of the Royal Festival Hall, we might never have known ∎

Pl. 165.  The Royal Festival Hall, London 1951, with its picture window and view of the River Thames.
Photograph by Colin Westwood/RIBA Collections.

# 16 The Unitarian
## *Notes*

1  Mary Jane Hamilton, *The Meeting House* (Madison: Friends of the Meeting House, First Unitarian Society of Madison, 1991), p. 6.

2  The Solar Hemicycle was designed on passive solar principles, decades before those principles were codified.

3  Olin Terrace was later renamed Monona Terrace. An impressively convincing interpretation of the 1953 version was eventually built on the intended site nearly forty years after his death. He won in the end.

4  *The Unitarian Yearbook 1909* (Boston: American Unitarian Association, 1909), p. 110.

5  M. E. Curti, 'Our Golden Age', in *Landmarks in the Life of the First Unitarian Society of Madison* (Madison: Friends of the Meeting House, First Unitarian Society Madison, 1999), pp. 9–11.

6  M. J. Hamilton and D. V Mollenhoff, *Frank Lloyd Wright's Monona Terrace: The Enduring Power of a Civic Vision* (Madison: University of Wisconsin Press, 1999), p. 43.

7  Mary Jane Hamilton, quoted in *Landmarks in the Life of the First Unitarian Society of Madison*, p. 55.

8  Joseph Siry, *Beth Sholom Synagogue: Frank Lloyd Wright and Modern Religious Architecture* (Chicago: University of Chicago Press, 2011), p. 249.

9  Hamilton, *The Meeting House*, p. 29.

10  Siry, *Beth Sholom Synagogue*, pp. 248–9.

11  The Society also had a Parish House on East Dayton Street, the same street as their church, dedicated in 1916.

12  Hamilton and Mollenhoff, *Frank Lloyd Wright's Monona Terrace*, p. 101.

13  Siry, *Beth Sholom Synagogue*, p. 257.

14  Siry, *Beth Sholom Synagogue*, p. 257.

15    *Capital Times* (Madison, 29 August 1951), quoted in Siry, *Beth Sholom Synagogue*, p. 271.

16    *Capital Times* (Madison, 29 August 1951), quoted in Siry, *Beth Sholom Synagogue*, p. 271.

17    The timber members are all 4"x 2" (100 x 50mm) or 6" x 2" (150 x 50mm).

18    Anthony Alofsin, *Wright and New York: The Making of America's Architect* (New Haven: Yale University Press, 2019), pp. 210–11.

19    Fuller patented his hexagonal '4D House' in 1928. See *Inventions: The Patented Works of Buckminster Fuller* (New York, St Martin's Press, 1983), p. 11

20    Siry, *Beth Sholom Synagogue*, p. 282.

21    One of Fuller's own foundation myths is that he constructed an 'octet truss' from toothpicks and dried peas during a kindergarten class when he was five years old.

22    Siry, *Beth Sholom Synagogue*, pp. 261–3. The Rev. Kenneth Patton was receptive to the idea. Early in the society's planning he had suggested that they might buy 100 acres of land to build an entire village, an ideal interracial community, but the members were not inclined to uproot themselves from Madison.

23    Hamilton, *The Meeting House*, p. 5.

24    Siry, *Beth Sholom Synagogue*, pp. 261–3.

25    M. D. Gaebler, 'Unitarianism in the Life and Work of Frank Lloyd Wright', in *Landmarks in the Life of the First Unitarian Society of Madison*, p. 59.

26    Hamilton, *The Meeting House*, p. 10 and p. 29, n. 30.

27    Gaebler, 'Unitarianism in the Life and Work of Frank Lloyd Wright', p. 64.

28    Siry, *Beth Shlom Synagogue*, pp. 298–9.

29    Anthony Cox et al., 'The Brynmawr Rubber Factory', *AA Files, The Annals of the Architectural Association School of Architecture*,10 (Autumn 1985), 3-12.

30    Andrew Saint, 'Wright and Great Britain', in Anthony Alofsin (ed.), *Frank Lloyd Wright: Europe and Beyond* (Berkeley: University of California Press, 1999), pp. 136–7.

31    Letter from Robert Furneaux Jordan to Frank Lloyd Wright, 30 May 1949. Frank Lloyd Wright Foundation archive reference A112A10.

32    Robert Furneaux Jordan, 'A Great Architect's Visit to Britain', *The Listener*, 44/1130 (28 September 1950), 415.

33    Victoria Perry, *Built for a Better Future: The Brynmawr Rubber Factory* (Oxford: White Cockade Publishing, 1994), p. 48.

34    Jordan, 'A Great Architect's Visit to Britain', p. 415.

35    Saint, 'Wright and Great Britain', pp. 136-7. The exchange, as Peter Moro recalled it, rings true, but on the issue of acoustics, Frank and the county architects were at cross-purposes. The acousticians of the Festival Hall had become preoccupied with reverberation time as an absolute. Frank was concerned with the projection and the clarity of music and voice, of which reverberation was just one aspect. A large part of the problem, solved by the 2007 remedial work, was that the reverberation time was actually too short. The original acousticians went too far in their effort to dampen it down, which in turn stripped energy and clarity from the sound. If they could have followed Frank's advice it would have led to a better outcome.

36    Curtis Besinger, *Working with Mr. Wright: What it Was Like* (Cambridge: Cambridge University Press, 1995), p. 216.

37    Siry, *Beth Sholom Synagogue*, pp. 291–2.

38    There are several unbuilt projects of the 1930s and 1940s that feature prominent glass elevations, most conspicuously the Elizabeth Arden Desert Spa, Phoenix, Arizona, 1945, and the Rogers Lacy Hotel, Dallas, Texas, 1946.

# 17

# The Welshman

The after-dinner conversation broke up as the train slowed to a stop. They had arrived at the border station, where they were instructed to take their baggage for inspection in the customs house. They were led to the counter where Olgivanna began to open their cases. One of the officers noticed that Frank was carrying a roll of drawings under his arm. When she asked him to open it, he refused. 'I am the invited guest of the International Architectural Convention ... I will not have you pawing through my drawings.' The angry dispute that followed was curtailed by Frank announcing that he was going back to America. He stormed out of the

customs house and strode down the platform. Seconds later he returned, walking up the platform with a rifle pointed at his back. The soldier was perplexed. Thankfully Olgivanna could speak in Russian. She explained that Frank wasn't aware that he couldn't just walk back over the border. Frank's mood had only darkened, 'What does this man think he's doing? Tell him that this sort of conduct will put warships on the Black Sea!' Olgivanna pleaded with him to calm down, then explained to the Russian officials, 'He is an American ... we have freedom of speech in America. Everyone there says what he feels.' Olgivanna recalled that the senior officer disappeared to make a phone call. Frank, she said, was

> *a free-spoken man and no-one can curb him .... The man came back from telephoning and said quietly 'You are ready now to continue your journey to Moscow.' Mr. Wright did not open his roll of drawings ... and I was proud of the way that he had upheld the dignity of the American citizen.*[2]

Frank and Olgivanna had travelled a long way. They had left The Valley a few days after the public testing of the Johnson Wax column. They sailed from New York on the *Queen Mary*, first to Southampton and then across to Cherbourg, where they caught a train for Paris. They rested there for a few days, allowing Olgivanna to make a visit to Gurdjieff, whose volatile behaviour only increased her unease.[3] From Paris they took a train to Berlin, where they found the city submerged in Nazism. They changed trains for the last stretch of their journey to Moscow, where Frank was to give a speech at a 'Congress of Architects' convened by General Secretary Stalin himself while, at the same time, he was secretly conducting his Great Purge. Olgivanna had fled Russia to escape the revolution. She was anxious at the prospect of returning, and as the train had approached Poland's eastern border she warned Frank: 'You had better be careful in what you say or else we may both land in prison.' Dinner was served a few hours before the border. Frank and Olgivanna were led by the waiter to a table that was already occupied by a slender, well-dressed man with distinguished features. Introducing themselves, Frank noted a crisp English accent, and the stranger noticed Frank's, 'very slightly Americanised English'.[4] They established quickly that they were connected in two unexpected ways. They were both architects, and they were both Welsh, born out of Wales. The stranger was Clough Williams-Ellis, the British delegate to the Moscow Congress.

This account of Frank's life and origins began as he dictated the opening words of the first edition of his autobiography. He was fifty-nine years old; his career had stalled. He was in the process of losing his beloved house. There had been no reason to assume he would build anything again. His autobiography was written in the knowledge that it might be his last word to the world. It is generally accepted that it was Olgivanna's idea. Gurdjieff, her spiritual mentor, developed his own self-mythology as an instrument of his teaching. Frank approached his memoir in the same way, writing it first for Olgivanna, casting himself as the indomitable hero, ensuring that it should be a good story, if not entirely factual, because the point of the exercise was to sell it, to earn money at a desperate time. In 1932, when it was first published, his situation had hardly improved. Although the early printings sold well, they were small editions. In the late 1930s he emerged, suddenly, from obscurity into the bright light of fame. His real story was extraordinary enough, but the wishful fictions within his published account were also celebrated and cemented as fact. From that point onwards, for both Frank and Olgivanna, myth-building became a perpetual project.

The second edition of his autobiography was published in 1943. Although it is longer than the first edition, the luxuriant narrative of his youth in The Valley was reduced, replaced by long accounts of the triumphs of his late career. Where the first edition ended with a rumination on his past and its vicissitudes, the later edition revelled in his overdue redemption and set out his vision for the American future. The last episode in the 1943 edition is a lengthy account of his visit to the Moscow Congress of 1937, which concludes with a declaration of his faith in a 'new organic Russia ... If Comrade Stalin ... is betraying the revolution then, in the light of what I have seen in Moscow, I say he is betraying

it into the hands of the Russian people.' Clough Williams-Ellis recalled an evening a few days into the Moscow visit. They had attended a 'vast outdoor opera performance that involved a squadron of cavalry. Frank had been so impressed that he, 'burst out with "These are the people! Theirs is the future!"'

Clough also recalled the events on the platform at Nieharelaje Station:

> my companion flatly refused to open anything at all and went off into the most uncontrolled fit (or show) of anger that I have ever beheld in a grown man ... When the tirade was over I walked him along the platform reviewing the actual facts of the situation and reasoning mildly ... what will you tell those you represent back in America? That you turned back rather than have your shirts and socks inspected? ... you can't possibly do anything so utterly silly – come and have a drink and tell these chaps they can get on with it. Grudgingly, he did so, and we reached Moscow without further incident.[5]

No guns, no triumph of American dignity, just reasonable pragmatism when it was needed. But it is Olgivanna's account of the 'border incident' that has entered the canon of Frank Lloyd Wright mythology. It first appeared in Our House, a late adjunct to his autobiography published a few months after Frank's death, its tone redolent of the late 1950s Cold War rather than the détente of the 1930s. It has been repeated many times since. Our House was not Olgivanna's first book. It was preceded four years earlier by a spiritual improvement manual, The Struggle Within, a soft exegesis of Gurdjieff's 'work'. Kamal Amin, one of the later apprentices, recalled in his own memoir that Olgivanna had gradually moulded the operation of the Fellowship until it was, 'duplicating the community in which she had lived with Gurdjieff'. Much as Frank was uninterested, fixated on his architecture, by the early 1940s the world around him, and his appearance to it, were both under Olgivanna's control.[6]

## 9 April 1959. St Joseph's Hospital, Encanto Village, Phoenix, Arizona

Dr Rorke told Olgivanna that Gurdjieff was to blame. Frank's heart stopped sometime in the mid-morning. Joe Rorke was the Taliesin physician. He'd been called to Frank's room by the night nurse.[7] They made an attempt to resuscitate, but he could not be brought back. Olgivanna had been with him too until the small hours, before leaving to rest in a spare room. She had been worried, but hopeful that Frank would recover as he had always done before. She was devastated that she hadn't been there, that there had been no 'last words', that she could not take him back home to die. Frank had suffered with gallstones for decades but he had never been properly treated. The fierce pain had seized him once in 1934, when Gurdjieff had been with them at Taliesin. The magus proposed his own therapy: 'You should show the gall bladder who is master: feed it more grease!' There was no wiser doctor, as far as Olgivanna was concerned. She made sure that Frank abided by the prescription through the uncomfortable years that followed, along a reliable path to rupture, sepsis and death.[8]

Easter was always celebrated at Taliesin West with a gathering of family, friends and Fellowship members, but the week had begun with a dark portent, Frank's son David arrived from Los Angeles with news that Catherine, Frank's first wife, the mother of six of his children, had been cremated that same morning. David could find no sympathy for his father's tears. On Easter Sunday there was the customary feasting, music and dance (Pl. 167). A film show and a piano recital brought the evening to its end. Frank had seemed tired as Olgivanna led him through the ceremonies, but there was no sense of anything amiss.[9] He began to struggle the following Saturday. As an audience waited on him for the start of a dance performance, Frank was being rushed to hospital. Iovanna recalled her father gasping, 'the pain. I can't bear it. Mother chop the old tree down.'

When news of his death got back to Taliesin West, it was met with incredulity. They all expected him to live out at least a century.[10] There is a passage in one of Uncle Jenkin's sermons, *Transformation of the Country*, in which he describes the advent of the 'Manny Reaper' on the Lloyd Jones farm,

Pl. 167.  Easter Breakfast at Taliesin West 1959. The Taliesin Choir is singing from the balcony in the background. Photograph by Herb Jacobs, *Madison Capital Times*.

the first intrusion of the machine age into their daily life. Frank would be born within the same decade, when the corduroy roads still ran for hundreds of miles across Wisconsin. He lived long enough to fly in luxury across the Atlantic, a life so dense with incident that it seems sometimes to have been more than one existence. There were certainly two careers. He completed as many built projects in his last thirty years as he managed in the previous sixty. William Storrer's *Complete Catalogue* includes 430 completed works, and there are more again unbuilt. His output was phenomenal in quantity, almost miraculous in quality.[11] There are indications, though, within the surge of late projects, that Frank was anticipating finality.

## October 1956. The Sherman Hotel, Chicago

A large audience was present for the unveiling of a bewildering proposal: a skyscraper of 528 floors, fully a mile in height.[12] Its exterior was a continuous skin of steel, a monocoque shell, to, 'absorb, justify and legitimise the gregarious instinct of humanity and ... mop-up what now remains of urbanism, and leave us free to do Broadacre City'.[13]

Frank explained that the first of these astonishing towers, 'The Illinois', would be built in the centre of Chicago, rendering the rest of the business district obsolete, to be returned to grass. Two more, constructed in Central Park, would do the same favour for New York.[14] Despite Frank's assurance that the 'mile high tower' was quite consistent with his dream of decentralisation, many friends and supporters were unconvinced. Others dismissed it as a publicity stunt, but they were wrong. Frank was entirely serious. One of the key drawings, a technical cross-section, had a prominent, carefully inscribed legend that listed the great modern engineers whose original ideas made 'The Illinois' possible. The name of Louis Sullivan was there, at the top, as the man who, 'first made the tall building tall', and at the end of the list, Frank's own name with his honorary 'engineering' degrees, one from Switzerland and the other from Germany.[15] His intention was to assure anyone who might be interested, and who had access to unlimited funds, that it could really be built.[16] He presented it as a technical, sociological and aesthetic enterprise, but the true meaning of the 'Mile High Tower' was entirely human and personal. It would be his marker, as eternal and as bold as any could be, outliving everyone he knew or could think of, like the Romeo and Juliet Windmill, defying them all.[17] Midway Gardens had gone long before, demolished in 1929, and the Larkin Administration Building had gone too, razed to the ground in 1950, just to make a car park. They were two of his greatest achievements. Of the many houses there were dozens that had burned, collapsed from neglect or worse still, been altered by other architects. Taliesin itself was destroyed twice. He, more than anyone, understood that buildings were fragile, transient things. It was too easy to imagine that all he had done would soon disappear. 'The grass withereth, the flower fadeth away', the verse so cherished by his grandfather, had always tormented him, but he knew it to be true.

The least plausible aspect of the Mile High Tower was that someone would come forward with the money to build

Pl. 168. Frank's presentation of 'The Illinois', a mile-high tower, at the Sherman Hotel, Chicago, 1956.

in contemporary terms, which, he explained, would enable it to soar to incredible heights (Pl. 168). It would provide space for 130,000 workers, to fulfil its ultimate purpose which was it. Then, early in 1957 another possibility fell into his hands. Out of the blue, a commission from the Development Board of Iraq to design a new opera house for Baghdad. He sensed a higher purpose at work again, the feeling of a circle being closed. His mother had loved *A Thousand and One Nights*, it had filled his boyhood imagination. He travelled to Baghdad, where he told his hosts that he considered himself a subject of Harun al-Rashid, the eighth-century caliph and hero of the tales.[18] By the end of the visit he had secured an audience with King Faisal II and been able to expand his commission to include a casino, a 'central postal-telegraph building' and a grand bazaar.[19] Royal patronage came with unlimited funds. It must have occurred to Frank that Faisal II was one of the few people who could even afford to build the Mile High Tower. The Baghdad projects would be an apt culmination, perhaps the enduring testament that he hoped for. But if realisation seemed a formality, it was without regard for the volatility of the region in the aftermath of the Suez Crisis. In one violent day, little more than a year after Frank's visit, the Hashemite Kingdom of Iraq yielded to a *coup d'état*. Young King Faisal was executed in the courtyard of his half-built palace. On 14 July 1958, like so many of Frank's cherished expectations, the Baghdad dream came to an abrupt end. It could have been later in that month that another idea took shape in Frank's mind, perhaps with a sense of resignation, something more modest but not so contingent on wild fates.

By the late 1950s Frank was in control of The Valley. The Fellowship owned more property than even Uncle James had managed to acquire. Uncle Enos, the last of the original Lloyd Joneses, had died in 1941, but Unity Chapel was still cherished by the younger descendants and it belonged to the Lloyd Jones family, not to Frank.[20] For his whole adult life he imagined that he would be buried there too, but in his ninety-first year he began to imagine a different resting place for himself and for those closest to him.[21] His mausoleum would be called Unity Temple (Pl. 169). It had a pure, square plan. Both the name and the form seemed inevitable.

The outline of the plan was defined by double rows of columns. There was a third layer behind the stone columns, full-height clear glass between hardwood posts. The space

inside was empty apart from a fireplace at one corner. Sarcophagi were set into the floor beneath a square of black marble and lit from above by a grid of skylights that closely resembled the *Go-Tenjo* lid of the original Unity Temple, far away in Oak Park, far away in time.

Frank revisited the design regularly over the following months, content to take his time with construction. Blocks of lustrous quartzite arrived from a quarry at Rock Springs, an avenue of conifers was planted along the road from Taliesin to the chapel, and on the site apprentices had marked out the lines of the footings.[22] The mausoleum was around seventy metres from Unity Chapel, far enough to stand on its own but close enough always to be linked. He drew a broad stone path between them and, on some of the sketches, a cenotaph with a bronze lantern located precisely on the, 'centre line of Grandfather Obelisk', the modest resting place of Richard Lloyd Jones.[23]

## Sunday, 12 April 1959. Unity Chapel, The Valley, Wyoming Township, Wisconsin

Frank's hearse was a farm trailer, pulled by a pair of heavy draft horses, black percherons, with Wes Peters and Gene Masselink at the reins. They had both joined the Fellowship nearly thirty years before, at its inception, arriving fresh from college. Neither had left. In 1935, three years after joining the Fellowship, Wesley married Svetlana, Olgivanna's daughter from her first marriage, and became Frank's son-in-law. Wes and Gene were the seniors of the Fellowship, 'Life Members' who had been allocated their own places in the future mausoleum.[24] It was Wes and Gene who had brought Frank's coffin to the Valley from Taliesin West, an unbroken, twenty-eight-hour drive. The arrangements were made quickly. There were many who wished that they could have made it to The Valley for the funeral, but who were too far away or found out too late. Photographs taken on that Sunday evening show around fifty mourners walking the mile from Taliesin to Unity Chapel in the rain, a loose procession behind the trailer. It was piled high with pine branches, the coffin completely

Pl. 169. Frank's intended mausoleum, to be called Unity Temple and built a short distance to the east of Unity Chapel, 1958. The pine branches on the left of the drawing indicate the edge of grandmother Mallie's pine grove.
FLWF/AAFAL.

hidden. The service was led by Max Gaebler, pastor of the First Unitarian Society of Madison. He read from *Self Reliance*, Emerson's famous essay, Frank's dependable touchstone (Pl. 170).

The apprentices brought a blade of rough limestone from the Taliesin quarry, to plant at the head of his grave (Pl. 171). There was no other marker. It was assumed that his burial there would be temporary, for as long as it took for the mausoleum to be built. Assumed by everyone except Olgivanna. There is another episode in Olgivanna's book *Our House*, in which she recounts a conversation with Frank. They were discussing monuments. He says, 'If it's a beautiful monument, let us have it.' Olgivanna demurs: for her there was no kind of monument worth having 'except that in the hearts of those who knew us we remain an inspiring memory'.[25] Within a day of the funeral, she revised Frank's plan for the succession of his practice. Connections to the first Wright family were cut. Wes Peters and Gene Masselink were promoted to Vice-President and Secretary. Just as she had transferred her own loyalty from Gurdjieff to Frank, the lifetime of loyalty that Wesley and Gene had devoted to Frank would now be devoted to her. Plans for the mausoleum were dropped. The spiritual heart of the Fellowship shifted, for as long as Olgivanna lived, from The Valley to Arizona, where she had always felt more at ease.

There would seem a sort of righteousness in the way that Frank's mausoleum was forgotten, leaving him to rest in the yard of Unity Chapel among his true people. It's where he should be, where he had often said he intended to be. He now has a handsome slab below the shard of limestone that still marks the head of his grave. Both are brushed in soft moss, embedded in the moist soil of the gentle grove. A sense of resolution pervades, but it deceives. Frank's remains are no longer there. Olgivanna moved him.

Olgivanna lost her own life to tuberculosis on 1 March, 1985.[26] Dr Joe Rorke, who had witnessed Frank's death, was there too with Olgivanna at her end. Frank had left no last words. Olgivanna's last words would create a schism. Frank had expected that she would be buried alongside him, but the prospect of a grave in The Valley was unacceptable to her. Her dying wish, Rorke told the apprentices, was that Frank's remains should be exhumed, cremated and then brought to Taliesin West so that she and Frank could share eternity together in the sun, where *she* wanted *him* to be. As the *New York Times* reported, 'Friction within the community of Wright relatives, apprentices, students, artists and friends was already heated before the opening of the architect's grave … [the] source of friction lay in Mrs. Wright's dominance of Taliesin West after her husband died.' Frank's descendants were uniformly appalled.[27] Robert Lloyd Wright, then aged eighty-one, called it an, 'act of vandalism', and he pointed out that the Fellowship 'knew all about my father's wishes and they should have prevented it'. Frank's granddaughter Elizabeth, an architect herself, was more specific. She told the press that her grandfather belonged in Wisconsin, 'that is the heartland of Frank Lloyd Wright … the heartland is

Pl. 170.  The funeral of Frank Lloyd Wright at Unity Chapel. Wes Peters is the pall-bearer leading on the left, Pastor Max Gaebler is to his right. Gene Masselink is behind the pastor. Olgivanna is behind the coffin. Wisconsin Historical Society WHS-45511.

where his spirit is, where the ideas were formulated, where the genius was born.' She was right, but Wesley Peters was right to remind them, also, that Frank would usually accede to Olgivanna's wishes.[28]

Olgivanna had suppressed her own nationhood. She had fled Montenegro as the revolution encroached, and then shed her identity, willingly, during her time with Gurdjieff. She loved Frank, but they saw the world differently. Frank's cultural identity was vigorous, unshakeable. At the forefront of his thought and behaviour, he was American, Welsh and Unitarian. Everything he did, everything he was capable of, had grown and branched from radical, intellectual roots and a fiercely defiant attitude. By nurture and by nature, this 'blood knowledge' as Olgivanna called it, was 'such as streamed through the veins of his druid-Welsh ancestors'.[29] She knew this about him, and admired him for it but, in the end, could

Pl. 171. Frank's memorial at Unity Chapel, with the Lloyd Jones cemetery and pine grove beyond. The standing stone was the original head-stone. The small slab directly behind is for Svetlana, Frank's stepdaughter, and at the base of the pine tree immediately behind is the last resting place of Mamah Borthwick.

not be reconciled with the reality that Frank was not really hers, that he was 'more than any other thing, a Lloyd Jones'.[30]

## Mid-July 1956. Snowdonia National Park, Wales

Nineteen years had passed since their tense conversation on the floodlit platform of Nieharelaje Station. Clough Williams-Ellis was wary of Frank's demanding nature, but he need not have been anxious. Frank was, according to Olgivanna, 'as gay and happy as a young boy to be in that wildly picturesque country'.[31] It was a typical summer in Wales, sun and high cloud, the occasional shower. Snowdonia was a beautiful part of the land. Frank's only other visit, six years before, had been to the industrial anglicised south-east. Caernarvonshire was in the far north-west, blessed with a magnificent landscape, where the English language was rarely heard. Frank had travelled, as usual, with his wife and his daughter, Iovanna. Outside Frank's family, Clough was one of the few Welsh acquaintances they had made. Frank could not have hoped for a more capable host. Clough drove with them through the mountains, recalling later that the rocks, 'called forth his constant commendation as consummate examples of divine cantilevering, the mountains themselves having, he declared, no peers for miniature majesty ... in all the world save possibly Japan'. While he was in Frank's company, Clough was impressed continually by his 'open-armed and zestful appreciation of all things authentically Welsh'. He recalled Frank's particular delight at the trees: 'he rejoiced in their stalwart grace ... insisting that American trees had no such vigorous individuality.' Frank had, at last, found the Wales that he had been imagining for the whole of his long life.[32]

The University of Wales chose to award higher doctorates in only a few disciplines. Outstanding achievement in the field of theology could be rewarded with a Doctorate in Divinity. Exceptional writers might be endowed as Doctors of Literature. The pinnacle in every other field of learning in the arts and humanities was a Doctorate in Laws. This was the distinction that was to be bestowed upon Frank. As Clough put it, he had come 'to receive belated honour in his ancestral country – Wales – at the hands of its University', before reflecting that 'he was, I felt, much less my private guest than a venerable public monument temporarily removed from its transatlantic pedestal to have an overdue laurel wreath laid at its foot, a view with which he seemed to concur'.[33]

Frank had been awarded medals and memberships of academies in Japan, Cuba, Brazil, Germany and Belgium. Latin American and European institutions were particularly appreciative. He had been given the Gold Medal of the RIBA in 1941, apparently as part of the British wartime effort to build sympathy in the American establishment. It was ironic that Frank, an ardent isolationist, was drawn into the exercise. His first academic honour was an MA, which came in 1939, ironically, from the Wesleyan University in Connecticut.[34] Princeton and Yale followed a decade later with honorary doctorates. Florida Southern College awarded him a doctorate in 1950, to acknowledge the decade of intermittent work that Frank had contributed to the rebuilding of their campus. He accepted an honorary doctorate in fine arts from the University of Wisconsin with a sense of deserved restitution. It had been a hope that he had nurtured for decades.[35] When he received the invitation, he responded with gratitude and asked if he could be awarded his undergraduate degree at the same time, a proposal which the university had to decline with as much tact as it could muster. The Wisconsin ceremony was in June 1955. A month later he flew to Switzerland to receive his honorary Doctor of Engineering award from the Eidgenössische Technische Hochschule, Zürich, Albert Einstein's alma mater, one of the finest technical universities in the world. He went to Darmstadt, in southern Germany, during the same trip, to receive the second of the honorary 'engineering' doctorates that were later proclaimed, in bold capitals, on the drawings of the 'Mile High Tower'.[36] The invitation from Wales reached him the following spring. It was 'received with pride and pleasure'. Frank declared:

*Of the many honours the spirit of Man has bestowed upon me, none touches me more closely where I live than that Wales, my mother's own native country, should count me one of her sons.*[37]

The University of Wales was a confederation of four university colleges, situated in Aberystwyth, Cardiff, Bangor and Swansea. Each had its own degree ceremony, but the honorary degrees were awarded on behalf of the University as a whole, and the venue was moved between the colleges each year, to coincide with the summer meetings of the University Court. It might have suited Frank to have received his doctorate at Aberystwyth, within a few miles of the Unitarian *Smotyn Du*, but in 1956 the Congregation was to take place at Bangor University, in the far north west. Being in north Wales had compensations, however: the sublime landscape of course, and the hospitality of Clough Williams-Ellis.

Frank, with Olgivanna and Iovanna, arrived in north Wales in the second week of July They stayed first at Bangor's most reputable hotel, The Castle, on Bishops Close, directly facing the cathedral and downslope from the university.[38] A few days later they transferred to Clough's hotel at Portmeirion.[39] Clough had steeled himself for what he was sure would be a stinging critical assessment of the decorative, set-piece village that he had designed and built across the cliffside on the Dwyryd estuary. It stood against every principle of modernism, just as Clough intended it to, but Frank would only ever judge on his own terms. 'He took it all in without a blink, seeming instantly to see the point of all my wilful pleasantries', Clough recalled. 'Having paid handsome tribute to the situation he then proceeded to abash me by praising my exploitation of its violent variations in level; whereafter he took *me* on a tour right round the place, pointing out features that he particularly liked' (Pl. 172).

The Lloyd Wrights stayed in north Wales until 19 July. Clough was with them for most of their stay, and was astonished by Frank's energy. 'The mileage he covered ... was immense, the sight seeing gargantuan ... one way or another every day was chock-full ... so that high official occasions were barely reached in time after breathless scrambles.'[40] The first of the nearly missed events was the banquet for the twelve honorary graduands, held in Bangor on the evening of 17 July. Frank was one of two international recipients, the other was Vijaya Lakshmi Pandit, the first woman President

Pl. 172. Frank with Clough Williams Ellis at Portmeirion, July 1956. The urn is now a fountain in the pond at the centre of the village.
Courtesy of Portmeirion.

place the following afternoon beneath the lofty barrel vaults of the Prichard-Jones Hall. Frank was robed in a magnificent gown of scarlet cloth with 'silk facings and sleeve linings of red shot with purple'. In a short ceremony, bracketed by the enthusiastic doffing of hats, Frank received his doctorate from the Principal of University College of Wales Aberystwyth, Goronwy Rees, a man of idiosyncratic brilliance, and a firebrand in Frank's own vein.[41] His Presentation Address touched on Frank's deepest sentiments:

> I have the great honour and pleasure today of presenting Mr. Frank Lloyd Wright for the degree of Doctor in Legibus honoris causa, and all the more so because I feel that in honouring him we are also honouring his Welsh grandfather and grandmother who, well over a century ago, with their seven children, made the long journey by ship and canal-boat and lake-steamer from Wales to Wisconsin, taking with them their family motto, which has been Mr. Wright's own, 'The Truth against the World,' 'Y Gwir yn erbyn a Byd.'
>
> And certainly the grandson of the Welsh emigrants has brought great glory to the land of his fathers. It is no exaggeration to describe him as the greatest of living architects and one of the founding fathers of modern architecture ... For Mr. Wright is not only an architect of genius; he is also a revolutionary who has given his revolutionary ideas tangible form in his buildings. They give a local habitation, here and now, to ideas of a freer and a more humane society which are common to us all and are the hope of the world. They make us feel as if a new world were already with us; but they also give us the deep conviction that the new world will be better than the old.[42]

of the UN General Assembly. They were honoured with a toast, to which each gave a reply, Frank's ending with a fond tribute to the nation of his forebears. The Congregation took

That evening, after the ceremony, he was driven to the seaside town of Rhyl, thirty miles along the north Wales coast, to give a live broadcast interview for the Welsh service of BBC Television.[43] Clough recalled the 'highly intelligent interviewer'.[44] This was John Ormond, who would become one of the finest Welsh poets working in the English language. Frank later sent Ormond a telegram thanking him for their enjoyable conversation.[45] On 19 July, their final day in north Wales, they travelled through Snowdonia National Park to Colwyn Bay, to meet Clough's friend, the architect Sidney Colwyn Foulkes. Colwyn Foulkes's son Ralph recalled that Frank, 'just walked into our offices in Pwllycrochan Avenue, and everyone was dumbfounded.' The party was invited to Colwyn Foulkes's house for tea, where Frank found himself distracted by a large beech tree. They watched as 'he stood in silence for several minutes looking up and then, with both arms outstretched ... started to stroke the bark with both hands'.[46] The Lloyd Wrights left Wales late in the afternoon of the 19th, travelling onwards from Colwyn Bay. Frank, on their second encounter, had made a more positive and more lasting impact upon Clough than he had made in Russia those many years before:

> my impression from my happily renewed acquaintance with him was that he was far broader in his sympathies than I had supposed, a poetical philosopher indeed, who, viewing the whole world with tolerant interest, saw architecture and the arts generally as but parts, yet utterly essential parts, of humanity's equipment for climbing up to the higher level he still believed it would one day reach.

Frank was in London on the morning of 20 July, at the Stafford Hotel in St James's. Clough had booked it on their behalf, taking pains, as he had throughout their visit, to keep Frank's presence out of the public eye.[47] A reception had been arranged for him at the headquarters of the Incorporated Association of Architects and Surveyors in Belgrave Square. The President of the Association had been delighted to receive a letter from Frank in the autumn of 1955, accepting the offer of an honorary membership. 'I appreciate the compliment paid to me by the I.A.A.S. The British in me is still British', Frank told them, choosing the identifier with care. Other senior members were astonished, because 'the greatest architect of our day ... has hitherto displayed unmistakeable reluctance to be identified with professional bodies'.[48] Council members went on from the

reception, with Frank, to a relaxed lunch at the Coq D'Or in Mayfair.[49] A few hours later he was on the other side of St James's Park, at the Bride of Denmark, a private bar in the basement of the offices of the Architectural Press, publishers of the *Architects' Journal*. He was joined there by an eager crowd of journalists and English modernist latecomers, who beset him with questions that he had been answering since the 1930s. It pleased him, still, to swat them away[50] (Pl. 173).

In the summer of 1956 Frank was resident at the Plaza Hotel in New York. The contract for construction of the Guggenheim Museum had been signed in May (Pl. 174 and Pl. 175). Building was due to start in mid-August.[51] It would be reasonable to assume that Frank flew back to New York over the weekend that followed his commitments in London, ready to pick up work on the Monday, in keeping with the relentless pace of his practice and his life. The whole of his British visit could have been wrapped up within a week. There is, however, a recollection in Olgivanna's memoir that suggests there was more to the visit than has been presumed until now:

> once, when we came across an old cemetery, we looked for some of his ancestors' graves. We tried to read those complex Welsh names which were almost impossible to pronounce even for him, though he did not want to admit it: Evrawc, Manawyddan, Wledig, Llevelys, Fflwch. At last we found one tombstone with the name WRIAETH inscribed on it. He was overjoyed.[52]

Olgivanna must have assembled her list of names from one or more books written in Welsh. The first two are names of major characters in the Mabinogion. The three that follow may come from the same source, but they are not names, just words that seem randomly chosen. Wright was, of course, the name of Frank's father, not Welsh at all. He may have been looking for 'Lloyd' or 'Jones' or possibly John Enoch, but certainly not for 'Wright'. The most intriguing aspect of this story is that Frank was looking for his ancestors in a cemetery. Even allowing for Olgivanna's

Pl. 173. At the 'Bride of Denmark', the private bar of the Architectural Press. At left is Ove Arup, the great structural engineer, and at right are Jane Drew and Maxwell Fry, the prominent English modernist architects. 20 July 1956.
Courtesy of Architects Journal.

Pl. 174. The Guggenheim Museum, New York, 1959.

embellishment, the recollection implies that they did, at some stage in the course of their visit to Britain, make their way to south Cardiganshire to find Frank's Unitarian roots. There is another source that removes any doubt.

## July 1956. Prengwyn, South Cardiganshire, Wales

There is a set of inscribed slabs mounted on the inside of the stone walls of the New Chapel at Llwynrhydowen, the walls that David Timothy built. They are memorials to previous ministers. One of them pays tribute to the Rev. Aubrey Martin, who died in 1990. From 1972 he was minister at Pantydefaid Chapel, built on the village square of Prengwyn. Aubrey Martin was married to Nansi. Both were scholars and both had work published on the history of the founding chapels. There are many in the neighbourhood of Prengwyn and Rhydowen with fond memories of their music lessons with Nansi. She had a vivid memory of her own, of a summer day, when she was 31 years of age, which by good fortune, she related to the local author, Jon Meirion Jones, in 1998.[53] If she had not done so at that time there might be no surviving memory of the occasion. Nansi Martin died in 2002. On that Sunday in July 1956, she was at Pantydefaid Chapel for a special meeting of the elders and the local ministers to welcome an important visitor. Frank Lloyd Wright arrived in a chauffeur driven car:

> After being shown the interior of the chapel ... I saw him, carrying his hat and mingling amongst the members outside the chapel and in the village square. He spoke a few short phrases in Welsh but his accompanying driver, who was a mature Welsh speaker, assisted in translating the contents of the conversation.[54]

Pantydefaid Chapel would have appeared then much as it had done when his mother and sister had visited at the beginning of the century, but there was a notable addition to the interior that the elders would have been eager to show him. It was a large stone carving, unveiled in December 1922, a memorial to his uncle, Jenkin Lloyd Jones (Pl. 176). Inscribed in Welsh and English, it had been sent to Cardiganshire by the American Unitarian Society, based in Boston, Massachusetts, 'as an appreciation for sending Jenkin to America'.[55] It was one of two inscribed stones from America; the second was mounted on the outside of the farmhouse at Blaenralltddu, Jenkin's birthplace, also the birthplace of Frank's mother, just two miles away. Some planning had gone into the visit. The chapel community had been there ready to greet him and they would surely have helped him to find his way. It seems inconceivable that he would not have gone to the old farmhouse, to Llwynrhydowen Chapel and to the church at Llanwenog too, just another three miles along the road. If he had gone looking in a churchyard for the names of his forebears, he would have found them at Llanwenog alongside the beautiful church of the Lloyds of Llanfechan. Did he see the verse on John Enoch's headstone? Did he recognise the name of 'Iolo', inscribed beneath it? Olgivanna recalled that Frank, 'kept reminiscing ... tracing the memories back to his grandfather and grandmother who had come out of [that] poetic environment. "I can now understand" he said "the greatness that my uncles and aunts possessed ... a vague sense of belonging here comes over me."'[56]

## May 1958. Sarah Lawrence College, Yonkers, New York

Frank had been invited to give the Commencement Address to the new graduates. It was a prosperous liberal arts college, a half-hour drive north of Central Park, established to cultivate the daughters of wealthy parents, a lush campus set out along a hilltop thickly planted with specimen trees. The ceremony was held on the lawn in front of 'Westlands', the first college building, a large brick manor house in the Tudor revival style that hid its awkwardness behind a cloak of ivy. Two years had passed since Frank's visit to Wales. He was a few weeks short of his ninety-first birthday.

A journalist from the *New Yorker* magazine was waiting beneath the pergola outside for the scholars' procession. He recalled

Pl. 175.  The Guggenheim Museum, New York, 1959.
Photograph by David Heald, courtesy of the Solomon R. Guggenheim Foundation.

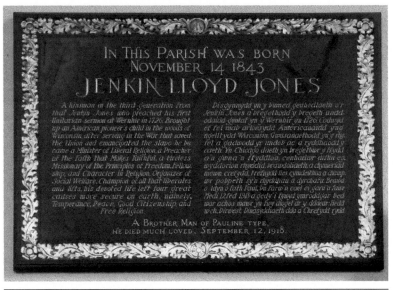

Pl. 176.  The memorial to Jenkin Lloyd Jones inside Pantydefaid Chapel, installed in 1922.

Pl. 177. Frank and apprentices making hay at Taliesin, 1953.
Photograph by Pedro Guerrero, courtesy of Dixie Guerrero.

*two men in academic gowns approaching … One was Dr. Harold Taylor, then president of the college; the other was Wright … Dr. Taylor was wearing a red gown that but for his companion would have served to make him the most conspicuous sight for miles around, but Wright had disposed of all imaginable competition by wearing a scarlet and purple gown so rich and soft that it might have been run up out of fuchsia blossoms.*

Frank explained that it had been awarded to him by the University of Wales, adding, 'Don't get much chance to wear it in my line of work.'[57] Frank concluded his Commencement Address with these words:

*The things we have to depend on for our culture, if we are ever to have one that is indigenous, are art, architecture*

*and religion … You know we have no religion to go with the Declaration of Independence, to go with the sovereignty of the individual … The only thing we have to go with it … is the saying of Jesus that the Kingdom of God is within you. The greatest of all poetic students of human nature gave us the key to the religion that would be ours someday and be appropriate to the brave status we have taken before the world … The principles that build the tree will build the man, and the principles that you find activating nature everywhere are those that will build the man, the woman and the spirit. That is why I think nature should be spelled with a capital 'N' … because all that we can learn of God we will learn from the body of God, which we call Nature.*[58]

There is, as there so often was, a little mischief in this declaration. The religion that Frank posited did exist. It existed in his life and in the lives of his forebears, the 'Liberal Christianity' of the Lloyd Joneses and the Transcendentalism of Emerson: 'The happiest man is he who learns from nature the lesson of worship',[59] but it was a form of worship that had never been more than the faith of the liberal fringe. In its conclusion his advice to the young graduates embodied the fundamental revelation of Unitarianism, the truth that had been conveyed to him in his childhood, and which inspired him still as a 91 year-old man, that God was present physically in the natural world that surrounded them (Pl. 177). The centrality of this idea had seeped back into his thinking in the months before. In September 1957 he had told Aline Saarinen, the *New York Times* critic, 'You put a capital "G" on God. All my life I've been putting a capital "N" on Nature. I know in my heart that it is all the body of God that we're ever going to see.'[60] His famously robust televised interview with the journalist Mike Wallace was broadcast in the same month. When asked about his faith, Frank said: 'I always considered myself deeply religious … I go occasionally to this [church] and then to that one, but my church – put a capital "N" on Nature, and go there … you spell God with a "G"… I spell Nature with an "N" – capital.'

In his contribution to the *Myvyrian Archaiology of Wales,* Iolo Morganwg set out an ambition to *reanimate the genius of our country ... by [affording] our writers models of writing that are more natural and truly beautiful than awkward imitations can ever be ... The ANCIENT BRITONS ... have a species of poetry peculiarly their own; of indigenous growth, founded on principles which ... are undoubtedly those of* Nature.[61]

'Nature' with an 'N' – capital.

The idea of Nature, of the organic and the primitive had passed to Frank unmodified, pristine artefacts from the revolutionary Unitarian and Romantic polemic of the late nineteenth century. They were ideas that were never given fuller expression than they were in the life and art of Frank Lloyd Wright. To Frank it was a simple, unambiguous fact, no less than God's own will, that he should create according to his own intuition, that his own voice was the only one that he should heed, that conformity was the enemy of Truth. Frank understood his own creativity in terms that were identical to Iolo Morganwg's. Both built their reputation on a platform of creative defiance. Each was determined to be defined in those terms, offering their defiance as a spark to ignite a greater collective cause. Iolo's vision was of a new Wales, restored to unspoilt freedom in almost prelapsarian terms. He gave serious thought to the possibility that the Wales he dreamed of might actually be found in America. Richard and Mallie Jones went to America looking for it, and in time they found their new Wales. Their grandson Frank was born into their task of forging a new nation from the elements of its unique Nature, and he was born to share their spiritual convictions, guided by the same ancient truths. As Wales was to Iolo Morganwg, so America was to Frank Lloyd Wright. The new nation became transposed upon the old through the agency of Richard and Mallie Jones's migrant generation, but the lifelong, uncompromising drive to reform was the same, as was the determined attitude of creative defiance.

# CODA

In the first edition of his autobiography, published in 1932, Frank had written that his grandfather had a 'family crest, the old Druid symbol: /|\ "TRUTH AGAINST THE WORLD"'. For the vast majority, if not all of his readers, the symbol and the words meant the same thing, and it has been inferred, understandably, that Frank believed that too. A close reading of the second edition, published in 1943, reveals that he had always known that the symbol /|\, *Y Nod Cyfrin*, had its own, distinct meaning. There were not many people in Wales who knew this, let alone in America.

As Iolo Morganwg had explained, the world and the Almighty came into existence simultaneously, and God's 'Shout of Joy' was manifested as three rays of light.

In the closing section of *An Autobiography* of 1943 Frank is diverted by reminiscence. He sets out his feelings as an allegory:

The Title of this Allegory is 'Truth Against the World'...

*As I sat disconsolate on a low grass-covered mound in the chapel yard, I wondered and pondered and remembered as twilight deepened into dusk and darkened under the evergreens – the sacred chapel evergreens. They were sighing, stirring to and fro in the gentle breeze. As I carelessly listened I thought I heard ... Was it possible? A human sigh, then the whisper of my name. Listening now intently, I heard ... the gentle human whispering of intelligible words ... pale blue wraiths were wreathing upward out of the family graves ... all around me ... taking on familiar human shapes ... all seeming to sit there on their own headstones ...*

*Nearby a shade arose in shimmering silver, head bent forward, hands folded in her lap ... I whispered, 'Mother ... why are you here like this ... my mother ... surely* you are a *spirit in heaven!'*

*A pause ... 'A spirit in heaven, yes, my son: but spirits in heaven cast blue shadows here on the green earth as the golden sun casts the blue shadows of the green trees ...*

*'When gentle breezes fan your cheek or stir your hair my son, it may be the gentle touch of those whom you love but have lost upon the earth, those who still love you in heaven ... their caress may be upon your head ...'*[62]

Frank's allegory is deliberately and playfully overwrought. In *An Autobiography* the short verses alternate with text in small italics recalling the contemptuous reactions of his wife and daughter as they listen to him reading it aloud, *'Pah! Frank, you are gone, gone, gone. This must never get into print.'* The episode has its own title: *The Allegory that Failed to Convince Even the Author.* He goes out of his way to invite doubt upon the truth of its conclusion, uncertain if he should reveal the meaning of /|\ or whether it should remain hidden. It was not until Frank reached his very old age that he seemed comfortable to give full expression to the spirituality and the cultural identity, the Welshness, of the Lloyd Joneses as it flowed within him. His experience of building the Unitarian Meeting House in Madison may have moved him towards his open reconciliation. His visit to Wales in 1956 surely completed it. God in Nature; Nature with an 'N'. Uncle Enos, the last of the original Lloyd Joneses, had died in 1941, while Frank was rewriting *An Autobiography.* In its self-deprecation the allegory recalls Iolo Morganwg at his most ambivalent, unsure about the responsibility that he bore for his people and his faith, the responsibility that he worked so hard to impose upon himself. In the early 1940s Frank wrestled with similar conflicted feelings: should he let the Lloyd Joneses fade into history? Or should he accept that he was one of them, and embrace the spiritual challenge that came with the Lloyd Jones name? It made him uneasy, but the answer was never in doubt.

*The silver shade gently lifted the semblance of a beloved, venerable head, eyes hidden deep in shadow as, more faintly than ever, now that the breeze was dying, scarcely audible whispered ... 'You will know what your beloved want you to know, my son, if you turn to look at the symbol on the chapel gate'* (Pl. 178).

*... I got up and went out by the way I came in. Wondering still and remembering I looked back at the gate. There it was in stone ... the revered, ancient Druid symbol old Timothy had carved there on the gatepost for the Lloyd-Joneses ...*

*Strange ... a new meaning ... Why had I not seen it so before? ... The downward rays of the sun were Joy! Joy! Set against*

Pl. 178. The meaning of *Y Nod Cyfrin* is 'Joy'. The gatepost of Unity Chapel. Photograph by Huw T. Walters.

*and dispelling the mean hatreds that were the sorrows of this world.*

*That then was what the old Druids knew?*

*'The truth to set against the woes of this world is Joy!'*

*Joy it is that elevates and transfigures Life* ∎

# 17 The Welshman
## *Notes*

1    The location of the railway station at the 1937 border between Poland and the USSR is now near the centre of Belarus, a few kilometres north-east of the city of Stowbtsy.

2    Olgivanna Lloyd Wright, *Our House* (New York: Horizon Press, 1959), pp. 37–40.

3    The 1937 Paris Exposition was at its midsummer peak, clustered around the base of the Eiffel Tower and dominated by the pavilions of Soviet Russia and Nazi Germany. If he did make time to visit, Frank would have been dismayed by the clumsy edifice that was supposed to represent America. Alden Dow, one of Frank's recent apprentices, won the 'grand prize for residential architecture', for a house designed in undisguised imitation of his erstwhile master.

4    Clough Williams-Ellis, *Architect Errant: The Autobiography of Clough Williams-Ellis* (Portmeirion: Golden Dragon Books, 1980), pp. 187–8. Clough was mistaken in assuming that Frank was the American delegate. Frank had been specifically invited to the congress by the Union of Soviet Architects, not sent as a national representative.

5    Williams-Ellis, *Architect Errant*, pp. 187–8.

6    Kamal Amin, *Reflections from the Shining Brow* (Santa Barbara: Fithian Press, 2004), pp. 14–15.

7    Meryl Secrest, *Frank Lloyd Wright: A Biography* (Chicago: University of Chicago Press, 1998), p. 12.

8    Roger Friedland and Harold Zellman, *The Fellowship: The Untold Story of Frank Lloyd Wright and the Taliesin Fellowship* (New York: HarperCollins, 2006), p. 526. There are also well-attested accounts of Olgivanna taking care to limit Frank's diet in his later years. When they were invited to dinners, she would insist that Frank should only be served white fish and baked potato. Unfortunately she also insisted that he should only drink milk, which in those days would always be full-fat.

9   It would actually be his ninety-second birthday. Frank began taking two years off his age around the time that he first met Olgivanna. His family knew of the deception, but it was not made known to the public until long after his death. See Secrest, *Frank Lloyd Wright: A Biography*, p. 334

10  Friedland and Zellman, *The Fellowship*, p. 525.

11  William A. Storrer, *The Architecture of Frank Lloyd Wright: A Complete Catalogue (Third Edition)* (Chicago: University of Chicago Press, 2002).

12  Frank Lloyd Wright, *A Testament* (New York: Horizon Press, 1956), p. 239.

13  Bruce Brooks Pfeiffer, *Wright: Complete Works 1943–1959* (Cologne: Taschen, 2016), p. 463. Transcript of a 'Taliesin Sunday Morning Talk' delivered by Frank Lloyd Wright, 30 December 1956.

14  P. J. Meehan (ed.), *The Master Architect: Conversations with Frank Lloyd Wright* (New York: John Wiley and Sons, 1984), p. 299. Transcript of the Mike Wallace TV interview.

15  Architectural qualifications in Germany and Switzerland are classed within the engineering disciplines. Frank's honorary Doctor of Engineering (Dr.-ing.) degrees were for his architectural achievements.

16  Bruce Brooks Pfeiffer observes, in *Wright: Complete Works 1943–1959*, p. 463, that Frank made a note on one of the drawings that the Mile High Tower could cost $60 million to build. In his book *A Testament* Frank gives the gross internal floor area of the tower as 18,462,000 sq. ft (1,715,161 sq.m.). Applying a realistic unit cost ($/sq.m.) to this area suggests that the construction cost in 1956 would have been in the region of $600 million, or $5.7 billion at 2021 prices. The Burj Khalifa, the world's tallest building at the time of writing, cost $1.5 billion to build.

17  The rapier-like form of 'The Illinois' has been cited as the inspiration for the Burj Khalifa. Frank's design is, of course, far more beautiful.

18  Friedland and Zellman, *The Fellowship*, p. 518.

19  Pfeiffer, *Wright: Complete Works 1943–1959*, p. 485.

20  Frank Lloyd Wright, *An Autobiography (Edition 2)* (New York: Duell, Sloan & Pearce, 1943), p. 437.

21  There is at least one account that Frank was prepared to see Unity Chapel demolished – see Secrest, *Frank Lloyd Wright: A Biography*, p. 14. As it wasn't his property, this would not have been possible without the Lloyd Jones family's assent. His plans for the mausoleum show a concern for the precise alignment of the two buildings that strongly suggests he intended the two buildings to complement each other.

22  Secrest, *Frank Lloyd Wright: A Biography*, pp. 13–14. Quartzite is the chief product of the quarries at Rock Springs, and the only obvious reason to source the stone from that location. At that time the road between Taliesin and Unity Chapel ran from the I-23 public road diagonally across a field and bridging over the Taliesin lake. A few of the trees still mark its line.

23  Pfeiffer, *Wright: Complete Works 1943–1959*, p. 550.

24  Masselink was Frank's personal assistant, and a gifted artist. Peters was the most trusted of Frank's architectural protégés, a veteran of Fallingwater and Johnson Wax. Wes Peters's marriage to Svetlana ended tragically. She died in September 1946 in a car accident near to Taliesin, along with the younger of their two sons. In 1970, at Olgivanna's bidding, Wes Peters married another Svetlana, the Russian defector Svetlana Alliluyeva, Joseph Stalin's daughter. That marriage lasted for three years.

25  O. L. Wright, *Our House*, p. 152.

26  There is a strong possibility that she had contracted tuberculosis during her time at Gurdjieff's commune, and that it was passed to her by the novelist Katherine Mansfield, who was cared for by Olgivanna during her own last days before her death from the same disease.

27  The exception was Iovanna. The disinterment would have been impossible without her approval. She was receiving treatment for a long-term psychiatric illness, and yet her signature was seen to have legal weight.

28  I. Peterson, 'Reburial of Frank Lloyd Wright Touches off a Stormy Debate', *New York Times – Section A* (10 April 1985), 14.

29   Olgivanna Lloyd Wright, *Frank Lloyd Wright: His Life, His Work, His Words* (New York: Horizon Press, 1966), p. 13.

30   Maginel Wright Barney, *The Valley of the God Almighty Joneses* (New York: Appleton Century, 1965), p. 13.

31   O. L. Wright, *Frank Lloyd Wright: His Life, His Work, His Words*, p. 16.

32   Clough Williams-Ellis, *Portmeirion: The Place and its Meaning* (Portmeirion, 1973), pp. 44–7.

33   Williams-Ellis, *Portmeirion: The Place and its Meaning*, pp. 44–7.

34   Donald Leslie Johnson, *Frank Lloyd Wright Versus America: The 1930s* (Boston: MIT Press, 1990), p. 35.

35   Frank's own time there had been brief, but the University had been a significant presence in his life. Three of his sons had studied there, and his uncles James and Enos had both served on the Board of Regents.

36   The various medals and honorary degrees are listed chronologically in Donald Langmead, *Frank Lloyd Wright: A Bio-Bibliography* (Westport: Praeger, 2003), pp. 19–34 – although, surprisingly, the Doctorate of Laws from the University of Wales is omitted. This opens up the possibility that there are other omissions from what appears a comprehensive list.

37   Letter, Frank Lloyd Wright to Sir Emrys Evans, 12 April 1956. Frank Lloyd Wright Foundation archive reference E085C05.

38   Purchase order letter from the BBC Welsh Programme Executive to Frank Lloyd Wright, 12 July 1956. Frank Lloyd Wright Foundation archive reference W259D01. The letter is addressed to Frank at the Castle Hotel, Bangor. He was paid ten guineas for the interview, and it was broadcast from Rhyl Town Hall.

39   Letter from Cynthia Judah (BBC, London), to Frank Lloyd Wright, 17 July 1956. Frank Lloyd Wright Foundation archive reference W260A05. The letter is addressed to Frank at the Portmeirion Hotel, Penrhyndeudraeth.

40   Williams-Ellis, *Portmeirion: The Place and its Meaning*, pp. 44–7.

41   *North Wales Chronicle* (20 July 1956). Goronwy Rees's role as Principal lasted only four years. He was dismissed in 1957 because of the unwanted attention that followed from his exposure of the spy Guy Burgess in a low-grade newspaper, *The People*. Rees himself had spied for Russia in the early 1930s.

42   From the record of the Congregation of the University of Wales (July 1956), p. 37.

43   Letter, John Ormond Thomas to Frank Lloyd Wright, 8 June 1956. Frank Lloyd Wright Foundation archive reference B192C10.

44   Williams-Ellis, *Portmeirion: The Place and its Meaning*, pp. 44–7.

45   Sadly, there appears to be no surviving film or written record of 'Outlook', as broadcast at 10 pm, in Wales only, on 18 July 1956. It is listed in the *Radio Times*, 1705 (13 July 1956). The existence of the telegram from Frank Lloyd Wright to John Ormond is confirmed by its current owner, the author Rian Evans, John Ormond's daughter and editor of his *Collected Poems*.

46   Mari Jones, 'The Day American Architect Frank Lloyd Wright Came to Colwyn Bay', *North Wales Daily Post* (9 June 2011).

47   Letter from Clough Williams-Ellis to Frank Lloyd Wright, 19 July 1956. Frank Lloyd Wright Foundation archive reference W263D04.

48   Editorial, *Architect and Surveyor*, journal of the Incorporated Association of Architects and Surveyors, 1 (January–December 1956), 4, 70.

49   *The Times* (21 July 1956), 8.

50   K. J. Robinson, 'From Taliesin to Shepherd's Bush', *The Architects' Journal*, 125/3204 (26 July 1956), 65–7.

51   Debra Pickrel and Jane Hession, *Frank Lloyd Wright in New York: The Plaza Years 1954–59* (New York: Gibbs M. Smith Inc., 2007), pp. 102–4.

52   O. L. Wright, *Frank Lloyd Wright: His Life, His Work, His Words*, p. 16.

53   The most likely date of the visit is Sunday, 22 July, 1956. Frank had returned to London by the evening of the 24th. He sent a telegram to Harry Guggenheim that evening, concerning changes to the design of the Guggenheim Museum (Guggenheim NY Archives Collection A0006, Folder 1).

54   Record of a conversation with Nansi Martin by the author Jon Meiron Jones of Llangranog, and quoted with his kind consent.

55   Rev. E. O Jenkins, *Yr Ymofynydd* (January 1923), translation by Rev. Cen Llwyd.

56   O. L. Wright, *Frank Lloyd Wright: His Life, His Work, His Words*, p. 16.

57    This account appears in Brendan Gill, *Many Masks: A Life of Frank Lloyd Wright* (London: Heinemann, 1988), pp. 20–2. It is a reworking of his article 'Commencement' for the *New Yorker* magazine (14 June 1958), 26–7.

58    Gill, *Many Masks*, p. 27 with additional lines sourced from a partial transcript at *http://wright-up.blogspot.com/2011/02/wright-reflective-at-sarah-lawrence.html* (April 2021).

59    Ralph Waldo Emerson, *Nature* (Boston: James Monroe and Co., 1836), pp. 76–7.

60    Hession and Pickrel, *Frank Lloyd Wright in New York*, p. 108. Extract from Aline Saarinen, 'Tour with Mr. Wright', *New York Times Magazine* (22 September 1957).

61    Edward Williams (Iolo Morganwg), Preface, in *The Myvyrian Archaiology of Wales* (London: Gwyneddigion Society,1801–7), vol. 1, p. xiii.

62    F. L. Wright, *An Autobiography (Edition 2)*, p. 43.

# Timeline

| | |
|---|---|
| 1733 | Rev. Jenkin Jones establishes Llwynrhydowen Chapel, the first non-Trinitarian (Arminian) chapel in Wales. |
| 1742 | Rev. David Lloyd assumes leadership of Llwynrhydowen Chapel, and the Arminian cause in south Cardiganshire following the death of Jenkin Jones. |
| 1774 | Theophilus Lindsay establishes the first Unitarian Chapel in Britain, at Essex Street in London. Iolo Morganwg is among the congregation. |
| 1779 | Rev. David Davis assumes leadership of Llwynrhydowen Chapel following the death of David Lloyd. Davis leads the community to the more radical Arian tradition. |
| 1791 | Joseph Priestley, the most famous British Unitarian, is driven from his home before it is destroyed by arson. He later escapes to America where he helps to establish American Unitarianism. |
| 1792 | Iolo Morganwg convenes the first modern *Gorsedd* of Bards at Primrose Hill, London. The proceedings commence with the call *Y Gwir yn Erbyn y Byd* – Truth Against the World. |
| 1794 | Publication of Iolo Morganwg's *Poems, Lyric and Pastoral*, with the first appearance of the 'Genius Triad' that was frequently quoted, in his later life, by Frank Lloyd Wright. |

| | |
|---|---|
| 1796 | Tomos Glyn Cothi establishes the first Unitarian chapel in Wales, at Brechfa, Carmarthenshire. |
| 1802 | Rev. Charles Lloyd leads a Unitarian secession, setting up the first Unitarian Chapels in Cardiganshire. He is supported by Iolo Morganwg.<br><br>Frank Lloyd Wright's great-grandfather and great-granduncles are among the founders. |
| 1802 | Establishment of the South Wales Unitarian Society. Iolo Morganwg is a leading organiser, and is responsible for drafting the rules of the society. |
| 1813 | The UK Parliament passes the Doctrine of the Trinity Act, allowing Unitarian worship legal status for the first time. |
| 1829 | Marriage of Richard Jones and Margaret 'Mallie' Thomas, Frank Lloyd Wright's grandparents. |
| 1844 | Richard and Mallie Jones migrate to America with their seven children. |
| 1845 | Richard and Mallie settle in the east Wisconsin township of Ixonia, where they join Richard's brother Jenkin, who migrated two years before. |
| 1846 | Death of Jenkin Jones, from malaria. |
| 1850 | c.1850 Richard Jones begins to restore the name 'Lloyd' to his family. From then on they would be known as 'Lloyd Jones'. |

| | |
|---|---|
| 1857 | The Lloyd Jones family moves from Ixonia to Spring Green, Wisconsin. Their new property becomes known as the 'River Farms'. |
| 1863 | The Lloyd Jones family sells the River Farms and buys land at The Valley. They rent land close to Lone Rock, in the neighbouring county, while their property at The Valley is cleared for farming.<br><br>Hannah Lloyd Jones meets William Wright. |
| 1866 | Marriage of Hannah Lloyd Jones and William Wright. Hannah changes her name to Anna Lloyd Wright. |
| 1867 | Frank Lincoln Wright born at Richland Center, Wisconsin. |
| 1870 | Death of Mallie Lloyd Jones, Frank's grandmother. |
| 1878 | After six moves to different homes across America, the Wright family settles in Madison, Wisconsin. |
| 1878 | Jenkin Lloyd Jones leads the establishment of the First Unitarian Society of Madison. |
| 1878 | Frank makes the first of his summer moves to live with his Uncle James and work on his farm in The Valley. He does the same for the next six summers. |
| 1882 | Jenkin Lloyd Jones makes his visit to south Cardiganshire. He preaches at Pantydefaid and Llwynrhydowen chapels. |
| 1885 | Divorce of Anna and William Wright. Frank changes his middle name from Lincoln to Lloyd. |
| 1885 | Frank starts work as a junior in the architectural office of Prof. Allan Conover in Madison. |

| | |
|---|---|
| 1885 | December: death of Richard Lloyd Jones, the patriarch. |
| 1886 | Dedication of Unity Chapel in the Lloyd Jones Valley. |
| 1886 | At the end of the year Frank leaves home and moves to Chicago. He lives with his uncle Jenkin Lloyd Jones and begins work with Joseph Silsbee. |
| 1887 | Under Silsbee's supervision, Frank works on the conversion of his grandparents' old home into a dormitory for his aunts' Hillside Home School. |
| 1888 | Frank moves to work for Adler and Sullivan as assistant to Louis Sullivan. |
| 1888 | Anna Lloyd Wright moves to Oak Park, Chicago, with her two daughters. Frank moves there to live with them. |
| 1889 | Frank Lloyd Wright marries Catherine Tobin. |
| 1890 | Frank completes his own house on the Oak Park property, his first independent design. He moves in with Catherine just before the birth of Lloyd, the first of their six children. |
| 1893 | After working secretly on nine 'bootlegged' house projects of his own, Frank is dismissed from Adler and Sullivan. He starts his own architectural practice. |
| 1893 | The World's Columbian Exposition at Chicago: a watershed moment for American architecture. |
| 1894 | Completion of the Winslow House, at River Forest, Illinois. The first project of Frank Lloyd Wright, Architect. |

| | |
|---|---|
| 1895 | Frank extends his Oak Park house to include a small studio for himself and a large playroom for his family. It becomes known as the 'Home and Studio'. |
| 1898 | Frank constructs a new, large studio alongside his Oak Park home. |
| 1901 | Anna and Maginel Lloyd Wright make their visit to south Cardiganshire. |
| 1901 | Completion of the B. Harley Bradley House in Kankakee, Illinois. The first house in the Prairie style. |
| 1902 | Completion of the Ward Willits House, Highland Park, Chicago, considered to be the first of the great Prairie houses. |
| 1903 | Completion of the Edwin Cheney Residence in Oak Park, the beginning of Frank's involvement with Mamah Cheney. |
| 1904 | Completion of the Dana Thomas House in Springfield, Illinois. |
| 1905 | Frank Lloyd Wright makes his first trip to Japan. Completion of Darwin Martin Residence in Buffalo, New York. |
| 1905 | Frank is commissioned to design Unity Temple at Oak Park. |
| 1906 | Completion of the Larkin Administration Building, Frank's first large commercial project. |
| 1909 | Dedication of Unity Temple. Frank leaves his wife and children and travels to Europe with Mamah Cheney. |
| 1910 | Frank and Mamah Cheney spend the summer in Fiesole, on the outskirts of Florence. Frank begins work on the *Wasmuth Portfolio*, his first architectural monograph. |

| | |
|---|---|
| 1911 | Frank and Anna Lloyd Wright buy land in the Lloyd Jones Valley. Frank begins work on his new house, Taliesin. |
| 1912 | Mamah Cheney divorces her husband. Taliesin is completed. It becomes Frank's new home and studio. Mamah moves there to live with him. |
| 1913 | Frank makes a second visit to Japan to collect antique prints and to pursue the commission for the Tokyo Imperial Hotel.<br><br>Receives commission for Midway Gardens, Chicago |
| 1914 | July. Completion of Midway Gardens. |
| 1914 | Taliesin destroyed by arson. Mamah Borthwick and two of her children are murdered, along with four members of Frank's staff. |
| 1914 | December: Frank begins a relationship with Miriam Noel, a Chicago socialite. |
| 1915 | Construction of Taliesin II, completed incorporating the remains of the original house. |
| 1916 | Frank is commissioned to design the Imperial Hotel, Tokyo. Most of the following six years are spent in Japan. |
| 1921 | Completion of the Hollyhock House for Aline Barnsdall in Los Angeles, California. |
| 1922 | Frank Leaves Japan for the last time, with the Imperial Hotel near completion. Opens an office in Los Angeles. |
| 1922 | Catherine Lloyd Wright grants Frank a divorce, twelve years after Frank's abandonment of their marriage. |

| | |
|---|---|
| 1923 | Marriage of Frank and Miriam Noel.<br><br>Completion of the Alice Millard Residence, the first of the four Los Angeles 'Textile Block' houses. |
| 1923 | On the day of the formal opening of the Tokyo Imperial Hotel most of the city is destroyed by an earthquake. The hotel is one of the few buildings to survive. |
| 1923 | Death of Anna Lloyd Wright. |
| 1924 | Miriam Noel leaves Frank in May. In November Frank meets Olgivanna Milanov and begins a relationship with her. |
| 1925 | Taliesin substantially destroyed by fire for the second time. Olgivanna gives birth to Iovanna. Frank is her father. Miriam Noel launches several legal actions against Frank and Olgivanna. Frank's bank forecloses his mortgage on Taliesin. |
| 1926 | Frank and Olgivanna arrested at a Lake Minnetonka holiday cottage. Unable to return to Taliesin following their release from prison, they move to La Jolla, California. |
| 1927 | Friends and patrons establish Frank Lloyd Wright Incorporated, to pay off Frank's legal costs and to support Frank in restarting his career.<br><br>Frank and Miriam divorce. |
| 1928 | Trustees of Frank Lloyd Wright Incorporated manage to buy Taliesin back from the Bank of Wisconsin. Frank and Olgivanna move back to The Valley. They marry in August. |
| 1929 | The Wall Street Crash. Work dries up for Frank. |

| | |
|---|---|
| 1932 | Frank and Olgivanna launch the Taliesin Fellowship. The first apprentices arrive in September.<br><br>First publication of *An Autobiography*, a mix of memoire and self-mythologising. Several reprints follow. |
| 1935 | Opening of the 'Broadacre City' exhibition in New York City. |
| 1937 | Completion of Fallingwater, at Bear Run, Pennsylvania.<br><br>Construction of Taliesin West begins in the desert near to Phoenix, Arizona. From hereon it will be his winter home and studio. |
| 1937 | Completion of the Jacobs House at Madison, Wisconsin, the first of the 'Usonian houses'. |
| 1937 | Attends the International Architects' Convention in Moscow. |
| 1938 | Frank rejoins the First Unitarian Society of Madison. He had last been a member in 1886. |
| 1939 | Completion of the Johnson Wax Administration Building, at Racine, Wisconsin.<br><br>Frank visits Britain for the second time, to deliver a series of lectures. |
| 1939 | World War II breaks out in Europe. Frank argues for American isolationism. |
| 1941 | America enters World War II. Three apprentices from the Taliesin Fellowship are imprisoned for refusing the draft. |
| 1942 | The FBI begins to investigate Frank, suspecting him of sedition. |

| | |
|---|---|
| 1943 | Commissioned to design the Solomon R. Guggenheim Museum, New York City. |
| 1946 | A major revision of *An Autobiography* is published. |
| 1950 | Frank's third visit to Britain, and his first to Wales. |
| 1951 | Completion of the Meeting House for the First Unitarian Society of Madison, Wisconsin. |
| 1954 | Frank leases a suite at the Plaza Hotel, New York City, his third 'home and studio'. It becomes known as Taliesin East. |
| 1956 | First presentation of the 'Mile High Tower' project at the Sherman Hotel, Chicago. Construction of the Guggenheim Museum finally commences. |
| 1956 | Frank visits Britain to receive an honorary doctorate from the University of Wales. He spends most of the visit in Wales and makes time to travel to south Cardiganshire in search of the roots of the Lloyd Jones family. |

| | |
|---|---|
| 1958 | Visits Iraq. Commissioned to design an opera house and other civic buildings for Baghdad. The project comes to a sudden end later in the year when the Iraqi royal family is overthrown. |
| 1959 | Easter: death of Frank Lloyd Wright following abdominal surgery in Phoenix, Arizona. His body is returned to The Valley and buried at Unity Chapel. |
| 1959 | The Guggenheim Museum is opened later in the year. Several other large projects are completed in the three years following Frank's death. |
| 1985 | Death of Olgivanna Lloyd Wright at Taliesin West. In accordance with her dying wish, the remains of Frank Lloyd Wright are exhumed, cremated and sent to Taliesin West to be reinterred with Olgivanna's. |

# Select Bibliography

Abernathy, Ann, *The Oak Park Home and Studio of Frank Lloyd Wright* (Chicago: Frank Lloyd Wright Home and Studio Foundation, 1988).

Adolphson, Svea, *A History of Albion Academy* (Beloit, WI: Rock County Rehabilitation Services Inc, 1976).

Aiken, Andrew. J., *Men of Progress: Wisconsin* (Milwaukee: The Evening Wisconsin Company, 1897).

Alofsin, Anthony (ed.), *An Index to the Taliesin Correspondence* (New York: Garland Publishing, 1988).

Alofsin, Anthony, *Frank Lloyd Wright: The Lost Years, 1910–1922: A Study of Influence* (Chicago: University of Chicago Press, 1993).

Alofsin, Anthony (ed.), *Frank Lloyd Wright: Europe and Beyond* (Berkeley: University of California Press, 1999).

Alofsin, Anthony, *Wright and New York: The Making of America's Architect* (New Haven and London: Yale University Press, 2019).

Amin, Kamal, *Reflections from the Shining Brow* (Santa Barbara: Fithian Press, 2004).

Barney, Maginel Wright, *Valley of the God Almighty Joneses* (New York: Appleton Century, 1965).

Barrows, John H. (ed.), *The World's Parliament of Religions* (Chicago: Parliament Publishing Co., 1893).

Besinger, Curtis, *Working with Mr. Wright: What it Was Like* (Cambridge: Cambridge University Press, 1995).

Birk, Melanie (ed.), *Frank Lloyd Wright's Fifty Views of Japan* (Chicago: Frank Lloyd Wright Trust, 1996).

Brierly, Cornelia, *Tales of Taliesin: A Memoir of Fellowship* (Portland, OR: Pomegranate Communications, 2000).

Butterfield, C. W., *History of Crawford and Richland Counties, Wisconsin* (Chicago: Union Publishing Company, 1884).

Chamberlain, Everett, *Chicago and its Suburbs* (Chicago: T. A. Hungerford & Co., 1874).

Charnell-White, Catherine, *Bardic Circles: National, Regional and Personal Identity in the Bardic Vision of Iolo Morganwg* (Cardiff: University of Wales Press, 2007).

Chase, Mary Ellen, *A Goodly Fellowship* (New York: The Macmillan Co., 1939).

Chidlaw Benjamin W., *Yr American* (Llanrwst: John Jones, 1840).

Chulak, T.A., *A People Moving thru Time: A Brief History of the Unitarian Universalist Church in Oak Park, Illinois* (Chicago: The Unitarian Universalist Church in Oak Park, 1979).

Cole, Harry Elseworth, *A Standard History of Sauk County Wisconsin* (Chicago: Lewis Publishing Co., 1918).

Cooper, Kathryn J., *Exodus from Cardiganshire: Rural–Urban Migration in Victorian Britain* (Cardiff: University of Wales Press, 2011).

Crunden, R. M., *Ministers of Reform* (Champaign: University of Illinois Press, 1984).

Davies, Edward, *The Mythology and Rites of the British Druids Ascertained by National Documents* (London: J. Booth, 1809).

Davies, D. Elwyn, *They Thought for Themselves: A Brief Look at the History of Unitarianism in Wales* (Llandysul: Gomer, 1982).

Davis, Mike, *City of Quartz* (New York: Verso, 1990).

Dowling, Andrew Jackson, *The Architecture of Country Houses* (New York: D. Appleton, 1851).

Emerson, Ralph Waldo, *Essays: First Series* (New York: Houghton Mifflin & Co, 1899).

Evans, Evan, *Some Specimens of the Poetry of the Antient Welsh Bards* (London: R. and J. Dodsley, 1864).

Flinn, John J., *Official Guide to the World's Columbian Exposition* (Chicago: The Columbian Guide Co., 1893).

Friedland, Roger and Zellman, Harold, *The Fellowship: The Untold Story of Frank Lloyd Wright and the Taliesin Fellowship* (New York: HarperCollins, 2006).

Fuller, R. Buckminster, *Inventions: The Patented Works of Buckminster Fuller* (New York: St Martin's Press, 1983).

Gaebler, Max D. et al., *Landmarks in the Life of the First Unitarian Society of Madison* (Madison, WI: Friends of the Meeting House, 1999).

Gill, Brendan, *Many Masks: A Life of Frank Lloyd Wright* (London: Heinemann, 1988).

Gordon, Alexander, *Addresses Biographical and Historical* (London: The Lindsey Press, 1922).

Graham, Thomas (ed.), *Trilogy: Through Their Eyes* (Spring Green, WI: Unity Chapel Publications, 1986).

Graham, Thomas E., *Unity Chapel Sermons* (Winnipeg: New Colgrove Press, 2002).

Gravil, Richard, *Wordsworth's Bardic Vocation* (London: Palgrave Macmillan, 2003).

Gurdjieff, George I., *Meetings with Remarkable Men* (London: Routledge and Kegan Paul, 1963).

Hague, Judy and Graham, *The Unitarian Heritage: An Architectural Survey* (Sheffield: Unitarian Heritage, 1986).

Hamilton, Mary Jane, *The Meeting House* (Madison, WI: Friends of the Meeting House, 1991).

Harvey, Samantha J., *Transatlantic Transcendentalism: Coleridge, Emerson and Nature* (Edinburgh: Edinburgh University Press, 2013).

Heinz, Thomas A., *The Vision of Frank Lloyd Wright* (Menai Bridge: S. Webb and Son, 2002),

Hendrickson Paul, *Plagued by Fire* (London: Bodley Head, 2019).

Hertzberg, M., *Frank Lloyd Wright's Penwern* (Madison: Wisconsin Historical Society Press, 2019).

Hitchcock, Henry-Russell et al., *Modern Architecture: International Exhibition* (New York: Museum of Modern Art, 1932).

Hoffman, Donald, *Frank Lloyd Wright's Fallingwater* (Mineola, NY: Dover, 1978).

Hoffman, Donald, *Frank Lloyd Wright's Robie House* (Mineola, NY: Dover, 2012).

Hovey, Richard, *Taliesin: A Masque* (Boston: Small Maynard and Co., 1900).

Huxtable, Ada Louise, *Frank Lloyd Wright* (London: Penguin Books, 2004).

Ives, Halsey Cooley, *The Dream City: Photographic Views of the World's Columbian Exposition* (St Louis: N. D. Thompson Publishing Co., 1893).

Jenkins, Geraint H. (ed.), *A Rattleskull Genius: The Many Faces of Iolo Morganwg* (Cardiff: University of Wales Press, 2005).

Jenkins, Geraint H., *Bard of Liberty* (Cardiff: University of Wales Press, 2012).

Johnson, Donald Leslie, *Frank Lloyd Wright Versus America* (Boston: MIT Press, 1990).

Johnson, Donald Leslie, *Frank Lloyd Wright: Early Years: Progressivism: Aesthetics: Cities* (Abingdon: Routledge, 2017).

Jones, Chester Lloyd, *Youngest Son* (Madison, WI: Self-published, 1938).

Jones, Edward, *Y Teithiwr Americanaidd (The American Traveller)* (Aberystwyth: E. Williams, 1840).

Jones, Jenkin Lloyd, *An Artilleryman's Diary* (Madison: Wisconsin History Commission, 1914).

Jones, Richard Lloyd et al., *A Lloyd Jones Retrospective* (Spring Green, WI: Unity Chapel Publications, 1986).

Kakudzo, Okakura, *The Hō-ō-den* (Tokyo: K. Ogawa, 1893).

Knight, Charles, *Old England: A Pictorial Museum of Regal, Ecclesiastical, Baronial, Municipal and Popular Antiquities* (London: Charles Knight & Co., 1845).

Langmead, Donald, *Frank Lloyd Wright: A Bio-Bibliography* (Westport, CT: Praeger Publishing, 2003).

Lanier, Sidney, *The Boys' Mabinogion* (New York: Charles Scribner & Sons, 1881).

Leslie, Frank, *Illustrated Historical Register of the Centennial Exposition 1876* (New York: Frank Leslie, 1876).

Levine, Neil, *The Architecture of Frank Lloyd Wright* (Princeton: Princeton University Press, 1996).

Lewis, W. J., *An Illustrated History of Cardiganshire* (Aberystwyth: Cymdeithas Lyfrau Ceredigion, 1970).

Lewis, Gyneth and Williams, Rowan, *The Book of Taliesin: Poems of Warfare and Praise in an Enchanted Britain* (London: Penguin Classics, 2019).

Lipman, Jonathan, *Frank Lloyd Wright and the Johnson Wax Building* (New York: Rizzoli, 1986).

Lloyd, Charles, *Particulars of the Life of a Dissenting Minister* (London: Self-published, 1813).

Manson, Grant Carpenter, *Frank Lloyd Wright to 1910: The First Golden Age* (New York: Van Nostrand Reinhold & Co., 1958).

McCarter, Robert, *Frank Lloyd Wright* (New York: Phaidon, 1997).

McCrea, Ron, *Building Taliesin: Frank Lloyd Wright's Home of Love and Loss* (Madison: Wisconsin Historical Society Press, 2012).

Meech, Julia, *Frank Lloyd Wright and the Art of Japan: The Architect's Other Passion* (New York: Harry N. Abrams, 2001).

Meehan, Patrick J. (ed.), *The Master Architect: Conversations with Frank Lloyd Wright* (New York: John Wiley & Sons, 1984).

Menocal, Narciso (ed.), *Wright Studies*, vol. 1: *Taliesin 1911–1914* (Carbondale: Southern Illinois University Press, 1992).

Mollenhoff, D. V. and Hamilton, M. J., *Frank Lloyd Wright's Monona Terrace: The Enduring Power of a Civic Vision* (Madison: University of Wisconsin Press, 1999).

Morse, Edward S., *Japanese Homes and their Surroundings* (Boston: Ticknor & Co., 1886).

Muirhead, Findlay (ed.), *The Blue Guides: Wales* (London: Macmillan & Co., 1926).

Mumford, Lewis, *Sketches from Life* (New York: The Dial Press, 1982).

Nute, Kevin, *Frank Lloyd Wright and Japan* (New York: Van Nostrand Reinhold, 1993).

Ott, John Henry (ed.), *Jefferson County, Wisconsin and its People* (Chicago: S. J. Clarke Publishing Co., 1917).

Peabody, Elizabeth Palmer & Mann, M. T. Peabody, *Moral Culture of Infancy and Kindergarten Guide* (Boston: T. O. H. P. Burnham, 1864).

Perry, Victoria, *Built for a Better Future: The Brynmawr Rubber Factory* (Oxford: White Cockade Publishing, 1994).

Pfeiffer, Bruce Brooks, *Frank Lloyd Wright Selected Houses 3: Taliesin West* (Tokyo: ADS Edita Co. Ltd, 1992).

Pfeiffer, Bruce Brooks (ed.), *Frank Lloyd Wright Collected Writings*, vols 1–5 (New York: Random House, 1992–4).

Pfeiffer, Bruce Brooks (ed.), *Wright: Complete Works 1943–1959* (Cologne: Taschen, 2009).

Pfeiffer, Bruce Brooks (ed.), *Wright: Complete Works 1917–1942* (Cologne: Taschen, 2010).

Pfeiffer, Bruce Brooks (ed.), *Wright: Complete Works 1885–1916* (Cologne: Taschen, 2011).

Pfeiffer, Bruce Brooks and Nordland, G., *Frank Lloyd Wright in the Realm of Ideas* (Carbondale: Southern Illinois University Press, 1988).

Pfeiffer, Bruce Brooks and Wojtowicz, Robert (eds), *Frank Lloyd Wright and Lewis Mumford: Thirty Years of Correspondence* (New York: Princeton Architectural Press, 2001).

Pickrel, Debra and Hession, Jane, *Frank Lloyd Wright in New York: The Plaza Years 1954–59* (New York: Gibbs M. Smith Inc., 2007).

Plomin Robert, *Blueprint: How DNA Makes Us Who We Are* (London: Allen Lane, 2018).

Quinan, Jack, *Frank Lloyd Wright's Larkin Building: Myth and Fact* (Chicago: University of Chicago Press, 2006).

Raymond, Antonin, *An Autobiography* (Clarendon, VT: C. E. Tuttle, 1973).

Riley, Terrance (ed.), *Frank Lloyd Wright: Architect* (New York: Museum of Modern Art, 1994).

Scully, Vincent, *Frank Lloyd Wright* (New York: George Braziller Inc., 1960).

Scully, Vincent, *The Shingle Style and the Stick Style* (New Haven: Yale University Press, 1971).

Secrest, Meryl, *Frank Lloyd Wright: A Biography* (Chicago: University of Chicago Press, 1998).

Shapiro, Michael S., *A Child's Garden: The Kindergarten Movement from Fröbel to Dewey* (University Park: Pennsylvania State University Press, 1983).

Shepp, J. W., *Shepp's World's Fair Photographed* (Chicago: Globe Bible Publishing Co., 1893).

Siry, Joseph, *Beth Sholom Synagogue: Frank Lloyd Wright and Modern Religious Architecture* (Chicago: University of Chicago Press, 2011).

Smith, Norris K., *Frank Lloyd Wright: A Study in Architectural Content* (Englewood Cliffs, NJ: Prentice Hall, 1966).

Sokol, David M., *The Noble Room* (Chicago: Top Five Books, 2008).

Storrer, William A., *The Architecture of Frank Lloyd Wright: A Complete Catalogue – Third Edition* (Chicago: University of Chicago Press, 2002).

Sullivan, Louis H., *The Autobiography of an Idea* (Washington, DC: The Press of the American Institute of Architects, 1924).

Tafel, Edgar, *Album of Recollections by Those Who Knew Frank Lloyd Wright* (New York: Dover, 1993).

Tenorio-Trillo, Mauricio, *Mexico at the World's Fairs: Crafting a Modern Nation* (Berkeley: University of California Press, 1996).

Theakston, Lucy (ed.), *Some Family Records & Pedigrees of the Lloyds of Allt yr Odyn, Castell Hywel, Ffos y Bleiddiaid, Gilfach Wen, Llan Llyr and Waun Ifor* (London: Fox, Jones & Co., 1913).

Thoreau, Henry David, *Walden and Other Writings* (New York: Bantam Books, 1962).

Thwaites, Reuben G., *The Story of Wisconsin* (Boston: D. Lothrop Co., 1890).

Twombly, Robert C., *Frank Lloyd Wright: An Interpretive Biography* (New York: Harper Colophon, 1974).

Unwin, Simon, *Twenty-Five Buildings Every Architect Should Understand* (Abingdon: Routledge, 2015).

Waring, Elijah, *Recollections and Anecdotes of Edward Williams* (London: Charles Gilpin, 1850).

Wijdeveld, Hendrik. T. et al., *Frank Lloyd Wright: The Early Work of the Great Architect* (New York: Gramercy Books, 1994).

Williams, Edward (Iolo Morganwg), *Poems, Lyric and Pastoral*, vols 1 and 2 (London: J. Nichols, 1794).

Williams, Edward (Iolo Morganwg), *Salmau yr Eglwys yn yr Anialwch* (Merthyr Tydfil: J. James, 1827).

Williams-Ellis, Clough, *Portmeirion: The Place and its Meaning* (Portmeirion: Portmeirion Publishing, 1973).

Williams-Ellis, Clough, *Architect Errant: The Autobiography of Clough Williams-Ellis* (Portmeirion: Golden Dragon Books, 1980).

Williamson, Roxanne K., *American Architects and the Mechanics of Fame* (Austin: University of Texas Press, 1991).

Wilson, Colin, *G. I. Gurdjieff: The War Against Sleep* (London: Aeon Books, 2005).

Wright, Frank Lloyd, *Modern Architecture: Being the Kahn Lectures for 1930* (Princeton: Princeton University Press, 1931).

Wright, Frank Lloyd, *An Autobiography* (New York: Longman, Green & Co., 1932).

Wright, Frank Lloyd, *An Autobiography* (New York: Duell Sloane & Pearce, 1943).

Wright, Frank Lloyd, *Genius and the Mobocracy* (New York: Duell Sloane & Pearce, 1949).

Wright, Frank Lloyd, *The Natural House* (New York: Horizon Press, 1954).

Wright, Frank Lloyd, *A Testament* (New York: Horizon Press, 1957).

Wright, John Lloyd, *My Father Who is on Earth* (New York: Putnam, 1946).

Wright, Olgivanna Lloyd, *The Struggle Within* (New York: Horizon Press, 1955).

Wright, Olgivanna Lloyd, *Our House* (New York: Horizon Press, 1959).

Wright, Olgivanna Lloyd, *Frank Lloyd Wright: His Life, His Work, His Words* (New York: Horizon Press, 1966).

# Image Accreditation

The following abbreviations are used in the image captions.

| © Crown copyright: RCAHMW | Reproduced with the permission of the Royal Commission on the Ancient and Historical Monuments of Wales under delegated authority from The Keeper of Public Records |
|---|---|
| NLW | National Library of Wales |
| LOC | US Library of Congress |
| FLWT | Courtesy Frank Lloyd Wright Trust |
| FLWF/AAFAL | Courtesy Frank Lloyd Wright Foundation, Scottsdale, Arizona/Avery Architecture and Fine Arts Library, Columbia University, New York. |
| FLWF | Courtesy Frank Lloyd Wright Foundation, Scottsdale Arizona. |
| CC | Creative Commons |

All images without accreditation are in the public domain or are the work of the author.

# Index

**Note**: *illustrations are shown by the use of **bold** text. Notes are referenced by the suffix 'n'.*

Humphreys, Emyr 249

Huron, Lake 59, **60** (fig. 4.1)

Husser, Helen and Joseph 178

Husser House, Buena Park, Chicago 178-9, **179** (fig. 11.5), **180** (pl. 79), 184, 185, 186

# I

Ianelli, Alfonso **245** (pl. 128)

'The Illinois' (Mile High tower) 298-300, **299** (pl. 168), 304

Imperial Hotel, Tokyo 79, 241-42, 253, 254-8, **255** (fig. 15.1), **256** (pls 135, 136), **258** (pl. 137), 270

*Inland Architect and News Record* (journal) 139

Iolo Morganwg (Edward Williams) **14** (pl. 4), 16-20, **17** (pl. 6), 24-6, 27-9, 31-2, 33, 103, 249, 310, 311

Capel y Groes, stone inscription at 16, **17** (pl. 7)

*Hymns for the Church in the Wilderness* 28, **28** (pl. 9), 38-9, 49

and the Lloyd-Jones family 14, 16-18, **28** (pl. 9), 29, 30, 31, 39-40, 49, 240, 308

and Pantydefaid chapel 16-17, 41

*Poems, Lyric and Pastoral* 24-6

Unitarian Rule Book 49

Iraq 298

Irish emigration 48, 131, 133

Isaiah 29, 214, 270

Italy, Frank in 228-229, **229** (pl. 117), 231, 246

Ixonia, Wisconsin 60, **60** (fig. 4.1), 61, **62** (fig. 4.2), 63-5, 70-4, 78, 86, 131, 141

Welsh cemetery 51n3, **62** (fig. 4.2), 64, **64** (pl. 26), 72

# J

Jackson County, Ohio 48

Jacob, Enoch 46

Jacobins 16, 19, 20

Jacobs House, Madison, Wisconsin 277-8, **277** (fig. 15.3), **278** (pl. 156)

Jacobs, Katherine and Herb 277, 278, 282, 289

James, David and Thomas 17, 47

Japan 76, 282-3, 303, 304

Frank in 210-11, 241-42, 253, 254-8

Hō-ō-den Palace at 1893 World's Fair 158, **159** (fig. 10.3), **160** (pl. 67), 166, 214, **214** (pl. 103)

Imperial Hotel, Tokyo 75, 241-2, 253, 254-8, **255** (fig. 15.1), **256** (pls 135, 136), **258** (pl. 137), 270

Taiyū-in Reibyō mausoleum, Nikko 211, **213** (fig. 13.3), **212** (pl. 102)

Japanese art 134, 158, 21, 241, 242

Japanese influence on Frank's architecture 192, 193, 194, 211-14, **216** (pl. 107), 235, 244

Jefferson County, Wisconsin 70-4

Jenkin, John (d. 1759) 9, 10, 45

Jenney, William Le Baron 134, **135** (pl. 46)

Johnson, Donald Leslie 30, 85, 102, 206

Johnson, Hib **273** (pl. 152), 274, 275

Johnson, Philip 271, 272

Johnson Wax Administration Building, Racine, Wisconsin 236, 273-5, **273** (pl. 152), **274** (pl. 153), **275** (pl. 154), 278

Jones, Chester Lloyd 41, 57, **118** (pl. 40), 156

*Youngest Son* 41-5, **42** (pl. 15), **43** (pls 16, 17), **43** (pls 18, 19), 84

Jones, David 40, **47** (pl. 21), 49, 73

Jones, Eleanor 'Nel' (1809-1872) 40, 71-2

Jones, Enoch Lloyd (1816-1873) 40, 71, 72, 73

Jones, Frederick B. 190

Jones, Hannah (1803-1885) 40, **41** (pl. 14)

Jones, Rev. Jenkin (1700-1742) 9-11, 16, 45

Jones, Jenkin (1807-1846) 7, 59, 63, 64-5, 70-1

death and burial 40, 64-5, **64** (pl. 26), 72

emigrates to America 40, 41, 48, 49, 60-1, 85, 86

Jones, John 40

Jones, Jon Meirion 307

Jones, Margaret (1770-1854) (née Lloyd) *see* Lloyd, Margaret (1770-1854)

Jones, Margaret (d. 1858) 71, 82n8

Jones, Nany 49, 57, 58-9

Jones, Owen (Owain Myfyr) 19

Jones, Owen (son of Owain Myfyr) 140

Jones, Rachel (1812-1859) 40, 48, 49, 58, 71

Jones, Rachel (1815-1899) 71

Jones, Richard (Lloyd) (1799-1885) 2, 7-9, **8** (pl. 1), 17, 18, 57, 63-6, 70-4, 77, 78, 117, **118** (pl. 40), **119** (pl. 41), 120, 127n25, 156

at Blaenralltddu **39** (fig. 3.1), 42, 44, **44** (p. 19)

childhood **10** (pl. 2), 42, 46-7

death and burial 96, 121, 300

emigrates to America 18, 20, 33, 39-40, 41, 45, 47, 48-50, 57-61, **58** (pl. 22), **60** (fig. 4.1)

faith 8-9, 33, 39-40, 47, 49, 50, 65, 70, 214, **215** (pl. 104)

hat-making business 7-8, 29, 47, 48, 73

marriage 47, **47** (pl. 21)

name 46

Jones Valley, Wisconsin *see* The Valley, Wyoming Township

Jonesville, Spring Green, Wisconsin 72-3

# K

Kankakee, Illinois 191-3

Kaufmann, Edgar Junior 107, 175

Kaufmann, Edgar Senior 172-3, 175-6, 288

Price, Bruce 150

Price, Richard 9, 19, 32

Price Tower, Bartlesville, Oklahoma 238, **240** (pl. 124)

Priestley, Joseph 9, 12, 13, 19, 32, 103, 138, 141

Princeton University 74-5, 287-8, 304

Puerto Rico 15

## Q

Quakers 51n12, 163n13

Queen Anne style 137, 152, 163n22, 191

quilt from Carmarthenshire 200-1, **201** (pl. 96)

## R

railroad in America 57-8, **60** (fig. 4.1), **62** (fig. 4.2), 71, 78, 132, 141, 192

Rand, Ayn 69n29

Rational Dissent 30-1, 38, 43

Raymond, Antonin 259

Rebecca Riots 43-4

Rees, David Jenkin 13-14, 16

Rees, Goronwy 305

*Remittance* (clipper) 50, 57, **58** (pl. 22), 68n4

Rhode Island 90, 93

Rhydowen, Cardiganshire 22n14, 200, 307

Rhydyceir, Cardiganshire 44, 46

Rhys ap Gruffydd, Lord 22n18

Richards, Arthur 249, 264

Richardson, Henry Hobson 119, 138

Richland Center, Richland County, Wisconsin 91-2, **92** (pl. 32), 101, 262, **264** (pl. 142)

Richland County, Wisconsin 78, 89, 90, 91

Reider family 231, 233, 246

River Farms, Spring Green, Wisconsin 73-4, 77, 78, **79** (fig. 5.1), 80, 104

River Forest township, Illinois **142** (pl. 52), 165, 167, 242

    Roberts House 62-3, **63** (pl. 25)

    Williams House 167, **168** (pl. 71)

    Winslow House 62, **62** (pl. 23), **160** (pl. 66), 165, 166, **166** (pl. 69), 167, **167** (pl. 70), 168, 178, 193, 242

Roberts, Charles 197, 212

Roberts House, River Forest, Illinois 62-3, **63** (pl. 25)

Roberts, Isabel 62-3, 189

Robie, Fred 225, 226

Robie House, Woodlawn Avenue, Chicago **223** (pl. 114), **224** (fig. 13.5), **224** (pl. 115), 225-6, **225** (pl. 116)

Robinson, Sidney K. 215

Romanticism 25, 31-2, 103

Rome, New York 58, 59, **60** (fig. 4.1)

Romeo and Juliet Windmill, The Valley 169-72, **170** (fig. 11.1), **172** (pl. 74), 198-9, 299

Rookery Building, Chicago 180, 186-7

Rorke, Dr Joe 298, 302

Rousseau, Jean-Jacques 36n27, 103, 109

Royal Festival Hall, London 292, 293, **293** (pl. 165)

Roycrofters Community, Aurora, New York 76

Ruskin, John 109, 110

Russia/USSR 19, 296-7

## S

Saarinen, Aline 309

St Louis, Missouri 106-7

San Marcos in the Desert, Arizona 74, 236

Sarah Lawrence College, Yonkers, New York 308-10

Sauk County, Wisconsin 71, 72-3, 77-81, 89

Scandinavia, migrants from 89, 119, 131, 133

Schenectady, New York 58, **60** (fig. 4.1)

Schiller Building, Chicago 161, 180, 206

Schindler, Rudolf 259

Schlesinger & Mayer department store, Chicago **187** (pl. 81)

'School of the Middle-West' 225

Scully, Vincent 150, 193, 273

Second World War 19, 282-3, 304

Secrest, Meryl 81, 97

*Sedd Fawr* (the Great Seat in Welsh chapels) **217** (pl. 108), **218** (pl. 109), 219

shingle style 150, 192

Silsbee, Joseph Lyman 34, 136-7, 138, 140, 145, 150, 152, 167-8

    All Souls Church, Chicago 120, 123, 133, **133** (pl. 45)

    Frank disparages 139, 140

    Frank works for 34, 123-4, 133-4, 135, 136-7, 139, 152

    Hillside Home School 137, **137** (pl. 48)

    introduces Frank to Japanese art 134, 158

    Lakeside Building, Chicago 134, **134** (fig. 9.1)

    Unity Chapel, The Valley 120, 121, 123, **124** (pl. 42), **125** (pl. 43), 138

Silsby, J. R. 50

Sioux City Unitarian Chapel, Iowa 127n18, 137-9, **138** (pl. 50)

Siry, Joseph 292-3

skyscrapers 134, **135** (pl. 46), 299

slavery 20, 33, 78

Smith, George 220

Smith, Kathryn 258

Smith, Norris K. 102-3, 188

South Cardiganshire (now Ceredigion), Wales 7-14, **8** (fig. 1.1), 16-20, 46

    Anna and Maginel visit 190-1

    Frank visits 307-8

    Jenkin Lloyd Jones visits 41-2